EQUALITY
AND ACHIEVEMENT

AN INTRODUCTION
TO THE SOCIOLOGY
OF EDUCATION

SECOND EDITION

Cornelius Riordan

Providence College

Upper Saddle River, New Jersey 07458

Library of Congress Cataloging-in-Publication Data

Riordan, Cornelius H.
  Equality and achievement: An introduction to the sociology of education/Cornelius
Riordan.—2nd ed.
    p.   cm.
  Includes bibliographical references and index.
  ISBN 0-13-048177-7 (pbk.)
    1. Educational sociology—United States.   2. Educational equalization—United States.
  3. Academic achievement—United States.   4. Education—Social aspects—United States.
  I. Title.

  LC191.4.R56 2003
  306.43'0973—dc21

                                                                    2003043872

AVP, Publisher: Nancy Roberts
Executive Editor: Chris DeJohn
Project Coordination: Interactive Composition Corporation
Copyeditor: Melissa Messina
Prepress and Manufacturing Buyer: Mary Ann Gloriande
Senior Marketing Manager: Amy Speckman
Marketing Assistant: Adam Laitman
Editorial Assistant: Veronica D'Amico
Electronic Art Creation: Mirella Signoretto
Cover Image Specialist: Karen Sanatar
Cover Photos: Mike Crockett/Dorling Kinderslay (*left*); Stephen Ferry/Getty Images (*right*)
Cover Director: Jayne Conte
Cover Designer: Bruce Kenselaar

This book was set in 10/12 New Aster by Interactive Composition Corporation,
and was printed and bound by Hamilton Printing Company.
The cover was printed by Phoenix Color Corp.

© 2004, 1997 by Pearson Education, Inc.
Upper Saddle River, New Jersey 07458

Printed in the United States of America

10 9 8 7 6 5 4 3 2 1

ISBN 0-13-048177-7

Pearson Education LTD., London
Pearson Education Australia PTY, Limited, Sydney
Pearson Education Singapore, Pte. Ltd
Pearson Education North Asia Ltd, Hong Kong
Pearson Education Canada, Ltd., Toronto
Pearson Educación de Mexico, S.A. de C.V.
Pearson Education—Japan, Tokyo
Pearson Education Malaysia, Pte. Ltd
Pearson Education, Upper Saddle River, New Jersey

*For poor, desperate, and powerless children everywhere
who truly do benefit from high-quality teachers
and effective schools*

CONTENTS

CHAPTER 3
Differences Between Homes   66

CHAPTER 4
Differences Between Schools: The Early Studies   105

PREFACE

Most people sense that our educational system is in trouble. The clients of our schools—parents and students alike—realize that something beyond the control of individuals is wrong. Those on the front lines must constantly confront the reality that schools appear ineffective, that little knowledge of subject matter is gained over the course of a year, and that even less is retained in the long run. We are bombarded daily with studies and media reports demonstrating how little students learn and retain, across virtually every type of subject, and the increasing problems associated with student dropouts, misbehavior, and violence.

Teachers are experiencing profound frustration with their work. Their students are disinterested and ill-prepared, and their classrooms have come to be characterized by mediocrity and accommodation. Studies show that increasingly teachers wish that they had chosen some other career. An "oppositional" adolescent subculture has emerged, and it has now become sufficiently powerful that academic standards can only be as high as students will allow. And all of these problems are exacerbated by major transformations of the family that circumscribe the schools.

This crisis in schooling has precipitated a change in the way that we have come to explain human behavior within an educational framework. Heretofore, both professional and lay people sought answers to human problems from the field of psychology. A problem was defined as a problem of the individual. Today, most people realize that the problems of schooling are far beyond the control of *individual* students, teachers, administrators, or policy makers. The problems do not lie either within or between individuals, but rather between and within organizations and institutions. More precisely, the problems and the potential solutions are to be found in the rules and the policies of institutions and organizations which transcend individuals, and in the relationships between schools, families, and communities.

All of this points toward an "arrival" at last of the field of sociology on the educational front. Indeed, a central area of sociological expertise is the study of the influence of communities and organizations on human behavior. In fact, over the past fifty years, sociologists have amassed a vast storehouse of knowledge on what kinds of organizational arrangements work most effectively in schools and which ones do not work (see *What Works*, 1987).

The sociology of education is perhaps the richest domain in all of sociology. It focuses on a single social institution, part of which is a central large organization. At the same time, it is related in critical ways to the family, the economic and political systems, the mass media, and the mass culture. It has access to an abundance of recorded and relatively reliable and valid information regarding students, teachers, and administrators of this organization. Likewise, there is more than adequate information regarding the physical and social characteristics of the organization as a social unit, and of peripheral institutions such as the family. It has rather definitive starting and ending points, making longitudinal and some experimental research possible. There exists a highly developed and directly applicable theory base. It is perhaps the easiest way to teach or learn sociology in the broadest sense. For students in sociology, it can provide the easiest and most convincing materials favoring a sociological way of thinking. For students embarking on a career in education, it can provide important practical information about their chosen craft.

This book is an *introduction* to the sociology of education. It is not intended to cover the entire field. It does address, however, the central topics of the discipline—the sociological influences of school outcomes. This topic is sufficiently rich, complicated, broad, and important to merit a book of its own. In sociology of education (and social foundations of education) courses, students are interested in the study of "outcomes." Yet, they are often frustrated by the sheer magnitude of information and the complexities that arise regarding between and within

school effects, "selection bias" in the study of school effects, the applicability of functional and conflict theories, and the relative effects of the home and the school. Thus, this book is designed to serve as a short core textbook which may be supplemented by (or supplementary to) other readings or activities in a one-semester course in either Sociology of Education or Social Foundations of Education.

The strategy employed in this book is to examine a selective set of studies and theories in the sociology of education. This strategy means that many studies and theories are excluded. Moreover, as I have indicated above, the book is selective in the topics that it covers. And the book has a decidedly empirical emphasis. I believe that readers will learn more about the topics that are covered when the presentation is ample rather than superficial. This is true even when readers may disagree with the analysis and/or the conclusions of some of the studies.

The book draws heavily upon the work of James Coleman. Although some readers may find this confining, I believe that Coleman's work is representative of the major issues and captures the major research questions in the field. The sociology of education is clearly more advanced in part because of his direct contributions, but also as a result of the many criticisms that have been raised in response to his work. Thus, much can be learned by simply reading the critical literature that surrounds nearly everything that Coleman wrote.

The substantive issues in this book are presented within a simple "causal model" framework. The emphasis is on conceptualizing the relationships, rather than the numbers. Quantitative methodologists may fear that it will lead to an oversimplification of path analytic techniques and that students will be misinformed. Qualitative sociologists may feel that quantitative thinking is overemphasized. These fears are not trivial and they are not without some bases. The strategy here, however, is to help the student to conceptualize the process of schooling; it is not to sell a methodology. Surely, anyone overly concerned about these matters can supplement the text with other points of view.

Some of my colleagues in the sociology of education may feel that I have oversimplified some issues that actually remain unresolved. Undoubtedly, this is true. The purpose of the book is to provide an *introduction* to the sociology of education. Nonetheless, I have made every effort to avoid misrepresenting or misleading and I believe that I have been successful in this endeavor. Some teachers may feel that the material is actually more complicated than they would prefer. To them, I would say that students are remarkably capable and that soft sociology can be its own burden.

PREFACE
TO THE SECOND EDITION

The second edition of *Equality and Achievement* is a faithful continuation of the first edition. The purpose is to make available the best empirical research on the sociology of education in a single volume that is readable and coherent to undergraduate and graduate students. One of the main advantages of the opportunity to produce a second edition is to remove some of the warts in the first edition, for which I am grateful. Readers should discover that the current edition improves and updates the 1997 version of the book. More than thirty new empirical studies are included and discussed in detail in the second edition, and over 200 new citations have been added. Moreover, the majority of the book now centers on the sociology of education in the 1980s, the 1990s, and the 2000s.

Readers of this book who have read the first edition will find much improvement, but the basic framework has been retained, including the chapter titles. One chapter has been added that splits between school studies into the earlier studies and the current research. A great deal of the earlier material has been removed because it is no longer relevant or it has been shown to be inconsistent or simply not true. I have also removed extraneous material that I now believe was not in the mainstream of the sociology of education. I have not hesitated, however, to retain older material going back as far as 1951 that presents points of departure, theoretical ideas, and/or empirical findings that are relevant, verified, and essential to the formation of sound education policy in 2002.

Although much is new, I have retained some of the classic findings, many of which derive from the late James Coleman. Research on Catholic and public schooling conducted during the 1980s and early 1990s established a benchmark in the sociology of education. Coleman's theory of social capital, and later with Thomas Hoffer on functional communities, provide the student in sociology with more than just quality data and technical analysis. Rather, these are solid theoretical ideas that have provided the launching pad for later work. The fact that social capital is now a highly scrutinized concept is evidence of the enduring impact of Coleman. But this edition is also full of the new sociologists of education who demonstrate the enduring legacy of Coleman.

The book tries to tell a coherent story about how the sociology of education can be usefully employed in educational policy and administration. It reminds the reader in every chapter that the goals of formal schooling are both greater equality and higher achievement. It ties together studies that consistently show that school effects are greater for disadvantaged students. Every chapter points in the direction of a theory of social reproduction that occurs either before school, after school, during the summer, or during school. It tries to show the reader that educational research and policy are never simple—that research findings are often contradictory, often underresearched, and often not applied to educational policy because policy is often controlled by educational politics.

❖ ACKNOWLEDGMENTS

I owe a large debt to many people who have helped me to reach a point where I could write this book. Several of my early teachers from whom I acquired a theoretical foundation in social science were Philip Olson, Maurice Stein, and Arthur Vidich (at Clark University). Later, Allan Mazur, Marshall Segall, and Howard Taylor (at Syracuse University) introduced me to the empirical side of the discipline.

From 1979 to 1981, I had the treasured opportunity to do postdoctoral work in the Department of Sociology at Johns Hopkins University. This experience allowed me to develop a much greater appreciation for and familiarity with the analysis of large national data sets on education, which form a central core of this book. I learned to look over the edge and truly experience the world of sociological research. I am grateful for the opportunity and the mentoring

and the friendships provided by Doris Entwisle, Karl Alexander, James McPartland, Edward McDill, Richard Rubinson, David Baker, Aaron Pallas, Thomas Reilly, Joyce Epstein, Laura Salganik, Pamela Walters, and many others at the Center for the Study of the Organization of Schools.

Another experience that contributed to the format of the book was a summer seminar at Harvard University under the direction of James Davis, who has long been a spokesperson for an empirically based sociology, especially as it is taught to undergraduates. In addition to those mentioned above, in one way or another, all of the following people have contributed directly or indirectly to the writing of this book: Adam Gamoran, Elizabeth Cohen, Ian Westbury, Annette Lareau, Bruce Fuller, Kathryn Schiller and Richard Ingersoll, Roger Shouse, and George Farkas.

Of course, hundreds of people who are found in this bibliography also contributed to this book. I am grateful for their research and their thoughts, and I hope that I have used their work in an appropriate and reasonable manner. I also wish to acknowledge the large contribution that was made by Janice Schuster and Francine Mancini, who provided innumerable specifics for the hundreds of citations in the bibliography, and the help of Marcia Battle, who provided first-rate secretarial assistance throughout the life of the book. Paul Reilly, Michelle Sagan, and James McShane were especially helpful in various stages of the second edition. I am particularly grateful to Stephanie Magean, who worked to make the first edition more accurate and more readable and to Melissa Messina, who copyedited the second edition. Finally, I want to acknowledge the support from beginning to end that was provided by

Alan McClare and Margaret Loftus at Addison Wesley Longman, Jade Moran of Interactive Composition Corporation, and Christopher DeJohn at Prentice Hall.

I have the good fortune to be able to discuss the issues that form the basis for this book on a regular basis with my entire family. Many of the attempts to synthesize and present this sociology of education were greatly improved by their contributions. Thank you Arline, Kate, Julie, and Dave.

Over the course of the development of the book, each of the following individuals reviewed one or more chapters (in some cases the entire book): Karl Alexander, Johns Hopkins University; David Baker, Pennsylvania State University; Jean Daniels, California State University-Northridge; Doris Entwisle, Johns Hopkins University; Joyce Epstein, Johns Hopkins University; Lawrence G. Felice, Baylor University; William A. Firestone, Rutgers University; Arthur Harkins, University of Minnesota; Maureen Hallinan, University of Notre Dame; Walter Konetschni, Shippenburg University; Aaron Pallas, Michigan State University; Lester J. Roth, California State University; Richard Rubinson, Emory University; Maryellen Schaub, Pennsylvania State University; and Lala Carr Steelman, University of South Carolina. I am grateful for the support and input of all of these colleagues.

Cornelius Riordan
Providence, RI

Chapter 1

EQUALITY
AND ACHIEVEMENT
IN EDUCATION

This book is about schools, students, parents, and society. Its main objective is to try to determine who succeeds and who fails in school and beyond, and why. The approach is entirely sociological, relying upon both theory and research. We will draw upon the best social facts regarding education that we can obtain, and we attempt to explain these facts on the basis of sociological theory. We also avoid the temptation to psychologize about success and failure in school. We do this not because psychology is useless to furthering our understanding, but rather because it is overused. Most assuredly, an understanding of psychology will improve our understanding of school success and failure, and for this you should take a course in psychology. Since much of the educational process is organizational and communal, however, sociology is the social science of choice.

This chapter examines the goals of schools and their clients (parents and students) within the current context of controversy and reform that has emerged over the past several decades. These goals of schooling in modern society are complex and often conflicting: In democratic societies, citizens demand both greater

equality and greater quality from schools. They desire both the simple transmission of basic knowledge and skills and the selection of certain students to pursue specialized and functional roles in society; but also our society demands equity and equality of educational opportunity for all citizens. Some of the goals have become more salient in response to certain social structural and historical transformations. If we look closely at these broad objectives of schools and students, we will discover that more often than not, they are contradictory and conflicting.

❖ EQUALITY OF EDUCATIONAL OPPORTUNITY

Pivotal to the entire book is a working definition of *equality of educational opportunity*. Without this, one might easily claim that the schools *do* "equalize" or overcome the effects of the home, if one's definition of equality was simply that everyone was provided with a free public school education. There was a time, in fact, when this was the working definition of equality of educational opportunity. Today, of course, this definition would fall far short of how most people would conceive it. In a seminal article, Coleman (1968) traces the evolution of the concept of equality of educational opportunity, noting that it has gone through at least five stages of development or evolution: (1) equal access, (2) common curriculum, (3) differential curriculum, (4) desegregated schooling, and (5) equality of results.

◆ EQUAL ACCESS

Schools may provide "a *free* education up to a given level which constitutes the principal entry point to the labor force" (Coleman, 1968: 11). This concept has roots in America at least as far back as the eighteenth century when towns were required to establish and maintain free public schools. Although the starting point for this conception of equality varies from society to society, Coleman argues that the driving force behind this development was the Industrial Revolution, which ultimately led to a situation in which the family lost its economic and educational functions, and factory owners increasingly came to depend upon people who had to be given a general education. According to this definition, equality of educational opportunity is measured by the degree of *access* that all people have to schools. To whatever extent people are excluded, therefore, inequality exists.

In the Western world, we have come to take this definition for granted. By this definition, however, there is considerable educational inequality in developing and underdeveloped countries. Females, in particular, are excluded from all levels of education in some countries. Figure 1.1 reports the percentage of males and females in least developed, developing, and

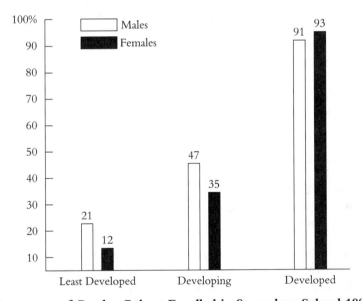

FIGURE 1.1 **Percentage of Gender Cohort Enrolled in Secondary School 1986–1990**
Source: United Nations Children's Fund, *The State of the World's Children, 1993* (New York: Oxford University Press, 1993), table 4, p. 75.

developed countries who were enrolled in secondary school during the period 1986–1990. Least developed countries include Ethiopia, Bangladesh, and Chad; developing countries include Turkey, Kenya, Vietnam; developed countries include Germany, France, and the United States.

Figure 1.1 displays inequalities in access to schooling (access to the ninth grade and beyond) across both countries and gender. In the least developed countries, both males and females are generally excluded from a secondary school education, but males in these countries do have slightly more access. The same is true for the developing countries. In the Middle East, North Africa, and Southeast Asia, the male/female difference can be as much as 20 percent (UNICEF, 1993). In developed countries, females have obtained parity with males in terms of access. Yet, even in the most economically developed countries, including America, women in college are still more likely to graduate from education, arts, humanities, social sciences, and law, and men are more likely to graduate from natural sciences, mathematics, and engineering (Bradley, 2000). But in the United States, the gender gap is nearly at parity judging from recent 2000 reports (Willingham and Cole, 1997; U.S. Department of Education, 2000).

It is also useful to consider the concept of access as a measure of equality with reference to curriculum allocation within schools. Access to schools per se may not guarantee full access to all the advantages provided by them. Oakes (1985) argues that curriculum differentiation is a violation of the equal protection clause of the Fourteenth Amendment to the Constitution. "Tracking is a governmental action that classifies and separates students and thereby determines the amount, the quality, and even the value of the government service (education) that students receive" (Oakes, 1985: 173). Conceived in this manner, tracking can serve as an obstacle to equality since it seems to provide unequal opportunities to students *within* the schools themselves.

◆ COMMON CURRICULUM

Another effort to equal educational opportunities for every student was made when schools provided a *"common curriculum* for all children, regardless of background" (Coleman, 1968: 11). During the nineteenth century, the free public schools in the United States became the common schools; these schools provided the same curriculum for everyone and were attended by students representing all classes of the community, except for the truly upper class, who attended private schools, or the truly poor, who did not attend school, and Native Americans and Southern blacks, who were excluded from school. Until 1954, of course, blacks attended segregated schools with a common curriculum under the "separate but equal" doctrine. Despite the extent of equality provided by the sameness of curriculum, it is remarkable that any remaining unequal educational opportunities of access (due to class, gender, and race) were relatively unchallenged until well into the twentieth century.[1] That is, general access to the schools and the sameness of curriculum (either in separate or desegregated schools) was commonly accepted to provide equality of educational opportunity.

---

[1] The debate over the equality of separate schools for blacks and whites dates back as far as 1787 (Bell, 1980).

The first challenge to the common curriculum came from the National Education Association in 1918 (Coleman, 1968: 12) in a report arguing that a common classical education may provide unequal educational opportunity to those students who were not likely to go on to college. By this time, such students composed the majority and were mostly immigrant children. According to Coleman (1968: 13) this "inequality" was defined as the use of a college curriculum that served only a minority and was not designed to meet the needs of the majority. In 1908, the superintendent of schools in Boston criticized the common school concept for providing "equal opportunity for all to receive *one kind* of education" (cited in Powell, Farrar, and Cohen, 1985: 247). The problem with this arrangement, he argued, was that students' abilities differed and the educational needs of various specialized occupations differed as well. Very shortly, this led to the idea of the comprehensive high school in which schools would provide a variety of academic curricula.

◆ DIFFERENTIAL CURRICULUM

Schools may provide a *differential (diverse) curriculum* (college, general, vocational) which, in theory at least, allowed students, regardless of their background, to "choose" which curriculum best suited their occupational goals and interests. The comprehensive high school offered advanced academic courses, along with those in vocational and business instruction, and remedial courses in basic skills. This became the Shopping Mall High School (Powell et al., 1985). This process occurred during an era of school reform and school expansion in the early decades of the twentieth century, and was brought about largely because of the increased immigrant population in the schools, coupled with economic and technological transformations and new laws restricting child labor (Cremin, 1988; Conant, 1967; Tyack, 1974).

In practice, of course, this is not the way it worked, for a student's home background obviously entered, then as now, into the placement (not choice) of curriculum. Behind the policy, however, was the assumption that all students would not benefit equally from a common education; that for many students, a classic college-oriented education might be a deterrent to occupational success, especially if there was little likelihood that these students could or would attend college. "An important objective of the comprehensive curriculum was, and still is, to keep students in school until graduation" (Lee, 2000).

Although this was an attempt to establish a greater extent of equality of educational opportunity, it led quickly to the institutionalization of "tracking" in the comprehensive high school, and soon became *de rigeur* in elementary schools as well. Retrospectively, in view of the steady decline in student academic performance, the persistent wide gap between the educational outcomes of various subgroups in the society, and the reform efforts of the past two decades, this particular evolution of the concept may have been ill-advised. In any event, during these first three stages very little concern was expressed as to how the factors of race, gender, and social class might affect the concept of equality of educational opportunity.

Table 1.1 shows the distribution of seniors in various tracks in public high schools in 1982 by socioeconomic status (SES). Clearly, the American high school curriculum is differentiated and influenced by the variables of race and class.

TABLE 1.1

PERCENTAGE OF 1982 PUBLIC HIGH SCHOOL SENIORS IN EDUCATIONAL PROGRAM BY SOCIOECONOMIC STATUS*

Socioeconomic Status	High School Program		
	College	General	Vocational
Bottom 50%	30	30	40
Top 50%	55	23	22

* Estimates are for 1982 public high school seniors in the High School and Beyond (HSB) survey. Estimates were computed by the author and are based on the weighted sample.

Overall, about one-third of the students enroll in each of the three program types. Middle-class students are more likely to be found in a college preparatory curriculum (55 percent) whereas working- and lower-class students are more likely to complete a vocational program. This pattern remained unchanged during the 1990s.

◆ DESEGREGATED SCHOOLING

Eventually, the concept of equality of educational opportunity was dramatically changed, providing by legal mandate that children from diverse backgrounds attend the same schools. This concept was implicit in the earlier conception of a common or same curriculum. Yet, for a variety of familiar and regrettable rationales, it was not until the Supreme Court decision of 1954 that this conception was added to the list. Until that time, the doctrine that schools could be "separate but equal" had held sway. Note also that the "separate but equal" belief (affirmed by the Supreme Court in 1896) was in full accord with the prevailing conception of equality of educational opportunity as described in the first three stages above.

However, according to Coleman (1968), it was in debating the pros and cons of the "separate but equal" doctrine during the middle decades of the twentieth century that the concept of equality of educational opportunity took on a different form. Until then, providing equality of educational opportunity meant providing equal *inputs*—free schools, a common curriculum, a comprehensive curriculum, and equal facilities and resources (as per the separate but equal policy). Yet, implicit in the concept are the *outcomes* or results of schooling. This had remained hidden in the concept until the 1954 Supreme Court decision. In formulating that decision, the Court compared the effects of schools that were, in fact, "separate but equal" and concluded that these schools produced results that were exceedingly unequal.[2] In this case, the outcomes or effects that were considered were self-esteem and prejudice.

It is interesting to note that by today's standards of research, the evidence upon

[2] The Supreme Court decision also utilized information regarding the inputs to schools in formulating its decision (Kluger, 1976).

which the decision was made was questionable. This is not to say the Court made the wrong decision, but only that it really did lack sound social science evidence (see Stephan, 1978; Rist and Anson, 1977; Kluger, 1976). In fact, the next stage in the development of the concept involved a mandate by Congress in 1964 to accurately determine the full extent of inequality in educational opportunity. In any event, the fourth stage essentially claimed that equality of educational opportunity could *not* be achieved via separate schools for blacks and whites. It was still a concept consisting mostly of inputs (racial composition of the student body), but with some attention paid to student outcomes in the form of possible negative psychological effects for blacks.

◆ EQUALITY OF RESULTS

Today, equality of educational opportunity is conceived as the extent to which schools are able to provide equality of educational *results* given different student inputs. This definition of the concept evolved as part of a study conducted by Coleman et al. (1966) to provide answers to a congressional mandate. This study was published under the title of *Equality of Educational Opportunity* but also came to be known as the Coleman Report. It was a milestone in education and in educational research, and we will consider the specific results in Chapter 4. Here, we want to emphasize that in designing the study, Coleman systematically dissected the concept (along the lines presented above) and investigated five different definitions of equality of educational opportunity. The first three were organized around the older views concerned mainly with "inputs" or "resources," the fourth and fifth were concerned with the "effects" or "outcomes" of schooling:

1. the degree of access to the school, the quality of the physical plant, the curriculum, the teachers (were they equal or unequal?);

2. the background characteristics of students (for example, an all-black school would not provide equality by any working definition except that of "separate but equal");

3. the social and academic "climate" existing as a result of the interrelationships of the first two inputs and other intangibles such as the nature of school-community relations;

4. the consequences (results) of schooling for individual students with equal backgrounds and abilities (Here the concern was the extent to which schools made a difference; that is, were some schools more effective or productive than others?);

5. the consequences (results) of schooling for individual students of unequal backgrounds and abilities (Here the concern was the extent to which the school was able to overcome or reduce the unequal effects of the home.).

In his analysis of these five dimensions, Coleman found that the differences (inequalities) between blacks and whites were smallest for facilities and curriculum, followed by teachers, and then by background characteristics of other students. The differences were greatest by far with regard to academic achievement. Much more importantly, he demonstrated that the inputs of schooling had only small effects upon the outputs, when conceived either as school effectiveness (as per definition 4 above) or as reducing initial inequalities (as per definition 5 above). But the crucial point is that the study advanced our understanding of the concept of equality of educational opportunity. In the final analysis, Coleman (1968: 18) concluded "that *effects* of inputs have come to constitute the basis for assessment of school quality (and hence equality of opportunity) in place of using certain inputs by definition as measures of quality (for example, small classes are better than large, higher-paid teachers are better than lower-paid ones, by definition)."

In the twenty-first century, all five of these definitions come into play in discussions of equality of educational opportunity. Although access to schools is no longer a major issue in the Western world, access to high-quality resources, courses, curriculum, and teachers *within* schools is now seen as critical to equality. Of course, access to schools is still a problem in other parts of the world. The matter of a core versus a differentiated curriculum is one of the current burning debates, and we examine this in detail in Chapter 6. You should readily see that these latter two definitions are the ones that receive considerable attention today as we try to compare the relative effects of charter schools, private schools, magnet schools, privatized schools, restructured schools, and so on.

❖ EDUCATIONAL REFORM

Today, the concept of equality of educational opportunity continues to undergo scrutiny and further evolution. Among the reforms of the 1990s and the twenty-first century is "school choice." Ironically, it parallels the "choice" movement of the Progressive Era described above, that led eventually to the comprehensive high school. Thus, "school choice" is a refor-

mulation of "subject and curriculum choice" within schools. Under a policy of school choice, students may select the school that they wish to attend. The choice may be made either within a district, or in some cases, within as large a geographic region as a state. In either case, the choice process must be made within the guidelines for racial balance operating within the state or district. In any event, the issue is whether equality is possible when some students are constrained to attend poor inner-city schools while others attend affluent suburban schools that, in effect, have been chosen by their parents.

Concomitant with the school choice movement are several major reforms moving in the opposite direction and implying greater control by the state and the school. In some districts, efforts are under way to abolish the "tracking" system of curriculum differentiation. Tracking (the grouping of students by ability) was the by-product of the comprehensive high school, and according to many critics (Oakes, 1985; Rosenbaum, 1976) led to increasing *inequality* of educational opportunity. For this reason, some reforms now are shifting back to a common curriculum. An extensive discussion of tracking is taken up in Chapter 6.

Similarly, in many states, new policies are being implemented regarding the redistribution of state funds to local communities. These plans call for greater equity in the distribution of funds: Poorer communities would get a greater percentage of state (and possibly federal) monies than more affluent communities. This would allow the poorer communities to provide school facilities and resources that were more equivalent to the more advantaged communities. Note that this reform actually relies on the older "input" model, which has been previously refuted by the Coleman study (see above). Proponents, however, point to problems with the earlier studies and to newly emergent data. We will examine this further in Chapter 5.

Along somewhat different lines, several reform proposals aim to lengthen the school day or the school year. A moment's thought will reveal why these ideas are clearly related to equality of educational opportunity. Let's assume that we have reached a point where equality is truly available in the schools and that the differences between groups have been reduced as a result of school; or more realistically perhaps, let's assume that the schools minimally maintain whatever differences were there to begin with between racial or gender or class groups. Then, the longer time that schools are in session, the more likely that differences will decrease, and vice versa. This assumes that there are no other serious fallouts attributed to school per se.

During the 1990s, states initiated accountability programs whereby students and schools undergo testing to assure that standards are being met in terms of achievement and equality. This has now become a national agenda. This has arisen in response to what many have perceived as a crisis in education, a concern on the part of families for more accurate information and assessment of how well their children are doing and how their money is being spent, and the fact that education is now fully entrenched in the formal taxation networks at the local, state, and federal levels. Thus, both families and the state have a vested interest in assessment and accountability. At this time, accountability is conducted in ways that may have consequences for students (they may not receive their diploma if they do not pass state examinations) and for schools (they will not receive incentive money if they do

not meet the standard over several years, or in extreme cases, they may be taken over by the state government). In Chapter 8 we examine a study by Muller and Schiller (2000) that examines the extent to which achievement and equality are increased by accountability measures.

Is it possible to provide equality of educational opportunity with a policy of school choice? Or, is school choice a way of providing better quality of schooling for only some students? School choice implies greater control of the school by parents, but this control may be limited to parents of high socioeconomic status. Is choice perhaps antithetical to equality of educational opportunity? How does the idea of school choice compare to the idea of curriculum choice? Does choice imply something different for those who are most and least advantaged in society? What are the best ways to provide equality of educational opportunity? Common curriculum? School choice? Integrated schools? Accountability? Redistribution of state funds? Is access to schools or to school programs a necessary and sufficient condition to provide equality of educational opportunity? Why or why not? Can you create a definition of equality of educational opportunity that is acceptable to you? What indicator(s) would you use to measure your concept of equality of educational opportunity?

❖ EQUALITY VERSUS QUALITY: CAN WE BE EQUAL AND EXCELLENT?

In the United States, and in other countries as well, two fundamental questions have been posed in recent years:

1. Can the schools foster more *equality* of educational opportunity?

2. Can the schools simultaneously produce greater achievement or *quality* of results?

It is obvious that these are, in fact, twin goals for schools in a democratic society. Are these goals fundamentally in conflict? Coleman (1988a: 377) posed the issue as follows: "Is inequality necessarily produced in pursuing a goal of excellence? Is mediocrity necessarily produced in pursuing a goal of equality?" This question was raised more than thirty years ago by John Gardner (1961) in a book entitled *Excellence: Can We Be Equal and Excellent Too?*

These two goals have always been part of educational thought in Western democratic countries, but both issues have intensified in recent years. The issue of equality arose in the United States initially with regard to blacks and in Europe in relation to the lower classes. Later, on both continents, the issue broadened to include all disadvantaged ethnic groups, the physically handicapped, and women. The challenge has been to induce a more equitable distribution of academic achievement among a broad and diverse range of students. The matter of excellence has come about largely as a result of a decline in a variety of achievement test scores. It was observed initially in the Scholastic Aptitude Test (SAT) scores, later in tests conducted by the National Assessment of Educational Progress (NAEP), and recently by international comparisons of mathematical and scientific achievement tests made available from studies by the International Association for the Evaluation of Educational Achievement (IEA). Most recently, we see the issue embodied in the reauthorization of the Elementary and Secondary School Act of 2002 (ESEA), commonly referred to as the "No Child Left Behind Act." These twin goals create an educational puzzle: How can we establish and maintain schools that produce high average achievement accompanied by social equity? One solution is *not* to equalize schools in which everyone does poorly. What is known empirically about the difficulties associated with this dilemma?

◆ **MEASURING EQUALITY AND QUALITY**

According to Brown and Saks (1975) there are indeed two major and conflicting goals in American education:

1. The democratic ideal of the nineteenth-century common school emphasizing equality of educational opportunity, attainment, and curriculum. (In the twentieth century, this ideal was expanded considerably to include integration of students from diverse racial, ethnic, and religious backgrounds.)

2. The twentieth-century ideal of excellence and efficiency that emphasizes the greatest degree of individual cognitive development via a process of objective selectivity in a merit-based organization of schooling. Contained in this goal is the notion that schooling enhances individual differences, thereby increasing the variation between students on achievement outcomes.

To attain the first goal, the variance or spread of student achievement should be narrow, whereas to reach the second goal, a wider dispersion of achievement within a school or system may be necessary to allow those at the top to excel. Following this logic, Brown and Saks advocate the use of both the mean (average) scores and the standard deviation (dispersion) in studies of student

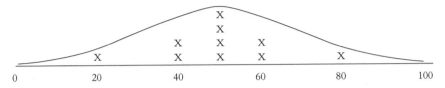

FIGURE 1.2   **Hypothetical Distribution of Test Scores for Ten Students**

achievement and school effectiveness.[3] Perhaps equality is best measured by attention to variation in achievement, but excellence is best measured by the use of both average scores and measures of dispersion. Note that both goals employ outcome measures in this example. Can you think of other, perhaps better ways to measure equality and quality?

Consider the hypothetical distribution of test scores shown in Figure 1.2 for ten students at the beginning of ninth grade. In order for a school to demonstrate effectiveness in reaching the goals of both equality and excellence, what should the distribution look like at the end of the twelfth grade? Plot your results onto Figure 1.2.

Under this kind of model, an effective or productive school would be one having a high mean achievement relative to otherwise comparable schools (suggesting that the school was successfully performing its goal of excellence) *and* a low dispersion or variation of scores relative to other schools (suggesting that this school was successfully attaining its goal of

equality).[4] Is it possible for schools to exhibit such results, or are these goals mutually exclusive? Is it possible for school systems to have it both ways—equality and excellence? Are there schools and school systems that are characterized by a relatively low spread or variation in test scores and are also characterized by "high achievement" of students on average? Are these schools integrated and diverse along class and race lines, or are they segregated? Are they public or private? Can you think of another way to demonstrate empirically that schools are accomplishing both goals?

◆ SOME EMPIRICAL EXAMPLES

One way to approach this question is to compare schools having unusually high achievement with those having unusually low achievement. Perhaps the easiest way to find such schools is to compare student outcomes in Japan and the United States. Over the past several decades, the International Educational Association has conducted cross-national studies of academic outcomes (FIMS, SIMMS, and TIMMS). In all of these studies, students in the United States consistently scored lower than their

[3] Test scores distribute themselves from high to low along a normal curve. For any distribution of scores, a standard deviation is the average amount of test score units that all scores deviate from the mean score. If all the scores cluster around the mean, the standard deviation would be small, and one might reason that this was evidence of greater equality of achievement. Hence, higher standard deviations of educational test scores are evidence of greater inequality.

[4] This interpretation departs from Brown and Saks (1975), who argue that a high degree of school effectiveness is indicated by either a high mean score or a high degree of dispersion of individual scores. They do concur, however, that a low dispersion of scores is indicative of greater equality of educational opportunity for all students in the school.

counterparts in Japan. It is quite conceivable that Japan emphasizes achievement at the expense of equality, while the opposite is true in the United States.

We have already noted that historically, the United States has had a system of *common* schools in which a higher value was placed on equality. Consequently, we might hypothesize that schools in Japan (and in Europe) would emphasize achievement goals whereas in American schools we might find evidence of egalitarianism. Efforts to generate equality are likely to constrain achievement at the top and to decrease the number of academically disadvantaged students at the bottom. Efforts to generate high achievement are likely to increase academic standards, causing students at the top to excel and possibly forcing those at the bottom to drop out.

Baker (1993) examined this issue empirically by marshaling evidence from the Second International Mathematics Survey (SIMS), which was conducted in the early 1980s using standardized tests of mathematics in nineteen countries (see Westbury et al., 1994). Baker plotted the simple change of the posttest (end-of-year score) minus the pretest (beginning-of-year score) for Population A in the SIMS data among *classrooms* in the sample. The students in the study were random samples of eighth grade classrooms in the United States and seventh grade classrooms in Japan. (The difference in grade level is due to the fact that the seventh grade curriculum in Japan was most implicitly related to the cognitive tests.) Figure 1.3 displays a striking difference between the two distributions.

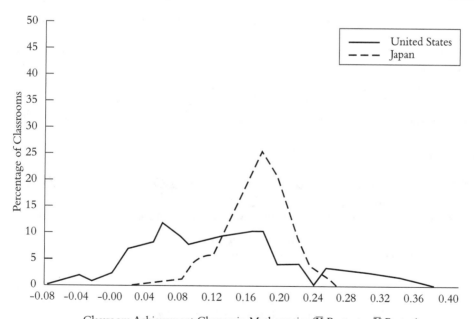

FIGURE 1.3 Distribution of Change in Mathematics Achievement in Japanese and American Classrooms

Source: David P. Baker, "Compared to Japan, the U.S. Is a Low Achiever . . . Really." *Educational Researcher* 22 (April 1993): 20. Copyright 1993 by the American Educational Research Association. Reprinted with permission.

The average achievement gains over the school year in Japan are much higher than the average achievement gains in the United States classrooms. At the same time, the scores are narrowly distributed in Japan as compared with the United States, where the scores are widely spread across the classrooms. Although the unit of analysis here is the classroom, the same results would hold even if the students were the unit of analysis (although the degree of variability would be greater in both countries). Thus, contrary to our hypothesis regarding greater egalitarianism in American schools, Baker found that schools in Japan were able to generate a greater degree of quality (achievement) and equality at the same time. (For contradictory results, see Coleman, 1988a.) In Chapter 6, we will return to these data again to inquire further as to how Japan is able to attain both high quality and equality in its schools.

Another comparison of schools along these dimensions of equality and quality can be observed from the High School and Beyond (HSB) survey of 1982 high school graduates in public and Catholic schools. Students in the HSB survey were tested first as sophomores and then as seniors (see description of HSB in Chapter 2). Coleman and his colleagues (1982) found that high achievement growth and low inequality *did* exist in Catholic schools in the United States. In a comparison of public and Catholic schools, they found that students in Catholic schools obtained higher levels of achievement than students in public schools, *and* at the same time, displayed smaller differences in achievement between high-performing and low-performing students, between blacks and whites, and between students from high and low socioeconomic home backgrounds.

Let's consider the case of minority and white students who attend Catholic and public high schools using the High School and Beyond data. Bryk, Lee, and Holland (1993) examined this question and reported the results (using the mathematics test only) shown in Table 1.2.

We can immediately see the larger gains made by students attending Catholic schools over the two-year period. We can also see that the largest gains of all

TABLE 1.2

AMOUNT OF MATHEMATICS LEARNING BETWEEN SOPHOMORE AND SENIOR YEAR (EXPRESSED IN TERMS OF YEARS OF LEARNING)

	White Students	Minority Students
Catholic Schools	2.5	3.3
Public Schools	2.1	1.5

Source: Adapted from Bryk, Lee, and Holland (1993), table 10.1. Data are from the High School and Beyond (HSB) survey. These figures were computed from the sophomore to senior raw gain in mathematics for each group, divided by half of the average gain made by public school students, which is taken as the benchmark. Reprinted by permission of the publishers from *Catholic Schools and The Common Good* by Anthony S. Bryk, Valerie E. Lee, and Peter B. Holland, Cambridge, MA: Harvard University Press, Copyright © 1993 by the President and Fellows of Harvard College.

were made by minority students attending Catholic schools. By contrast, minority students in public schools made the smallest gains. Catholic schools produced the largest gains in achievement and, at the same time, reduced the gap between whites and minorities. Public schools, on the other hand, were characterized by lower achievement levels and an increasing gap between whites and minorities. The increasing gap between the racial groups is a measure of inequality. Thus, another way to estimate the degree of equality in a school is to examine the gap between low-performing and high-performing students at two points in time. If one can demonstrate that the initial performance gap is reduced in some schools relative to others, a claim may be made that the former schools are producing more equality.

Of course, students attending Catholic schools are more homogeneous. Hence, the schools are more selective and less diverse at the outset. There is less inequality to overcome. Yet, Table 1.2 shows that students in Catholic schools become even more equal compared to students in public schools, while outperforming them at the same time. These results do not change substantially even when controls are added to account for home background differences, although about half of the greater gain in Catholic schools is due to the fact that these students come from higher SES homes (see discussion in Chapter 4).

Thus, it appears that Catholic schools are able to overcome this general incompatibility between educational quality and equality. Coleman, Hoffer, and Kilgore (1982) concluded that this twofold effectiveness of Catholic schools was due to a combination of stronger academic demands, a more disciplined and orderly environment, and less tracking or differentiation of students. In later work, Coleman and Hoffer (1987) argue that these school policies are the result of a more effective authority and control structure that is made possible through the existence of a functional and value community that is shared by parents, students, and teachers in Catholic schools.[5] Critics of this research have faulted it on both theoretical (McPartland and McDill, 1982; Salganik and Karweit, 1982; Riordan, 1985) and methodological (Willms, 1985; Alexander and Pallas, 1985) grounds. In Chapter 4, we consider this study in more detail.

♦ BALANCING QUALITY AND EQUALITY

The goals of excellence and equality may be incompatible and difficult to achieve simultaneously. Yet, it is equally clear that this conflict is not universal or inherent in all educational systems. Assuming that both objectives are equally important (this assumption should be worth at least a moment's thought), we face a key question: What conditions are necessary to bring about high levels of achievement among the top and average students without leaving other students too far behind? Some people (Oakes, 1985; Carnegie Council on Adolescent Development, 1989) feel that a less differentiated (untracked) core curriculum that is

---

[5] In a similar analyses, Bryk, Lee, and Holland (1993) concluded that the Catholic school advantage was due to an academic core curriculum; an extended communal organization between parents, teachers, and students; a decentralized school governance; and an inspirational ideology.

equally demanding for all students is part of the solution (see Chapter 6). Critics (Greenberg, 1990; Beck, 1990) of "untracking" argue that it will lower scores at the top, creating mediocre results similar to those depicted for the United States in Figure 1.3. Slavin (1983) argues that a greater degree of compatibility can be obtained by changing the technology of teaching and learning, as emphasized in the use of games and teams to establish an environment more appealing to low-performing and poorly motivated students. Cohen (2000) emphasizes the need for cooperative learning and group work along with the ongoing modification of student expectations for each other in the classroom.

In any event, to achieve greater equality conditions must be established that will allow disadvantaged and low-performing students to increase their achievement growth on an equal rate to better-performing students, and ideally, their achievement gains should exceed that of the initially stronger students. Focusing on how this would work at the classroom level, Cohen (2000: 276) summarizes what has to happen:

> [I]n an equitable classroom, teachers and students view each student as capable of learning both basic skills and high-level concepts. All students have equal access to challenging learning materials; the teacher does not deprive certain students of tasks demanding higher order thinking because they are not ready; classmates do not block access to instructional materials or prevent others from using manipulatives. Students who cannot read or understand the language of instruction have opportunities to complete activities and to use materials. The interaction among the students is "equal-status," that is, all students are active and influential

participants and their opinions matter to their fellow students. Finally, the achievement of students does not vary widely between the stronger and the weaker students. Whereas the more successful students continue to do well, the less successful students are more closely clustered around the mean achievement of the classroom rather than trailing far out on the failing end of the distribution. Thus, there is a higher mean and a lower variance of achievement scores in more equitable classrooms as compared with less equitable classrooms.

In order to accomplish this, the influence of the home (and other nonschool factors) must be mitigated while the influence of the school is increased. The difficult task is to identify schools that are able to meet this challenge (see Chapters 4, 5, and 6).

Some critics of school reform (McDill, Natriello, and Pallas, 1986: 416) have reservations about its "failure to give balanced emphasis to the ideas of quality and equality" (see also Gardner, 1961; Linn, Madaus, and Pedulla, 1982; Stedman and Smith, 1983; Sedlak et al., 1986). Reform measures, such as more rigorous and restricted curricula, greater demands for student time in school and on homework, and minimum competency testing, the critics argue, may spawn greater student stratification and failure. Critics fear that the negative effects of such reforms would fall disproportionately upon those most in need of help from the schools. Indeed, the concern is that some reforms might be inegalitarian and elitist. It is understandable, therefore, that any educational reform that carries the risk of a reduced commitment to equality, in the name of quality, will be viewed with suspicion. The critics are concerned that a latent effect of this type of reform is to create a more elitist school (more like the European model) and to reduce the likelihood of increasing equality.

❖ STATE VERSUS FAMILY AGENCY: WHO CONTROLS THE SCHOOLS?

Historically there have been two other conflicting orientations toward schooling in America. To what extent does the government (nation, state, or society) control the school? To what extent is the family (or local community) able to influence what goes on? This is a different (although related) question from the previous one above where we inquired about the capacity of the school to bring about quality and equality. Here we examine the conflicting interests of schools and families. To what degree are schools able to reduce (or at least maintain) the levels of inequality that children bring with them from their homes? To what extent are children entitled to the full benefits of their own family resources?

> The first orientation sees schools as society's instrument for releasing a child from the blinders imposed by the accident of birth into this family or that family. Schools have been designed to open broad horizons to the child, transcending the limitations of the parents, and have taken children from disparate cultural backgrounds into the mainstream of American culture. They have been a major element in social mobility, freeing children from the poverty of their parents and the low status of their origins. . . . [The] second orientation to schooling sees school as an extension of the family, reinforcing family values. The school is *in loco parentis*, vested with

> the authority of the parent to carry out the parent's will. The school is, in this orientation, an efficient means for transmitting the culture of the community from the older generation to the younger. (Coleman and Hoffer, 1987: 3–4)

Thus, in the first orientation, the school serves as an agent for the larger society; in the second orientation, the school acts as an agent for the family. Coleman and Hoffer point out that there is yet a third orientation in which school serves the interest of a particular community, such as a religious community or a group of like-minded families who share certain collective values regarding education or some other areas of interest. The demand in some cities for single-sex schools, or an Afro-centric curriculum, or "charter" schools are examples of this idea. This third orientation could also be a local community, although there are very few residential neighborhoods remaining that qualify as "communities" in any functional sense (see below).

Generally, these orientations are incongruent except in the unusual situation in which the needs and values of the family (or community) are entirely consistent with the needs and values of the larger society. Such a society would necessarily be religiously and ethnically homogeneous and essentially classless. It would require a "perfect cultural consistency and social continuity between family and school" (Coleman and Hoffer, 1987: 5). Such a social environment would occur only in the absence of social change and perhaps only in the historic past.

◆ RAWLS VERSUS NOZICK

Fundamentally, the issue involves two contrasting images of a "just" society.

These images are exemplified by two books on moral philosophy: *A Theory of Justice* by John Rawls (1971) and *Anarchy, State, and Utopia* by Robert Nozick (1974). This discussion draws largely from an article by Coleman (1976) entitled "Rawls, Nozick, and Educational Equality."

> Rawls's theory of justice addresses the question of . . . whether inequalities are justified in society. Rawls's answer is that only those inequalities are justified which are to the advantage of the least advantaged. . . . Beginning with the assumption that each person has a set of natural rights, Nozick argues that justice demands neither equality nor inequality that must benefit the least advantaged, but rather the full entitlement of each person to what he has justly acquired. Whereas for Rawls, a central authority is entitled to distribute the fruits of everyone's labor, for Nozick, only the individual is entitled to the fruits of his own labor, and he has full rights to the use and disposal of them. (Coleman, 1976: 121)

For Rawls, creating equality is the objective of a just society; for Nozick, the preservation of individual liberty is the most important goal. These polar positions are useful because they identify the ultimate goals of each philosophy, and thereby, they sensitize us to what is gained or lost by moving in either direction.

What do these two philosophical positions imply for education? Rawls suggests that equality would be achieved by removing a child from influences of the home to the greatest possible extent. Since families provide unequal resources, equality is difficult to achieve unless the child is extricated in large part from the home. Nozick implies, by contrast, that public education should be dispensed with altogether.

> For public education is redistributive, and by Nozick's "entitlement" principles, each child is entitled to the full untaxed benefits of his family's resources, insofar as it chooses to use those resources for his benefit. Thus, for Nozick, all education is private, paid for individually by each family according to its resources and preferences. (Coleman, 1976: 122)

The educational structures implied by either of these views, perhaps once viewed as extreme, are today the vogue of educational policy. Some of the attempts to implement forms of private schooling, including vouchers and charters, are policies founded on Nozick's philosophy. Exceptions to this are those where the charter or voucher constrains the school to serve only disadvantaged students (for example see Howell et al., 2000; http://www.brighterchoice.org). All efforts to extend the school day or the school year in terms of day care, preschool, after school, and summer school are grounded in the philosophy of Rawls. Likewise, all efforts to increase access to the full range of schooling and the curriculum are based on Rawls. Taken together then, these two philosophies dominate the educational reform landscape, even though they are at opposite ends of the continuum.

◆ PUBLIC AND PRIVATE SCHOOLS

To some degree, these orientations have been the bases for public and private schooling, respectively. In eighteenth-century American society, community and family were in fact consistent in ethnicity, religion, and cultural values. All that changed, however, as America became the "melting pot" for one immigrant group after another, each with its own unique set of family, religious, and community values. Within this context, the values of schools, families, and communities became increasingly inconsistent and conflicting. Of particular concern to families and communities of different religions and ethnic backgrounds was the fact that the values of the larger society were dominant in the schools.

This gave rise to an increase in private schools charged with maintaining certain particularistic religious, ethnic, communal, or family values. Of course, this organizational differentiation protected more than simply family values. More importantly, independent "elite" private schools provided a "better" education, thereby ensuring the economic interests of families and individuals, rather than supporting the broader interests of the society. In this way, wealthy families were most easily able to pass on their class position to their children. This line of thinking is the basis for a sociological perspective called "social reproduction" theory (Carnoy and Levin, 1976; Bowles and Gintis, 1976; Bourdieu, 1977).

The very nature of the public schools has resolved this dilemma most often in favor of the values of the larger society. In the United States, the "common school" was formed on the basis that schools were meant to serve the interests of the wider society. Equality and inclusiveness were the values of choice in the public school:

> It was a choice against schools organized along class lines. It was a choice against schools organized along religious lines and against schools organized along ethnic lines. . . . It was a choice in favor of schools organized along residential lines and governed by the local community. (Coleman and Hoffer, 1987: 13–14)

Of course, to a significant degree, suburban public schools are similar to private schools. Here, parents exercise their choice by moving to the suburbs rather than living in the city and sending their children to private schools. Nonetheless, ideologically and practically in the cities, public schools were common schools.

In the early years of the common school movement all students completed a common curriculum. By 1920, however, despite the protests of critics (Sizer, 1964), the comprehensive high school emerged and offered a differentiated curriculum that quickly became the standard fare. This provided an element of "choice" for students attending the public schools. Also, in the early years of the common schools, students came from relatively homogeneous residential areas. Thus, they brought with them a common set of values, many of which were compatible with the values of the school.

During the twentieth century, however, residential areas have become increasingly heterogeneous and so have the public schools. As this occurred, the conflict between family (or community) values and the values promulgated in the schools increased accordingly. And as this occurred, families and communities pressed for "choices" and "control" in the schools: choices of teachers, curriculum, textbooks, amount of homework, length of the school day and the school year, type of extracurricular activities, and most recently, choice of school. In some cities today, private firms now operate public schools (Bennett, 1992). Hence, the issue is no longer confined to the simple bifurcation of public and private schools.

I am not referring to racial or social class heterogeneity. Research has shown that residential communities in the

United States are at least as racially homogeneous as they have always been. Rather, I am referring to the values and beliefs that people hold. These are no longer sustained by an intense interaction within a local residential community. More often today, values are created and then held in place by individual reactions to broad issues and events as they are depicted in the mass media. Hence, within residential communities are people of different religions and political perspectives living side by side with one another. They are advocates for and against abortion, nuclear energy, desegregated schooling, feminism, greater equality, homosexuality, and on and on.

◆ THE INFLUENCE OF THE HOME

The plans *and* the results of court-ordered racial desegregation in the schools are pivotal to this entire issue. If families rather than the state controlled the public schools, desegregated schools might not ever have come into existence. Integrated schools came about as a result of state- and court-ordered mandates. Family responses to these mandates have often been to reassert family control by changing family residence—that is, moving to a school district outside the practical enforcement of state-ordered busing or enrolling children in private schools. In fact, public schools today are just as segregated as they were prior to 1954 largely as a result of "white flight" from the central cities (Orfield and Monfort, 1992; Simon-McWilliams, 1989; for disagreement on this, see Taeuber, 1990). There is perhaps no better evidence of the power of the family.

This conflict between school as an instrument of society versus school as an extension of the family pivots around the matter of control. Generally, in the

United States and in other democratic countries, conflicts between these two forces have been resolved in favor of the larger society. For example, federal laws and legislation empower school districts to make decisions regarding school assignments of students, employing busing when necessary. For another example, the Supreme Court has ruled that separation of church and state prohibits religious activity of any kind in the public schools, despite the fact that the majority would probably favor it (*Engle v. Vitale*, 1962; *Abington School District v. Schempp*, 1963). Nonetheless, these issues never have been completely resolved. Today, there is increasing dissatisfaction among both whites and minorities regarding the benefits of desegregation. And the issue of school prayer surfaces persistently at both the local and national level. Recently, the Supreme Court ruled that prayer be disallowed even at school graduation ceremonies (*Lee v. Weisman*, 1992). Most school districts have abandoned busing programs and desegregation efforts as we enter the twenty-first century.

◆ SOCIAL REPRODUCTION THEORY

There have always been ways, however, for parents to have their own way despite the hegemony of the schools. Those parents who could afford it could send their children to private schools chosen specifically because they mirror the values of the family. Or, as long as they could afford it, they could choose a residence on the basis of the excellent reputation of the public schools in a certain geographical area (typically, wealthy and exclusive suburban communities). To a lesser extent, it has always been possible for parents to influence the curriculum placement of children, thereby ensuring a modicum of consistency between family and school values, at least in the classroom.

But social class influences achievement mostly in terms of how parents prepare children for school and monitor their progress by providing a place for homework to be done and ensuring that the homework is completed. In this way, middle-class parents provide a home advantage for their children and control the process of social reproduction regardless of the type of school, the location of the school, or the student composition of the school. By the beginning of school, reading and mathematical ability are strongly related to social class. Table 2.1 in Chapter 2 shows that among students entering kindergarten for the first time in 1998, students in the upper SES quartile outperform their counterparts in the lower SES quartile quite substantially and significantly. In Chapter 3, we pursue this in detail.

In any event, all of the mechanisms by which parents can exert greater control over the educational process have been employed. And there has been growth in the public schools in the idea of magnet schools in which parents and students choose a school on the basis of a specialized curriculum. Moreover, in states such as Minnesota and Oregon, students are able to choose whichever public school they wish to attend regardless of curriculum (subject only to restrictions regarding violations of state regulations for racial balance in the school; see Glastris and Toch, 1989). In Detroit and Milwaukee, some students are even able to choose between a public and private school (Wells, 1990). In Oregon, students can actually select either a public or a private school anywhere in the state (Celis, 1990). And now in Michigan, which is the first state to abolish the use of property taxes as the primary means of financing public

education, teachers and parents can actually propose to "charter" their own schools with self-defined curriculum, personnel, scheduling, and self-governance (Garber, 1994).

At the same time, schools have been expanding to take on some functions that formerly were the business of the family. For example, schools offer an increasing amount of day care for children both before and after school, during the summer, and during the preschool years. Martin (1992, 1995) advocates removing the barriers of school and home entirely. As more and more parents enter the workforce on a full-time basis, the traditional concept of home and family becomes devalued. Martin argues that a reevaluation of domesticity is in order. She advocates a "schoolhome" that can provide the safe and nurturing environment once provided by the traditional family. All of this suggests that the conflict between state and family agency is very salient in the schools today.

It is important to recognize that this conflict contains more than simply a case of state versus parental control. The alert reader may have noted already that the plea for family control is at the same time a mechanism by which middle- and upper-class families can pass on their wealth to their children. If schools completely control what is going on, and if schools are committed to equality (which they are by law and by educational theory), the relationship of the social class of parents to the social class destinations of their offspring would be attenuated in public schools. In situations where parents control the educational process, even in part, they are better able to pass on whatever advantages they have to their children. This is typically the case in "elite" private schools (Cookson, Jr. and Persell, 1985) but also is true in public schools, reflecting the fact that parents continue to exert control. Only in Catholic schools is the relationship of parental social class mitigated in the United States (this is reflected in Table 1.2 and pursued further in Chapter 4).

Consider that in private schools, wealthy parents are capable of paying for the best teachers and equipment available, whereas in public schools, parents may have to accept whatever is there.[6] Also, in private schools, most students will come from wealthy homes and most students will have positive attitudes regarding the value of education; public schools, on the other hand, accept all comers including many students who are poorly motivated and prepared. In more affluent suburban communities, the resources and motivation of students in public schools will resemble private schools in many respects. By contrast, public schools in the inner city with fewer resources are attended by those students with the fewest home resources and the greatest academic needs. In Chapter 3 we explore in detail the many ways in which the socioeconomic status of the home influences educational, and ultimately, occupational outcomes.

Given a voice and a choice in the matter, upper- and middle-class parents will encourage, cajole, persuade, and, if necessary, pay to make sure that their children get the best that school has to offer. In sociology, we call this process whereby children pass through the educational system and end up in economically in the same place as their parents "social reproduction." To the extent that this process is dominant in a society, the people making up the social structure would be replicates of the previous generation. Professional parents would "reproduce" children earmarked for the professions; unskilled laborers would similarly "reproduce" their children for laboring occupations. In Western democratic societies, "social reproduction" theory runs contrary to a commonly held ideology maintaining that everyone has an equal chance to succeed. And, in fact, people are mobile in such societies; it is possible and not unusual for very successful people to have come from very poor homes.

One of the interesting and important questions in the sociology of education is the prevalence of "social reproduction" in a given society at a particular historic point. It is widely believed that to some extent social reproduction increases in a linear fashion with increases in the family control of education, and vice versa. Social reproduction theory implies (actually requires) greater control by families of higher socioeconomic status. You can see immediately that this theory aligns with the philosophy of Nozick discussed above. In lieu of this control, schools would presumably institute and maintain a system of meritocracy and equality of opportunity. Public schools, in theory, are in accord with the philosophy of Rawls. Many public school teachers, being frightened of Marx as a protégé, fail to recognize that the mandate and the current practice of public schools (excluding affluent suburban schools) follows the philosophy of Rawls, certainly not that of Nozick.

---

[6] The salary of teachers in "elite" independent schools is significantly lower than in public schools, and private school teachers have fewer teaching credentials than their public school counterparts. They are, however, highly motivated and work extra hours both before and after school. For this effort, they generally receive full tuition for their own children at the private school, which undoubtedly increases their commitment to the school.

Another complication to the debate has been raised by Coleman and Hoffer (1987). They argue that private schools are value communities—that is, that teachers, parents, and students share the same values about education. Public schools, on the other hand, because they are based on residence, are lacking in value consistency. Hence, they are contentious and divisive. In a value community, there is a clear and consistent set of norms that express dominant values and which determine behavior. According to Coleman and Hoffer (1987: 11), being a principal in a value community is easy— "discover the dominant set of values in the community and the norms supporting those values, and then exercise authority accordingly, imposing sanctions to enforce the norms."

In today's public schools, this is not possible because attendance is still largely based on residence, and the schools operate without a dominant set of shared values. Being governed by the law, schools attempt to implement the dominant state value of equality, but this value is not always shared and embraced by parents and students. Coleman and Hoffer conclude that this objective of the public schools to overcome the influence of the home is greatly hampered by a lack of value consistency. They argue further that this is a major stimulus to the idea of "choice" in the public schools.

♦ TRADITIONALISTS AND
REVISIONISTS

This idea of school and family control has been conceptualized in various ways. Selakowich (1984) compares and contrasts educators and educational critics— the traditionalists and the revisionists. Traditionalists have maintained that the whole purpose of American education

was to provide universal, common, free, and equal education to everyone and that this has been accomplished (early traditionalists such as Cubberly thought that the matter was closed in 1919). In contrast, the "revisionists" have reached a very different conclusion regarding schools and the democratic idea. They argue that despite reform and an ideology to the contrary, the schools have actually promoted the social class interests of the elite of the society, and that they have been quite instrumental in preserving what is basically an educational system of inequality.

The revisionists' argument is bolstered by studies such as Colin Greer's *The Great School Legend* (1972), which demonstrates that between 1920 and 1960, certain ethnic/racial groups (Slavic people, Italians, blacks) made little or no progress in the educational and occupational ladder of the United States. Likewise, in their much read and discussed book, *Schooling in Capitalist America*, Bowles and Gintis (1976: 35) declared "that United States education is highly unequal, the chances of attaining much or little schooling being substantially dependent on one's race and parents' economic level."

As part of their exhaustive analyses, Bowles and Gintis examined the relationship between parental socioeconomic status and educational attainment among white males for whom full data was available, including IQ scores that were used as controls. Under a scenario of low family control in the schools, the relationship between parental SES and educational attainment should be low when IQ is taken into account. Figure 1.4 shows that this relationship is extremely strong even when IQ scores are controlled. Males from the lowest SES decile attained five full years less education (9.9) than their

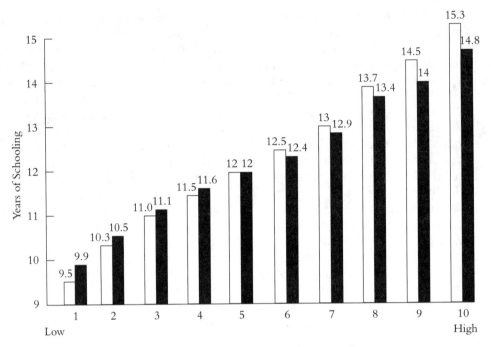

FIGURE 1.4   Educational Attainments Are Strongly Dependent on Social Background Even for People of Similar Childhood IQs

Notes: For each socioeconomic group, the left-hand bar indicates the estimated average number of years of schooling attained by all men from that group. The right-hand bar indicates the estimated average number of years of schooling attained by men with IQ scores equal to the average for the entire sample. The sample refers to "non-Negro" men of "nonfarm" backgrounds, aged 35–44 years in 1962.

Source: Samuel Bowles and Herbert Gintis, *Schooling in Capitalist America* (New York: Basic Books, 1976), 31. Reprinted by permission of Basic Books, a division of HarperCollins Publishers, Inc.

counterparts in the highest SES decile (14.8), even when their IQ scores were equivalent. Bowles and Gintis present a very cogent theoretical and empirical case, showing that the schools have maintained the inequality that is vital to a capitalistic system (docile and obedient workers who are not overly critical of the system and have learned to accept their place).

Before proceeding further, we should note that it is never simply a case of educational outcomes that concern us;

rather the "bottom line" on this issue of equality is usually taken to be occupational outcomes, as shown in Figure 1.5. In more recent work, Bowles and Gintis (2002) reviewed current studies on intergenerational inequality (social reproduction), and based on studies in the United States only, concluded that the average intergenerational correlations (between parents and children) were .35 and .38 for family income and education, respectively.

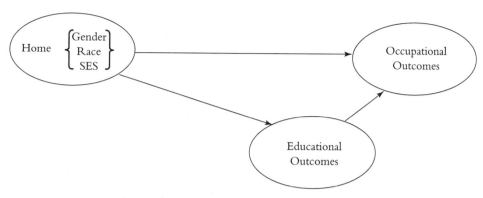

FIGURE 1.5   Model of Status Attainment

If school did nothing to alter the advantage or disadvantage provided by the home, then the SES, race, or gender advantage would be passed on to the next generation (that is, through social reproduction, as the revisionists maintain). It would not matter if the effect were direct or indirect. In fact, the effect would be largely indirect through educational outcomes, which were determined mostly by the influence of home background. Note that there is no question here whatsoever that educational outcomes strongly influence occupational achievement. Hence, when we talk about the matter of equality, and the role of school and home in the process, we are ultimately talking about a reduced influence of home background on occupational achievement. In this book, we often simplify matters by looking only at the extent to which the home affects educational outcomes.

❖ CULTURAL TRANSMISSION VERSUS SELECTION AND ALLOCATION: WHAT IS THE BUSINESS OF THE SCHOOLS?

Beyond the questions of whether schools can be equal and excellent, and how they are controlled, is the question of what they actually do: How do they operate on the inside? Assuming a set of schools with a given degree of equality and quality, and a certain degree of state and family control, what are the schools all about? What is their central business? Is it to socialize all students in a given school to a common set of values and skills considered to be important in society? Or is it to sort and channel students in such a way as to ensure, for the good of society, that all the specialized occupational and family roles will be filled? Or is it a bit of both?

◆ THE FUNCTIONS OF SCHOOLS

There has always been debate regarding the most appropriate and critical *functions* of the school. Here we employ the notion of functions in a more focused manner than previously conceived. In this case, we are concerned with the day-to-day activities of the school. The following list of school functions, suggested by Spady (1974), is fairly inclusive:

1. *Instruction*—transmission of knowledge and technical skills; with goals of ensuring cultural literacy and cultural progress;

2. *Socialization*—transmission of attitudes, values, and interpersonal skills;

3. *Custody and control*—care and monitoring of student behavior;
4. *Certification*—maintaining and forwarding of credits, diplomas, and credentials as evidence of competency levels for use by other institutions;
5. *Selection*—sorting and channeling of students toward certain educational and occupational opportunities.

The first two functions might be viewed as the "manifest functions" of school. They correspond quite closely to goals held by parents, students, and educators. They are the goals likely to be found in local, state, and federal documents that serve as guides for education. In his book *A Place Called School*, John Goodlad (1984) further specifies these two functions as follows: (1) academic goals; (2) vocational goals; (3) social, civic, and cultural goals; and (4) personal goals. The remaining three goals from Spady's list might be viewed as the "latent functions" of schooling. By this we mean that they represent the business of school that is often overlooked.

It is worth noting, however, that all of the functions are surely part of the everyday business of the school, regardless of whether the school is controlled by the state or the home, and regardless of whether the school is high or low on the twin issues of quality and equality. For this reason, it may be useful to think of this set of conflicting goals as occurring "within" schools. The issue of inequality will arise again in this section, but bear in mind that the source of inequality in this case lies "within" schools rather than "between" schools or "between" homes. Chapter 2 will help to distinguish these different types of school and home effects.

Few would argue with the view that one of the central functions of school is cultural transmission. Schools are held responsible, in large part, for the transfer of society's values, beliefs, knowledge, and behavioral patterns from one generation to another. Students receive instruction in a curriculum containing the basic knowledge and beliefs of the society. Minimally, students learn to read and write, to divide and multiply, to become literate regarding civic laws and customs, to have at least a rudimentary knowledge of the history of the country and the world, and finally, to have a working knowledge of the natural sciences (the nature of the galaxy, the human body, and so on).

But the process of cultural transmission involves much more than knowledge and cognitive skills. It also includes value socialization.

> Basic to the process of cultural reproduction is teaching youth to love and revere the established and traditional institutions of society. These usually include the family, religion, the government and the general economic system.... Schools present children with highly idealized pictures of their social institutions. They encourage the expression of allegiance through colorful rituals, oaths, songs, drama, and dance. (Parelius and Parelius, 1987: 22)

In addition, socialization in the proper attitudes toward adult work is considered to be an important part of the process. Students learn to be responsible, obedient, cooperative, and some students are selected and trained in leadership roles (Bowles and Gintis, 1976, 2002).

In carrying out its socialization function, schools also help to maintain social control in the society. As individuals internalize the values and morals of the society, they come to exercise self-control and become supportive and committed to the existing order of things. They are less likely to rebel, deviate, or otherwise threaten the social order. Sociologists view the process of socialization or internalization as the primary basis of social control (Berger and Berger, 1978; Berger and Luckman, 1967).

The school contributes to the maintenance of social control in a direct sense as well. Students are required to attend school from approximately age five through age sixteen, five days a week, ten months of the year. (There is variation, of course, from state to state and from country to country.) Through compulsory school attendance, schools function as custodial institutions for young people. School attendance keeps children off the streets and generally out of trouble. In this context, schools are able to carefully monitor intellectual, social, and personal development. When confronted by nonconforming, recalcitrant, or criminal behavior, the school employs counselors, social workers, and psychologists to "treat" the potential offender. In this regard, the school serves as one of many forms of secondary social control (Berger and Berger, 1978). All of this leads to a view as Meyer (1977: 55) notes, that schools "are organized networks of socializing experiences which prepare individuals to act in society."

◆ FUNCTIONAL AND CONFLICT THEORY

Schools are thus charged with the serious business of developing citizens who will be ready to support society's values and institutions. Certainly, the preservation of any society is dependent upon the schools to meet this challenge. Further-more, and especially in modern democratic, industrialized societies, schools are asked to deliver an adequate supply of literate and competent workers who are able to meet the sophisticated demands of jobs in a highly technical and specialized society. But some jobs are more difficult than others; some are more dangerous; some require special talent and training; and some provide more prestige and rewards. Thus, jobs in modern societies are rarely equal, in either importance or in financial reward. Hence, the question arises as to the role of the schools in sorting, channeling, preparing, and placing students in differential career projectories. This matter requires us to consider the "functional" and "conflict" theories of education.

According to the structural functional theory of society, schools accept the existing arrangements of society including the class system, differential values, and the political and economic system. The functions of schooling include *both* "socialization" to adult roles and "allocation" to educational and occupational training according to ability (see Kerckhoff, 1976). Functional theory argues that education provides a mechanism for individual mobility, and perhaps more importantly, that schools ensure that the most qualified people ultimately get the best jobs in the society. People move up or down in school and in the occupational world beyond, according to their ability and motivation. The theory further assumes that schools serve a very important societal function by channeling and allocating the most able and appropriate people into professions and other key occupations on the basis of ability. From the perspective of society, the process ensures not only that very important and often difficult job positions

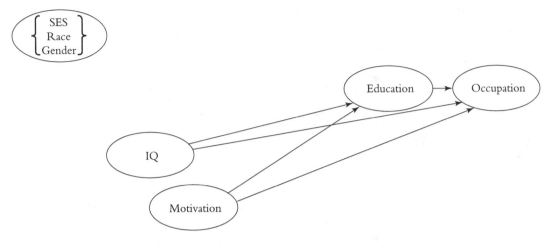

Figure 1.6   **Model of Functional Theory**

are regularly filled but also that they are occupied by the most qualified people. According to this theory, teachers and administrators act as agents for the society as a whole. Functional theory rejects the notion that social reproduction is a dominant process in society. In fact, functional theory assumes that the meritocratic principals of school overcome social reproduction. A model of functional theory is shown in Figure 1.6.

Conflict theory, on the other hand, argues that education serves to reinforce and reproduce the inequalities of a society. It does not entirely allocate according to ability, but rather according to race and class and gender, thus acting to constrain social mobility. Conflict theory is quite similar to social reproduction theory, except that it also emphasizes that the results of social reproduction are to increase the conflict between groups that must compete for scarce resources. In this view, allocation exists to serve the interests of the dominant and advantaged elites of the society, and contributes to the conflict that separates groups in society.

Conflict theory (or Marxism) is actually constituted by those who emphasize the reproduction aspects and another group who emphasize conflict (see Carnoy, 1974; Dougherty and Hammack, 1990). The conflict model is displayed in Figure 1.7.

Bernstein (1975) elaborated conflict theory into what he called code theory, in which he posited that the communication codes of working- and middle-class children differed substantively and that this was the basis for the lower performance of working-class students. Bernstein (1996) argued that this was not a deficit theory, as his critics maintained, but rather that working-class students possess one type of language codes but that schools required an elaborate language code for success.

Teachers and administrators act as agents to protect the interests of the dominant groups at the expense of the others. This does not necessarily (or even likely) involve deliberate discrimination; rather it simply means that schools (teachers) do not actively implement a selection process that *deactivates* the influence of

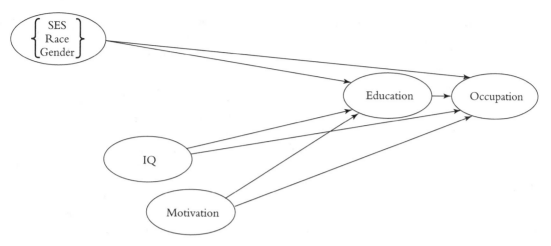

FIGURE 1.7   Model of Conflict Theory

socioeconomic status, race, and gender. Some researchers (Rist, 1970; Cicourel and Kituse, 1963), have reported instances in which the sorting of students was directly related to social class. Other research (Eder, 1981; Heyns, 1974) demonstrates, however, that the impact of social class on track placement becomes insignificant once tested ability is taken into account (which tends to support functional theory). The simple existence of tracking as a form of organization in a school, however, may contribute to increased inequality (Gamoran, 1992).

Gender, race, and socioeconomic status are the three major determinants of inequality in society. Despite all of our efforts to eliminate their effects, these variables persistently influence the status outcome variables of education, occupation, and income. These relationships are prima facie evidence of the conflict theory of stratification in sociology. When status origin variables strongly influence status destinations, categories (or groups) of people in society remain divided and in conflict with each other. In

ideology, if not always in practice, our society is committed to reducing and eliminating these invidious relationships.

At issue, therefore, is whether schools are able to allocate students on a fair and just basis, providing equal protection. Once again, it is important to emphasize that this is an entirely different issue from how schools are controlled (relative influence of home/state). It is a "within" school process.[7] There is considerable evidence, which we consider in Chapter 6, that home, socioeconomic background, and the personal attributes of gender and race play a significant role in the allocation process. Also at issue here is the question of when the allocation process begins. Most people are aware that high schools and junior high schools provide a differentiated curriculum. Students are enrolled in either a college, general, or

[7] Conflict and functional theory are by no means limited to the analysis of within school issues. Both theories are widely used throughout the discipline.

vocational track. Although students and parents might be deluded into thinking they have a "choice" of track placement, the evidence suggests otherwise (see Chapter 6). Schools, in the form of teachers and counselors, allocate students to tracks (Rosenbaum, 1976; Lucas, 1999). Increasingly, it appears that the allocation or tracking process may begin much earlier—perhaps, at the very beginning of school (see Rist, 1970; Entwisle and Hayduck, 1982; Entwisle, Alexander, Pallas, and Cadigan, 1988; Pederson, Faucher, and Eaton, 1978). And at the other end of the educational ladder, there is evidence that colleges extend the allocation function by "cooling-out" the educational aspirations of students in junior colleges (Clark, 1960; Dougherty, 1987), and making the cost of private education prohibitive to all except the children of the elite.

It seems, therefore, that the allocation function of schooling is at least as dominant as the socialization function, possibly more so. And that allocation may be based partly upon irrelevant ascribed status characteristics. To the extent that this is true (and we will pursue it further in Chapter 6), schools are implicated in maintaining or reproducing the structural inequalities of the society. Thus, the allocation function may be in conflict with the goal of equality as well.

❖ THE POLITICS OF EDUCATION

Throughout this chapter, we have discussed a variety of philosophies and strategies for defining what is wrong with schooling and the proposed policy solutions. Perhaps unlike any other topic in sociology, everyone has very definitive and relatively knowledgeable views about schools. After all, there is no other social institution, except the family, for which we have accumulated so much direct experience. Virtually no one could ever be lost for words in any discussion about the issues of education. The problem, however, is that many of our individual views lack empirical and/or theoretical support.

For example, if students had their way, the academic aspects of school would be greatly reduced, as would the length of school. They would probably argue, not without some basis, that it would become a more meaningful experience if school were more vocational and practical and shorter. Of course, most educators and parents would focus on other considerations, such as the custodial functions of schooling that we discussed in this chapter. Nonetheless, there are all sorts of political opinions as to possibly restructuring the curriculum (some educators do agree that it should be more practical, with more internship-type experiences) and the length of the school year (here many educators think it should be longer rather than shorter). How do we determine which is the best course of action?

Consider another example: If some parents and educators had their way, schools would never have been racially integrated. The pros and cons of segregated and desegregated schooling are colored by racial attitudes and experiences. In fact, nearly fifty years after the Brown decision, the future of school desegregation remains subject to the values and beliefs of parents and students. As we noted earlier in this chapter, the promises of desegregation are largely unfulfilled. The schools are just as segregated as they were in 1954 as a result of "white flight" to the suburbs.

Consider the various policy solutions discussed in this chapter alone. Who is to say if any of these claims are true or false?

1. School choice is better than assignment based on residence.

2. School assignment based on racial quotas is better than school assignment based on residence.

3. Integrated schools are better than segregated schools.

4. Catholic schools are better than public schools.

5. Equality and quality of educational opportunity are best achieved when student progress is assessed at key points during the K–12 educational career via accountability programs.

6. To achieve greater equality, the system of "tracking" should be abolished.

7. To achieve greater equality, poor communities should receive a greater share of state and federal funds than affluent communities.

8. To promote higher achievement, the school year should be lengthened.

9. Parents should have greater control of the schools.

10. The state must assume greater control of the schools since parents are increasingly unable to carry out basic parental functions.

This book attempts to provide the necessary research and theory that can lead to informed rational choice between these political options. Surely, there are determinable consequences for any of the above policy choices. The book provides a compendium of empirical information on many of these issues. Most of the issues cannot be resolved by social science research alone. Ultimately, moral choices will form the bases for educational decisions. This was certainly the case when the Supreme Court ruled in 1954 that the public schools of America be desegregated "with all deliberate speed." Yet, en route to this decision, social science research provided valuable information, allowing the Court to transcend political ideologies.

❖ HOME AND SCHOOL EFFECTS

At this point, it is clear that these sets of conflicting goals are not independent of one another. In fact, they all tie together around the concepts of equality and achievement that might be thought of as the master set of conflicting goals of school. Moreover, these conflicts arise because the outcomes of schooling are largely dependent upon *both* the home and the school. Whenever, and to whatever extent the home influences educational outcomes (either directly or indirectly), the results are increased inequality and family control and represent class- and race-based allocation. Whenever we can observe a decrease in the influence of the home, we should see an increase in equal opportunity and equal results in the educational process. This might be thought of as a "common school effect" in which greater equality is achieved by minimizing the effects of the home and irrelevant ascribed status characteristics.

❖ SUMMARY

Thus, we see that the basic model of the schooling process involves equality and achievement. In fact, all of the conflicts of education pit the goal of equality against some other goal or function of schooling. For this reason, functional and conflict theory (or variants thereof) are used often in the sociology of education. Together, they allow us to identify and understand the multiple goals of schooling and the ineluctable tensions that exist between these goals.

Added to this is the conflict between students and teachers—the conflict between the profession of education and its clients. At some level of schooling, a large percentage of students demonstrate little interest in academic work. Some of these students drop out, while others reluctantly remain in school. Both in and out of school, extracurricular activities of a nonacademic nature dominate the culture and the media (which often creates but always reflects the culture). The conflicts between students and schools are considered in Chapter 7.

Within this context, therefore, to what extent is the school able to overcome, or lessen, or at least hold in control the influence of the home? When we say the "home" we mean here the separate and collective influence of the factors of socioeconomic status, race, gender, religion, and family structure. These variables constitute differences among students due to differences in their homes. Given the conflicting goals of school regarding quality and inequality, and the confounding influences of home and school, it is no small task to isolate the effects of the school or the home. Yet, these questions are critical since goals like equality are directly related to the effectiveness of schools among the disadvantaged. Sorting out some answers to these questions is the central task of this book.

❖ KEY CONCEPTS

equality of educational opportunity
equal access—some empirical international results
common curriculum
differential curriculum (tracking)—results from HSB
educational resources (inputs)
educational results (outcomes)
reforms—school choice, untracking, redistribution of funds
measuring equality and quality of educational results—empirical results from the SIMS and HSB studies

state versus family control of schooling
philosophies of educational justice—Rawls and Nozick
social reproduction theory
"schoolhome" (Martin)
functions of the school
role of the school in social control
conflict and functional theories of schooling
politics of education
effects of the home and the school

❖ KEY STUDIES

Baker (1993)
Bryk, Lee, and Holland (1993)

Coleman (1968)
Bowles and Gintis (1976, 2002)

❖ REVIEW QUESTIONS

1. Discuss the pros and cons of a school or school system that values quality education over equality of educational opportunity, and vice versa.

2. Are the goals of equality and quality of the same importance in education? Explain.

3. Discuss the pros and cons of a school or school system that operates largely under state control as opposed to private (family) control, and vice versa.

4. Contrast and compare the views of Rawls and Nozick with regard to equality/inequality in society. What is lost or gained by moving in the direction of either Rawls or Nozick?

5. Coleman identified a newly emergent definition of equality of educational opportunity. Define and contrast this concept with earlier views.

6. Identify and explain two ways to operationalize (measure) the concept of equality of education attainment beyond simple access.

7. In the SIMs study of mathematics, describe Baker's findings with regard to Japan and the United States. Contrast and compare with the findings by Bryk, Lee, and Holland.

8. Discuss the pros and cons of a school or school system that emphasizes selection and allocation and specialization rather than the transmission of a common set of knowledge and skills to all students, and vice versa.

9. Describe and contrast functional and conflict theory as they apply to educational and occupational attainment.

10. Describe the relationship between SES and educational attainment according to Bowles and Gintis (Figure 1.4). Note the effect when IQ is controlled. Describe the theoretical explanation.

11. Contrast and compare the intended and unintended consequences of raising standards in school reform (McDill, Natriello, and Pallas).

12. Given the overall discussion of reforms, theories, data results, and the conflicts of equality and quality, family and state control, and the functions of schooling, identify two reform strategies that you think will succeed and two which you think will fail.

Chapter 2

METHODOLOGICAL ISSUES

After twelve years of primary and secondary schooling, students vary considerably in virtually every possible outcome that might be attributable to either home or school, that is, grades, test scores, attitudes toward schools, attitudes toward society, or feelings about one's self. In fact, this "variation" generally follows the pattern of a normal curve. The sociology of education addresses the question of what accounts for this variation in educational outcomes. In so doing, we focus upon explanations provided in the model depicted in Figure 2.1. Generally, educational outcomes in this book are confined to learning outcomes, often based on standardized tests of achievement. This narrow focus is justified to some degree by the fact that both parents and policy makers alike limit their own concerns to factors such as average mathematical and verbal test scores in making decisions about where to live (in the case of parents) or school funding (in the case of policy makers and legislators).

Of course, there are other factors that influence educational outcomes, and we must also consider them along the way. These would include: (1) student inherited IQ; (2) differences within students' homes (for example, birth order); (3) regional differences; (4) cross-national differences; and (5) governmental policies and funding. For the most part, however, this book concentrates on the variables shown in Figure 2.1. Note that teacher training and quality are viewed as aspects of both between and within school differences.

❖ THE BASIC MODEL

If we ignore the "other factors" for now, we can simplify the model as shown in Figure 2.2. In sociology, a "model" is a schematic diagram that depicts the way we think the world works. In this case, we are modeling educational outcomes from the perspective of sociology. In words, the model shown in Figure 2.2 claims (theorizes) that children from higher socioeconomic homes (more affluent) attend better schools (either private or suburban) and associate with friends holding similar values and attitudes. Moreover, the model hypothesizes that homes, schools, and peers are directly related to educational outcomes. Note that there is a sense of time order to the model. An educational career begins in the home (time 1) and is followed by the selection of a school (time 2). These two events are then followed by friendship choices (time 3) and finally by educational outcomes (time 4). Note also that if we thought the variables were negatively related, we would use a minus sign to designate this.

In this book, we will assume that the vast majority of variability in educational outcomes is due to the factors of home,

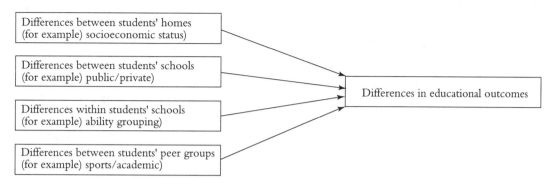

FIGURE 2.1   Factors Influencing Educational Outcomes

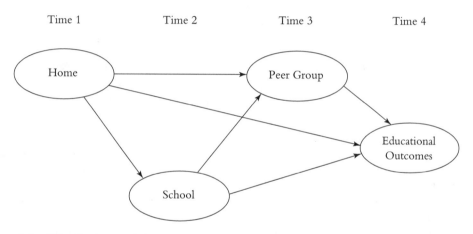

FIGURE 2.2   The Basic Model

school, and peer group. The goal is to unpack the relative influence of each of these factors and to understand the nature of these interrelationships. For example, if the influence of the home is large and the effect of the school is small, educational outcomes will closely resemble whatever inequalities exist between homes. On the other hand, if the impact of the home decreases and that of the school increases, there exists the possibility of greater equality in educational opportunity (assuming the school is strongly committed to this goal). Educational outcomes might be educational

attainment in years, or standardized tests scores, or grades or class rank, or self-esteem or leadership behaviors.

The idea is to uncover the relative strength of the relationships between the possible causes and outcomes of schooling: for example, we will explore in detail the relationships shown in Figure 2.3. Here we see that the influence (or the effect) of parental socioeconomic status (SES) amounts to about a two-year difference in educational attainment, whereas the influence of school type is about one year. Students from high-SES homes attain about 14.5 years of education while

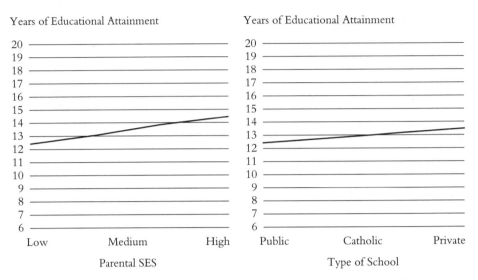

Years of Educational Attainment   Years of Educational Attainment

FIGURE 2.3   Educational Attainment by Socioeconomic Status and School Type

Source: Based upon estimates computed by the author from the High School and Beyond (HSB) Sophomore Cohort covering the period from high school graduation (1982) through 1992.

students from low-SES homes attain about 12.5 years. Students who attended other private schools obtain 13.5 years of education compared to only 12.5 for public school attendees. These are uncontrolled bivariate relationships and might change when controls are added. For example, the influence of school type might be larger among low-SES or minority-group students. In fact, this is the case as we have already demonstrated in Table 1.2 of Chapter 1. Controlling for a third variable can be very important in the sociology of education. Later in this chapter we will discuss the difference between controlled and uncontrolled relationships.

Consider other examples: What are the cognitive, affective, and educational outcomes for students who return each day to a transformed family structure? What are the educational results when parents divorce, when both parents work,

in single-parent families, or when students work, and how do each of these variables interact with school quality?

These questions—in fact, most of the questions in the sociology of education—require students to conceptualize the world in a multivariate mode. To facilitate this type of thinking, these questions are given extensive attention in this book. It is never simply a case of the influence of SES on educational outcomes; students who live in a certain SES home are also male or female, white or nonwhite, and they attend either a public or private school. Usually, we want to estimate the effect of SES on outcomes, assuming that students are similar in every other respect. Sometimes, however, we wish to know the effects of SES on outcomes, separately for blacks and whites, or for those who attend public versus Catholic schools (again, as in Table 1.2 of Chapter 1). In the second half of this chapter, you will learn the rudimentary logic of multivariate survey analysis. This will provide sufficient background for you to be able to interpret the research that is presented throughout the book.

❖ THEORY AND RESEARCH

Students often find the term "theory" to be a burden. But it need not be so. In sociology, theories are simply explanations for our behavior. They are statements that describe how and why several concepts are related. In sociology, most of our concepts are either events or attributes. For example, most people know that on average whites score higher than blacks on standardized cognitive tests such as the SAT. The interesting thing about this "social fact" is that no one really knows exactly why it is so, that is,

there is no commonly accepted theory. So if you want to become famous overnight, think up a theory that will explain this relationship. Of course, the theory will have to be persuasive and will have to undergo close scientific empirical scrutiny.

Let's consider another example for which a simple theoretical explanation is available. To some minimum extent (if you are reading this book) you are motivated to pursue more education. Why? Because it's always great fun to sit in classrooms, especially in April and May. Wrong! Theoretically, education pays off in the long run economically. Thus, the promise of a better economic future may "explain" why most people stay in school, even though it is a grind at times.

Someone once said that science walks on two legs—theory and research. This process is depicted in Figure 2.4. The scientific process involves two

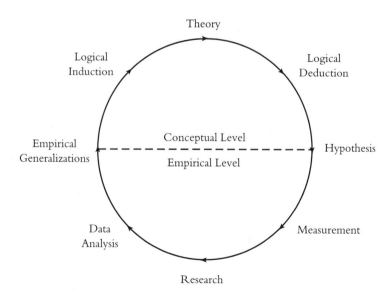

FIGURE 2.4   The Scientific Process
Source: Adapted from Walter Wallace, *The Logic of Science in Sociology* (Chicago: Aldine-Atherton, 1971).

levels—the theoretical (conceptual) level and the empirical (research) level. Note that the process moves in a one-way direction only—clockwise in the diagram. Note also that one might conceivably begin anywhere along the cycle. In this book, we often begin with a research finding (an empirical fact) based on a research study. We call this an empirical generalization. In the example of Figure 2.4, the empirical generalization might be that men make more money than women.

The real question, of course, is *why* do men have higher incomes? What theoretical explanation can account for these gender differences in earnings? Continuing the example, we "induce" that men may obtain more education or spend more time in the work force, or, perhaps, the difference is due to discrimination. Theoretically, each of these is possible and so in the scientific process we might propose a formal hypothesis that states that among men and women with equal educational levels, there are no differences in income. In doing this, we have proposed a theoretical model. Can you diagram the model in a manner similar to Figure 2.2?

The next step is to test the hypothesis by obtaining empirical measures for education, gender, and income among a representative group of people. These measures are our observations that numerically become the data. Finally, we analyze the data and make a revised empirical generalization. If we found that the male-female differences were just as great even among people with equal educational levels, we would have to propose an alternative model. In most occupations today in 2002, women possess at least as much education as their male counterparts (U.S. Department of Education, 2000), so some other hypothesis would have to be pursued.

❖ TYPES OF SOCIOLOGICAL RESEARCH IN EDUCATION

There are many ways to do educational research. Some researchers pore over historical or government documents, others attend classes for months or years to observe the behavior of teachers and students. Other researchers employ the experimental method (both in the classroom and in the laboratory). But a great deal of research explores social patterns in large data sets of census returns or questionnaire interviews. This latter approach—the analysis of large data sets—is called "survey research," and it is the method that is emphasized in this book. The other "methodologies" are entirely necessary and legitimate. In fact, for certain types of research questions, survey research is clearly inappropriate. At various points in the book, we will have occasion to draw upon the findings of the other methodologies. Nonetheless, I believe that one can gain a greater initial understanding of the subject matter by emphasizing the quantitative survey approach.

The most daunting task in determining the influence of schools on educational outcomes is separating the effects of schooling from the effects that are caused by all the other institutions of society, primarily the family. In certain selective areas such as calculus, learning can be easily isolated and attributed to the school. But, for most topics and especially in the earlier grades, it is very difficult methodologically to clearly disentangle the effects of the school from other societal influences. The survey approach is especially well suited to overcoming this obstacle of separating the influences of schooling from the influences of the home. Another type of research that might be able to disentangle these multiple causes (if we could use it) is the classic experiment. Unfortunately, experiments are rarely employed for educational research.

Consider the following scenarios: If we could simply take a sample of schools with differing types of organization (public/private) or different types of teaching methods or different levels of funding, and then randomly assign students to each school, we could easily determine which type of school was more effective in producing student learning. Random assignment to an experimental condition ensures that the students will be equal on all the other extraneous factors (on average) except for the experimental treatment. Although there have been a few randomized experiments in educational research, they are difficult to implement because you would have to withhold an experimental treatment (a teaching method) from some students. Some people would view this as unethical and some parents would quickly object to the experiment once they discerned that their children had been assigned to the hypothesized lesser-quality classroom. I would emphasize to the reader that these objections are unfortunate and usually ill-advised, since experiments provide the best ways to determine which type of school or teaching method is most effective. The great advances in medicine are due in large degree to experimental clinical trials in which a patient is randomly assigned to either a treatment or a placebo condition.

In any event, most educational research is nonexperimental or quasi-experimental rather than experimental, and is either qualitative or quantitative. However, a brief discussion of each of the primary methods used in the sociology of education is useful because each contains valuable insight into the main goals of the science of sociology, including some concepts as well as the philosophy of social science.

◆ EXPERIMENTS

Many people believe that an experiment properly conducted is the gold standard in scientific research. In a true experiment, the researcher randomly assigns individuals to either an experimental or a control condition. This ensures that the average attributes and predispositions of individuals in each condition are equal at the outset. Then, the researcher might expose the experimental group to a learning technique such as memorization with immediate rewards while the control group was engaged in memorization without rewards. Hypothetically, the experimental group would learn more effectively. The advantage of an experiment is that it controls for all the extraneous factors that might influence the outcome by randomizing the subjects at the beginning. The possibility of spuriousness (other factors which might influence the dependent variable) is ruled out. Also, the experiment controls the environmental conditions so that they are the same for each observation.

In a true experiment done well, the internal validity of the results is secured. *Internal validity* refers to the causal influence of the independent variable on the dependent variable. The extent to which we can generalize the results of a finding to a larger population refers to *external validity,* and experiments are often weak in this latter regard. Another problem with experiments is that subjects often are able to detect the purpose of an experiment and might change their behavior as a result (either in a positive or negative manner). True experiments in education are difficult to perform and more often than not, experiments are performed in the field where control and randomization are often not possible. These later experiments are referred to as quasi-experiments (Campbell and Stanley, 1966).

The Tennessee Star Experiment (Nye, Hedges, and Konstantopoulos, 2000) on the effect of class size is one of the best examples of an experiment in educational research (we discuss the actual findings in depth in Chapter 5). The research was designed to test the hypothesis that students in small classes learn better than in larger classes, and the research found strong support for this hypothesis. Since it was a large statewide study that randomized both teachers and students, it is considered "one of the great experiments in education in U.S. history" (Mosteller, 1995: 814). But here we will discuss only the problems of implementing this great experiment in the field in education. Note that its internal validity is actually limited to Tennessee.

This study was conceived in 1985 by the Tennessee state legislature and implemented by a consortium of Tennessee universities (Nye et al., 2000). Initially, all Tennessee school districts were asked to participate but only one-third of the schools across the state expressed interest. This initial expression of interest by 100 schools was further reduced by an assortment of criteria including the fact that the research required at least 57 students in each grade in order to sort the grade into classes of three sizes mandated by the research design. Districts also had to agree to allow site visitations for four years (K to 3) for interviews and data collection, as well as the random assignment of both students and teachers to class types during these four years. In the end only 79 elementary schools became the sites for the experiment. Hence, implementation and conclusions are limited by this initial set of constraints.

The research required that three types of classes be established in each grade: small (13–17 students), larger (22–26 students), and larger classes with a teacher aide (22–26 students). The researchers were able to do this quite successfully. However, there was attrition from these classes in each grade in each year of the study. Approximately 20 to 30 percent of the students in each grade left the study each year. Of course, new students also entered into the experiment in each grade in each year. In addition, there was some degree of switching of classes. Very early on, parents in the larger-size control classes were unhappy and adjustment had to be made. These adjustments are not often cited in the discussions of this study that appear in the broader media or even in many professional books (see Mosteller, 1995 in Chapter 5). By and large, however, the experiment was able to retain adequate fidelity of implementation, and I sight these problems here only to point up the difficulties of conducting experiments in education even when they are mandated by the state government and provided with adequate funding.

As this book goes to press, another ambitious educational experiment is just getting under way (Slavin, 2002a). Success for All (SFA) is a whole school curriculum that has been developed over the past 20 years. It is a comprehensive program for students in grades pre-K to five consisting of a schoolwide curriculum (with a reading emphasis), tutors, eight-week assessments, family support teams, and a program facilitator. The main objective is to ensure that all student reach third grade with adequate basic skills. SFA is used in more than 1,600 schools in 48 states and four other countries.

Although earlier research has been overwhelmingly positive in terms of student achievement, there is increasing interest on the part of the curriculum developers, teachers, principals, and educational policy makers to put reform curricula such as SFA to the true experimental test. Previous studies have used a quasi-experimental method of *matched samples*, which means that schools using SFA were matched in the aggregate to schools not using SFA, but similar in many ways in terms of their student body composition, size, past performance, etc. But the reauthorization of the Elementary and Secondary School Act (ESEA) of 2002 (called No Child Left Behind) has raised the level of research to a higher level, calling for more studies that use rigorous scientifically based objective procedures to obtain valid knowledge. Specifically, ESEA calls for experimental research designs, preferably with random assignment. Responding to this challenge, SFA asked a third-party agency (National Opinion Research Center) to develop a proposal to conduct randomized experiments on SFA. This proposal was then funded by the U.S. Department of Education.

Originally, the research design proposed to recruit 60 schools across the nation and randomly assign them to either receive the Success For All curriculum for 3 years or the control condition (nothing). The schools were offered $30,000 as an incentive. For the experimental group, this was a $30,000 discount off the price of SFA, which has a first-year price of $75,000 for a school of 500 students. The control group could use its $30,000 for any purpose. According to Slavin (2002b), this design was unsuccessful as only six schools were willing to participate on these terms. Schools were either unwilling to take a chance on being assigned to the control group (which meant that they could not do anything different for three years) or they could not afford the program cost beyond the $30,000. A few schools wanted the $30,000 but did not wish to implement SFA (in the event that they were chosen to be in the experimental condition).

This design had to be abandoned and replaced with an alternative. The experiment had to be delayed for a year while the research was redesigned. Beginning in September 2002, schools willing to participate will be randomly assigned to use Success For All either in grades K–2 or 3–5. Schools in the K–2 condition will be the experimental group while those in the 3–5 condition will be the control group since they will receive nothing new during the K–2 period. Note that the actual experiment will involve those schools assigned to receive SFA in K–2 grades and they will be compared to the other 30 schools that will not get SFA until grades 3–5. What goes on during grades 3–5 is not part of the experiment. Schools will pay only $10,000 for SFA (whenever they adopt it) for materials and training worth much more than this. Under this design, it appears that there will be an adequate number of schools to conduct the randomized experiment.

Note that this is clearly not a perfect plan as only schools with some degree of interest and desire for SFA will ask to be considered, and schools in the control group, which have to wait until grades 3–5, may still do a variety of things to prepare for the curriculum that they might otherwise not do. And the experimentally designed research cannot proceed beyond the second grade. Although now redesigned and somewhat compromised, we examine this ongoing experiment for several reasons. First, it demonstrates the commitment of the federal government toward making experimental studies de riguer in education research during the twenty-first century. Second, it demonstrates the problems of implementing experiments. And third, it shows how these problems can be overcome with a little ingenuity.

♦ QUALITATIVE RESEARCH

Some of best studies in the sociology of education employ a strategy of gathering data by observing behavior in natural settings such as classrooms, schoolyards, living rooms, hallways, and virtually anywhere where students, teachers, parents, and administrators gather. The data can be observations of behavior, communications or relations, or artifacts such as documents. A fundamental tenet of qualitative research is that the data must be understood on its own terms and rarely is suitable for quantitative analysis. Qualitative studies share several important theoretical and methodological assumptions about human behavior: (1) there is an emphasis on naturally occurring behavior as experienced by participants rather than how they respond to or fit into categories developed by the researcher; (2) there is an orientation to understanding the social context of events and behavior—so with Thorne's (1993) study of boys and girls, she assumes that you can only understand

the behavior by being out there on the park bench with the kids as they play as boys and girls; and (3) there is an emphasis on understanding the subjective meaning that participants attach to events— this is similar to the first assumption but is much deeper, assuming basically that people are constantly redefining who they are and who others are and their behavior. All of this is summarized by Geertz (1973: 9), who observed, "What we call our data are really our own constructions of other people's constructions of what they and their compatriots are up to."

Qualitative research is often conducted using *participant observation* that involves developing a sustained relationship with people while they go about their normal activities. Participant observation might range from complete observation to complete participation or something in between these extremes. Some problems with this approach include the difficulty of taking notes, asking questions, not being found out, ethical issues, and maintaining objectivity. Qualitative research can also be done through the use of intensive interviews or focus groups. The idea that this research allows the study of subjective meaning is important and should receive much greater attention. In a survey or an experiment, we define the meaning of events for participants. For example, we ask people whether they would vote for a woman for president, or whether it is good for a woman to work full time outside the home, and we induce from this something about their attitudes toward women. We structure the question and the answers and usually do not provide conditions that might alter the response. In naturally occurring events, we can observe how men and women might actually act on their attitudes. There is a fundamental theoretical issue at work here, and it is this: To what degree do people define social situations uniquely (as individuals) and how does their response to this symbolic defining and evaluation differ from their response to objectively conceived norms?

One of the central questions that we address in this book is how middle-class parents pass on their educational advantage to their children. A simple answer, easily quantified, is to argue and demonstrate that middle-class parents have the capacity to purchase more cultural capital resources for their children, including trips to museums, computers, travel, and tutors. But the simple answer is not adequate to explain the process that we identified as social reproduction in Chapter 1. In actuality, it is clear from close order qualitative studies that language development is an important cultural capital resource which is not easily measured (Bernstein, 1975; Heath, 1983). Most children arrive at the schoolhouse door with language skills that are adequate, but often they are not the language skills valued by the school.

"A key finding from qualitative research is that the forms of capital available to families must be activated by schools to influence children's educational experiences and outcomes" (Riehl, 2001: 118). In her qualitative study of two schools (one working class and the other middle class) involving observations and interviews with first graders and their parents, Lareau (1989, 1995) reveals that parents hold the same high values and educational expectations for their children in each school. Contrary to the incorrect stereotype about working-class (and lower-class) parents, they value education as much if not more than middle-class parents. They differ in their relationship to schools. Working-class parents are disconnected from school just as they are disconnected from their work. Middle-class parents, by contrast, are connected to school as they are to their work. Working-class parents punch a time clock and go home, while middle-class parents bring some of their work home. These two value systems lead working-class parents to expect teachers to educate their children in school while middle-class parents expect to be involved in the education of their children. This value differential works against working-class (and lower-class) parents because the school has adopted an operational model which values parental involvement in school.

◆ QUANTITATIVE SURVEY RESEARCH

Unlike qualitative research, quantitative studies proceed under the assumption that social reality can be defined in measurable ways by the researcher. Questions can be developed and asked of students or teachers, and the data can be organized and analyzed to determine the relationships among variables in a quantitative manner. Some variables, such as sex, race, and age, are easier to measure than others, such as student attitudes toward schools and behavior patterns after school. But a great deal of data is a matter of record in a student's file. Quantitative research understands that this method overlooks some of the subtleties and richness of events, and that this is provided by qualitative research.

Survey research can be either cross-sectional or longitudinal. Since the central focus of interest in the sociology of education is student growth over time, longitudinal studies are clearly preferable. Until recently, however, longitudinal studies were scarce, mainly due to the cost of following students over time. Beginning in 1972, however, the National Center for Education Statistics (NCES) embarked on a series of longitudinal studies that now have become the standard in quantitative survey research in the sociology of education.

◆ THE DATA SETS

We often use four data sets in this book, each of which was commissioned by the National Center for Education Statistics. NCES is a branch of the United States Department of Education, and its purpose is to collect and disseminate statistics and other data related to education in the United States and in other nations.

In 1972, NCES began an ambitious program of research with a project called the National Longitudinal Study of the high school class of 1972 (NLS). NLS is a longitudinal study of 22,652 graduating senior students in 1,318 private, public, and church-related secondary schools. These students were randomly selected through a two-stage stratified sampling strategy. First, schools were randomly selected and then students from each school were randomly identified. In 1972, these students completed a base-year questionnaire and an extensive test battery. In addition to the student questionnaires, a variety of valuable data were gathered from the high school records. Follow-up studies on these students were conducted in 1973, 1974, 1976, 1979, and 1986.

In 1980, NCES initiated a second long-term study of high school students which came to be called High School and Beyond (HSB). HSB is a longitudinal study of 58,270 high school sophomores and seniors who were randomly selected through the same type of two-stage strati-fied sampling strategy as described above for the NLS data. In this book, we use only the HSB sophomores, who as seniors became the high school graduating class of 1982. These students (N = 29,737) were selected from 1,015 public, private, and church-related secondary schools. As with the NLS study, the HSB data contain a broad set of student and school-reported information. The last survey of the HSB sophomores was in 1992.

In 1988, NCES began a third survey among a sample of 26,000 eighth graders in public, Catholic, and other private schools in the United States. Like the previous surveys, these students will be followed as they move into high school, college, and beyond. These students eventually became the high school graduating class of 1992. To distinguish it from earlier studies, it is called the National Educational Longitudinal Study (NELS). It has several unique features, including the base-year eighth grade measures, a parent survey for each student, a survey of two teachers of each student, an administrator survey, and special oversample of Asian, black, and Hispanic students. The last year of this survey was 2000 and this data has just now become available.

In 1998, NCES initiated the Early Childhood Longitudinal Study-Kindergarten Class of 1998–1999 (ECLS-K). ECLS-K began in the fall of 1998 with a nationally representative sample of about 22,000 children enrolled in kindergarten in about 1,000 programs (schools). These children will be followed longitudinally at least through the fifth grade, but at this time the available data is confined to the first two years only (K–1). Students were first tested at the beginning of school in the fall of 1998, and again in the spring of 1999. ECLS-K is a complex multistage sample with counties being the primary sampling units. Schools within counties were then randomly selected, separately from a public and private school sampling frame, and students were randomly selected from within schools. At the outset, approximately 23 kindergartners were sampled from each school.

A critical component of ECLS-K is the assessment of children along a wide range of outcomes including cognitive development, social and emotional development, and physical and psychomotor development. In both kindergarten and first grade, children demonstrate their competency in each of these domains through one-on-one untimed sessions with a trained child assessor. Additional information on a child's skill in reading, mathematics, and general knowledge is gathered from the child's teacher. We will also know the extent of each child's physical activity and patterns of misbehavior from the teacher questionnaires and school records. Parents/guardians are also interviewed twice during the kindergarten and first-grade school years to obtain information about family demographics and child rearing practices. Finally, a school administrator completed a questionnaire concerning the physical, organizational, fiscal, and pedagogical characteristics of the school. Another critical element of ECLS-K is the availability of excellent data on the organization of both schools and classrooms, the structure and functioning of families, and the activities of children during the summer.

What kinds of questions are the respondents asked in these surveys? Of course, the respondents are students, parents, teachers, and administrators. Among the things asked about respondents' backgrounds are their race and gender, the socioeconomic characteris-

tics of their parents and features of the place where they themselves were raised, the characteristics of their family, and their home and neighborhood activities. Both students and parents are asked questions concerning the students' school work—their coursework, homework, curriculum, grades, and extracurricular activities; their academic progress and plans; and the attitudes they hold toward themselves and others. In NELS and ECLS-K, we have detailed information about what was taught in the class from the teacher questionnaire, and school records and school resources from the administrator's questionnaire. Among the most interesting research done with the data is that relating background to foreground, for example, "what kind" of respondents are more likely to graduate from college or to score low on the SAT; or schoolground to foreground, for example, the effect of teachers' expectations or type of curriculum on current academic ability or final educational attainment. Of particular interest in the sociology of education is the capacity in the data to relate school and classroom organization to the social distribution of achievement (the relationship of factors such as race and SES to academic achievement).

There are certain limitations to these data sets. They are limited to school experiences in the United States. There are many topics that are not considered by NLS, HSB, NELS, or ECLS-K. Among these are the processes of language acquisition, student and teacher interaction in the classroom, the characteristics of effective teachers, and international comparisons. To provide coverage in these areas, we will refer occasionally to other empirical studies. NLS, HSB, NELS, and ECLS-K, however, form the core of the empirical studies employed in this book.

❖ SAMPLES AND POPULATIONS

It always seems mysterious how social scientists or pollsters can interview a sample of only 1,500 (or even 15,000) people and have the results accurately reflect the attitudes and behaviors of the whole American population—how people feel about X, or how often they do Y. While the results of a good survey are not perfectly accurate, they are usually pretty close. You might ask how we know they are close, since we usually haven't asked the whole population how they feel about X or how often they do Y.

The key to drawing a good sample that reflects the whole population is called *random sampling*. This simply means that every person in the whole population has the same chance of being interviewed as every other person. Random samples have a remarkable property. Their "accuracy" depends on the size of the sample and not on the size of the population (assuming that the population is much larger than the sample).[1] Thus, a random sample of 1,500 residents of Syracuse, New York (population about 180,000) is no more or less accurate than a random sample of 1,500 residents of the United States (population about 220 million). If we asked respondents whether they were for or against X, *in both cases* the percentage of our sample that was for (or against) X would "usually" be within about 3% of the "population value" (that is, the percentage we would have gotten if we had interviewed the whole population).

[1] The accuracy of a sample also depends on the degree to which measured characteristics vary in the population.

When we say the result would *usually* be within 3% we are waffling a bit for simplicity. To be technically correct, there is a .95 probability that the sample percentage will be within 3% of the population value. Notice that sometimes (5 times out of 100) the sample result will be *further* than 3% from the right answer; occasionally it will be way off. There is always some chance that a perfectly well-done survey will miss the mark by a lot, and that chance depends on the sample size. The larger the sample, the more likely the poll result will be close to the population value. Mathematical sampling theory tells us that if a random sample size is 150, then the survey result will "usually" (95 times out of 100) fall within 9% of the population value. If the sample size is 1,500 (the usual size of a Gallup poll), the result will usually be within 3% of the population value: And if the sample is more than 15,000 (which is the case in the NCES studies), then it will usually fall within 1% of the population value. (Of course, if you use only a subset of your sample, say the men, then the accuracy of your result is determined by the number of men, not of the whole sample.) Despite these cautionary remarks, I want to emphasize that within the limits described above, survey results provide valid and reliable estimates of the strengths of relationships between variables.

Good representative samples, such as those drawn by the NLS, HSB, NELS, and ECLS-K studies, are random samples. Actually, in practice there are usually several important deviations from simple random sampling that actually improve the precision of the survey. First, the sample is drawn from a restricted group (in the case of ECLS-K, only kindergartners were considered) and certain groups of students (minorities) are oversampled to ensure an adequate sample size. In addition, samples are drawn proportionally from certain strata with known proportions—this increases the accuracy of the sample. Also, since it would be too expensive to send interviewers all over the country to visit every randomly drawn student, it is schools that are first selected randomly, and the respondents themselves are then selected randomly from within those schools. Technically, this is referred to as two-stage (schools, then students) stratified random sampling. In the case of ECLS-K, the first stage was actually a clustered sample.

❖ SIMPLE BIVARIATE RELATIONSHIPS

Everyone has theoretical notions of how schools work and how educational outcomes are influenced by events that occur both in and out of school. The home, the school, and the peer group are all deeply implicated in the matter of educational outcomes. Some people will conceptualize these forces in conflict with each other. Others may theorize that the influence of the school is very small. Still others may think that all three forces work in close concert with one another.

Every reader of this book has a working theoretical idea of the extent to which your own educational outcomes were influenced by family conditions, school conditions, and the conditions of peers. I emphasize the word "conditions" here because I want you to recognize the variability of these conditions. Something that is conditional is at the same time variable. Thus, as you visualize the conditions which have shaped your own educational career, you should recognize

that these conditions could have been more positive or negative than what they were.

As you come to recognize this, you begin to enter sociological space. That is, you come to possess the idea that these positive and negative conditions of family, school, and peers *vary* considerably across neighborhoods and communities, throughout the society, and even more considerably across societies. C. Wright Mills (1959) called this "the sociological imagination." These social conditions, external to ourselves, influence our lives to a prodigious extent. The sociology of education investigates this influence in a systematic way. In fact, these conditions represent the differences between homes, schools, and peers that form the core of this book in Chapters 3 to 7. The examples that follow provide an introductory window into the empirical analysis of these sociological conditions as they relate to educational outcomes. The examples also contain ample substantive and theoretical ideas. Each of the examples sets the stage for fundamental conceptual issues that underlie the sociology of education— the theory of social reproduction and theories of school effects. As we explore the examples, therefore, try to focus equally upon the theoretical implications of the findings and the methodological logic that governs the empirical analyses.

In these examples, we will examine the relative effects of important variables that influence academic achievement. These variables are socioeconomic status (SES), race, school type, and curriculum. These variables measure and indicate differences *between* homes, differences *between* schools, and differences *within* schools. SES refers to the socioeconomic status of the student's family. It is often a composite of five equally weighted (and standardized) components—yearly household income of the student's family, father's education, mother's education, and father's and mother's occupational prestige scores. Curriculum (track) refers to the type of curriculum that a student is exposed to in school—vocational, general, college. In the NELS study, information on track placement was obtained from both school records and from the students themselves. The student is the measure employed here. Some degree of inconsistency exists between the two measures so that in professional-level research, both indicators should be examined (see Rosenbaum, 1980; Fennessey et al., 1981). High school type is the kind of school attended by each student (Catholic/public/private/other religion/private nonreligious). The last variable is the reading ability as measured by a standardized test and expressed in the table as those students scoring in the upper quartile (upper 25 percent). Thus, in Tables 2.1 and 2.2, reading ability is the dependent variable and each of the other variables is an independent variable.

TABLE 2.1

PERCENTAGE OF FIRST-TIME KINDERGARTEN STUDENTS WITH HIGH READING SCORES (UPPER QUARTILE) BY PARENTAL SES, RACE, AND SCHOOL SECTOR*

Parental SES		Race		School Sector	
Bottom Quartile	6	Hispanic	17	Catholic	33
26%–50%	16	Black	14	Public	20
51%–75%	27	White	27	Private Other Relig	40
Top Quartile	44	Asian	38	Private Non Relig	47

* These estimates computed by the author using appropriate weights. The number of cases is approximately 17,000 across the three relationships.

TABLE 2.2

PERCENTAGE OF STUDENTS ENTERING KINDERGARTEN FOR THE FIRST TIME BY SES, RACE, AND SCHOOL TYPE*

	Catholic	Public	Pri. Oth. Rel.	Pri. Non Rel.
% in Upper SES Quartile	37	18	48	57
% White	73	57	77	68

* These estimates computed by the author using appropriate weights. The number of cases is approximately 17,000 across the three relationships.

❖ BIVARIATE RELATIONSHIPS AT THE BEGINNING OF SCHOOL

In Table 2.1, we examine the influence of socioeconomic status (SES), race, and school sector on the reading scores for students entering kindergarten for the first time. These data are taken from the Early Childhood Longitudinal Survey-Kindergarten Cohort (ECLS-K) and allow us to examine the influence of several variables on student ability at the very beginning of school. In ECLS-K, kindergarten students were tested in reading, mathematics, and general knowledge by independent assessors during the first few weeks of school. Reading scores are used here since reading is of great importance during the first years of school. It is immediately apparent that students do not begin school on an equal playing field. Forty-four percent of high-SES students compared to only 6 percent of low-SES students score in the upper quartile of the reading test score. Likewise, 27 percent of white students but only 14 percent of black students score in the upper quartile on the test.

The extent of the influence of SES can be estimated by calculating the percentage difference across the categories of SES. Thus, we could say that there is an effect of 36 (44–6) percentage points for SES from the bottom to the top quartile. Similarly, there is a percentage difference of 13 points between whites and blacks. If the percentage difference is large, there is a strong relationship between the two variables. Values or categories of the independent variable would predict values of the dependent variable, as is the case with SES. Thus, knowing that a student is in the lowest SES quartile allows us to estimate that it is unlikely that he or she would be in the upper quartile of the reading test. A percentage difference of less than 10% is small; between 11% and 29% is moderate; and anything greater than 30% is large.

Table 2.1 also shows that students in Catholic schools are more likely than students in public schools to be in the upper quartile (33% versus 20%). This is true to a greater degree for students attending other types of private schools. This finding suggests that students attending Catholic and other private schools must come from higher-SES homes or differ in other ways that make them better readers when they arrive at the schoolhouse door. In any event, this private-public difference is not due to anything that has been taught in the classroom, since we are measuring student performance during the first few weeks of school. This would not necessarily mean that students might learn more in private schools than public schools, but only that they begin with a clear reading advantage. We will make much of this home-school issue throughout the book.

This leads us to want to know more precisely the demographic makeup of private and public schools. To do this we can examine a simple cross tabulation of social class, race, and school type. This is shown in Table 2.2. We can discern that indeed 37 percent of students in Catholic schools come from the upper quartile of SES compared to only 18 percent of students in public schools. Students attending the two other types of other private schools are much more likely to come from upper quartile SES homes. Likewise, nearly three-quarters of students attending kindergarten in Catholic schools are white (73 percent) compared to the public schools in which 57 percent are white.

❖ BIVARIATE RELATIONSHIPS AT THE END OF SECONDARY SCHOOL

How do these variables influence student achievement after twelve years of schooling? To answer this, we cannot use the ECLS-K data since this survey began in 1998 and the students are just beginning to make their way through their educational careers. We can, however, utilize the National Educational Longitudinal Study (NELS) of the high school class of 1992. Here we repeat the analysis for ECLS-K for high school seniors in 1992 using the SES variable, school sector, race, and school curriculum. For this analysis we use SES measured in the 8th grade; track, race, and school type as measured in the 10th grade; and reading ability as measured in the 12th grade. Once again, we see in Table 2.3 the large SES effect (virtually identical to the difference at the beginning of school as shown in Table 2.1), a large difference according to curriculum (32 percent), and once again a smaller difference of 9 percent between the Catholic and public schools (32%–23%). The effect of race is disconcerting: The gap between whites and blacks and Hispanics has increased substantially and this is the result of a smaller percentage of blacks and Hispanics scoring in the upper quartile. Of course, we cannot conclude with any certainty that the 1998 kindergarten students will show the same pattern when they graduate, but the data results are consistent with previous studies.

Of course, this difference between school types is now more complicated than in Table 2.1, for it is possible that the difference (9 percent) may be due to either the effect of SES or race, or perhaps due to something about the schools themselves, or all of these things. That students score higher on a reading test in the twelfth grade may be a result of having an SES advantage at the outset or it may be due to the fact that they receive a more effective education in Catholic schools, or both factors may be operating. We will pursue this conundrum at a later point in the chapter.

TABLE 2.3

PERCENTAGE OF 1992 SENIOR HIGH SCHOOL STUDENTS WITH HIGH READING SCORES (UPPER QUARTILE)*

Parental SES		Race		School Sector		Type of Curriculum	
Bottom Quartile	7	Hispanic	11	Catholic	32	Vocational	7
26%–50%	16	Black	8	Public	23	General	14
51%–75%	23	White	26	Private Oth Rel	49	College	39
Top Quartile	41	Asian	28	Private Non Rel	48		

* These estimates computed by the author using appropriate weights. The number of cases is approximately 15,000 across the three relationships.

Although we often use percentage differences to measure the strength of relationships in this book, there are occasions where we employ other statistics. In Table 2.1, it would be possible to express the value of each category of each variable as a mean or average score. That is, we could determine the average reading score for each school type or each category of SES. In fact, we did this in Figure 2.3 where the average years of educational attainment for students from Catholic school was 13.0 and the mean score for students from public schools was 12.5. In which case, we would say there is a mean difference of one-half (.5) year. And we could compare this to the difference in SES just as we did for the percentage difference.

Another statistic that we use occasionally is called a correlation. A correlation is very similar to a percentage difference—it is a measure of the strength of a relationship between two variables. Correlations range from +1.0 which is perfect positive relationship down to 0.0, which means there is no relationship (just like a percentage difference of zero), and then up to −1.0 which is a perfect negative relationship. A negative relationship simply means that the variables are inversely correlated—a high value on one variable is associated with a low value on the other variable. Social class and family size are inversely correlated. Correlations have several advantages over percentage differences: (1) they can be either positive or negative; (2) in most cases, they are more precise; and (3) they can be employed in the calculations of more advanced statistics. In many instances, I have used correlations for all of these reasons. Just as with percentage differences, correlations less than .10 would normally be considered small.

❖ EFFECT SIZES AND STATISTICAL SIGNIFICANCE

Most readers of this book probably have heard the term statistical significance. Some readers will know, quite correctly, that we use this term to claim that the mean difference between two groups (an experimental and control group or Catholic and public schools) is probably not due to chance factors. Formally, a statistically significant result tells us that the null hypothesis (that there is no difference between the groups) can be rejected at some level of probability, usually .05 or .01. That is, we can reject the null hypothesis and accept the research hypothesis with the understanding that we will be wrong in doing so 5 percent (.05) or 1 percent (.01) of the time. Statistical significance can and does apply also to correlations and regression coefficients in basically the same way: namely, that the null hypothesis of no relationship between the independent and dependent variables can be rejected at the specified level of significance. Rejecting the null hypothesis means that we accept the alternative or research hypothesis that the difference or the correlation is real and not due to chance.

An effect size (ES) is a general term for various statistics that estimate the magnitude of the relationship between an independent variable and the dependent variable. A percentage difference is perhaps the simplest way to express this estimate of an effect. A correlation is another way to express an effect size. Note that just as a percentage difference ranges from 0 to 100, a correlation ranges from 0 to plus or minus 1.0. Typically, the difference between two groups on some dependent variable such as a test score is converted into an effect size by dividing the test score difference in raw units by the pooled standard deviation. This transforms the difference into a metric that ranges between 0 and plus or minus 1.0. In fact, it is easy to convert all the variables into standardized scores prior to the analysis (by using Z scores which have a mean of zero and a standard deviation of 1.0) and then the mean differences will as a matter of course become effect sizes. Likewise regression coefficients can be converted to effect sizes.

In educational research, we often are interested in beginning-to-end of year test score gains, and how these gains differ between schools or subgroups. This difference in "raw" test score units is not very helpful. For example, consider a situation where students in Catholic schools gain 8.5 points and students in public schools gain 7.5 points on a standardized mathematics test over the course of one year (see the results for nonwhites in Table 2.4 on page 54). Without further clarification, we have no way of knowing if this one point difference is small or large. It is known, however, (from basic mathematical statistics) that a difference amounting to a standard deviation is large. In fact, a standard deviation difference between two groups means that the average score of the higher scoring group is at the 84th percentile while the average score of the lower scoring group is at the 50th percentile (Cohen, 1988). Thus, if you had a 1.0 raw score difference between two groups and the standard deviation of the scores was 2.0, the standardized difference would be .5 or one half of a standard deviation. In fact, this means that the average score of the higher scoring group is at the 69th percentile compared to the average score of the lower-scoring group that would be at the 50th percentile. This

is a large effect and this transformation is called an effect size.

The use of effect sizes is increasingly used in social science research because it allows a standard for judging the magnitude of an effect across studies and across methods. Although there is some room for variation, most researchers interpret the magnitude of effect sizes as follows: large if ES is .5 or more; moderate if ES is .3–.5; small if ES is .1 to .3; and trivial if ES is less than .1 (Rosenthal and Rosnow, 1984). This is even more conservative than the rule of thumb provided above for percent differences but gives the reader several options.

❖ CONTROL VARIABLES

In Table 2.3, we found that students from low-SES homes achieve lower reading scores than students from high-SES homes. We found also that students in low-ability groups or tracks read less well than students in higher-ability groups, and that students in Catholic schools outperformed students in public schools on this test. Now we want to look further into these results. These findings reflect the effects between homes (SES), within schools (curriculum), and between schools (school type), respectively. And herein lies one of the great challenges involved in educational research.

Probably the single greatest difficulty of educational research is to distinguish between academic outcome differences that are due to differences in the kinds of students (home background) that attend schools, from differences that are due to something about the schools themselves (curriculum, school type, teacher quality, and so on). The problem is always salient because students from high-SES families are always more likely to attend good schools and more likely to be in higher-level tracks. The only solution is to control the effects of the home with school variables, and likewise, to control the effects of the school with home variables.

A control variable is one that is held constant while we reexamine the relationship between the independent and dependent variables. For example, a question that immediately presses upon us is whether the racial or school type differences observed in Table 2.1 are true when we hold SES constant. We could do this by simply reexamining the race-to-reading relationship among low-SES students only, and then for medium-SES students only, and finally for high-SES students only. If the original findings of Table 2.1 remained, we would say the race effect held, after controlling for SES.

There are actually three major purposes for adding control variables:

1. An antecedent control variable is added to *verify* that the original relationship between the independent and dependent variable is true. If the effect of school sector on reading achievement disappeared (the percentage difference was reduced to zero) after controlling for SES, we would conclude that the relationship was spurious. The reading gap would not be due to school type, but rather to SES. If the relationship was reduced by 50 percent, we would say that 50 percent was spurious. Spurious relationships are common in educational research and social science, and determining how much of a relationship might be spurious is usually a first step in analysis.

2. An intervening control variable is added to *explain* the relationship between the independent and dependent variable. In one of the examples below we will examine the relationship between race and achievement. Whites have higher test scores than blacks at all levels of school and this effect is large and seemingly imperious to change. And this raises the question as to why this is so. To answer this question, explanations must be sought and these explanations are variables that intervene between the independent and the dependent variable. Thus, it might be that whites are more likely than blacks to live in homes of higher socioeconomic status and that the variation in SES explains part of the racial gap in test scores.

3. Often, a control variable (either antecedent or intervening) specifies the conditions under which the independent variable influences the dependent variable. In this case, the control variable provides a *specification* or an *interaction* effect by revealing the conditioning results. For example, in one of the examples below you will discover that teachers' ability to assess attention deficiency hyperactivity disorder (ADHD) of students in their classes is conditioned by the social class of the student. One might think that the assessment of (ADHD) is generally consistent among teachers for all students, but this is not true. SES conditions the assessment process, and we can determine this by using SES as a control variable.

In summary, the sociology of education is interested in determining the existence of a relationship between an independent variable such as school type (Catholic or public) and a dependent variable such as reading ability. To do this, some sort of association must be revealed in the form of a significant percentage or mean difference, a correlation or an effect size. Second, to establish causal validity we must be able to show that the independent variable precedes the dependent variable (this is not clear in the case of school type). Third, we must determine how much if any of the relationship is spurious; that is, is it caused by another antecedent variable such as SES or race? Finally, assuming that the relationship was not spurious, we would try to explain the relationship; specifically, why is it that students in private schools score higher on the reading test? Three examples of this logic are presented below.

❖ RESEARCH QUESTION #1: ARE CATHOLIC SCHOOLS MORE EFFECTIVE THAN PUBLIC SCHOOLS?

There is a widely held view that some schools are better than other schools. These are the schools that parents search out for their children. They are the schools that educators point to as models. Virtually everyone has an intuitive sense that there is a discernible difference between schools in terms of quality and effectiveness. And virtually everyone, students, parents, and educators, think that it is relatively easy to distinguish a "good" school from a "bad" school. In reality, however, it appears that schools are more alike than different (Coleman et al., 1966; Goodlad, 1984) and identifying a "good" school is an elusive task even among professional educators and researchers. In Chapters 4 and 5, we take up this issue in detail. Here we simply present an example that illustrates the dilemma.

In 1980, James Coleman was asked by the National Center on Education Statistics to test the relative effectiveness of public and private schools on academic outcomes using the High School and Beyond (HSB) data. In this research, it was assumed and hypothesized that private schools, in particular, were more effective. Conceivably, Coleman reasoned, private schools might provide clues of how a good school works, clues that might be adopted by other (less successful) schools. Critics contended, however, that the relationship between school type and achievement would prove to be spurious, resulting from the fact that the socioeconomic status of the home and initial ability are common causes of both school type and academic performance; that is, better-performing students from high-SES homes are more likely to attend private schools and to do better academically (not because of the school but rather because of the home).[2] These preexisting or antecedent variables are the source of "selection bias" and represent a central problem in all studies of school effects. The results predicted by the critics are depicted in Figure 2.5.

Coleman and his colleagues, on the other hand, hypothesized that SCHOOL TYPE would affect OUTCOMES, after controlling for SES of the home. Acknowledging that selection bias would play a role, Coleman hypothesized that the relationship would not be spurious. This model is shown in Figure 2.6.

We already know from Tables 2.1 and 2.2 that the critics may be correct since we determined that students entering Catholic schools in kindergarten are more likely to have higher reading scores and are more likely to come from

---

[2] Technically, the term "spurious" relationship is reserved for a case in which the appearance of a relationship between an independent and dependent variable is explained by an antecedent control variable. The antecedent variable is viewed as the "common cause" of the spurious correlation.

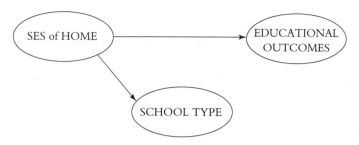

FIGURE 2.5 Model Showing a Spurious Relationship Between School Type and Educational Outcomes

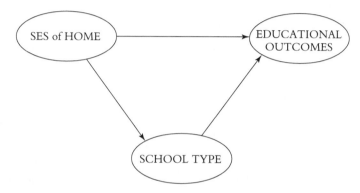

FIGURE 2.6 Model Showing Nonspurious Effect of School Type on Educational Outcomes

higher-SES homes than students in public schools. But, this information is often not available. Most statewide testing programs, for example, including those now mandated under the ESEA Act of 2002, only provide test results for the end of school in the spring. Moreover, even knowing what we do from Tables 2.1 and 2.2, it is still possible that students in Catholic schools progress at a faster learning rate than students in public schools. Using ECLS-K, however, we can get to the bottom of this question, at least for kindergarten students in 1998.

One of the major issues is the need to control for initial ability since that variable is certainly part of selection bias.

One way to overcome the difficulties of controlling for initial ability is to obtain a measure of ability before the students start school. This is probably as close as you can come and we can do this by using the ECLS-K data set. Previous research on this issue has concentrated on secondary schooling using either an 8th or 10th grade measure of initial ability (see Table 1.2 in Chapter 1). But this approach may be flawed since this is not a true measure of initial ability and may already have been strongly influenced by SES and earlier schooling. One of the disadvantages of using ECLS-K, especially during the kindergarten year, is that the difference between schools (classrooms)

TABLE 2.4

MEAN GAINS IN READING AND MATHEMATICS DURING THE KINDERGARTEN YEAR BY SCHOOL TYPE AND RACE*

School Sector	Mathematics		Reading	
	Whites	Nonwhites	Whites	Nonwhites
Catholic Schools	8.2	8.5	9.9	10.3
Public Schools	8.5	7.5	10.2	9.6
Number of Cases	7,665	3,205	7,665	3,205

* These estimates computed by the author using appropriate weights. Students are first-time kindergarteners only with the same school and same teacher for entire year. Nonwhites are African Americans and Hispanic Americans.

in Catholic and public schools would be much less than in the 10th or 12th grade. At the secondary school level, the quality of textbooks, laboratories, teacher credentials, and other school resources may differ to a greater degree than they do at the kindergarten level. This means that we do need to be careful about generalizing these results to secondary schools.

Bearing this in mind, consider Table 2.4 that displays the mean reading and mathematics test score gains in public and Catholic schools for kindergarten students over the course of the academic school year (1998–1999). These scores were obtained by subtracting the beginning-of-year scores from the end-of-year scores. The results are presented separately for whites and nonwhites (African American and Hispanic American students). Note first that whites in public schools gain .3 of a point more that whites in Catholic schools in both reading and mathematics. This fraction is quite trivial. Since the overall standard deviation is about 8 points (not shown), the effect size is only .04 (.3/8). Moreover, the

difference is not significant and actually becomes smaller when SES is controlled. The conclusion is simple: White students gain approximately the same amount in reading and mathematics in Catholic and public school during kindergarten.

The results for African American and Hispanic American students, however, are a bit different and parallel the results shown in Chapter 1 for secondary school students (see Table 1.2). These nonwhite students do gain more in Catholic schools than in public schools, but again the differential gains are small. In mathematics, however, the gain is one full point that would be about .13 of an effect size. One can see that several years of such growth would quickly amount to a substantial greater gain for minorities who attend Catholic schools. These gains are reduced slightly when SES is controlled.

Assume for a moment that we did not have access to the fall scores and had to rely solely on the spring results. The test score differences between students in Catholic and public schools in reading and mathematics would be about 3.5 points. This translates into an effect size of about .4 (not shown in Table 2.4), suggesting that students in Catholic schools learn more than students in public schools. But we can see immediately that this would be a spurious finding. In fact, it is clear from Table 2.4 that white students in both school types learn about the same amount in both reading and mathematics. As you can see, the results clearly show that there is no Catholic school advantage (when all the controls are added, white students in public schools gain slightly more but it is insignificant and should be treated as zero). The results for nonwhites do favor Catholic schools. We call this type of conditional finding an interaction or a specification.

So the answer to our research question is: Yes and No. Catholic schools are not more effective than public schools (at least not during the kindergarten year) for white students but there is a small advantage that accrues to African American and Hispanic American students. Compare these findings to those obtained by Bryk, Lee, and Holland (1993) presented in Chapter 1 (Table 1.2). Their analysis is fundamentally the same as shown in Table 2.4 except that they examined the gain from the 10th to the 12th grades.

❖ RESEARCH QUESTION #2: CAN WE EXPLAIN THE BLACK-WHITE TEST SCORE GAP?

One of the most troubling facts about school outcomes is that African American and Hispanic American students consistently score lower than white students on standardized tests at every level of schooling. In this section, I confine the discussion to the black-white gap only. Social scientists have been trying to understand the black-white test score gap for the past century. Historically, blacks have scored about one standard deviation (1.0 ES) lower than whites on typical standardized academic tests across all content areas. This gap appears before children enter kindergarten and it persists until adulthood (Jencks and Phillips, 1998: 1). Over the course of time, debate has raged as to what the test scores actually measure and what is the cause of the test score gap.

Although some researchers (Jensen, 1969; Herrnstein and Murray, 1994) have argued that the gap is largely biological and hence immutable, most researchers have argued otherwise (Jencks and Phillips, 1998; Neisser et al., 1996; Fischer et al., 1996; Hallinan, 2001). The fact is that "no one has found genetic evidence indicating that blacks have less innate intellectual ability than whites" (Jencks and Phillips, 1998: 2). By contrast, sociologists have demonstrated that some of the gap is explained by differences in social class between whites and blacks, differences in family structure and functioning, access to formal and informal education, and long-term discrimination against blacks (Jencks and Phillips, 1998; Fischer et al., 1996; Hallinan, 2001; Walters, 2001). It is also true, however, that no one has been able to fully explain the test score gap by employing family and cultural background characteristics or school organizational characteristics (see Jencks and Phillips, 1998).

We do know, however, that the test score gap between whites and blacks plays a large role in educational, occupational, and income attainment. After controlling for other variables, students with high test

TABLE 2.5

BLACK-WHITE DIFFERENCES IN ACHIEVEMENT (MATH/READING/VOCABULARY COMPOSITE) 1972–1992, ADJUSTED FOR SOCIAL CLASS

Survey and Year	Unadjusted Effect Size	SES Adjusted Effect Size
NLS 1972	1.12	.71
HSB 1982	.95	.73
NELS 1992	.82	.65

Source: Adapted from Larry V. Hedges and Amy Nowell. 1999. "Changes in the Black-White Gap in Achievement Test Scores." *Sociology of Education* 72: 111–135, Table 1.

scores (whatever it is that they measure) are more likely to obtain educational and occupational success. Assuming that racial equality is an important goal,

> [R]educing the black-white test score gap would probably do more to promote this goal than any other strategy.... Reducing the test score gap is probably both necessary and sufficient for substantially reducing racial inequality in educational attainment and earnings. Changes in education and earnings would in turn help reduce racial differences in crime, health, and family structure. (Jencks and Phillips, 1998: 3–4)

In this example, we will look at the extent to which socioeconomic status helps to explain the test score gap and the degree to which the gap has changed between the years of 1972 and 1992.

Hedges and Nowell (1999) employed NLS, HSB, and NELS to examine the black-white gap for students graduating from high school in 1972, 1982, and 1992. Their purpose was to determine how much of the racial gap can be attributed to social class differences and how much of the gap had changed over the time

period. Table 2.5 shows the results they obtained for the three data sets.[3] Hedges and Nowell used effect sizes (see discussion above) to describe their results. Effect sizes are especially useful here because the raw tests are not the same across the years, but effect sizes standardize the scores so that the size of the gap can be compared across the years. The composite test score measure shown in Table 2.5 is a combination of tests in reading, vocabulary, and mathematics.[4]

An examination of Table 2.5 reveals three important findings: First, the size of the gap is large regardless of year and whether it is adjusted or not. All of the effect sizes are highly significant. Second, the gap has narrowed considerably since

[3] Hedges and Nowell actually used seven data sets in their article covering a time period from 1965 to 1996, but I have limited this presentation to the three data sets that I have described earlier in the chapter. The conclusions are the same using either only three or the entire seven data sets.

[4] The original paper by Hedges and Nowell shows the results for each of these separate content areas as well as the composite.

1972. In fact, the researchers concluded that the gap is narrowing by .15 effect size per decade. This reduction in the size of the gap from 1972 to 1992 clearly demonstrates that the gap is not immutable or inevitable, and it suggests that greater educational access and opportunities for blacks during 1972 to 1992 have been effective in reducing the gap. If the gap were to continue to narrow along the lines shown in Table 2.5, it would be eliminated in about sixty years! Unfortunately, however, more recent research (Campbell et al., 2000) has demonstrated quite conclusively that the gap actually increased from 1992 to 1999, with the average black 17-year-old reading only about as well as the average white 13-year-old.

Third, controlling for social class reduces the size of the gap. Here, social class is held constant statistically, which means that the researchers are examining the race gap under the assumption that all students are in the exact same social class.[5] Consider how this must work: Since the effect size is reduced in each year when social class is controlled, it implies that part of the unadjusted gap is due to the fact that whites are more likely than blacks to come from higher socioeconomic homes. It is easy to estimate how much of the gap is "explained" by social class differences among the races. In 1992, the unadjusted gap is .82 and this is reduced to .65 in the adjusted column. Social class reduces the gap by .17 ES (.82 − .65) and .17 is 20 percent of .82. This allows us to conclude that social class differences explain about 20 percent of the racial gap. Obviously, the addition of other control variables such as family

structure and functioning, type of community, school quality, type of curriculum, quality of child care, teacher expectations, etc. will reduce the gap even further. Each of these variables is a potential partial explanation for the race gap and the addition of these variables together will explain about 50 percent of the gap (Jencks and Phillips, 1998). It is important to point out that there is no model that has been analyzed employing all of the possible explanatory variables. More often than not, variables such as IQ and discrimination are not available as measured variables in the data set. Either one (or both) of these variables could explain the remaining 50 percent. So in the end, we can conclude that SES explains part of the gap, along with other family and school quality variables.

❖ RESEARCH QUESTION #3: HOW ACCURATE ARE TEACHERS' JUDGMENTS OF ADHD BEHAVIOR?

Let's examine an entirely different type of situation in the sociology of education. At the classroom level, teachers are required to make evaluations of children from the very beginning of school. These assessments range from grades for cognitive achievement to deportment and also include recommendations for special education of individualized educational programs (IEP). One of the most important evaluations involves decisions regarding the placement of a student into a reading or math group. Typically, these groups are arranged according to an assessment that the teacher makes of the student's reading or mathematical ability. Among other things, the sociology of education raises

---

[5] Social class was measured using mother's and father's education and family income.

the question of the accuracy of teachers' judgments in ability group placement and other types of evaluative decisions.

Miech, Essex, and Goldsmith (2001) conducted a study which examined the accuracy of teachers' assessment of attention deficit hyperactivity disorder (ADHD). The major focus of their study was to examine the relationship between a child's self-regulatory behavior and adjustment to school. One of their main concerns was whether self-regulatory behavior was spurious since it is influenced by social class (high-SES children are less likely to have problems self-regulating their behavior). If it were spurious, this would imply that children's ability to regulate their behavior is a function of social processes rather than biophysiological processes. If the results were spurious, it would direct "research and policy away from the individual child and toward social processes within the school" (Miech et al., 2001: 104). Determining whether the relationship was spurious simply required controlling for parental SES, and when this was done the results showed the relationship was not entirely spurious. But in this example, we are more interested in another phase of the research.

The research employed a data set entitled the Wisconsin Study of Family and Work, which was primarily interested in family issues as they relate to work patterns. But there is excellent data on the parents and children from the second trimester of pregnancy until entry into kindergarten, which is the time period for this study. The key measures as they apply to this example are as follows:

• *Children's self-regulatory behavior*— measured at age four and one-half using a very reliable and valid scale to measure child temperament (Miech et al., 2001: 106). An example of one of the items is, "When practicing an activity, the child has a hard time keeping her/his mind on it" with an answer that ranged from 1 (extremely untrue) to 7 (extremely true). These questions were completed by the mother.

• *Teachers' assessments of children as attention deficit hyperactivity disorder (ADHD)*—utilized another well-known scale with high reliability and validity. In the analysis, the attention deficit hyperactivity disorder measure is those children who fell in the upper quartile of the teacher scale indicating a high probability of ADHD. The authors caution (2001: 107) that this is not formal medical diagnosis of ADHD but is "similar to a 'screening' measure by which teachers and parents— who generally have little training in formal psychiatric diagnosis—designate children for further testing by professionals."

• *Family SES*—measured by a composite of mother's and father's education and family income prior to the birth of the child and again at age four and one-half.

Other variables were included in the study but our interest is confined to these three.

For our purposes, the most interesting part of the research is that the researchers investigated the extent to which teachers' assessments of ADHD were conditioned by the social class of the children. Recall that we have an independent measure of the child's propensity for ADHD before the child enters kindergarten, which is then followed by the teacher's independent assessment after the child had been in school for about six months. And of course, we have the

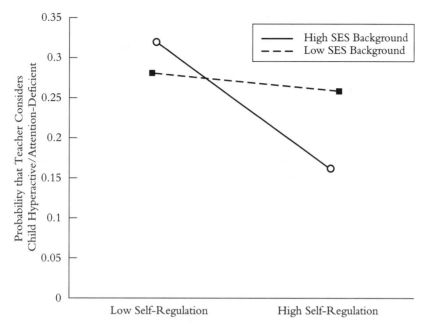

FIGURE 2.7 **Relationship Between Self-Regulation and Teachers' Reports of ADHD, by Children's Socioeconomic Backgrounds**

Note: High-SES background indicated by children whose mothers completed sixteen or more years of education; low-SES background indicated by children whose mothers completed twelve or fewer years of education; low self-regulation indicated by children at the bottom third of the self-regulation distribution; high self-regulation indicated by children at the top third of the self-regulation distribution.

Source: Richard Miech, Marilyn J. Essex, and H. Hill Goldsmith, 2001. "Socioeconomic Status and Adjustment to School: The Role of Self-Regulation During Early Childhood." *Sociology of Education* 74: 102–120, Figure 1. Reprinted with permission.

measure of family SES. Figure 2.7 displays the manner in which family SES (high and low) influences the relationship of a child's score on self-regulation to the teachers' assessment of the same behavior as it manifests itself in the classroom.

Note carefully that we are not examining the simple influence of an independent variable on a dependent variable, but rather the way in which a control variable (SES) effects the relationship between an independent and dependent variable. *The*

relationship between mothers' and teachers' assessments of ADHD is really the dependent variable in this analysis. Examine first the relationship among high-SES children: Here the relationship is what one might expect; namely that if a child's self-regulatory behavior was low, the probability is high that a teacher will recognize this as shown in Figure 2.7. This is what we would expect to find for all the children in the study. If a child's mother indicates that the child has problems in self-regulation, it seems reasonable that the child's teacher will observe the same pattern of behavior.

We can see immediately, however, that this finding does not hold true for low-SES children. Here, teachers seem less able to correctly differentiate between the low- and high-self-regulating children. Most important perhaps is that there is a high probability that teachers will consider a child ADHD even when the independent measure has found that there is no evidence for this. We say of this finding that SES conditions the relationship between self-regulating behavior and teachers' assessments of that behavior. And the importance of the finding is that this may occur elsewhere in classroom assessments such as grading, assignment to ability groups, and everyday reactions to a child's behavior. The research is not saying that teachers should make these assessments of ADHD, since this is the work of specially trained professionals in this area. In fact, it is clear that they should not, since they would do a questionable job, badly conditioned by a child's SES.

❖ RESEARCH PERSPECTIVES

In sociology, there are a variety of both theoretical and research perspectives. Theoretical perspectives provide thematic models (see the definition of a model above) regarding how to conceptualize the sociological nature of education. Research perspectives, on the other hand, provide models and techniques on how to go about studying it.

Currently, there is no single dominant theoretical perspective in the field. Although one might wish for one single

sociological theory, the complexity of society and education has produced several theories, each of which is true in part, but each of which is also incomplete. Consequently, throughout the book, we will call upon each of the major theoretical perspectives. These perspectives are functionalism, various forms of Marxism (social reproduction and conflict), and the theories of Weber, Bourdieu, and Meyer. This list is by no means complete, and indeed, other theorists are included in the book to lesser degrees, and some other theorists are omitted. Willie (1993) argues that "single paradigms usually offer insufficient explanations for complex situations. . . . By reconciling multiple, integrated paradigms, we have a better chance of achieving a good educational outcome and true educational reform."

There are two rather distinctive research perspectives in the sociology of education. Quantitative research obviously involves numerical measurement of variables which have been operationalized from theoretical concepts, and it provides numerical estimates of the degree of association between variables. Quantitative research assumes that observable events and expressed words (via questionnaires or interviews) are adequate measures to produce a scientific knowledge base in the sociology of education. Countering the quantitative paradigm is the qualitative research perspective.

Qualitative methodologies assume there is value to an analysis of both the inner and the outer perspective of human behavior. In German, the word is *verstehen*. This inner perspective or "understanding" assumes that a complete and ultimately truthful analysis can only be achieved by actively participating in the life of the observed and gaining insights by means of introspection. Emphasis is placed upon the ability of the researcher to "take the role of the other," to grasp the basic underlying assumptions of behavior through understanding the "definition of the situation" from the point of view of the participants, and upon the need to understand the perceptions and values given to symbols as they are manipulated by man. (Rist, 1977: 44)

Currently, most researchers from either camp agree that there are certain advantages and disadvantages to each perspective. Furthermore, most would concur that there are circumstances in which one methodology is clearly more appropriate than the other. For example, the numerical measurement of dropouts does not require the study of inner meaning. On the other hand, a *verstehen* approach may be very helpful in learning more about the process by which individuals come to actually make the decision to drop out of school. Nonetheless, according Rist (1977: 42):

Quantitative research is *the* dominant methodology in educational research. It is the more widely published, taught, accepted, and rewarded in educational circles than any other approach.

Moreover, Rist (1977: 43) makes an important point when he writes that "the selection of a particular methodology is profoundly theoretical" in the sense that "each method reveals peculiar elements of symbolic reality."

The purpose of this chapter has been to articulate a specific sociological perspective. This perspective emphasizes quantitative, empirical data analysis in conjunction with sociological theory and concepts. If you reexamine the concepts

that are embedded in the models, you should easily discover that the ideas of inequality (operationalized as socioeconomic status and race) and the organizational effects of schools are emphasized. This perspective examines the relative influence of ascribed and achieved characteristics of students and the characteristics of their schools upon various short- and long-term measures of educational and developmental outcomes, including tests scores, self-esteem, educational aspirations and attainments, occupational status, and eventual earnings.

This perspective takes its direction from a research tradition commonly referred to as *educational productivity* (Hallinan, 1989).

The study of educational productivity is the investigation of factors that affect the academic productivity of students in schools and its effects on their future educational and occupational attainment. . . . Interest in educational productivity is motivated by a number of pressing societal concerns: the quality of schooling . . . the extent of our nation's monetary investment in education . . . the relationship between education and employment or occupational attainment, the disparity between educational achievement and occupational attainment for minorities and women. Underlying these concerns is the basic belief that schools should equalize opportunities for learning and attainment for all students, regardless of race, ethnicity, social class, religion, or other family background characteristics. (Hallinan, 1989: 23)

Hallinan notes also that the study of educational productivity has developed largely within two interrelated research programs: the study of school effects and the study of status attainment. It is important to reemphasize that the educational productivity perspective is both substantive and methodological in character (for further elaboration on this see Karabel and Halsey, 1977; Hallinan, 1989).

One problem with educational productivity is that the research results sometimes are inconsistent. Some of this is due to the complexity of the research and the fact that very few studies contain exactly the same variables. This criticism, however, is true of virtually all social science research. In fact, there is clearly more consistency in this research tradition than any other in the field. Hallinan (1989: 35) concluded that educational productivity research "is among the best in the field in terms of scope and rigor."

Nonetheless, readers of this book should be aware that there are limitations to the kinds of questions that quantitative survey research and experiments can answer. The outcomes of schooling are related, in no small degree, to the social context of schools and classrooms; to the complexities of structure and interaction in the school, home, and peer group; and to the larger ideological, political, and economic context of the society. Surveys and experiments are not very good at measuring class, gender, and race antagonisms; the internal politics of schools and classrooms; the daily life of students and teachers; and especially the complexities of interpersonal interaction. For example, consider the many subtleties of teacher-student and peer interaction that occur on a microscopic, minute-by-minute basis in schools. Teachers and students may systematically, though unintentionally, hold negative expectations for certain types or certain groups of students. Such expectations, quite impervious to

large-scale survey research, undoubtedly will affect the educational productivity of these students.

❖ SOCIOLOGY AND EDUCATIONAL POLICY

Today, nearly everyone is interested in the qualities of a "good" school, and nearly everyone has ideas of what these qualities should be. Over the past fifty years, empirical social science research has become the dominant paradigm for decision making in educational policy. This is, I believe, as it should be.

Bear in mind that there are four primary interest groups in education: (1) consumers, (2) providers, (3) social science researchers and jurists, and (4) policy makers. These are shown in Figure 2.8. Each group has its own vested interests and relates to other groups in various ways. Although every group is concerned with the educational and developmental well-being of students, each is inspired by its respective identities and responsibilities. Consider for a moment what things would look like in the absence of legal scholars and jurists. It is unlikely that large-scale school desegregation would have occurred without desegregation laws. Similarly, the actual process of racial desegregation would probably be a fait accompli were it not for the fact that desegregation involves more than court decisions—it requires general compliance with those decisions on the part of students and parents.

There may have been a time when policy makers ignored the work of researchers, but that time has long since past. Educational decision makers—from the highest levels of the educational

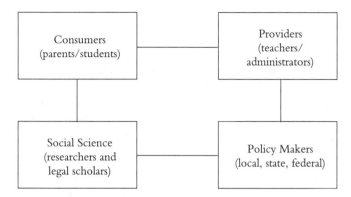

FIGURE 2.8   **Educational Interest Groups**

establishment on down to teachers in the classroom and parents in the home—are constantly looking for social science research. Practitioners, unlike scientists, however, consume research with at least two drawbacks. First, they tend to look only at research that "scientifically" justifies the views they already hold or those that they would like to institute. Second, practitioners are not trained researchers. Alas, many policy makers cannot recognize excellent and sound research studies from those that are questionable. (In many respects, the methodological issues have become so technical, that even educational researchers have trouble sorting out the wheat from the chaff.)

These two obstacles facing consumers of educational research are intensified by the rapidity with which research (mostly bad research) is rushed into practice. A good part of the blame for this state of affairs may be placed on school administrators who do not understand why a program that had good results with suburban eleventh graders may not necessarily work for urban eleventh graders. Blame also goes to researchers who are pressed into early "publish or perish" situations, and to research grant

foundations who set unrealistic deadlines for final reports. If medical research were rushed into policy and practice as rapidly as educational research, we would all be dead by now.[6]

With this brief introduction to research matters, we are now ready to move into the substantive areas of the book. Chapters 3 to 7 examine in detail the effects that occur between homes, between schools, within schools, and between peer groups, respectively. Finally, in Chapter 8, we attempt to synthesize the many differential effects discussed throughout the book. Given this understanding of educational outcomes, we ask what students, parents, and educators might do to further their respective interests in educational matters.

---

[6] Much of the above two paragraphs draws upon the thoughts of Bella Rosenberg as expressed in a presentation given at a Conference on Equity and Excellence in Education: The Policy Uses of Sociology, jointly sponsored by the United States Department of Education and the Sociology of Education Section of the American Sociological Association, June, 1993. These ideas were later communicated in personal correspondence.

❖ SUMMARY

In this chapter, we have reviewed some of the essential principles of research methods in the sociology of education. In addition, we have introduced several substantive ideas concerning school and home effects. Also, issues of sociological theory and educational policy have been discussed. After completing this chapter, you should have an understanding of each of the key concepts.

❖ KEY CONCEPTS

sociological model
differences between homes and between schools
differences within schools
independent and dependent variables
scientific process (Figure 2.4)
experiments
internal and external validity
quasi-experiments
qualitative research
participant observation
bivariate relationships
control variables
explanation
specification (interaction)
spurious relationship
antecedent variables
intervening variables

National Longitudinal Study (NLS)
High School and Beyond (HSB)
National Educational Longitudinal Study (NELS)
Early Childhood Longitudinal Survey (ECLS-K)
random sample
schoolground
two-stage stratified random sample
effects sizes
statistical significance
qualitative research and "verstehen"
educational productivity
empirical research and educational policy
Catholic-public school effects
black-white test score gap

❖ KEY STUDIES

Nye et al. (2000)
Slavin (2002a, 2002b)
Lareau (1989, 1995)
ECLS-K Beginning of School Results
NELS End of School Results

ECLS-K Catholic-public school Kindergarten Results
Hedges and Nowell (1999)
Miech, Essex, and Goldsmith (2001)

❖ REVIEW QUESTIONS

1. Describe several models in the sociology of education using both words and a schematic diagram.

2. Drawing upon Figure 2.4, describe the relationship between theory and research.

3. Describe the advantages and disadvantages of experimental research in education.

4. Describe the advantages and disadvantages of qualitative research in education.

5. Describe the results of the Tennessee experiment on class size.

6. Identify and describe the following data sets: NLS, HSB, NELS, and ECLS-K.

7. Describe the advantages and disadvantages of survey research in education.

8. Define and describe random sampling and two-stage stratified random sampling.

9. Based on the simple bivariate crosstabs in this chapter, what are the relative effects of SES, race, school type, and curriculum at both the beginning and end of school?

10. Define the meaning of statistical significance.

11. Define the concept of effect size.

12. Identify and describe the three purposes of using control variables.

13. Are Catholic schools more effective than public schools (Research Question #1)?

14. Can we explain the black-white test score gap (Research Question #2)?

15. How accurate are teachers' judgments of ADHD behavior (Research Question #3)?

16. You have been asked to demonstrate that an intervening variable "explains" the bivariate relationship between an independent and dependent variable. What must you be able to show from the data?

Chapter 3

DIFFERENCES BETWEEN HOMES

The sources of inequality of educational opportunity appear to lie first in the home itself and the cultural influences immediately surrounding the home; then they lie in the schools' ineffectiveness to free achievement from the impact of the home.

JAMES S. COLEMAN (1966)

It takes more than good schools and good teachers to do well in school. This chapter considers the influence of a student's home background on achievement in school. Students differ on a variety of home background measures. Jencks et al. (1972) has demonstrated that family background as a whole "explains" about 50 percent of the individual differences in educational achievement. Virtually everyone agrees that socioeconomic status is the most powerful home background characteristic. What is the extent of this influence and exactly how is it mediated? And to what extent do gender and race affect success in school? What, if any, are the effects of religion? And, how does family structure and family functioning influence school outcomes?

These questions raise a set of basic issues in the sociology of education and in sociology generally. Namely, is inequality necessary or inevitable in society? More specifically, to what extent are schools able to reduce the inequalities that students bring with them from their home?

Are status (occupational) destinations simply determined by status origins (parental SES)? Do schools exacerbate the inequalities that students bring with them? If the latter is true, then schools are involved in "reproducing" social inequality. These questions address the dilemmas posed in the above quote from Coleman—namely, To what extent is the school capable of overcoming the various influences of the home backgrounds of students? To begin to answer these questions, we must first consider in detail the differences that do exist *between* students' homes, and the extent to which these differences impact upon educational outcomes.

Aside from these questions of "ascriptive" effects, it is now thought that school outcomes may be dependent upon a rapidly changing family structure. The vast majority of students go to school each day and return to a home constituted by either a single parent, a two-parent home reformulated from a previous divorce, and/or a home in which both parents work. The implications of this major transformation of family structure are extensive. Coleman (1987: 32) notes that "school as we conceive of it, implies family as we conceive it. Yet family as we conceive of it no longer corresponds to family as it now exists." Thus, the parental structure and parental work patterns must be considered in conjunction with the ascriptive factors of socioeconomic status and race. And, as with SES and race, how are these family variables mediated? That is, what is the actual process by which children of divorced or working parents do less well in school? Amidst many possible explanations, language development, parental values and involvement, the amount of homework done, and TV watching are considered in this chapter.

Regardless of how disadvantaged students are identified and defined, some critics (Wehlage and Rutter, 1987) have cautioned that we run the risk of locating problems within the students themselves or their families or their neighborhoods, rather than within the schools. Focusing on categories of students directs attention away from the problems of schools and runs the risk of "blaming the victim" (Ryan, 1976). Others (Grannis, 1975; Rist, 1970) argue that identifying students of disadvantaged characteristics sets into motion the likelihood of a self-fulfilling prophecy whereby students, teachers, and family may lower their expectations for school performance (see also, Wasserman, 1970). Other critics are even more radical in their concerns, noting that the problems of so-called disadvantaged students lie in the inadequate and ineffective schools that these students must attend (see Baratz and Baratz, 1970; Valentine, 1968). Valentine (1971: 144–145) goes further, arguing that "poor Afro-Americans—far from being either

deficient or merely different in culture— often possess a richer repertoire of varied life styles than their ethnically nondescript social superiors." Thus, in addressing the home background characteristics of students, we must be careful to avoid any of the implications wisely offered by these critics. Our aim is to examine those factors beyond the immediate control of the school that influence the outcomes of schooling.

❖ HOME BACKGROUND

There are several types of home background variables that must be considered. Homes or families vary according to a number of *social characteristics*. Among these are socioeconomic status, race/ethnicity, and religion. Sociologists distinguish between characteristics of individuals and characteristics of groups or organizations. Factors such as socioeconomic status or race are actually *characteristics of individuals*, even though they are derived from one's family (group) of origin. These variables are commonly classified as social categories. In the case of students, of course, these social categories (or individual characteristics) are derived from differences between homes or families, or parents if you will. These variables are also defined as *ascribed* characteristics of individuals. For this reason, we include gender as one of the variables to be considered here as well.

Families or homes are groups, and as such, they possess certain *group characteristics*. Family structure varies according to such factors as the number of parents, the number of children, the number of marriages for each parent (this effects the extended family structure, see

Cherlin, 1992), the working patterns of each parent, and even the spacing patterns between children in the family. It is especially true in our society today that many of these variables of family structure will vary widely. And, it is important to note that family structure is often influenced by one or more of the social categories noted above (for example, race or social class).

Other key home background variables involve the *community and neighborhood characteristics* of students. Sociologists refer to these as "contextual" variables— variables of ambience or atmosphere or climate. Thus, communities maintain norms for appropriate and expected behavior regarding work, recreation, education, and so forth. Wilson (1987), for example, argues that the inner-city underclass community is characterized by extreme unemployment, crime, drugs, and anomie (normlessness). There is an absence of middle- and working-class black and Hispanic families that previously used to live in these inner-city neighborhoods. The result is a severe weakening of basic social institutions, values, and norms. This state of normlessness becomes part of the social milieu of the inner-city child. Contextual effects are discussed in greater detail in Chapters 4 and 7.

These home background variables constitute advantages or disadvantages that students bring with them to school. They become the basis for the "gifted" and the "disadvantaged" child. Taken as a whole, the configuration of these variables measures the *differences between homes* that exist among students in school. During the 1960s and 1970s, the disadvantaged student was defined and identified largely in terms of individual characteristics derived from the social categories of

socioeconomic and racial/ethnic status. This gave rise to the theory of cultural deprivation (Riessman, 1962; Havighurst, 1965; Lewis, 1966). During the 1980s, this concept came to be redefined under the rubric of "children at risk" (McCann and Austin, 1988). Often, categories for "children at risk" have included measures such as family structure (single/two parent) as well as race/ethnicity and socioeconomic status.

Recently, Coleman and Hoffer (1987) have proposed a set of important conceptual distinctions. Traditionally, social scientists have defined the disadvantaged as those families and individuals characterized by low education and low income. These are *human capital* resources in the home background of children that are viewed as critical for educational development. Children who are racial and ethnic minorities are also often characterized as "disadvantaged" by virtue of the strong correlation between race and education or race and income. Coleman and Hoffer (1987) suggest this approach:

> We will use the term "deficient" meaning certain resource deficiencies that were once, but are no longer, largely confined to families of low education and low income. An increasing fraction of families has structural and functional deficiencies. The structural deficiencies lie in what were once called "broken homes," but are now called "single-parent families." It lies secondarily in the increasing involvement of women in the corporate world of work institutions from which children and youth are excluded. The functional deficiencies lie in the increased self-interest of parents, the decreased personal investment in activities of the family as a unit, and the decreased parental involvement with the children. (p. 119)

Thus, families can be conceptualized as disadvantaged or structurally deficient or functionally deficient, or any combination thereof. What is especially compelling about these distinctions is that they open up a concern for families and children who might otherwise have been judged to be adequate. Advantaged and structurally adequate families may be functionally deficient. Disadvantaged and structurally inadequate families might be functionally efficient. What are the effects of each type of family condition for children?

The idea of "functional deficiency" is truly the newest part of the above distinction. The possibility of structural deficiencies in the family have been recognized for a long time, and there is considerable research examining the effects of these structural changes on children (Milne et al., 1986; Cherlin, 1988). Functional deficiencies, however, have been overlooked. The concept captures the motivation, values, and behavior of parents. It goes to the center of whether children may be at risk by changes in the modern family. Even a severe proponent of the negative outcomes accruing to children from increasing structural deficiencies in the family must recognize that some single parents who work full time are able, by virtue of their commitment to children and possibly the limited demands of their jobs, to compensate for structural deficiencies (through day care, super-parenting, or whatever) and to raise healthy children. Yet, by the same logic, even the most ardent supporter of family change must agree that children are very likely at risk when parent(s) are more interested in their own self-realization and success in the workplace than they are in the ultimate success of their children.

❖ PHYSICAL, HUMAN, CULTURAL, AND SOCIAL CAPITAL

One of the most important developments in the economics of education in recent years has been that the concept of physical capital can be usefully and easily extended to include human capital (Schultz, 1961; Becker, 1964; Mincer, 1974). Physical capital includes land, tools, machines, and other productive equipment. The possession of physical capital facilitates the production of goods and services. Initially, physical capital is created by working with materials to produce tools, machines, and fertile land. Likewise, human capital is generated by educating and training people to provide them with skills to increase their productivity. Hence, human capital is the possession of knowledge and skills. Schools are the main social institutions for creating and maintaining human capital. Physical capital and human capital are alike in that decision making is based largely on the expected rate of return from capital investments.

A concept closely related to human capital is *cultural capital*—the cultural resources possessed by individuals with varying degrees of human and physical capital (Bourdieu, 1987). These cultural advantages, which are held by people of high rather than low socioeconomic status, include tastes in furniture, home decorations, and the arts, as well as the capacity to appreciate and participate in certain high-status cultural experiences such as lectures, symphonies, and art exhibits. Cultural capital has also been defined more expansively as middle-class cultural values including hard work and basic skills (Farkas et al., 1990) and possessions such as books and computers (Roscigno and Ainsworth-Darnell, 1999). The idea of cultural capital is usually employed as an explanatory variable in attempting to describe exactly *how* social class influences life outcomes. (for an example of this, see Lareau, 1989; Cookson and Persell, 1985; DiMaggio, 1982). We will come back to the idea of cultural capital later in this chapter.

Coleman and Hoffer (1987) argue that the idea of human capital can be extended further by incorporating the concept of social capital:

> If physical capital is wholly tangible, being embodied in observable material form, and human capital is less tangible, being embodied in the skills and knowledge acquired by an individual, social capital is less tangible yet, for it exists in the *relations* between persons. Just as physical and human capital facilitate productive activity, social capital does as well. . . . Students' families differ in human capital, as, for example, measured in years of parental education. And research shows . . . that outcomes for children are strongly affected by the human capital possessed by their parents. But this human capital can be irrelevant to outcomes for children if parents are not an important part of their children's lives, if their human capital is employed exclusively at work or elsewhere outside the home. The social capital of the family is the relations between children and parents (and when families include other members, relationships with them as well). That is, if the human capital possessed by parents is not complimented by social capital embodied in family relations, it is irrelevant to the child's educational growth that the parent has a great deal, or a small amount of human capital. (pp. 221–223)

Coleman and Hoffer go on to cite several classic examples of family situations where human capital is low but social capital is high; the result is often successful socialization outcomes for children. One such example is that of many Southeast Asian refugee families with extremely low physical and human capital. It has been widely noted that children from these families often purchase an extra textbook for each school subject. The extra book is for the parent(s), who are determined to provide maximum help with schoolwork. Coleman and Hoffer (1987: 223) note, however, that these examples "contrast greatly with the situation in which many children of well-educated parents find themselves today. The human capital exists in the family, but the social capital does not."

Thus, social capital consists of relationships between adult family members (parents, grandparents, aunts, uncles, guardians) and children. The presence of some adult members in the family unit is a necessary condition for providing social capital. It is not, however, a sufficient condition. Some degree of *intergenerational* communication, commitment, and relationship is required.

> It is the absence of social capital within the family that we have labeled "deficiencies" in the family. What we have labeled as *structural* deficiency is the physical absence of family members. . . . What we have labeled as *functional* deficiency in the family is the absence of strong relations between children and parents despite their physical presence in the household. (Coleman and Hoffer, 1987: 224)

The presence of adult family members in the household is the cornerstone of this

Social Capital

Family Structure

Human Capital	Adequate Family Functioning		Deficient Family Functioning	
	Adequate	Deficient	Adequate	Deficient
High SES	1	2	3	4
Low SES	5	6	7	8

FIGURE 3.1   **Families Characterized by the Presence or Absence of Human and Social Capital**

Source: Adapted from James S. Coleman and Thomas Hoffer, *Public and Private High Schools* (New York: Basic Books, 1987), Fig. 8.2, p. 225.

model. All things being equal, the model implies that one parent is better than none, two are better than one, and the inclusion of an extended family is even better yet. But the model recognizes that presence alone is insufficient. Two parents who are never home, or who are abusive, are functionally deficient. The key is intergenerational communication, or simply providing "care" for children. Some minimum degree of adequate structure is necessary to provide some minimum degree of adequate functioning.[1]

The social capital concept takes on added significance when it is properly configured with the idea of human capital. Let's consider the eight cells identifying eight family types in Figure 3.1.

[1] The social capital concept also can be applied to the larger society. For example, Putnam (1995) has argued that deficiencies in political and social participation in America over the past fifty years reflect the erosion of social capital, broadly conceived. Some critics (Portes, 1998; Foley and Edward, 1999; Schaub and Baker, 2002) have cautioned that the social capital concept, although clearly providing a much needed social construct, requires more careful definition and measurement.

Cell 5 represents families of low socioeconomic status but with strong family relations. Such families often include immigrants and refugees who hold very traditional values from less-developed countries. Cell 8 represents families that possess very little human and social capital, families that lack both education and income, and families that are characterized also by structural and functional disorganization. Cell 1 represents families that possess adequate amounts of both human and social capital. These family units are structurally and functionally sound, and the adult members are educated and capable of maintaining effective intergenerational relations. Cells 2 and 4 represent problematic families that are increasingly prevalent in modern society. These are middle-class families with adequate human capital, but lacking in either structural or functional social capital for a variety of reasons (divorce, excessive parental self-involvement, overinvolvement in work, and so on).

In a related article, Coleman (1987: 37) demonstrated persuasively that over the past twenty-five years there has been a steady and "extensive erosion of social capital available to children and youth, both within the family and outside of it." By contrast, in this age of "advanced individualism," human capital within the family has grown extensively as reflected by increased levels of education.

> All of this would not matter, of course, in a society in which social capital was abundant. . . . But the world has changed. In the individualistic present, each (parent) narcissistically attends to self-development, with little attention left over for children. (Coleman, 1987: 37)

Social capital, therefore, is the capacity of a family (or other social institutions such as the church or the school) to "invest" a wealth of attention, advice, support, interest, values, and care in children. A precondition is a minimum degree of adult presence, but the investment process obviously is grounded in parent-child relationships. Normally, this investment involves regular intergenerational communication, a minimum amount of time and selfless effort exemplified by reading to children, helping with homework, listening to their problems, applauding their successes and comforting their failures, building self-control and social skills, and teaching basic values. Unlike physical and human capital where personal investment leads to an increased productivity of the self (in terms of educational and occupational achievement, fame and fortune), social capital is an investment in the productivity of others. Social capital is a parental outlay (investment) utilized as an input by children toward the production of their own physical, human, and social capital. Coleman (1988b: S119) calls this the *public good aspect* of social capital: "The actor or actors who generate social capital ordinarily capture only a small part of its

benefits, a fact that leads to underinvestment in social capital."

The idea of social capital extends beyond the home and family to the neighborhood, community, and school. These larger institutions, just like families, must provide some degree of social capital to help in the production of human capital. In fact, research (see Porter, 1990; Tinto, 1987; Coleman and Hoffer, 1987) clearly shows that three factors consistently influence academic success in education: (1) academic resources (human capital), (2) financial resources (physical capital), and (3) social resources (social capital). Student academic success is a function of previous academic achievement and the academic quality of the school, and the amount of financial resources that students receive either from the home or the school or both. But schools must also provide order, discipline, encouragement, attention, security, comfort, trust, and identity. Social capital in schools is indicated by a high degree of interconnectedness between students, parents, and teachers. Teachers and parents, in particular, have a joint interest in the well-being of the student. They operate as functional communities. Of course, this is less likely when parents are not involved or teachers are alienated from their occupation.

Similarly, youth organizations can provide (or fail to provide) social capital. Head Start programs and day care, for example, are clearly in the business of providing social capital. In fact, their existence attests to the persistent decline in the availability of social capital in the home. Likewise, community organizations such as Girls Scouts and Boys Scouts, Future Farmers of America, and so on endeavor to engage and support children and adolescents (Heath and

McLaughlin, 1987, 1991). Finally, the various dimensions of social capital (care, intergenerational communication, and so on) may or may not exist in neighborhoods and communities.

❖ SOCIAL CHARACTERISTICS OF FAMILIES

◆ SOCIOECONOMIC STATUS AND RACE

The most important of the home background variables is socioeconomic status. The higher the social class of the home, the higher the achievement of students. This is true regardless of which indicators are used for SES or for achievement. This relationship has been found consistently in literally thousands of studies. Student SES is related to grades, achievement test scores, curriculum placement, dropout rates, college plans, and educational attainment. The relationship holds even when other background and school effects are controlled. And, the relationship has been demonstrated in virtually every Western society. Only in developing and less-developed countries is the relationship attenuated (Heyneman and Loxley, 1983; Fuller and Heyneman, 1989).

We have already examined the impact of race and class in Chapter 2 and concluded that the effects are large, especially for socioeconomic status (SES). Recall and perhaps reexamine Tables 2.1, 2.3, and 2.5. We discovered there that the SES gap from low to high on reading scores is nearly 40 percentage points both at the beginning and at the end of school. The race gap is smaller but increases over the course of 12 years of schooling. But, the race gap is actually quite large when

translated into effect sizes, being about .65 ES in 1992 even after adjusting for SES (see Table 2.5). Unlike race, SES is a continuous variable that ranges from individuals with the lowest SES values to the highest values. We can group this large range of values into categories such as quartiles as in Table 2.1 and 2.3. The gap between the lowest and highest quartile is larger than the black-white gap. And this SES gap would increase further if we employed quintiles and even greater if we used deciles.

Race and SES are inextricably correlated. Blacks and Hispanics are more likely to hold low socioeconomic status and whites are more likely to hold middle or high socioeconomic status. For this reason, some part of the race gap is at the same time an SES gap. In Chapter 2, we determined that SES "explains" about one-third of the race gap. But the impact of race and SES is both short- and long-term, and not at all limited to test scores.

The short- and long-term effects of SES and race are clearly revealed by the results of a study on college graduation rates among 1972 high school graduates. Using the NLS data, Alexander et al. (1982) examined the influence of gender, race, and socioeconomic status on educational attainment. The dependent variable was whether the student had graduated from college. The average controlled effect of SES on educational attainment was 22 percentage points, even after controlling for race and sex. That is, an average of 22 percent more students from high-SES homes graduate from college than students from low-SES homes. By contrast, the effects of race and sex on college graduation were very small. Note carefully that the effect of an independent variable may change in size as the dependent variable changes.

Although they found "null" effects for race on educational attainment, controlling for SES, it would be very misleading to conclude that these results will hold across all educational outcomes. In fact, most people are surprised by the results for educational attainment, which suggest that race is an insignificant factor. For virtually any other academic outcome, minorities obtain less than whites (test scores, curriculum placement, class rank; see Alexander et al., 1982).

All of this suggests that the effects of race on educational attainment are indirect. Race influences classroom outcomes such as test scores and type of curriculum (high or low track) and these outcomes in turn affect educational attainment. In the Alexander et al. (1982) study, the uncontrolled total effect of race on educational attainment was 10 percent favoring whites. After controlling for SES and gen-

der, the effect of race was zero. Alexander et al. also controlled for a variable that they termed "academic resources," which was a composite of test scores, class rank, and the likelihood of being in a college track. After controlling for academic resources, they noted that the direct effect of SES had been reduced to 10 percent (from 22 percent), indicating that most of the effect was indirect through academic resources, as shown in Figure 3.2. They also found that the influence of race on educational attainment had become 13 percent favoring blacks. That is, among students with equal SES *and* equal academic resources, blacks were actually more likely to graduate from college than whites.

On the other hand, the effect of race on academic resources was 20 percent (favoring whites) and the influence of academic resources in educational attain-

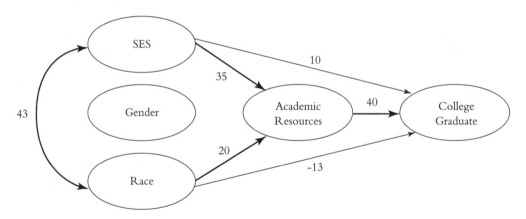

FIGURE 3.2 **Empirical Model of the Effects of SES, Race, Gender, and Academic Resources on College Graduation**

Source: These estimates were computed by the author using the same NLS data as Karl L. Alexander, Cornelius Riordan, James Fennessey, and Aaron M. Pallas. "Social Background, Academic Resources, and College Graduation: Recent Evidence from the National Longitudinal Survey." *American Journal of Education* 90 (1982): 325. Gender is related to class rank only and favoring females. Blacks are *less* likely to have high academic resources. Blacks are more likely to graduate (all other things being equal) and only after academic resources are considered.

ment was 40 percent. Thus, for most blacks the effect of race is indirect and negative—they obtain fewer academic resources and hence, achieve less education. For those blacks fortunate enough to possess equal SES and equal academic resources to whites, they are more likely to graduate from college. These results from Alexander et al. (1982), recomputed by the author, are depicted in Figure 3.2. Note that race and SES are highly correlated in Figure 3.2—whites being more likely by a percentage difference of 40 to be middle or high SES and blacks more likely to be low SES.

The findings regarding the direct effects of race on college graduation may be due to several factors. One possibility is that it indicates the results of affirmative action programs that were designed to provide greater opportunity and greater support to minorities who are otherwise equally qualified. This is not likely, however, since this finding has appeared in virtually every study on the issue, beginning with Rogoff (1953). Another possibility is that among students admitted to college, blacks may have greater academic ability. Assuming some degree of cultural bias in SAT test scores, point for point, any score on the tests would actually underestimate the true cognitive ability of blacks—that is, a score of 400 for a black student might actually be a true score of 500. This latter idea is only something to think about—there is no study that has actually shown this to be true.

The most likely and simple explanation, however, is that blacks with equivalent SES and school resource levels perform academically at an equal (or slightly higher) level with whites, on average. This situation does not occur often since most blacks have low-SES backgrounds

and low school resources, as shown in Figure 3.2. Thus, the effects of race on educational attainment are mostly indirect through academic resources such as test scores and track allocation.

◆ THE GENDER GAP

Note that in Figure 3.2 there are no gender effects on college graduation. Likewise, gender is not related to academic resources such as test scores and track allocation. Certainly, some studies have shown that females are disadvantaged in school. For example, an earlier review of nearly 1,000 studies concluded that schools shortchange girls in virtually all academic areas (American Association of University Women, 1992). More recently, however, it is commonly reported that girls do better than boys academically, except in the areas of science (Hedges and Nowell, 1995). In fact, females were more likely to have higher class ranking than males in the Alexander et al. (1982) study (Figure 3.2). In any event, the findings in Figure 3.2 have been sustained in follow-up studies across two decades (see Alexander, Holupa, and Pallas, 1987).

Despite the equalities in educational attainment and academic resources among males and females, however, there still remains concern regarding the treatment of females in school. Until recently, critics have argued that (1) women's cognitive development may be depressed or impaired; (2) their educational and occupational aspirations and ultimate attainment may be lowered; (3) their self-confidence and self-esteem may be damaged; (4) they may receive unequal treatment in the classroom and in curriculum opportunities; (5) teachers may devalue the work of female students relative to males;

and (6) sex segregation is the existing norm in coeducational schools anyway (for reviews, see Lockheed and Klein, 1985; Sadker, Sadker, and Klein, 1991; American Association of University Women, 1992; Sadker and Sadker, 1994).

Recent reports, however, have confirmed that boys, not girls, are increasingly on the unfavorable side of the gender gap in education and developmental matters. For example, enrollments in institutions of higher education in the 1990s favor females by a ratio of 54% to 46% (Green et al., 1995). As recent as 1980, the ratio was 50/50. Of course, in 1970 the ratio favored males by a margin of 59 to 41. Because of this large gap favoring males just 30 years ago, it is easy to understand how the reversal has gone unnoticed. Among African Americans and Hispanic Americans, the gap actually favored females in 1970 and has expanded substantially during these past two decades (Kopka and Korb, 1996).

A recent NCES report (Nord et al., 2000) concludes that the literacy and numerical scores for males are significantly lower than those for females in both 1993 and 1999. These gaps are approximately equivalent to a one-half-year difference in growth if compared to the gaps between 4- and 5-year-old children or 3- and 4-year-old children. Comparing four readiness variables in 1993 and 1999, these researchers show that the gender gap favoring females is equal or larger than the racial gaps favoring whites over blacks.

Educational Testing Service (ETS) has released a four-year study reinforcing this emergent view regarding the gender gap. In this report, Willingham and Cole (1997) analyzed data from 400 different tests from more than 1,500 different data sets. They found that for most subject matter tests, gender differences were very small and whenever a gender difference was found it "cut both ways." The researchers acknowledged that the results contradict the view that girls need to catch up with boys. In particular, they note (p. 10) that "12th grade girls have substantially closed the familiar math and science gap over the past 30 years but there continues to be a fairly large gap in writing skills that boys have not closed." A more recent report from Educational Testing Service (Coley, 2001) concluded that the above gender differences (or lack thereof) did not vary to any great degree across racial/ethnic groups.

In the spring of 2000, the U.S. Department of Education (2000) released a report entitled *Trends in Educational Equity of Girls and Women*, which reviewed evidence for 44 indicators of educational gender equity. These indicators covered many of the outcomes that other researchers had examined but provided some new data and new measures. The report (p. 2) concluded that:

> [I]n schools and in colleges, females are now doing as well or better than males on many of the indicators of educational attainment, and that the large gaps in educational attainment that once existed between men and women have in most cases been eliminated and, in others, have significantly decreased.

It now appears that boys enter school with significant academic readiness deficits that are not well understood or articulated (Riordan, 2002). Tyack and Hansot (1990) show that coeducation was established and flourished throughout the twentieth century, in large part, because educators saw it as a solution for the "boy problem." The above review suggests that some work still remains.

◆ RELIGION, RACE, AND ETHNICITY

In the above studies, the race variable is limited to whites and blacks. In view of the many varieties of race and ethnicity in America, this is a serious limitation. Moreover, race and ethnicity are often linked to religion. It would be informative to examine the influence of the various religio-ethnic groups on educational attainment. One of the most exhaustive studies of this nature was conducted by Hirshman and Falcon (1985), who investigated the relationship of ethnicity and educational attainment. Historically, certain religio-ethnic groups have been able to obtain greater educational achievement than have others. And since educational attainment is directly related to occupational attainment, the matter is of substantial importance.

According to one theory "some ethnic groups are able to achieve, in spite of discrimination, because their culture places a premium on ambition, persistence, deferred gratification, and social mobility" (Hirshman and Falcon, 1985: 84). This theory provides a "cultural" interpretation of differential values held by parents toward education and passed on to their children. Using this theory, the high educational aspirations and attainments of Jewish families are often compared to the lower achievements among Italians.

Following this theory, Zborowski and Herzog (1962) argued that the upward mobility of American Jews was "explained" by the favorable fit between the scholarly oriented culture of Jews and the educational and occupational opportunities in America. By contrast, Covello (1967) notes that the Italians who first came to America were almost exclusively peasant farmers. These people were from the south of Italy and were distrustful of

schools for several reasons. First, little of what was taught in school was of much importance to their lives as farmers. Second, the schools represented the subculture of Northern Italy. Covello concluded that these cultural values acted as obstacles to the educational and occupational progress of Italian Americans, especially when compared to the Jews. All of this is fairly reasonable and served as a basis for explaining differential patterns in educational and occupational achievement among religio-ethnic groups until the 1970s. (For other references on this theory, see Lenski, 1989; Rosen, 1959; Sowell, 1981; Kessner, 1977; Dinnerstein, 1982; LaGumina, 1982.)

This cultural theory can be challenged, however, by an alternative view holding that the differential attainments of these groups is due to prior educational and occupational differences. For example, Steinberg (1981) argues that Jewish immigrants had a substantial social class advantage relative to other immigrants from Eastern and Southern Europe at the turn of the century. Although all of these people came to America essentially penniless, Steinberg's theory is that Jewish immigrants brought with them prior experience, education, and occupational skills that better qualified them for highly skilled jobs. By examining immigration records, Steinberg found support for his theory. He found that only 3 percent of the turn-of-the-century immigrant Jews were farmers while 61 percent of the non-Jews were farmers. Moreover, he discovered that two-thirds of the Jewish immigrants were skilled laborers, far greater than any other immigrant group at that time. Hence, Steinberg concluded that Jewish mobility in America was explained by their initial skills and background, rather than by their cultural values. (For other references, see Lieberson, 1980; Duncan and Duncan, 1968; Greeley, 1976.)

There are two other theories that are at least as popular and as frequently cited as cultural values and SES background. Kramer (1970) has argued quite persuasively that the minority "community" (whenever it existed in an organized fashion) was the key to both the early stability of immigrants and the eventual mobility of second and third generations. Thus, the existence (or lack) of a functional community is a third possible explanation. Perhaps the most popular view on differential group mobility is institutional and cultural racism or discrimination. This theory points to the repressiveness of the social structure or the unwillingness of dominant groups to permit others to share in the fruits of the society. At this point, however, we want to return to the research of Hirshman and Falcon.

Attempting to find support for the theory of socioeconomic disadvantage, Hirshman and Falcon analyzed data from the General Social Surveys of 1977–1983. These surveys are conducted annually by the National Opinion Research Center and contain a wide range of general information on the U.S. adult population. The major purpose of the study was to test the notion that differences in the educational attainments of various religio-ethnic groups are due to prior educational and occupation differences of parents as described above. In their research, Hirshman and Falcon compared the differential education attainments for twenty-five religio-ethnic groups. As measures of parental SES, they used father's and mother's education, and father's occupational attainment, along with a number of other control variables (age, gender, region, generation, family structure). They also standardized the average educational attainments of each group so that the average educational level was equal to zero. Then, the standardized score of each group was either higher or lower than the average in years of education. This analysis is shown in Table 3.1.

The first column in the table shows that the uncontrolled educational attainment difference between the highest and the lowest religio-ethnic group is five full years. People of Jewish and Asian ancestry on average attained 2.3 years more than the average, which is 11.9 years. Mexican Americans, however, attained 2.7 years less than the average. After controlling for the home background variables, the uncontrolled gap of five years is reduced to 2.2 years of education (see column 2 of the table), a reduction of over 50 percent in the original uncontrolled difference. This holds generally even if we were to ignore the extreme values associated with Jewish, Asian, and Mexican American families. Comparing the gap between Scottish/Protestants and Spaniards/Portuguese, the uncontrolled gap of 2.7 is reduced to 1.4 after adding the background controls. Thus, there exists considerable support for the theory of SES disadvantage as an explanation for religio-ethnic differences in educational attainment. According to Hirshman and Falcon, (1985: 27) "these results give precious little room for an 'independent' cultural theory of achievement." However, only 50 percent of the difference has been "explained," leaving 50 percent "unexplained." This means that the "cultural values" theory or the "discrimination" theory or the "functional

TABLE 3.1

EFFECTS OF ETHNIC ORIGINS AND OTHER SOCIAL BACKGROUND
CHARACTERISTICS ON TOTAL YEARS OF COMPLETED SCHOOLING

Ethnic Origins	Uncontrolled	Controlled for Parental SES	Number of Cases
Jewish	2.3	0.8	174
Asian	2.3	1.6	47
Scottish Protestant	1.5	0.7	167
English/Scottish Catholic	1.5	0.4	71
Irish Catholic	1.3	0.2	250
English Protestant	1.2	0.7	746
French	0.9	−0.1	112
Non-French Canadian	0.6	−0.4	45
French Canadian	0.6	0.0	61
Scandinavian	0.5	0.1	320
Other Catholic	0.4	−0.3	206
German/Austrian/ Swiss Prot.	0.2	0.0	866
German/Austrian/ Swiss Cath.	0.2	−0.3	247
American Indian	−0.1	−0.6	140
Eastern European Protestant	−0.1	−0.3	88
Irish Protestant	−0.1	0.2	385
Eastern European Catholic	−0.1	0.0	142
Polish Catholic	−0.2	−0.2	156
Latin American/ Caribbean	−0.3	−0.1	82
Italian	−0.3	−0.5	310
Other Protestant	−0.9	−0.3	1050
Dutch/Belgian	−0.9	−0.5	108
African	−1.0	0.0	958
Spaniard/Portuguese	−1.2	−0.7	53
Mexican	−2.7	−1.4	101

Source: Adapted from Charles Hirschman, and Luis M. Falcon, "The Educational Attainment of Religio-Ethnic Groups in the United States," *Research in Sociology of Education and Socialization*, vol. 5, ed. Alan C. Kerckhoff (Greenwich, CN: JAI Press Inc., 1985), Table 4.

Note: Based on combined NORC General Social Surveys age twenty-five and above, from 1977 to 1983. Effects are expressed as deviations from the grand mean of the total sample = 11.9 years. SES controls include father's and mother's education, father's occupational attainment, mother's employment status, age, gender, and generation in the United States.

community" theory might contribute to the remaining explanations.

❖ FAMILY STRUCTURE

The configuration of roles within a household constitutes the family structure. This structure may contain one or more parents, one or more children, along with the possibility of extended family members. The parents may work at home or away from home, they may work part or full time, and children in the home may also work. The parents in a household may have been previously divorced and may be the parents of children from a previous marriage. These children may or may not reside with the parent(s) who have remarried. Despite the relatively small number of roles involved, therefore, family structure is a fairly complex social organization. In modern society, family structure is undergoing rapid transformation. Changes in family structure generate variables that may impact upon school performance. Some observers argue that these family changes are likely to be quite consequential for children. Moreover, changes in the structure of the family may necessitate changes in the structure and functions of schooling. Likewise, family functioning is complex and problematic. As regards the welfare of children, an adequately functioning family might expect at least one adult family member to devote considerable or at least minimal time and energy to the socialization of children in the home. In the traditional home, mothers usually performed this function with supplemental support from fathers. The traditional home no longer exists and the implications for schooling are of course extensive.

◆ PARENTAL PRESENCE IN THE HOME

Since the early 1960s, the divorce rate has roughly doubled to its current level, at which about one-half of all first marriages end in divorce (Cherlin, 1992, 1988). The level of out-of-wedlock births has increased dramatically since 1950. Among non-Hispanic whites, 15 percent of all births in 1985 were to unmarried mothers, up from 2 percent in 1950; among blacks, 60 percent of all births in 1985 were to unmarried mothers, up from 38 percent in 1970 (Zill and Rogers, 1988, Table 2.3). Nearly one-third (29 percent) of all first births in the United States in 1990 were to unmarried females (Usdansky, 1996). As a result of the increase in out-of-wedlock births and divorce, about 22 percent of all families with children are headed by a single parent, usually the mother (Cherlin, 1988). Another substantial percentage of children live in families in which either the mother or the father or both have been previously divorced. Of these, about half will experience a second divorce before they reach sixteen (Bumpass, 1984).

Table 3.2 shows the extent of parental presence among eighth grade students in the 1988 National Education Longitudinal Study (NELS). The problem of parental absence from households is significantly greater among African American and American Indian students. Yet, considering all students, fully 22.3 percent live in some form of a single-parent household and another 15 percent live in a restructured family.

◆ WORKING PARENTS

A related change in the family is the dramatic increase in the number of married

TABLE 3.2

PERCENTAGE OF EIGHTH GRADERS IN DIFFERENT TYPES OF HOUSEHOLDS BY RACE

Race/ Ethnicity	Mother Only	Father Only	Other Relative Only	Mother and Father Present	Mother/ Male Guardian	Father/ Female Guardian
Asian	8.3	2.4	3.6	78.4	5.4	1.9
Hispanic	17.7	2.2	3.5	63.5	11.2	1.9
Black	36.1	2.1	8.3	38.4	13.3	1.9
White	12.9	2.7	2.1	67.9	11.6	2.9
American Indian	21.1	3.6	6.4	55.6	11.8	1.5
Total	16.5	2.6	3.2	63.6	11.5	2.6

Source: Anne Hafner, Steven Ingels, Barbara Schneider, and David Stevenson. *A Profile of the American Eighth Grader:* NELS:88 *Student Descriptive Summary.* (Washington: U.S. Department of Education (OERI), Government Printing Office, 1990), Table 1.2, p. 6.

women in the labor force. Coleman (1987) notes that the movement of women away from the home and into the labor force began at the turn of the century and has paralleled a similar movement of men away from the home (farming) and into the labor force via industry and the corporation, which began a century earlier. In 1800, fully 87 percent of men worked in agriculture; today less than 3 percent are engaged in this home-based occupation. In 1900, fully 87 percent of women worked in the home, today, less than 40 percent do so (Coleman, 1987, Fig. 1). Cherlin (1988) documents the most recent trends in this transformation:

> By 1986, 61 percent of currently married women with children under age 18 were in the labor force compared with 41 percent in 1970 and 24 percent in 1950. Among currently married women with children under age 6, the labor force participation rate stood at 54 percent in 1986, compared with 30 percent

in 1970 and 12 percent in 1950. During the 1950s, the sharpest increases occurred among mothers of school-age children; in the 1960s and 1970s mothers of preschoolers had the highest rate of increase; and in the 1980s mothers of very young preschoolers have had the highest increase. By 1986, half of all mothers with children age 1 or younger were in the labor force. (Cherlin, 1988, pp. 5–6)

The pattern of this trend is clear: Since at least 1800, fathers first, and later mothers, have exited the home for work in the corporate world. This movement, like that of the increased incidence of divorce and out-of-wedlock births, has persistently decreased the presence of adult family members in the home. The NELS 1988 survey found that over 25 percent of eighth grade students were home alone for two or more hours each day (Hafner et al., 1990). What is not so clear is the effects of all of this for children.

◆ DIVORCE, WORKING PARENTS, AND OUTCOMES FOR CHILDREN

Some evidence (Milne et al., 1986) suggests that students from two-parent homes are more successful in school than students from single-parent households. Although the evidence is not conclusive, the loss of a parent, *through either work or divorce*, may be disadvantageous to academic progress. It is conceivable, of course, that the effects of family structure may be largely indirect. Family structure may influence family functioning, which may in turn affect academic outcomes. Certainly, it is necessary to control for socioeconomic status and race in this research. With regards to working mothers, it is a difficult task since working and nonworking mothers differ on just about every conceivable background variable.

In perhaps the most widely cited paper, Uhlenberg and Eggebeen (1986) empirically chronicle a steady deterioration in the well-being of children and adolescents between 1960 and 1980 using a wide range of indicators including suicide rates, test scores, crime rates, and premarital sexual activity. Uhlenberg and Eggebeen hypothesized that this deterioration was due to the increased participation of mothers in the labor force and to the increase in marital instability. Critics have argued that this hypothesis and the empirical analyses are flawed on several grounds. Many of the trends have actually leveled off since the mid-1970s (arrest rates, suicide rates, marihuana use, and premarital sexual activity), some of the measures are not valid indicators of well-being (sexual activity and test scores), and most importantly, there is no direct evidence of a causal relationship— that is, the possibility of spuriousness is very high (see Zill and Rogers, 1988; Furstenberg and Condran, 1988).

Using data from the NELS eighth grade sample, Lee et al. (1991), however, found that school-related behavioral problems were between two and four times as likely in single-parent and restructured (stepfamilies) as in intact families. Not surprisingly, children from intact families had higher test scores and grades and lower dropout rates than their counterparts from nontraditional families (see also Zimiles and Lee, 1991). The researchers also discovered that the emotional problems of children (as reported by their parents) were directly related to family structure—children in nontraditional family structures manifested more emotional problems. The study employed a full set of background statistical controls including race and ethnicity, mother's age, gender, socioeconomic status, and number of siblings. More recent research has also obtained detrimental outcomes for children in single-parent homes (Entwistle and Alexander, 1995; McLanahan and Sandefur, 1994; Zill, 1996).

Astone and McLanahan (1991) report similar results among students in the High School and Beyond survey. They hypothesized that the negative outcomes associated with single-parent and restructured families could be explained by differences in parental practices. Specifically, they reasoned that children raised in intact families would receive more encouragement and more help through greater parental involvement than children in other family types. Indeed, this was the case. Astone and McLanahan reported, however, that these differences in parental behavior did *not* explain much of the differences in educational attainment between students in intact and nonintact families. This suggests that the matter is more complex. According to Pong (1998), two basic explanations exist for the negative outcomes of single parenthood: one is the lack of economic resources in single parent families, and the second is the lack of social capital resources, as noted earlier in the chapter.

The work patterns of mothers and their possible influence on the cognitive and affective development of children are more controversial. Generally, the research on maternal work status has failed to produce consistent results. A review (Heyns, 1982) notes that the school achievement outcomes of children of working mothers differ very little from the children of nonworking mothers. A review by Hoffman (1980) of essentially the same literature concluded that the effects of working mothers were generally positive among low-socioeconomic students but negative among middle-class youth,

especially males. A review by Milne et al. (1986: 126) concurs that mother's employment "may have positive effects on lower-class and black children."

Two studies, in particular, have found remarkably consistent results among dual-parent families. Milne et al. (1986) report a study of elementary schoolchildren showing significant negative effects of maternal employment on the school achievement of children from *white* two-parent families. This effect is primarily direct and unmediated by other variables in their model. These results were replicated among secondary school students (Milne et al., 1986). In both studies, the magnitude of the effect directly relates to the amount of time mothers work. The empirical model for this research is presented (in modified form) as Figure 3.3.

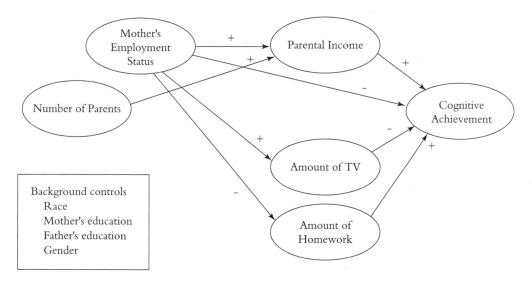

FIGURE 3.3 The Effect of Mother's Employment Status

Source: Adapted from Ann M. Milne, David E. Myers, Alvin S. Rosenthal, and Alan Ginsburg, "Single Parents, Working Mothers, and the Educational Achievement of School Children." *Sociology of Education* 59, (1986): 125–139, Table 1. More parental work is related to less homework (negative) and more television (positive). Homework is positively related to achievement and television is negatively related. Milne et al. used a variety of parental and student behaviors, including homework and TV.

Note that some of the effect of parental work is direct (and negative) and some of it is indirect (some positive and some negative). But the greater amount remained direct. This means that most of it is "unexplained" by such factors as time spent on homework or time spent watching television, parent-teacher conferences, parental homework monitoring, or increased family income. Note that the direct effect of mother's employment on cognitive achievement is significantly positive, rather than negative, among single-parent black families (not shown in Figure 3.3).

Unlike the effect of mother's employment, Milne et al. (1986) reported that the negative effects of living in a one-parent family occur primarily through the intervening variables in the model. That is, the effect is mediated or "explained" by the intervening variables—family income (and parental and student behavior, which are not shown in Figure 3.3). Milne et al. (1986) conclude:

> In general, students from two-parent families have higher scores on reading and math achievement tests than students from one-parent families. This is true for White and Black students in elementary and high school. . . . The negative effects on achievement of living in a one-parent family are almost entirely mediated by other variables, particularly by income. (p. 131) . . . We consistently find that mother's employment has a negative effect on achievement for White students from two-parent families. This is true for both reading and math and for both elementary school and high school students. Furthermore, the more the mother works, the stronger the effect. . . . [however] For Black elementary school students from one-parent families, the effects of mother's employment are positive and significant. (p. 134)

In traditional two-parent families where very low income is not a crucial issue, the loss of one parent's time as an educator is not offset by his or her added income (see also Bogenschneider and Steinberg, 1994). Presumably, parents may have positive effects on their children's achievement through educationally relevant activities in the home. Among low-income single-parent homes (especially minority homes), however, the effect of parental employment was confirmed to be positively related to achievement by Milne et al. (1986). The issue is obviously complex. (For a critique of the Milne et al. study, see Heyns and Catsambis, 1986.)

◆ FAMILY SIZE

Another component of family structure is size. On average, students from smaller families (fewer children) are more successful in school than students from larger families (Zajonc, 1976; Steelman and Mercy, 1980; Blake, 1985). Conceivably, however, this may be a spurious effect due to the prior influence of social class. The number of children in households has declined consistently over the past fifty years (U.S. Bureau of the Census, 1990).

The socioeconomic status of the home may temper or increase the effects of family size as such. Page and Grandon (1979) conclude that the effects of family size on ability are small after one adjusts for social class and ethnicity. Walberg and Marjoribanks (1976) found, however, that children from smaller families had higher cognitive ability, even after controlling for socioeconomic status. Generally, the research leans in the direction of an inverse relationship between family size and school achievement. Such a relationship suggests that parents with fewer children may be better able to provide the time, attention, and other resources conducive to an intellectually stimulating home climate than are parents with more children.

◆ FAMILY SIZE, MOTHER'S EMPLOYMENT, AND ACHIEVEMENT

In an earlier study, Mercy and Steelman (1982) provided an interesting insight as to why there may exist countervailing effects of two parents working. Their empirical resulting model (greatly simplified) is depicted in Figure 3.4.

The model shows that both parents working full time has a negative effect on family size. A negative effect simply means that the dependent variable decreases as the independent variable increases, and vice versa. Children of parents who work full time (more work) have fewer siblings. The model also shows that children who have more siblings have lower measured achievement. Thus, although the direct effect of parents' work status on achievement may be negative (as Milne et al. demonstrate), the indirect effect through family size is theoretically positive (a negative times a negative is a positive). The indirect effect is not just mathematical magic—mothers who work have fewer children, and children in smaller families have higher achievement. What are the hypothetical valences (positive or negative) for each of the remaining paths in Figure 3.4? You should obtain two negative indirect effects and two positive indirect effects. It is easy to see how countervailing views are held regarding the effects of women's employment on academic outcomes. A recent study, in fact, shows that the negative effects of changes in family structure between 1970 and 1992 were offset by the fact that parents were better educated, had fewer children, held higher incomes, and were older (Grissmer et al., 1994). Of course, there is also the unexplained direct negative effect of mother's employment reported by Milne et al. (1986).

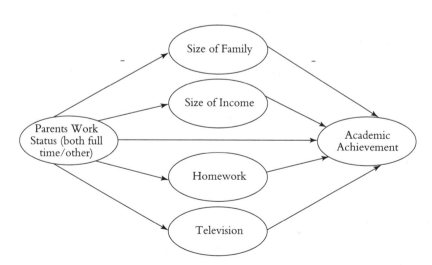

FIGURE 3.4   The Positive and Negative Effects of Two Working Parents

❖ FAMILY FUNCTIONING

In addition to family structure, we have previously identified family functioning as a critical factor defining differences that exist between homes. We can look at the NELS eighth grade data for some empirical evidence of the effects of family functioning on academic outcomes. Table 3.3 provides this analysis for a selective set of variables measuring parental involvement at home and in school. Each variable is a composite of three or more items in either the parent or the student questionnaire.[2] Some of the questions asked of parents and students are the same while others are different. Hence Table 3.3 provides the results for the parents' (P) and students' (S) responses separately.

In perhaps the most intriguing set of questions, parents only were asked if they knew the names of their child's first best friend as well as the names of the parents of this first best friend. They were then asked to do this for the second best friend and so forth up to five best friends. The amount of television watching per day is also included as a variable in Table 3.3. This variable does not directly measure either family functioning or parental involvement, but is indirectly related to both. All of the family functioning variables in the table are related to test score achievement and the weekly hours of homework. The effects vary in strength, and are stronger for test scores than for homework.

Family functioning is not totally defined by parental involvement. It would include many additional parental behaviors such as the absence of substance and child abuse, provision of a safe and secure home, meals and recreation, and a generally mature overall sense of responsibility. Nonetheless parental involvement measures certainly do tap an important dimension of family functioning, especially as related to a child's success in school. Parental involvement is

[2] The specific items for each variable are as follows:
Students discuss school with parents (student responses):
- Selecting course or programs at school
- School activities or events of particular interest to you
- Things you've studied in class

Parents discuss school with students (parent responses):
- About his/her experiences at school
- About his/her plans for high school
- About his/her plans for after high school

Parents attend school events (student responses):
- Attended a school meeting
- Phoned or spoken to student's teacher or counselor
- Visited student's classes
- Attended a school event such as a play, concert, etc., in which student participated

Parents attend school events (parent responses):
- Belong to parent-teacher organization
- Attend meetings of parent-teacher organization
- Take part in the activities of a parent-teacher organization
- Act as a volunteer at the school
- Belong to other organizations with other parents from school

TABLE 3.3

BIVARIATE CORRELATIONS OF FAMILY FUNCTIONING ON SELECTED OUTCOME VARIABLES AMONG EIGHTH GRADE WHITE STUDENTS IN NELS

Family Functioning	Reading/Math Test	Homework (hours per week)
Students discuss school with parents (S)	.30	.24
Parents discuss school with students (P)	.11	.07
Parents attend school events (S)	.12	.12
Parents attend school events (P)	.19	.10
Hours per day watching TV (S)	−.15	−.04
Parents knows names of student's friends and parents of friends (P)	.16	.07
Parental SES	.41	.15

Note: Estimates were computed by the author from the full sample for whites only. For all correlations, N = 11573. Correlations are based on the weighted sample. More attendance, more discussion, more rules, and more names are scored as high. SES is included for comparative purposes.

clearly a component of social capital, and we should not expect to find it to be plentiful in modern society, as per our early discussion. Coleman (1991: 14), draws this conclusion: "The effectiveness of schools in settings where the social capital of family and community is weak depends upon the rebuilding of that social capital ... This rebuilding requires something beyond parental involvement. It requires school involvement with parents."

♦ PARENTAL INVOLVEMENT
IN THE SCHOOLS

There is a growing literature on the importance of parental involvement for the success of students in school. It has been shown that parental involvement is directly related to both student and teacher performance in the classroom (see Clark, 1983; Epstein, 1987; Rich, 1987). Table 3.3 shows that parental involvement in the

school is significantly related to both cognitive achievement and amount of homework. This is true as measured by both the student and parent questionnaires.

Quite interestingly, Epstein also found that teachers' attitudes toward parents as a whole were positively influenced by the presence of even a small number of parent volunteers in the school. Unfortunately, Epstein also reported that parental involvement is a scarce commodity. The vast majority of parents manifest very little involvement either in the home or at school. Among low socioeconomic families, the involvement is critically low (Moles, 1990). In fact, Baker and Stevenson (1986) and Lareau (1989) have shown that higher-SES students do better in school partly because their parents are more involved in the school than working-class parents. This raises the possibility that parental involvement may "explain" part of the large effects of SES (for an opposing view, see Sui-Chu and Willms, 1996).

◆ PARENTAL INVOLVEMENT IN THE HOME

In a large study of 3,700 first, third, and fifth grade teachers and principals, Epstein (1987) found a significant improvement in student achievement and attitudes when parents assumed an educational role in the home (see also Becker and Epstein, 1982). Home activities include such things as tutoring, informal learning games, or just simply listening to their child read. Table 3.3 confirms that parental involvement in the home is significantly related to both cognitive achievement and amount of homework among eighth graders in the NELS study.

Several small studies with low-SES children have shown that programs that increase parental participation and interaction of parents with children and the school can be very important in raising the performance of these students (see Chall and Snow, 1988; Moles, 1990; Comer, 1988). This leads many educators to see parental involvement as a great untapped resource. And yet, the lack of involvement is viewed as an intractable problem. In addition, large-scale studies have been unable to clearly pinpoint the most valuable roles that parents play. Reviewing studies such as Head Start and other compensatory programs, Weiss (1987) notes that while the studies suggest the potential of family-oriented early participation, they do not clearly identify the specific components of programs that work, for whom, when, how, and why.

Table 3.3 shows that parental involvement in the home *and* in the school is related to both cognitive outcomes and homework. This is reflected in the measures for discussions of school activities at home, attendance at school events, the familiarity of parents with the friends of their own children (and with the parents of their children's friends), and by the amount of television viewing in the home. As with the other involvement measures, knowledge of children's friends and other parents is a measure of the social capital in the home and a good measure of family functioning. The same is true for television watching. Children who watch too much TV do less well on the cognitive tests. Likewise, parental involvement in the school is also important as indicated by the correlations between parental attendance at various school events and test scores and homework. These measures seem to be equally important except for the stronger correlations for the discussion of school activities (in the home) as reported by students. This parallels the results of a study by Peng and Lee (1992) which found that school involvement by parents is actually less important than frequent parent-child conversations and the availability of learning opportunities in the home (see also Sui-Chu and Willms, 1996).

◆ CONNECTING HOME, SCHOOL, AND COMMUNITY

An ambitious and promising line of theory and research in the sociology of education is that which attempts to link the effects of family, school, and communities on student achievement as illustrated by the work of Joyce Epstein and her colleagues at Johns Hopkins University. Of course, virtually all studies of "school effects" examine the impact of these variables on student achievement. But Epstein's objective, since the early 1980s, has been to probe the interconnections across these three overlapping spheres of influence.

Epstein and Sanders (2000) summarize this work that includes a sound theoretical framework, supportive research, and a proactive applied program of intervention. The theoretical component draws heavily on the concept of social capital, arguing that its currency increases when effective partnerships between families, schools, and communities interact in productive ways. The authors summarize several major research findings (2000: 288–289):

1. parents, teachers, and students do not understand each others' interests;

2. higher-SES families are more likely to be partners in their children's schooling, but teacher practices to involve families in their children's education are at least as important as "family background variables such as race, ethnicity, social class, marital status, or mother's education or mother's work status" (this seems a bit of a stretch);

3. "family practices of involvement are as important as or more important than family background variables for determining whether and how students progress and succeed at school" (this seems more plausible);

4. teachers who involve parents in their children's schooling rate parents more positively and in turn are rated more positively by parents and by principals;

5. and finally, they identify six different types of parental involvement covering a wide range of activities.

◆ THE RELATIVE EFFECTS OF FAMILY STRUCTURE AND FUNCTIONING

Of course, family structure and family functioning do not operate independently of each other. It is desirable to examine the independent effects of each of these variables. And it is necessary to control for socioeconomic status. To do this, we can return to the NELS data once again. Consider Figure 3.5 in which the effects of structure, functioning, and SES on cognitive test scores are presented.

Consequently, Figure 3.5 displays the results of a controlled analysis using percentage differences as the measure of an effect. All variables have been dichotomized into two categories and only white respondents were considered (for the sake of simplicity). The numbers shown in Figure 3.5 are the average controlled percentage differences. For example, 27 percent more high-SES students than low-SES students have high test scores. Because there were no significant interactions, the average effect is appropriate. The effects of SES on test scores, controlling for structure and functioning of the family, are large (27 percent) as per our previous discussion of this variable. SES affects both family structure and family functioning, but the effect on functioning is twice as large. The direct controlled effect of family structure on test scores is quite low (4 percent). We see also that family structure has only a small impact (7 percent) on family functioning. Clearly, the effect of family functioning (as defined here) significantly influences school outcomes. One way to think of the size of the functioning effect is that it is about one-half the size of SES, which we know is always very large.

Of course, family structure and functioning operate within a communal context. In our earlier discussion of the social capital concept, we noted that it implied the importance of a functional community that circumscribed the school and the family. Like families and schools, functional communities provide social capital

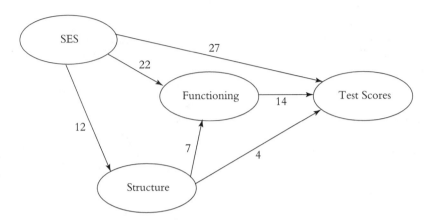

FIGURE 3.5   Model of Family Structure and Family Functioning

Note: Numbers are percentage differences for dichotomized variables. For example, 27 percent more high-SES students have higher test scores than low-SES students.

Family structure combines family composition and parental work status variables. Adequate is intact families and those with one parent at home at least part time; deficient is any other combination of these two variables. According to this breakdown, 45 percent of the families were adequate.

Family functioning combines the two student variables and the three parental variables on parental involvement. Television watching was not used. This produces a variable with a range of 13 (low) to 42 (high). This was collapsed into two categories high and low with 50 percent of the respondents in each.

Estimates were computed by the author from the full sample for whites only, based on the weighted sample.

to children. Unfortunately, there is widespread agreement that functional communities are scarce commodities in modern society. Functional communities are characterized by a clear set of values and norms, stable and functional relationships, and a willingness of community members to invest themselves in the well-being of the community. Communities in modern society are characterized by high levels of mobility and diversity and contentiousness. Few people are willing to invest social capital into the community because they are only temporary residents. Social analysts have raised concerns about the decline of functional

communities for some time now and its negative effect upon adults and children (see Stein, 1960; Nisbet, 1975; Riesman, Glazer, and Denney, 1951). In Chapter 4, we will return to this idea as we consider some possible reasons for the apparent efficacy of Catholic schools.

❖ THE INTERVENING EXPLANATORY VARIABLES

We have established that certain ascribed characteristics (SES, race, and religion) are strongly related to the performance of children in school. Moreover, the structure and the functioning of the family also predict success and failure in school. To some extent, these effects are "direct" and explainable within the variable itself. For example, to come from a lower-class home means to come from a home without a great deal of discretionary income for books, paper, tutoring, or higher education; likewise, to come from a single-parent family means to come from a low-SES home and one with only one parent to direct, control, and provide support. But to a larger extent, family structure and social category variables produce *indirect effects* by influencing a set of variables that "intervene"

between the background variables and educational achievement. These intervening variables help to "explain" how and why the status and family structure variables actually bring about success and failure in the schools. Of course, the family functioning variables represent many of the intervening variables. In addition, intervening variables such as student aspirations are the direct consequences of family functioning. Thus, there are dozens of indirect paths by which home variables may influence educational outcomes, as shown in Figure 3.6. In the remainder of this chapter, we will consider a select set of these many relationships.

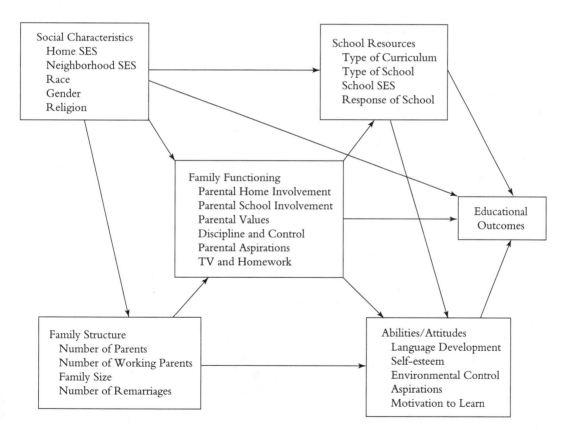

FIGURE 3.6 **Modeling the Effects of Differences Between Students' Homes**

◆ LANGUAGE AND EARLY COGNITIVE DEVELOPMENT

It may seem obvious that socioeconomic status and language development are inextricably linked—that is, students from low-SES homes may be disadvantaged in their verbal and written language skills relative to their counterparts from higher-SES homes. Since language skill is basic to virtually all schoolwork, this variable is critical, especially if it is linked to SES or race.

Basil Bernstein and others argue that low-SES children are not linguistically or cognitively in tune with the language of the school when they begin. According to Bernstein (1975), social class differences in families give rise to different modes of communication that he labels "linguistic codes." In middle-class homes, children learn an "elaborate" and "abstract" linguistic code that is congruent with classroom communication. Lower-class children, by contrast, are exposed to a more restrictive code, constrained both by social class and subculture. Aside from the notion of linguistic codes, children of higher-SES parents are likely to have been exposed to a greater range of typical academic ideas and vocabulary than their counterparts from lower-SES homes.

Recently, a study by Farkas and Beron (2001) has provided strong support for the position articulated by Bernstein and others. They argue and show empirically that the social reproduction process begins during the first 3 years of life and is mediated largely by oral language socialization (similar to Bernstein's codes). "The child's oral language skills and habits—including vocabulary and grammar as they are used respectively to understand others, expressively to make oneself understood, and analytically to represent the concepts that the child

employs for thinking—are the principal vehicles for cognitive development until the child learns to read" (Farkas and Beron, 2001: 2). They argue that oral language development differs according to class and race in the early years, and that these gaps establish a projectory for success and failure in the areas of schooling such as reading and mathematics that are not generally part of learning until school begins. Reading is largely dependent upon oral language development as are all other areas of school.

These researchers utilized data from the National Longitudinal Study of Youth (not the same as the NLS) which is a national panel study of men and women who were between 14 and 21 years of age in 1979 and have been followed up to the present time. The study examines the children of these respondents, using the Peabody Picture Vocabulary Test (PPVT) as the dependent variable, which is designed to measure oral vocabulary. The test consists of 175 words of increasing difficulty. The tester reads the words to the child and the child points to one of four pictures that best describe its meaning. Testing stops and the child's score is established when the child incorrectly answers six of any eight consecutive items.

Key to the research was a measure of the mother's linguistic cultural capital that was theoretically passed on to the child. They assumed that this measure should be composed of measured linguistic ability, the degree of parental instruction, and the degree of parental warmth toward the child. Note carefully the more expansive definition of cultural capital employed here. According to Farkas and Beron (2001: 23–24):

> For the mother's linguistic cultural capital to be transferred to her child it is not sufficient that she herself have a good

vocabulary; it is also necessary for her to *use* these skills in her interactions with her child in such a way that the skills are transferred. At least two conditions must be present: the mother must *instruct* by word and deed, and she must do so in a sufficiently *warm and attractive* manner so that the lesson takes.

Thus, this measure of linguistic cultural capital consisted of a verbal test (The Armed Forces Qualification Test), a cognitive stimulation scale, and an emotional warmth scale. Some of the results of this study are displayed in Figures 3.7 and 3.8.

Note that the black-white difference exists at 36 months, which is the starting point for the study, and that the gap in words has already been established at this point in the life cycle. According to the authors (p. 27): "During the first three years of life, the spoken vocabularies of African-American children grow at only half the rate of White children, leading to a White-Black vocabulary gap which is never made up in later life." Note carefully that this initial 36 month gap increases just slightly at the 60 month point when school begins, but that from this point on it essentially remains the same. Clearly, there would be no gap if all students were equal at the 60 month point when school begins. From the beginning of school, blacks and whites increase at

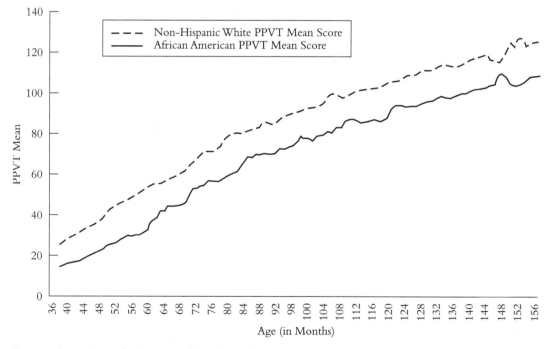

FIGURE 3.7 **Growth Curves of Oral Vocabulary, By Race (Means by Month of Age, Smoothed Via Three Month Moving Average)**

Source: George Farkas and Kurt Beron, 2001. "Family Linguistic Culture and Social Reproduction: Verbal Skill from Parent to Child in the Preschool and School Years." Paper presented at the annual meeting of the Population Association of America, Washington, DC. Reprinted with permission.

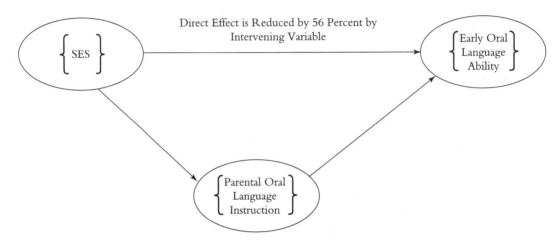

FIGURE 3.8   The Influence of Socioeconomic Status on Early Oral Language Ability Controlling for Mother's Oral Language Ability

the same rate on the test. The same pattern holds for the SES gap.

What role does family linguistic instruction play in the process? In their analysis, Farkas and Beron show that the gap between high- and low-SES students in words is about 8 points (but like race, this occurs mostly in the early period of life). In effect, the results for SES are similar to the effects for race. (They conducted their analysis separately for each race because the effects of SES and age differ quite a bit for each race.) The key question is whether the addition of family linguistics instruction of oral language reduces the impact of SES. When this variable was added to the equation, the influence of SES for whites is reduced by 56 percent. Following our causal model logic (developed in Chapter 2), the differences in oral language instruction between the classes "explains" about one-half of what becomes the long-term SES gap. For blacks, the amount of explanation is 45 percent.

Although Farkas and Beron found no increase in the size of the race and SES gap on vocabulary scores, previous research has documented that these early cognitive differences in race and SES do increase over the course of 12 years of schooling. Coleman et al. (1966), found that:

> At the 12th grade, results of tests in the same verbal and nonverbal skills show that, in every case, the minority scores *farther below* the majority than are the 1st graders . . . the deficiency in achievement is progressively greater for the minority pupils at progressively higher grade levels. (p. 21)

This suggests that the school, somewhat independent of the home, may exacerbate the SES and racial differences in educational outcomes. The difference is actually small at the outset, but increases the longer that students are in school. Note that Figure 3.6 reflects this possibility showing a path from school resources to language and cognitive development. And there is some evidence to support this school cause contention.

Rist (1970) reported that kindergarten children in his study were assigned "permanently" to different tables within the first eight days of their school life. The curriculum (reading) quality differed at each of the tables and Rist noted that these table assignments were often made inconsistent with reading readiness scores. In fact, he observed that lower-class children were more likely to be placed at the low-curriculum table, regardless of their pretest reading score. More recently, Pallas et al. (1994) studied the causes and effects of first grade reading-group placement. In this study of nineteen Baltimore public elementary schools, the first grade reading-group placements displayed a haphazard pattern:

> [C]hildren with comparable levels of measured academic performance and social backgrounds are often placed in reading groups that rank them anywhere from near the top of the class to near the bottom. . . . and that children in higher-ranked groups learned more and received higher grades than did children in lower-ranked groups. In this sense, instructional groups may have the unintended effect of increasing the inequalities in educational outcomes, largely by creating inequalities in educational resources and rewards. (p. 43)

Thus, the response to the student made by the school (see again Figure 3.6) can become a force that affects the trajectory of the student. We will return to this issue again in Chapter 5 as we consider school effects and the potential influence of "summer learning" on achievement growth in school and how these studies contribute to our understanding of the locus of race and SES cognitive differences.

◆ PARENTAL VALUES

As with language, it is in the family that most children acquire some of their most basic values. Melvin Kohn (1977) has conducted several studies regarding social class, parental values for children, and parental behavior, especially discipline. One study was conducted in Washington, another in Turin, Italy, and yet another was a nationwide U.S. sample. Kohn found that middle-SES families were significantly more likely than low-SES families to emphasize the values and behaviors of self-control and self-direction; by contrast, the behaviors and values that are most important to lower-class parents, relative to their middle-class counterparts, are conformity and obedience to external rules and authority. Kohn deduced this directly from survey questions and indirectly from the type of misbehavior that parents punished most severely. Boocock (1980) points out that the interpretation of these findings is not straightforward:

> The lesser emphasis by middle-class parents upon conformity to external authority does not mean that they do not value, and indeed expect, good behavior of the sort that will lead to success in school, but rather that they do not see these things as problematic. In the relatively secure environment of the middle-class home, it is more likely that cleanliness and orderly behavior can be taken for granted than in a lower-SES neighborhood, where simply keeping one's children and home neat and clean and trying to control children's behavior so that they will not get into trouble takes a strong commitment and continuous effort. (p. 44)

Thus, middle-class children come to school with conformity and obedience to authority as internalized norms; dealing with the rules of school is relatively unproblematic. They are able to concentrate on the subject matter at hand as well as further their development of self-control, which has already begun at home. Lower-class children, however, arrive at school still learning the norms of conformity and obedience. In fact, mastery of these norms is highly tentative on two accounts: first, they are likely to have been poorly trained and to have developed resistance to further polishing; second, the norms that they have learned to conform with are not necessarily the norms of the school. Hence, part of the visible difference that every teacher sees among students in the early grades may be simply due to a mastery or lack of mastery of conformity and obedience—essential behavior for success in school. Quite possibly, teachers may react to behavioral problems in such a way so as to jeopardize the development of language skills. This would occur, for example, if as in the Rist (1970) study, teachers might assign misbehaving, but cognitively competent, children to lower-ability groups.

In her book *Keeping Track*, Jeannie Oakes (1985) warns that unmanageable students are labeled slow learners and placed in slow tracks. These students then often make these classes unmanageable. She argues that we fail to distinguish two types of needy students: slow learners (not learning disabled) and misbehaving students. Further, that the goals of teachers in low-track classes often become directed (inadvertently) only at correcting misbehavior. What happens, Oakes argues, is "that we may saddle those who find it hard to learn with those who find it hard to behave" (p. 90). It is also useful to point out that differences in parental involvement also play a role here. Lareau (1989) demonstrates that working-class parents and school are characterized by "separation" or disconnectedness, unlike middle-class parents and the school, who are characterized by "connectedness." In lower- and working-class homes, the problems are multiple: parents are unable to observe the

potential problems for their child first-hand, the teacher is unable to demonstrate the problem to them, they have very little specific information about what is going on, and they are out of the loop of school-home communication.

Thus, schools operate out of a middle-class value model that assumes connectedness between the home and the school. For example, parental involvement in school and at home is a cornerstone of modern schooling. In the ideal world, few people would advocate less parental involvement, especially at home. But, this model does not match the reality of the human, cultural, and social capital available in most low-SES homes. Parents in these homes are often ill equipped to socialize children effectively and may not possess the resources necessary to engage in parental involvement at the level expected by the school. This suggests either extensive intervention (Epstein and Sanders, 2000) or an innovative model that more closely matches the needs of low-SES families (Lareau, 1995).

◆ PARENTAL VALUES, INVOLVEMENT, AND RESOURCES

Sewell and Hauser (1976) estimated that in America, high-SES children are four times more likely than low-SES children to enter college, six times more likely to complete college, and nine times more likely to attain some form of graduate- or professional-level training. Here we want to explore further why this is so.

Baker and Stevenson (1986) and Lareau (1989) have shown that higher-SES students do better in school partly because their parents are better connected to the school than working-class parents. This interconnectedness, in turn, allows the parents to manage the school careers of their children. At the first and second grade level, Lareau (1989) shows how it directly facilitates student success. In middle schools, Useem (1992: 263) reveals how the relationship between social class and track placement is explained, in part, "by the propensity of college educated parents to be knowledgeable about their children's placement, to be integrated into school affairs and parental information networks, to intervene in educational decisions that school officials make for their children, and to exert an influence over their children's preference for courses." In essence, there are a number of possible parental actions that may explain the large effect of socioeconomic status. We can turn once again to the NELS data for some hard evidence.

Figure 3.9 displays a model offering several parental variables as "explanatory" factors—parental involvement at school, parental involvement at home, parental aspirations and values, and cultural capital. The concept of cultural capital, developed by Bourdieu (1977),

argues that high-SES families possess key cultural resources that provide educational advantages. These resources include tastes in home decorations, recreational activities, and travel, which allow children (and adults) to better understand and appreciate certain cultural experiences, such as schooling. Perhaps the simplest example would be the fact that high-SES families are more likely to visit museums and libraries and to attend symphony concerts, activities that facilitate learning in school. In addition to these home and parental variables, Figure 3.9 includes a control for tracking, since we have had several occasions thus far to speculate that track allocation in school may be related to socioeconomic status and may be another way in which SES actually influences educational outcomes. Upper-middle-class parents monitor and manage the educational careers of their children, and this means ensuring that they obtain the highest track (ability group) placement whenever possible.

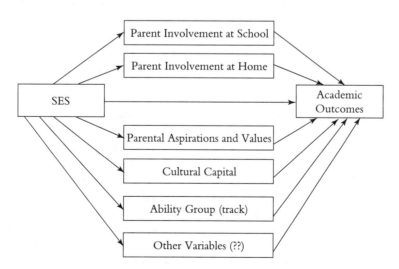

FIGURE 3.9   Explanatory Model of SES Effects on Academic Outcomes

TABLE 3.4

EFFECTS OF SOCIOECONOMIC STATUS ON TEST SCORES (READING/MATHEMATICS) CONTROLLING FOR VARIOUS PARENTAL ATTITUDES AND BEHAVIORS

	Standardized Coefficient
Uncontrolled effect of SES	.45
Adding controls for:	
Sex, family structure	.45
Parental involvement in home	.39
Parental involvement at school	.38
Parental educational expectations	.27
Cultural capital	.20
Ability group in four subject areas	.16
Remaining unexplained SES effect	.16

Note: These estimates were computed by the author from the sample of NELS eighth graders. Family structure is defined as adequate or deficient. Only whites are included. Parental involvement in the home is a composite of student/parent discussion variables and parents' knowledge of friends' names as defined in footnote 2. Parental involvement in the school is a composite of parental attendance at school activities also defined in footnote 2. Parental expectations is the parental response to how far in school they thought their child would go. Cultural capital is a composite of 19 items regarding whether the student attended a variety of cultural activities (art museums, public library, dance classes, computer class, etc.) outside of the school. Track is a composite of a student's response to which ability group (high, medium, low) she/he belonged in four subject areas.

Table 3.4 provides the results of a multivariate analysis using the NELS eighth grade data. The analysis shows that these parental variables do explain a fair amount of the SES effect. As variables are added to the equation, the direct effect of SES becomes smaller, which means that some of the SES influence is moving through the intervening variable as an indirect effect. The uncontrolled effect of SES is .45 (which is about what we obtained in Table 3.3). Parental involvement in the home reduces the direct effect to .39, which means that it explains about 13 percent of how SES influences test scores (.06/.45). Cultural capital explains about 16 percent, and parental aspirations another 25 percent.

Parental involvement in the school does not contribute much of anything to explaining the SES influence. Although tracking explains only about 7 percent of the effect, this may be due to the fact that it is added last to the equation. The lower effect for parental involvement in the school is *not* due to the order of entry; results are the same even if the order is reversed. Indeed, the effect of parental involvement in the home is fully four times as large as the effect of parental involvement in the school (see also Sui-Chu and Willms, 1996). This tends to confirm a view held by Lareau (1995) that working-class parents do not share the value of the importance of parental involvement in the school. According to Lareau, the model of family-school linkage is a middle-class value. Educators need to take more seriously the social class differences in what parents expect from the school. In any event, the large influence of socioeconomic status is explained to no small degree by a set of key variables: parental involvement (in the home), cultural capital, and parental aspirations.

❖ AFFECTIVE OUTCOMES

The primary objective of schooling is cognitive development. Another objective, however, is the social and personal growth of students. Elementary schools, in fact, emphasize and grade students on a variety of deportment characteristics, and secondary schools continue this procedure to a lesser extent. It is expected that students will indicate growth with regard to personal responsibility, initiative, industriousness, cooperation, poise, and maturity. It is generally assumed that these outcomes are positively related to academic progress as well as being independently meritorious.

Among the various affective outcomes that have been shown to be related to both home background and school experiences are the variables of self-esteem and locus of control, both of which have been studied almost exhaustively. Self-esteem is taken here to mean simply as liking and respecting oneself. It implies self-acceptance and a healthy, positive attitude toward one's own abilities and personal characteristics. There is little debate over whether it is better to have high or low self-esteem. There is debate, however, regarding the extent to which self-esteem influences school outcomes. Self-esteem is measured by such questions as: "Generally, I feel good about

myself" (strongly disagree, disagree, agree, strongly agree).

Internal-external locus of control refers to the extent to which people perceive that they have control over their actions and the consequences of their actions. People who believe they have some control over their destinies are called "internals"—that is, they believe that at least some control resides within themselves. "Externals," on the other hand, believe that the outcomes of their actions are determined by factors extrinsic to themselves—that is, by fate, luck, or the "system." Locus of control is measured by such questions as: "Every time I try to get ahead, something or somebody stops me" (strongly disagree, disagree, agree, strongly agree).

Although self-esteem is surely conditioned by the environment, it is experienced by the individual as being independent of the environment. Thus, a person may feel that "I am able to do things as well as most other people" knowing full well that there are many or few obstacles standing in the way of accomplishing certain tasks or goals. Feelings of high or low self-esteem are much like feelings that are associated with personality, such as feeling shy or extroverted. A feeling of environmental control, however, is something quite different. Unlike self-esteem, it directly indicates the extent to which an individual feels that the social environment either facilities or hinders the undertaking and completion of tasks and goals. Thus, an individual may possess high self-esteem and low environmental control. This may often be the case with members of minority groups.

Studies have found that factors such as race, social class, family structure, family size, birth order, and parental attitudes are related to both of these affective variables (see Rosenberg, 1965; Rosenberg and Simmons, 1972). Not surprisingly, minorities have been found consistently to be externally oriented. This seems to be a reasonable response to a subordinate situation in which one's life chances are often constrained by majority self-interest. With regards to blacks, research has shown that self-esteem decreases in racially integrated school settings whereas levels of internal control increase (Coleman et al., 1966; Rosenberg and Simmons, 1972). In addition, Coleman and his colleagues noted that locus of control is, in fact, strongly related to black achievement. The loss of self-esteem has been attributed to the loss of a protected and insulated environment provided by black schools. A more promising school environment, offering better physical resources, a stronger curriculum, and more opportunities, undoubtedly causes the gain in control.

Perhaps the most controversial question regarding self-esteem and locus of control, however, is whether either or both of these variables influence academic achievement. Some people argue that self-esteem improves academic achievement and that building self-esteem should be a school focus (Battle, 1981; State of California, 1986). The notion is that people who feel good about themselves will do better in school than people who have low self-esteem. In contrast, and more recently, scholars argued that there is no good reason to expect that academic success is dependent on self-esteem, rather that, academic achievement is more likely to be dependent on people having a strong sense of personal control over their lives. Of course, self-esteem and locus of control will increase as a result of success in school, but the question is, do they in turn influence subsequent successful achievement?

Ross and Broh (2000), following earlier work by Ross and Mirowsky (1989), theorize that there is no compelling reason to think that high self-esteem would be related to success in school. There is no need for people who already feel good about themselves to put forth the greater effort to succeed. In fact, according to Hewitt (1998: 18), it is possible that high "self-esteem makes people slacken their efforts because if they too easily feel good about themselves then they have no incentives to strive to meet higher standards of accomplishment." On the other hand, people with high levels of personal control feel that they are responsible for directing their own behavior and that they can control the results. People with low levels of control will have less motivation and will be less persistent, since they always worry that "someone or something will stand in their way." People with low personal control are likely to be passive learners and passive workers, whereas people with high personal control are likely to be proactive in their learning.

Ross and Broh (2000: 274) used the NELS data to test out the following hypotheses:

> Academic achievement (grades and test scores) increases the sense of personal control, which, in turn, increases achievement.
> Academic achievement increases self-esteem, but self-esteem does not affect subsequent achievement (grades and test scores).

The researchers were also interested in the determinants of self-esteem and locus of control and posited that supportive relationships at home would be more important for self-esteem than for locus of control. They employed the 8th, 10th, and 12th grade data available in the NELS

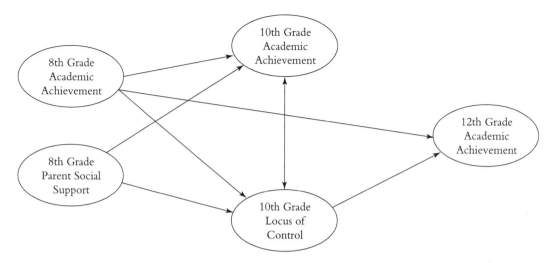

FIGURE 3.10 The Effect of Self-Esteem and Locus of Control on Academic Achievement

Source: Catherine E. Ross and Beckett A. Broh, 2000. "The Roles of Self-Esteem and the Sense of Personal Control in the Academic Achievement Process." *Sociology of Education* 73, adopted from Figure 1, p. 279.

surveys and controlled for a variety of background variables including parents' education, family income, gender, race, and family structure. The results shown in Figure 3.10 are the controlled coefficients after controlling for the variables in the model as well as the background variables. The paths mean that there is a significant positive controlled relationship between the two variables. They combined grades and test scores into a single standardized measure at each of the grade levels. Self-esteem and locus of control were measured using a set of items that correspond to those described earlier. Parent social support was measured by a set of items indicating the degree to which parents talked to their children about school (it might be viewed as a weak social or cultural capital variable).

They found that 8th grade achievement and parental support during the 8th grade influenced the levels of self-esteem and environmental control at the 10th grade. Interestingly, the effects

for 8th grade achievement and 8th grade parental support are about the same magnitude. Of course, the demographic variables also influence the 10th grade results and these are discussed below. The focus of the study, however, is the 12th grade results. As can be seen in Figure 3.10, 10th grade self-esteem does not influence 12th grade achievement, whereas 10th grade locus of control does. Thus, early achievement (8th grade) boosts self-esteem, but self-esteem in the 10th grade does not have any impact on 12th grade achievement. This confirms the theory that personal control and not self-esteem is more important in generating higher academic performance.

Ross and Broh also reported that males, blacks, and high-SES students had higher levels of self-esteem and personal control. This finding is generally in keeping with the earlier discussion with the exception of higher locus of control for blacks. Ross and Broh, however, found that blacks had higher levels of personal control, only after controlling for SES, as compared to lower levels without an SES control. This is similar to the finding reported earlier in the chapter regarding educational attainment (see Figure 3.2) where we found that blacks were more likely than whites to graduate from college after controlling for SES background and school resources.

Thus, the consequences of self-esteem and locus of control differ. One benefit of increased personal control appears to be greater academic achievement. All of this makes social psychological sense and resonates with sound learning theory and educational policy and practice. When students "feel good about themselves" and believe that they "are satisfied with themselves" there is less motivation to improve

or do better. The status quo is acceptable. On the other hand, positive feelings about personal control are likely to be conducive to growth and vice versa. Self-esteem undoubtedly has beneficial effects such as low levels of depression and greater general happiness, but its consequences for academic success are dubious.[3] Learning is likely to occur most effectively when students feel that they have control over their environment but feel just a bit uncertain about their self-worth and self-satisfaction. Quite possibly, self-esteem may contribute to personal control (the correlation was .1 in the Ross and Broh study) but the cause and effect is more likely to go the other way—higher personal control leads to high self-esteem, but this cannot be determined.

❖ SUMMARY

In this chapter we have considered the extent to which certain differences between the home backgrounds of students affect educational outcomes. In our review, we have observed that socioeconomic status, race, religio-ethnic status, and family functioning all have an important influence on academic and personal development outcomes. The effects of gender are more complex, having favored females in math and science in earlier years, but now those areas are nearly at parity, and males are disadvantaged in reading, writing, and other critical areas. We have also noted the importance of family functioning and the relatively small effect of family structure. Finally, we considered several intervening variables that were useful in explaining the effects of these home background variables. In Chapters 4, 5, and 6 we take up the extent to which differences between

and within schools have effects on student outcomes, over and above the influence of the home.

The ideas presented in this chapter can be set within the functional and conflict theories of education. Functionalists look for data that support the notion that status characteristics such as SES and race have little effect on the outcomes of schooling. They are especially delighted when the influence of schools can be

---

[3] An alternative view is that self-esteem is related to achievement if it is domain specific; that is, if the measure is academic self-esteem—the perception of how good a person is as a student (Marsh, 1993; Rosenberg et al., 1995). But this is entirely different from global self-esteem, which is the concept considered here. The fact that academic self concept is related to academic achievement seems to be a confounded and meaningless relationship.

shown to be of much greater magnitude than the effects of categories such as race and socioeconomic status that should be irrelevant to school outcomes.

Conflict theory, on the other hand, argues that home background influences the outcomes of schooling both directly and indirectly via the organization and the processes of schools. This chapter shows the larger influences of race, SES, ethnicity, religion, and family functioning on cognitive achievement, educational attainment, parental involvement, and other outcomes.

❖ KEY CONCEPTS

differences between homes
characteristics of individuals
characteristics of families as groups
characteristics of communities, organizations, neighborhoods
physical, human, cultural, and social capital
effects of SES, race, gender, religion, and ethnicity
the black-white test score gap
the gender gap

theories of status attainment
family structure and family functioning
parental presence in the home (divorce, working parents)
family size
parental involvement in the school and the home
effect of language development
direct and indirect effects
parental values
affective outcomes

❖ KEY STUDIES

Coleman and Hoffer (1987)
Alexander et al. (1982)
Willingham and Cole (1997)
Hirshman and Falcon (1985)
Uhlenberg and Eggebeen (1986)
Lee et al. (1991)

Milne et al. (1986)
Mercy and Steelman (1982)
Farkas and Beron (2001)
Kohn (1977)
Lareau (1989)
Ross and Broh (2000)

❖ REVIEW QUESTIONS

1. Drawing upon Coleman and Hoffer, distinguish among families that are disadvantaged, structurally deficient, and functionally deficient.

2. Certain changes have occurred in the family over the past century. Identify and describe five of these changes. Be specific.

3. How can the erosion of social capital in the home and the community best be remedied?

4. Carefully define the concepts of physical capital, human capital, social capital, and cultural capital.

5. Describe the results of the Hirshman and Falcon study and which theory it

supports. Discuss the other three theories and which one you think would be most applicable as another explanatory variable.

6. Demonstrate how it is theoretically possible to obtain both positive and negative results in academic achievement when both parents work.

7. Drawing on Figure 3.2, discuss the race, gender, and SES gap in educational outcomes.

8. Drawing upon the Milne et al. (1986) study, discuss the direct and indirect effects of number of parents and mother's employment on cognitive achievement.

9. Identify and describe three explanations for the effect of social class on academic achievement.

10. Contrast and compare black and white self-esteem (Rosenberg and Simmons). How are self-esteem and locus of control affected by school racial context? What is the influence of these affective variables on academic achievement?

11. Describe the research from Kohn regarding parental values. Describe the relationship of the studies by Kohn and Lareau. What are the implications of these findings for the organization of schools?

12. Describe the Farkas and Beron study and the implications for reducing the race and SES gaps.

Chapter 4

DIFFERENCES BETWEEN SCHOOLS: THE EARLY STUDIES

The effectiveness of the schools consists, in part, of making the conditional probabilities less conditional—that is, less dependent upon social origins.

JAMES S. COLEMAN (1966)

Most people think that the quality of a school does make a difference in the academic achievements of students, and that it is relatively easy to distinguish a good school from a bad one. In practice, this does not turn out to be true. For one thing, as Goodlad (1984: 247) points out, "the didactics of the classroom . . . are . . . very much the same from school-to-school." This is true, despite the fact that they are viewed as being very different by principals, teachers, students, and parents.

At the extremes, of course, good schools and bad schools are easy to identify. Everyone knows that an elite independent private school is a good school relative to a typical public school in the inner city. Everyone knows that a public school in which the average per pupil expenditure is $20,000 is a good school relative to a public school in which per pupil expenditure is only $4,000. Kozol (1991) properly calls these kinds of comparisons "savage inequalities." Within these extremes, however, it is much more difficult to discern inequalities between schools.

Yet even when the quality of schools does differ (as measured by physical facilities and teacher credentials), these differences are not related to student achievement. Initial uncontrolled differences between schools are often found to be "spurious" when the independent influence of the home and the community are taken into account. Recently, however, researchers are beginning to uncover greater "school effects" using new conceptual models and methodological techniques (see Lee and Bryk, 1988; Murchan and Sloane, 1994; Hedges, Laine, and Greenwald, 1994, Gamoran, Secada, and Marrett, 2000).

In this chapter, we focus on "school effects"—specifically, those effects on students that are the result of attending different types of schools. We examine closely the Coleman Report, a 1966 study by Coleman et al. entitled *Equality of Educational Opportunity* (EEO), and its aftermath, including definitions of school quality and contextual effects. The study of school effects is pursued further in light of recent theories and findings regarding public and private schools.

Various explanatory variables are considered as well as the problem of "selection bias" in school effects studies. Throughout the discussion, an important distinction is made between the size of school effects that exist for disadvantaged as opposed to advantaged students.

In due course, we will discover that between school effects are either null (zero) or small, with the important specification that the effects are consistently larger for nonwhites, disadvantaged, and otherwise at-risk students. Given these results, we will reconsider the issues of "equality" and "achievement" and the likely "reproductive" functions of schooling. The basic model of Home → School → Outcomes is reexamined so that we can begin to conceptualize what kinds of school effects would be needed to reduce, rather than maintain, social inequalities among students.

❖ SCHOOL EFFECTS

From the earliest days of both public and private schooling, everyone must have been aware that differences between homes affect school performance. Even in the first "public" schools in England (which were what we now call private schools), the home background of students varied among the very wealthy. Certainly, in the history of public schools in the United States and elsewhere, student home background varied greatly and was related to educational outcomes for all of the reasons we have discussed in the previous chapter. And to repeat, most people were generally aware of the "effect" even though they might not be able to systematically explain it or think of it in concrete terms. Literature and history

provide many descriptive examples of the educational paths of children from rich and poor homes.

By contrast, the idea of "school effects" is a recent construct. For school effects to occur, there must exist "school differences" which are real and recognized. For example, most people have assumed that real differences in material resources have always existed between public and private schools. With regard to public schools, however, at least in the United States, these possible differences were masked by an ideology and a policy of "common schools." Well into the twentieth century, it was thought that students attended schools that were very much the same in terms of resources, teachers, curriculum, and so on. This was prior to the great expansion of schooling and during a time in which most towns and cities had only a single high school. It is informative to note that in 1896 the Supreme Court ruled in *Plessey v. Ferguson* that schools (and other public service facilities) for blacks and whites were indeed "separate but equal." This decision exemplifies the prevailing view that differences between schools were nonexistent.

Although there is little hard evidence, it does seem that from 1900 to 1950, differences between schools began to arise and be recognized. I emphasize the importance of the differences being "recognized" because many sociologists, historians, and educators would argue that differences between predominantly black and predominantly white schools did exist in 1900 but were not recognized. Undoubtedly, then as now, there were differences in school and teacher quality between affluent and poor communities. It is interesting to note that prior to the 1980s, hardly anyone thought about comparing the relative effects of public and private schools. This will be considered later in the chapter.

There were several transformations of the educational landscape that actually created school differences and made possible the notion of a school effect. Perhaps the most important of these forces was the expansion of schooling at the turn of the century. This process soon led to the need for multiple junior and senior high schools, and further to the need for several different types of schools—the classical high school, the vocational high school, and the comprehensive high school. The differential curricula between each of these types of schools were sufficient to produce a school effect.

A related development was the creation of suburban schools. The development of the suburbs in America is coterminous with the exodus of the middle class from the central cities during the latter half of the twentieth century. This process has been characterized as "white flight" from the laws requiring school desegregation. In any event, suburban schools were initially white and middle class, with relatively higher property and income wealth than city schools. Consequently, suburban schools were provided with better resources than city schools. They were also newer, they had better facilities, and they were usually able to pay higher salaries to teachers. Over the past several decades, these social processes have proceeded to the extremes. Today, there are schools in America where the per pupil expenditure is as high as $27,896 (Barbanel, 1992) and as low as $3,000 (Celis, 1992a). This has prompted Jonathan Kozol (1991) to describe these suburban and inner-city differences between schools in America as "savage inequalities."[1] It has also prompted state officials and policy makers to initiate plans to reformulate and redistribute state aid to local communities. In Rhode Island and Texas, for example, plans have been implemented that will reduce allocations of state funds to more affluent local communities and will increase them for less affluent districts (see Celis, 1992a; Twenty-first Century Education Commission, 1992).

Robert Dreeben (2000) locates the study of school effects within the larger sociological context of the influence of social structure on individual conduct. He traces the history of this elementary social fact as it has developed from Durkheim to the present time and flourished in the Department of Sociology at Columbia University, especially in the work of James Coleman. He describes and dissects the importance of understanding that structural effects are both substantive and methodological, and (p. 107) that "these two considerations, . . . although analytically distinct, are not wholly so in reality. There is tension between them because some substantive formulations overburden the available methods, and some methods limit the range of testable substantive ideas." From the 1940s to the 1980s, these substantive and methodological issues were developed, debated, and polished, but it was during the late 1980s and the 1990s that structural effects took on an entirely new genre of educational

[1] The typical per pupil difference within a geographic area such as a small state or a large city is about $4,000 (see Kozol, 1991). The U.S. average per pupil expenditure in 1999–2000 was $6,835 (for more on this, see www.census.gov/govs/school/00fullreport.pdf).

policy reform. Most policy reforms employ the reasoning of structural effects. In the end, Dreeben cautions us regarding the conceptual vulnerability of structural effects. This occurs in two ways: first, there exists a rigidity in the false reification of the objectivity of the concept which our measures deceive us into believing; second, there is a rigidity that (p. 129) "derives from Durkheim's conception of social facts, where the order of causality runs from structure to individual conduct." Although the policy use of structural effects fits the Durkheimian perspective, Dreeben argues that it "does not justify the casual priority of school structure." The reader is advised to heed Dreeben's cautionary advice since in most research, causality does follow a path from social structure to the individual.

❖ THE COLEMAN REPORT

Yet by 1965, little was known about school differences and school effects. Nonetheless, it was clear at that time that there were widespread beliefs that differences did exist in schools according to race. That such perceptions existed is documented by the following resolution, voted on and passed in Congress, and incorporated into the Civil Rights Act of 1964:

> The Commissioner [of Education] shall conduct a survey and make a report to the President and the Congress, within two years of the enactment of this title, concerning the lack of availability of equal educational opportunities for individuals by reason of race, color, religion, or national origin in public educational institutions at all levels in the United States, its territories and possessions, and the District of Columbia. (Civil Rights Act, 1964)

This act was passed by a coalition of federal legislators who were determined to finally document the factual extent of segregation and inequality in American schools. Given the difficulties of implementing the law under the 1954 Brown decision, it was widely believed that the results of this mandated study would be used by the Justice Department to enforce the *Brown v. Board of Education* ruling (Miller, 1986). Moreover, educational policy makers assumed that the study would provide an empirical basis for channeling more federal money to schools attended predominantly by minority and low-SES students. In effect, everyone assumed that the study would support the conventional wisdom that the quality of schools was unequal and that the quality of schools was related to educational outcomes.

This study was conducted by James Coleman et al. (1966) and eventually published as a government document entitled *Equality of Educational Opportunity* (EEO). The main author became so well known that most people refer to the document as the Coleman Report. In designing and conducting the study, Coleman *reformulated* the conception of equality of educational opportunity (see Chapter 1), redirected the conception of "school effects," and reemphasized the influence of home background on educational outcomes. Also, in keeping with the governmental mandate of the study, Coleman proceeded to test an educational theory that was widely held at that time by a majority of educators, policy makers, and social scientists: Namely, if you want to achieve equality, good schools can make a difference. High-quality effective schools can erase the handicaps of birth (race, socioeconomic status, and so on). Coleman (and the U.S.

Congress which hired him) expected to find that minorities attended low-quality segregated schools and that educational outcomes were determined by the quality of the schools that students attended. (An overly simple two-variable relationship is implied here: School Quality → Educational Outcomes.)

◆ SCHOOL QUALITY

School quality in the Coleman Report was taken to mean such factors as annual per pupil expenditure, educational background of the teachers, age of the school, class size, and the quality of the science labs, libraries, and so on. Thus, the goals of the study were to determine each of the following:

1. the extent of equality in educational outcomes across various racial and socioeconomic groups;

2. the extent of equality in educational inputs—that is, the quality of the schools as judged by access, facilities, curriculum, and other resources;

3. the degree to which differences in school quality were related to differences in academic outcomes for students of equal backgrounds and abilities—that is, the effects of schools per se;

4. the extent to which the effect of the school was able to overcome the effects of the home and racial background (as shown by reductions in initial performance differences between racial or SES groupings).

Coleman surveyed 570,000 students and 60,000 teachers and principals in more than 4,000 public schools in the United States. Students were sampled from grades l, 3, 6, 9, and 12. Some of the major findings were as follows:

1. Most black and white students attended racially separate schools (80 percent of whites attended predominantly white schools and 65 percent of blacks attended predominantly black schools).

2. The gap in cognitive achievement (as measured by standardized tests) between white and black students was one to two grade equivalents in the early grades and had increased to three to four grade equivalents by the senior year of high school.

3. The physical facilities, the formal curricula, and the characteristics of teachers were surprisingly similar. Although the measurement of these variables was exhaustive, we will see later that they were not refined (see Ingersoll, 1999, 2001 in Chapter 6).

4. Whatever differences did exist in school quality (facilities, curricula, teacher characteristics) had very little influence on student test score performance.

5. The one school characteristic that displayed a consistent influence on test performance was the socioeconomic context of the school.

6. The racial context of the schools had a smaller though consistent positive effect—specifically, blacks in desegregated schools did slightly better on the cognitive tests than blacks in segregated schools.

7. Most of the variation in student achievement (test score performance) was found *within* the same school (showing, in part, an SES effect) and very little was found *between* schools.

8. The two largest effects on student achievement turned out to be home background and individual student attitudes,

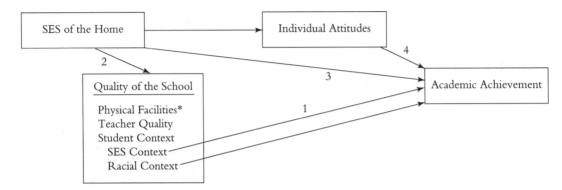

FIGURE 4.1 **Summary Model of Results from the Coleman Report**

* Included items such as annual per pupil expenditure, age of the school, age and quality of science labs and library, teacher/pupil ratio, and so on.

Note: The numbers in the paths correspond with column numbers in Table 4.1.

as discussed in Chapter 3. The school SES context effect was small by comparison. These results are depicted in Figure 4.1.

Coleman (1990a: 74) summed up the results as follows:

> The results clearly suggest that school integration across socioeconomic lines (and hence across racial lines) will increase Black achievement, and they throw serious doubt upon the effectiveness of policies designed to increase nonpersonal resources in the school. A simple general statement of the major result is that the closest portions of the child's environment—his family and his fellow students—affect his achievement most, the more distant portion of his environment—his teachers—affect it next most, and the nonsocial aspects of his social environment affect it the least.

At the time of the study, most people believed that school quality as measured by EEO would be strongly related to student achievement. It is possible that the relationship would have been established if

the difference in quality between schools had been greater. We can see immediately how the results led to a reconceptualization of equality of educational opportunity that emphasized outcomes rather than inputs. Differences in outcomes between the races were substantial even though school facilities were surprisingly similar.

The findings were directly contrary to the conventional educational wisdom (still popular today) that differences in financial resources between schools account for the differences that we observe between students. Invariably, the results of the Coleman Report led to the conclusion that the reason that children from lower-SES backgrounds did poorly in school had more to do with the students themselves, their families, their community, their culture, and possibly even their genetic makeup. This led to a whole set of student-centered explanations of inequality during the 1960s and 1970s (see Sadovnik, Cookson, and Semal, 1994, ch. 9; Dougherty and Hammack, 1990, ch. 6).

These findings, like others we have noted previously, tend to support the conflict theory or social reproduction theory of education and stratification. Educational achievement reflects and is determined mostly by existing social class inequalities. It is as if the purpose of education is to preserve or reproduce the existing social structure. Minimally, it seems that schools are unsuccessful at changing the patterns of existing social structures. Consequently, it does appear from these data that schools do not promote social mobility as the functional theory argues. Rather, it seemed that schools might channel students into tracks (curricula) in accordance with the social class and racial hierarchy of the wider society (Rosenbaum, 1976; Cicourel and Kituse, 1963; for an opposite view see Heyns, 1974; Alexander and McDill, 1976). This issue of tracking will be pursued further in Chapter 6.

EEO found very little relationship between school facilities and curriculum opportunities; that is, as noted above, the study found most of the variation between students to lie *within* schools (probably due to track placement), but that school quality was unrelated to tracking policies (see Smith, 1972). The effects of tracking, therefore, were independent of school quality.

◆ OUTCOMES FOR MINORITIES
IN THE COLEMAN REPORT

There are, however, some important differences in the relative effects of home and school for whites and minorities, as documented in Table 4.1. The percentages shown represent the amount of variation in student achievement that can be directly attributed to either home background, individual attitudes, or between school effects.[2] Thus, the table reports the relative effects of the same variables shown in Figure 4.1 for each racial/ethnic group. Column 5 shows the total amount of explained variation of all factors combined while columns 1–4 indicate the percentage of the total that can be attributed to each variable. Thus, column 4 indicates the amount of variation in achievement that can be attributed to individual variation in student attitudes (see path 4 in Figure 4.1). For social science research, the total amount of "explained" variation in this case is considered high, despite the fact that the majority of the variation is left unexplained (presumably due to other factors). Each numbered path in Figure 4.1 corresponds with each numbered column in Table 4.1.

The results shown in Table 4.1 for whites and Asians are the bases for concluding that the effects of school quality in this study were small relative to the effects for home background and individual attitudes. For whites, home background differences (column 3) explain at least twice as much as do school-to-school differences. (As indicated in Figure 4.1, some of the home background effects operate indirectly through schools by way of selection—good students tend to attend good schools—and this is depicted in column 2 of the table.) For Asians, the influence of the home is fully ten times the influence of the school. Thus, for these two groups, which together constituted nearly 80 percent of the U.S. population

[2] Technically, these percentages represent a statistic called the coefficient of determination (R^2).

TABLE 4.1

AMOUNT OF EXPLAINED VARIATION IN TWELFTH GRADE VERBAL ACHIEVEMENT BY RACIAL/ETHNIC GROUP

	1	2	3	4	5
Group	All School-to-School Variation Not Linked to Background[a]	School-to-School Variation Linked to Background	Individual Variation in Background	Individual Variation in Attitude	All Factors Combined
White	7.41%	2.08%	16.94%	13.38%	39.80%
Black	14.83	6.07	6.41	10.87	38.18
Puerto Rican	22.69	0.71	3.35	4.79	31.54
Indian	23.42	0.71	10.68	8.80	43.61
Chicano	17.75	2.32	6.02	8.24	34.33
Asian	2.20	0.13	19.66	10.05	32.04

Source: James S. Coleman, Ernest Q. Campbell, et al. *Equality of Educational Opportunity* (Washington: Government Printing Office, 1966), 229, Tables 3.221.1 and 3.221.2.

[a] Includes all school-to-school variation: (1) facilities, curriculum, and other characteristics of the school, (2) characteristics of the teaching staff, and (3) characteristics of the student body.

in 1966, between school effects are small, as noted above.

It is important to note, however, that the results are actually quite different for the other four racial/ethnic groups. Among blacks, Puerto Ricans, Indians, and Chicanos, Table 4.1 shows that the effects of the school are actually greater than the effects of the home. Moreover, they are quite substantial, representing on average nearly 50 percent of the total explained variation. To understand why this occurs, you must recall that the two most important school variables are socioeconomic context and racial context. For minorities, this translates into the difference between attending a predominantly white middle-class school or a pre-dominantly minority lower-class school.[3] Moreover, while home background is more important than school for whites and Asians, the effect of home background for other minorities is actually negative since a greater percentage of minorities lack the features of a home background (such as high SES, intact family,

[3] Column 1 of Table 4.1 does not allow us to examine the separate effects of the three components of school-to-school variation. Elsewhere in the report, however, Coleman et al. noted that "attributes of other students account for far more variation in the achievement of minority group children than do any attributes of school facilities and slightly more than do attributes of staff."

FIGURE 4.2   The Relative Effects of Home and School on Achievement by Race

and so on) that bring about positive effects for whites and Asians. These results are depicted in Figure 4.2.

It thus becomes clear that this between school difference is "large" for minorities, while it is quite "small" among whites and Asians. Coleman and his associates summarized this important distinction as follows:

> Improving the school of a minority pupil will increase his achievement more than will improving the school of a white child. Similarly, the average minority pupil's achievement will suffer more in a school of low quality than will the average white pupil's. In short, white, and ... [Asian] Americans, are less affected one way or the other by the quality of their schools than are minority pupils. This indicates that it is for the most disadvantaged children that improvements in school quality will make the most difference in achievement. (Coleman et al., 1966: 21)

Somehow, this finding received less attention at the time than one might have thought. In conjunction with research that has come later, however, these results are extremely salient in retrospect. Fuller and Heyneman (1989), for example, have demonstrated that the strength of home background (SES) on school outcomes is much weaker in Third World countries than is the case in Western countries. The clear implication here is that schools

"do make a difference" in reducing educational inequalities between advantaged and disadvantaged students. In the absence of schools, or in the presence of "bad" schools, racial and social class inequality in educational achievement is likely to increase. This is demonstrated most convincingly in the studies of "summer learning" reviewed in Chapter 5.

All of this raises some interesting questions regarding school choice and social reproduction. In terms of fulfilling the goal of equality, choice would make more sense if there were a guarantee that minority students rather than whites would be given first choice. At the same time, the data suggest that school choice will have limited impact upon outcomes among whites and Asians. The assurance of a first choice to any selected group, however, might be prohibited under the Fourteenth Amendment, unless there is a compelling state interest.

Recent research has shown that the matter is much more complex. Increasingly, minority parents and students seek out schools in which the SES and racial/ethnic context is similar to their own, rather than on the basis of the school's curriculum or effectiveness (see Elmore, 1990; Henig, 1994; Rasell and Rothstein, 1993). Moreover, as many people have feared, some research also indicates that minority parents are either misinformed or simply not informed at all about choice programs (see Rasell and Rothstein, 1993; Fuller, Elmore, and Orfield, 1995). A recent NCES (1995) study, however, reported that low-income and minority parents were more likely to have exercised the option of choosing a public school than high-income white parents. Thus, the opportunity to choose an effective school is not a simple panacea to socioeconomic and racial stratification. And yet, in the absence of school choice or any other comparable school reform emphasizing greater equity, the large influence of socioeconomic status on educational outcomes will continue the process of social reproduction.

❖ THE AFTERMATH OF THE COLEMAN REPORT

There were at least three major consequences of the Coleman Report. First, it became a highly scrutinized document among educators and social scientists and eventually led to a far better understanding of "school effects" and of the relative importance of home and school effects. It ushered in four decades of research on contextual effects, investigations of "within" and "between" school effects, studies of public and private schooling, and an entire "effective schools movement." These topics are taken up in the remainder of this chapter and in Chapters 5 and 6. It is interesting to note that at the time of the study, it was generally assumed that "the variation within schools is probably not the sort of thing a school can do much about as long as it tries to improve all equally" (Mosteller and Moynihan, 1972: 19). Twenty years later, educators and sociologists came to realize that within school differences in curriculum form the bases for a great deal of social inequality and social reproduction.

Second, the study led quickly and inevitably to the view that families and individuals were far more important than schools in accounting for variation in school success. Once again, this conclusion emanated out of the broad results showing only small school effects and large SES and individual attitude effects as shown in Figure 4.1. It bears repeating that mysteriously, the fact that this conclusion applied only to whites and Asians went relatively unnoticed.

Third, the Coleman Report had serious political consequences with regard to the findings for racial context. Although the data showed only small positive effects of integration on black achievement, this finding was frequently cited in court cases as "proof" that equal educational opportunity for minorities required integration, by means of busing if necessary. It is an interesting case in which a "lot" of political and educational mileage was obtained from a "little" effect. A 1984 study by the National Institute of Education confirmed that the effects of integrated schools on cognitive achievement are small at best. (For a more optimistic review of the effects of school desegregation see Wells, 1995; Teachers College Record, 1995).

During the 1970s and continuing into the 1980s, the likelihood of blacks attending a predominantly middle-class and racially integrated school diminished throughout the nation. Large urban centers became increasingly black (and Hispanic, Asian, and so on) in demographic composition as whites exited in vast numbers for the suburbs. Orfield and Monfort (1992) document the full probative degree of resegregation in a recent study showing that the segregation of black and Hispanic students in virtually every large city in America now exceeds the 1970 level of segregation. Given this changing demography, the small effect of integrated schools noted above, and the high rate of academic failure among African American youth, it has been proposed that all-black schools may provide a more effective education than integrated schools for African American students under certain conditions (Fleming, 1984; Bell, 1983; Murrell, 1992; Brookins and Lomotey, 1989). These conditions would include a middle-class SES context or some of the factors that have been found to characterize "effective schools" (see below), an Afro-centric curriculum, and a "caring" environment.

Prophetically, Coleman (1967: 22–23) anticipated this problem in remarks made shortly after the publication of EEO:

> The results indicate that heterogeneity of race and heterogeneity of family educational background can increase the achievement of children from weak educational backgrounds with no adverse effect on children from strong educational backgrounds. Such integration cannot be expected to bring about full equality of opportunity for achievement; but the evidence does indicate effects that are far from negligible. In the large cities, however, where lower class Blacks are both concentrated and numerous, this approach quickly exhausts its possibilities. There are simply not enough middle class children to go around. . . . the matter may be better dealt with by inquiring more fully into the question of *how* a child's achievement is affected by the educational resources brought to school by other children.

Coleman was *not* suggesting here that we abandon the goal of racial integration, but only that we recognize that racial integration and equal educational opportunity are two separable goals. To some extent (in some areas of the country), they can both be achieved via integrated schools. In a broader sense, however, more efficient methods for increasing the achievement of low-SES blacks may be found, without abandoning continued attempts to overcome de facto segregation. Nonetheless, some schools districts continue to pursue the goal of equality via integration. In Kansas City, Missouri, the nation's most expensive and controversial plan of school integration involves an unprecedented attempt to bring white, suburban students back into the city via a $700 million magnet school program (Atkinson, 1990). Recently, however, in a landmark decision, the Supreme Court ruled that this plan was unconstitutional (Schmidt, 1995a).

In addition, Coleman wrestled throughout his entire career with the dilemma posed by the conflicting educational practices that might be required to achieve equality of educational opportunity, given the large effects of race and social class that he uncovered. Hallinan (2000: 77) summarizes Coleman's final view on this quite well:

> The dilemma reflects the age-old tension between individual rights and the common good. On the one hand, if schools were to provide equal opportunities for all students, then the common good occasionally would have to take precedence over the goals of individual students. Schools would be forced to play a compensatory role, because students begin schooling with vast differences in background, ability, and skills. On the other hand, if schools were to be a meritocracy, then the needs and goals of individuals would be placed before those of the community in an effort to maximize individual talents and abilities.

Coleman (1990b) . . . rejected the goal of equality of educational opportunity for schools, regarding it as unrealistic and unattainable. Instead he suggested that the appropriate goal of education was to reduce, rather than to eliminate, the vast differences among students created by the variation in individual characteristics and social experiences.

We see here the philosophies of Rawls and Nozick acknowledged and understood and that the answer lies somewhere in between. We also can see that reducing (not eliminating) the "gap" between the high- and low-performing students is in itself a societal challenge.

The results of the Coleman Report led inevitably (and incorrectly) to the broad conclusion that "schools did not make a difference." Family background explained much more of the achievement difference between students than differences between schools. Moreover, achievement differences were far greater within schools than achievement differences between schools. Keep in mind that the "between" school differences were defined and limited here to differences according to physical facilities and teacher quality as noted above. Over the last four decades, however, studies of between school effects have persisted along the following lines of inquiry[4]:

1. the controversial "culture of poverty" or deficit theory of disadvantage along with an alternative theory of "cultural differences";

2. contextual effects, including the racial context and the value climate;

3. leadership, goals, school climate, teacher expectations, and student assessment (effective schools research);

4. the governance and social organization of schools (public/private schools; charter schools);

5. the physical facilities, resources, and costs of schools;

6. summer learning studies;

7. multilevel modeling techniques;

8. studies of school and class size.

We take the first four issues up in the remainder of this chapter and continue with the others in Chapter 5.

❖ THE CULTURE OF POVERTY AND THE BLACK FAMILY

The Coleman Report gave rise to a "culture of poverty" (Lewis, 1966) thesis, which claimed that the value system of minority children (especially blacks) was debilitated, dysfunctional, and the cause of poor school performance.[5] The theory argues that the culture of poverty results

---

[4] The Coleman Report also opened up the study of *within* school effects, such as tracking and teacher quality. These are taken up in Chapter 6.

[5] Even more controversial was a study published by Jensen (1969) purporting to demonstrate that unequal educational performance by minority and low-SES students is due to genetic differences in intelligence. Jensen marshaled an array of evidence to support this claim and concluded that efforts at changing the environmental, organizational, or social factors of schooling would make little difference in reducing the observed performance inequalities. Although some critics dismissed Jensen as a racist (Sowell, 1977) or at least guilty of a flawed analytic strategy (*Harvard Educational Review*, 1969; Kagan, 1969; McV. Hunt, 1969), more balanced assessments of the IQ controversy have concluded that the

(continued)

in a rejection of delayed gratification, hard work, and schooling itself as a means to success. In essence, "this perspective claims that black families fail to provide their children with the kinds of skills and educational attitudes and aspirations that support and encourage success at school" (Hallinan, 2001: 55).

The Coleman Report's finding on family influence was viewed as confirming this theory. Compensatory educational programs, such as Head Start (a preschool intervention program targeted for low-SES students), were implemented to address these purported shortcomings in the family and communal environment of nonwhite and low-SES students. The culture of poverty thesis is often referred to alternatively as a "deficit" theory or "cultural deprivation" theory.

During the 1970s, however, the culture of poverty thesis came under strong criticism primarily from a countertheory known as "blaming the victim" (Ryan, 1976; Baratz and Baratz, 1970). Here it was argued that society (including the schools) had created conditions that constrained the ability of minorities to succeed in school—that is, they had been

historically victimized. Studies such as the Coleman Report, overlooking the historical past, implied that the cause of failure was the minority family and community. One book in particular, *The Negro Family* by Daniel Moynihan (1965), appeared coterminously with the Coleman Report. Here, Moynihan described the black family as ineffectual and dysfunctional and identified it as the fundamental obstacle standing in the path of the successful experience for blacks in school and elsewhere. According to Ryan (1976), this was a case of blaming the victim. If schools had helped to produce inequalities (social reproduction), they could just as easily help to produce equality. In addition to this development, studies of teacher effectiveness, especially studies of "teacher expectations" (Rosenthal and Jacobson, 1968) pointed back toward positive effects associated with schools.

❖ CULTURAL DIFFERENCES THEORY

Another critique of the culture of poverty theory came from researchers who argued that some children do less well in school because they are an oppressed minority. Consequently, they must adapt to their oppressed position, and part of this adaptation is a realistic rejection of white middle-class school values, which simply do not apply them in the same way that these norms apply to white middle-class children. Research in this tradition is grounded in a theory of "cultural differences" rather than cultural deprivation. Although there are variations on the theory, racism and discrimination play a central role. Influenced by a strong

---

most significant factor influencing intelligence is social, even though a small amount of the difference between the classes and the races might be attributed to genetic factors (see Hurn, 1993: 142–152; Kamin, 1974; for research supporting Jensen, see Scarr and Weinberg, 1978; Herrnstein and Murray, 1994). This highly complex issue resurfaced in 1994 with Herrnstein and Murray's publication of *The Bell Curve*, which again attempts to demonstrate the genetic bases for racial and ethnic differences in intelligence. As was the case with Jensen, the book has been the subject of armies of critics (see Jacoby and Clauberman, 1994; Fraser, 1995).

antischool neighborhood culture (popularly referred to as Boys in the Hood), black students come to embrace the view that they will not profit from educational success, as will whites, because of racial discrimination.

Ogbu (1978) argues that students of color face a low "job ceiling," which they become aware of through home and community socialization, and which causes them to lower their aspirations to realistic employment opportunities that do not require success in school. In more recent work, Fordham and Ogbu (1986) demonstrate that African American students must deny their own cultural and racial identity and accept the dominant white culture of the school in order to succeed. Thus, they claim that African American students carry the burden of "acting white." Another form of cultural difference theory points out that working-class white students and nonwhite students alike often engage in a militant resistance and rejection of the dominant norms of the school. Willis (1981) shows that working-class boys in England consistently reject the middle-class norms of school in favor of a youth and antisocial subculture that eschews the values of schooling (see also Gaines, 1991; Devine, 1996).

Thus, in this view, it is the subculture of the community (especially the adolescent street community) that constrains blacks to reject the middle-class values of the school, rather than the family that fails to socialize via cultural deprivation. Although Fordham and Ogbu's conception seems compelling, their "oppositional culture" theory has not been substantiated with quantitative empirical research. Ainsworth-Darnell and Downey (1998) and Cook and Ludwig (1998) independently employed the NELS surveys of

1988, 1990, and 1992 (8th, 10th, and 12th grades) to test the theory. Both sets of researchers found that blacks do spend less time on homework and display more behavior problems than whites, but they do not hold different attitudes toward school. Blacks and whites were equally affected by peer group norms that opposed success in school, both perceived that their opportunities were equally limited or unlimited, and finally, both groups were equally engaged or alienated from school. Not surprisingly, both sets of researchers found that the differences in school behavior were the result of differences in family and neighborhood characteristics. Farkas, Lleras, and Maczuga (2002), however, report support for Ogbu's thesis (for a rejoinder see Downey and Ainsworth-Darnell, 2002). We will examine "oppositional culture" in greater depth in Chapter 7.

Over the course of the past several decades, both cultural deprivation and cultural differences theories have evoked multiple responses. As noted above, although intuitively compelling, cultural differences theory is not well supported empirically, despite enjoying wide acceptance (Fischer, et. al., 1996; Jaynes and Williams, 1989). Cultural differences theory provides a basis for "explaining" parts of the black-white gap not explained by socioeconomic status, cultural, or social capital (Alexander, 2001). The whole idea of compensatory education arose as a direct response to both theories; with this practice schools are viewed as the more promising avenue of change rather than families or neighborhoods. In large part, the continued reliance on Head Start is an $8 billion per year effort to overcome the consequences of both theories. Finally, theories and research emphasizing "expectations states" and "stereotype threats" emerged, which shifted the burden toward white society, claiming that it continues to impose traditional negative stereotyped expectations that influence the behavior of blacks and other nonwhites (see Cohen and Roper, 1972; Cohen, 2000, Steele and Aronson, 1998, see also Chapter 6 of this book). Both of these theories argue that black success is inhibited by expectations for failure that are held by whites and transmitted in subtle nuances. Moreover, stereotype threat assumes that blacks may activate the stereotype on themselves even in the face of contradictory information, in much the same way as senior citizens talk about having a "senior moment" for something that is quite normal. We see this vividly with seniors who often withdraw from interaction prematurely, for fear of forgetting and experiencing failure.

❖ CONTEXTUAL EFFECTS

Generally, this book has utilized what are often referred to as individual-, organizational-, or group-level variables. Some of these are called status variables or social category variables and they include race, gender, and socioeconomic status. This book has also focused on the effects of groups (families) and organizations (school facilities), and individual attitudinal variables such as self-esteem and environmental control. In addition, groups, organizations, communities, and societies can and do vary in the extent to which they are:

mostly male, mixed, mostly female;

mostly white, mixed, mostly black;

mostly Catholic, mixed, mostly Protestant;

mostly high SES, mixed, mostly low SES;

mostly religious, mixed, mostly non-religious;

mostly married, mixed, mostly divorced;

Gender is clearly a characteristic of an individual, but an all-male, all-female, or mixed-sex group is clearly a characteristic of a group or organization.

Each example provides three categories of a *contextual variable*—a characteristic of a group, organization, or society. Note that it would be easy (and useful) to increase the precision of the variable by increasing the number of categories. For example, we could break down racial context as follows:

90–100%	White	40–49%	White
80–89%	White	30–39%	White
70–79%	White	20–29%	White
60–69%	White	10–29%	White
50–59%	White	0–9%	White

Any group, school, neighborhood, or society can thus be categorized and measured in this manner.

A contextual variable operates at the same level as an organizational variable and is clearly a form of social organization. The logic of contextual effects derives from the notion that "students respond to the norms, performance standards, and rewards that are salient to the student body of which they are members, or to certain other students who serve as role models" (Boocock, 1980: 194). Thus, it is based upon reference group theory or the simple notion that people behave according to the norms of their membership groups. In the case of racial or socioeconomic context, it refers to the "unofficial" norms of the school. These are different from the "official" teacher-directed norms. In Chapter 7, we will pursue this idea further by considering the values of youth cultures, a set of contextual norms that are often anti-intellectual and that act as an obstacle to learning in most cases.

The idea of contextual variables is directly applicable to racial segregation and integration in schools. More importantly, and stemming directly from the Coleman Report, however, is the fact that the socioeconomic context of schools has been found to be the most powerful of all the variables differentiating schools. How exactly do contextual effects operate? Does having a majority of middle-class students in a school automatically establish a set of norms that are conducive to learning? Do all students stepping into such an environment learn at equal rates, allowing for home background differences? Unfortunately, placing blacks and whites, middle-class and lower-class students, or boys and girls in the same school does not provide a sufficient condition for significantly increasing the achievement levels of disadvantaged students. Nonetheless, it is apparent that contextual climate is a critical variable for some students. What then are the conditions that "mediate" the contextual influence of a school? Thus, we want to explore the model displayed as Figure 4.3.

◆ SES CONTEXT OF THE SCHOOL

According to the theory noted above regarding the "normative" environment, the SES context of a school has an independent effect upon the educational aspirations of students. In an early study, Wilson (1959) tested this theory in a study of eight public and private high schools on the West Coast. He limited the analysis to boys since at that time the educational and occupational aspirations of girls were more homogeneous and determined by other factors (of course, this would be much less true today).

Wilson hypothesized "that the values of the bulk of students in a high school provide a significant normative reference influencing the values of individuals within the school" (p. 836). He compared the aspirations and the achievement (grades) of students in three levels of school SES context (high, medium, low). The high-SES context schools were those containing a high proportion of students whose parents ranked high in educational and occupational status.

Wilson's research specifically examined the extent to which the SES context of a school influences academic outcomes, after controlling for SES of the

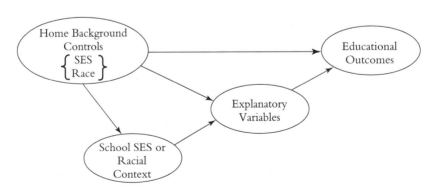

FIGURE 4.3   Modeling the Effects of Contextual Variables

home. "Concretely, are the sons of manual workers more likely to adhere to middle-class values and have high educational aspirations if they attend a predominantly middle-class school, and conversely, are the aspirations of the sons of professionals more modest if they attend a predominantly working class school?" (Wilson, 1959: 837).

Both home SES and school SES have independent effects upon educational aspirations. Wilson found that the aspirations of students from low-SES homes in high-SES schools *increase* by about the same amount that the aspirations of students from high-SES homes in low-SES schools *decrease*. Specifically, 93 percent of the sons of professionals who were attending a high-SES school planned to go to college while only 64 percent of similar students attending a low-SES school had such plans; in a like manner, only 33 percent of the sons of manual workers in low-SES schools held college aspirations while 59 percent of similar students in high-SES schools did. The SES context of a school clearly affects aspirations.

Although other studies have reported more skepticism regarding the impact of school SES context (see Hauser, 1971, 1974; Jencks et al., 1972), the idea remains intriguing. And, though school assignment had never been based upon student SES, it became a reality under a plan in La Crosse, Wisconsin, in September 1992. Family income has become one of the criteria that La Crosse employs for assigning elementary students to schools (Celis, 1992b). This is a local government plan that runs contrary to family control. This locally initiated educational reform is still in place and has had moderate academic success as well as positive results in terms of intergroup attitudes held by students (see Kahlenberg, 2000; Plank,

2000). In fact, Kahlenberg argues that economically integrated schools offer greater potential to increase achievement and equality for all students than vouchers, standards, class size reductions, or any of the other leading reform proposals. Recently, school boards in Cambridge, Massachusetts and Wake County, North Carolina have initiated plans to integrate by SES (Richard, 2002). Preliminary results from Wake County show positive outcomes (Vaishnav, 2002). What are the pros and cons of redistributing state funds versus redistributing students by SES in order to achieve greater equality?

Perhaps the most important study of school SES context is one that seriously calls it into question. In the early 1970s, McDill and Rigsby (1973) reported the results of research on "school climate." A model of this is shown in Figure 4.4. The purpose of the study was twofold: (1) to develop a measure of the academic normative and value climate of schools on the basis of questions other than the SES or racial characteristics of students and (2) to examine the influence of this measure of academic climate relative to the influence of school SES context. Thus, the underlying assumption was that factors other than SES (such as student and teacher attitudes, school policies, parental involvement) contributed to the academic normative and value culture of a school and that this climate influenced academic outcomes over and above the influence of school SES context. In fact, the researchers hypothesized that the climate measure would help to explain the school SES effect. Thus, they expected to discover no direct effect of SES context on achievement, after controlling for the school academic climate measure. School climate was measured by student answers to thirty-nine questions regarding

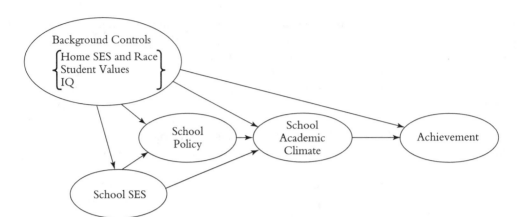

FIGURE 4.4 McDill and Rigsby's Model of Contextual Effects

the extent to which academic excellence and intellectual matters were emphasized in the school.

Indeed, McDill and Rigsby were able to demonstrate that virtually all of the bivariate effect of school SES context was "explained" by the academic climate variable. The relationship of school SES context and achievement is reduced to zero when controls are added for home SES, IQ, and the school climate measure. According to the authors (1973: 199), "In those schools where academic competition, intellectualism, and subject-matter competence are emphasized and rewarded by faculty and student bodies, individual students tend to conform to the scholastic norms of the majority and achieve at a higher level." To some degree, these schools do contain a higher percentage of students from higher-SES homes, but the researchers maintain that the academic climate explains most of the SES contextual effect and that the climate is generated by factors other than student body characteristics alone (including teacher attitudes, school policies, and so on). Thus, SES context seems to really be a proxy for the academic climate that exists in a school. The same reasoning applies to racial context. Coleman (1990a: 129) concurs:

> Middle class schools have their effects through providing a social environment that is more demanding and more stimulating. And once we consider this, we realize that integration is not the only means, nor even necessarily the most efficient means, for increasing lower class achievement. There may be other and better ways of creating such an environment.

We will pursue this in greater detail below. It is vital to note here, however, that this study was one of the first to incorporate school policy variables into an analysis that included typical sociological factors. We see that the sociological factors influence the policy variables, and the home variables, as always, effect achievement. But school policies can be established by legislative mandate (be it local, state, or federal) independent of the home background variables. Today, this is increasingly the case, and to no small extent, these mandates began with the Supreme Court decision of 1954 to integrate the schools across the country. The point is that school policies can be used to offset the negative impact of home variables.

Similarly, school policies can be used to offset the negative impact of contextual variables. For example, a recent data set has been established using state demographic and test score results which allows users to identify schools within any state with varying proportions of race and poverty context in the schools and to discover those schools that are performing above average for the state. These data are available at http://www.edtrust.org/main/index.asp and provide a user-friendly way to identify such schools, to examine characteristics of any particular school, and to even contact the school to determine what types of effective policies are in place. For example, Garfield Elementary School in Selma, California, with over 90 percent of the students from poverty homes (% qualifying for a free lunch), is outperforming schools with a more affluent SES context. The data show that the school is small (only 260 students) and operating with high teacher morale and a vibrant after-school enrichment program (see Archer, 2002b).

◆ RACIAL CONTEXT OF THE SCHOOL

Most studies investigating the effects of SES context have also examined the racial context of the school. Following the findings of the Coleman Report, most studies have reported small positive influences of integrated schools on the academic outcomes of minority students. These effects are clearly much less significant than the influence of either home SES or school SES context, though obviously the racial context of a school is correlated with the SES context of the school. Thus, to some

extent (possibly a substantial extent), the positive influence of school SES context includes a racial context effect, at least with regard to minority outcomes. Minority students attending a predominantly integrated school are at the same time attending a school of a higher SES context than they would if they were attending a predominantly minority school. Although we might discover that the influence of school racial context for minorities in such a school is only small, the influence of SES context is likely to be larger. And, of course, from McDill and Rigsby, we have learned that SES context is simply an indicator of school academic climate.

Perhaps because of the political and legal importance of racial integration as opposed to SES integration, the influence of racial context has received considerable attention. Also, there are some very important differences that complicate the two types of contextual effects. Some of these are test score performance for blacks and whites, curriculum placement *within* schools resulting from test scores, and interracial attitudes and behaviors (that is, racial tolerance or racism among both teachers and students). A racially integrated school does not necessarily guarantee integrated classrooms or positive interracial attitudes or unbiased tests.

The importance of direct contact with peers in classrooms was the focus of a 1967 study by James McPartland. McPartland argued that the academic advantage of being in an integrated school actually depended upon assignment to an integrated classroom. This model is shown in Figure 4.5. Using data from the original Equality of Educational Opportunity study, McPartland tested the relative influence of school and classroom integration, examining the influence of

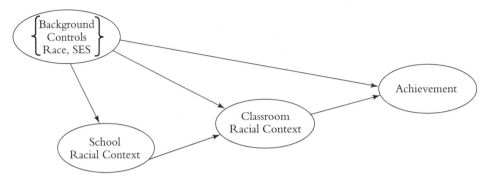

FIGURE 4.5   McPartland's Model of Contextual Effects

each variable while controlling for the other as well as for a typical set of home background factors. Note that the logic of this analysis is to establish classroom racial context as the "explanation" for the effects of school racial context.

McPartland found that school integration was indeed no guarantee of classroom integration. He observed that many fully integrated schools were just as fully segregated according to classrooms. Apparently, track placement in some schools, driven either by test score performance or racist and recalcitrant administrative attitudes, ensured the continued existence of racial segregation within schools. Yet, there were schools with classroom integration. McPartland offered this conclusion:

> It is desegregation at the classroom level which encompasses the factors having important influences on Negro student performance. . . . The only students who appear to derive benefit from attendance at mostly White schools are those in predominantly White classes within the school. As far as the differences in their achievement are concerned, the students in segregated classes may as well be in segregated schools as desegregated ones. (McPartland, 1967: 5)

These results indicate that racial integration provides only a necessary precondition for making possible the likelihood of contact by students of different races. Academic advantages only accrue, however, to minority students who contact middle-class white students in the classroom. Similar results have been found for the effects of SES context—namely, that the influence in school SES context occurs only among students who develop friendships at the classroom level with higher-SES students (see Campbell and Alexander, 1965). In summary, it is the personal contact with friends within a high school that brings about high or low academic outcomes (aspirations and achievement).

Research over the past four decades confirms these early findings. In fact, it is common today to discuss the effects of desegregation by separating the simple effects of racial composition at the school level from studies which examine "the racially correlated allocation of educational opportunities within school typically accomplished by tracking" (Mickelson, 2001: 216). Although it is unconstitutional (see *Hobson v. Hanson*, 1967) to use tracking or grouping to circumvent desegregation at the school level, research shows that this practice continues to persist.

The consequences of desegregation at the school level (without consideration to the correlation of race and track within a school) have manifested small and somewhat mixed results. Studies that focus on the long-term consequences in terms of educational and occupational attainment have found positive and significant results. Blacks who attended desegregated schools obtain higher educational and occupational attainment than their counterparts who attended segregated schools (Armor, 1995; Braddock and McPartland 1988; Wells and Crain, 1994).

The short-term results of desegregation in terms of test scores, grades, attitudes toward school, self-esteem, and personal control are mixed. The issue has been subjected to hundreds, perhaps thousands of studies, and yet the results seem to be consistent. The Coleman Report served as a good barometer as it found very small though positive outcomes in terms of tests scores, attitudes toward school, and the locus of control measure. In a review of studies through the mid-1970s, St. John (1975) found similar results, and this was followed by a review of studies through the mid-1990s by Armor (1995) with the same conclusion. The defining study was a meta-analysis of 19 studies judged to be most methodologically sound from among 157, many of which were flawed. This National Institute of Education (1984) report concluded that only 62 percent of comparisons between desegregated and segregated schools were more effective for black children. Although desegregation increased mean reading levels by a small but significant degree, it did not increase mathematical achievement (see also, Ascik, 1984; Walberg, 1985).

In addition to the relatively small positive effects associated with racial context (integration), a number of studies have reported negative findings for blacks and Hispanics in desegregated settings. For example, numerous studies have demonstrated that racial and ethnic minorities lose some degree of self-esteem in integrated environments (see Coleman et al., 1966; Rosenberg and Simmons, 1972). Recall from Chapter 3, however, that self-esteem is not a causal variable in achievement. Moreover, integrated schools may have contradictory effects upon a student's academic performance. On the one hand, they may raise educational aspirations and environmental control, but on the other hand, minorities and low-SES youth may be forced to deal with lower academic performance in a context of higher academic standards (see Jencks et al., 1972). Finally, desegregation is viewed as the central factor in the phenomenon known as "white flight," whereby whites have exited the cities undergoing desegregation for the suburbs (Armor, 1995; Clotfelter, 2001; Coleman, Kelly, and Moore, 1975; Rossel, 1992). Rivkin (1994: 279), however, concluded that white flight from the central cities occurred during 1968 to 1988 as a matter of course, and "school-integration efforts have had little long-term effect on residential segregation."

Beginning with McPartland (1967), researchers have consistently discovered that efforts to desegregate schools often result in resegregation in classrooms through tracking within schools (see again Figure 4.5). Officially, assignment to tracks within schools is done on the basis of meritocratic criteria with a goal of improving instruction (Hallinan, 1992; Mickelson, 2001). In practice, however, research has demonstrated that a variety of nonmeritocratic factors enter into the decision made by school officials to place a student into a given track. These other factors include the student's race, gender, and social class; parents' pressure on school decision makers; seat availability in a given course; and the racial and SES composition of the school. The weight of evidence, however, confirms that blacks and other nonwhites are disproportionately assigned to lower tracks that provide an inferior opportunity to learn and a segregated experience in school (Ferguson, 1998; Lucas, 1999; Mickelson, 2001; Oakes, 1985, 1994; Wheelock, 1992; Rosenbaum, 1976). We consider this matter in more depth in Chapter 6.

In the face of fifty years of small positive results from integration, along with the negative outcomes noted above, a certain degree of skepticism regarding the short-term value of integration does exist (for views strongly defending the success of school desegregation, see Crain and Mahard, 1983; Wells, 1995; Teachers College Record, 1995; Braddock, Crain, and McPartland, 1984; Mickelson, 2001). Moreover, the number of African American students attending predominantly black (segregated) schools has risen steadily since 1974 (Simon-McWilliams, 1989; Orfield and Monfort, 1992), prompting some educators to focus their efforts on establishing effective neighborhood schools, be they desegregated or otherwise (Bates, 1990). Some educators and researchers argue that the money saved on busing alone could be better spent directly for school resources in minority neighborhoods (Schmidt, 1994). A recent survey found that two-thirds of the urban school educators in America now believe that minority children can get a high-quality education in a racially segregated setting as long as these schools receive adequate financial and instructional resources (Schmidt, 1995b).

Thus, research on contextual effects has found that (1) the SES context of schools is the most important school-centered variable; (2) SES context is largely explained by the concept of school academic climate—that is, it is not the SES context per se that generates positive outcomes but rather the positive academic climate associated with high-SES (but this climate could be created via other means); and (3) racial context effects are small and appear to operate only when racial integration occurs at the classroom level.

◆ SES CONTEXT OF THE NEIGHBORHOOD

How does the influence of home-based individual-level SES compare with the influence of community (neighborhood) SES? In view of the everyday immediacy and the intimacy of the home, we might expect home SES to be the most powerful. On the other hand, it is on the streets of neighborhoods that students spend much of the day.

Recently, Duncan (1994) and Brooks-Gunn et al. (1993) have shown that reasonably powerful neighborhood SES effects do exist for childhood IQ, teenage births, school-leaving outcomes, and eventual educational attainment, even after control for the SES of families. Their studies were based on several theories originally reviewed by Jencks and Mayer (1990). The basic theory is fundamental: Social influences can be contagious either in a beneficial (as in an affluent community) or a detrimental manner (as in a troubled, low-income neighborhood). Neighborhood role models and institutions are critical components of the "collective socialization" of children. The collective behaviors and attitudes of neighborhoods establish norms that guide behavior either in a positive or a negative manner in terms of academic achievement along the full range of attitudes and behaviors.

Duncan (1994) used a longitudinal survey called the Panel Study of Income Dynamics begun in 1968 and continued through 1991. The dependent variable in the study was the years of school completed when an individual was in his or her mid-twenties. Measurements of family characteristics were obtained at the outset for each individual. Based on census data, Duncan used several variables that characterized the neighborhood SES context: the percentage of families in the neighborhood with incomes more than $30,000; the percentage of families in the neighborhood with incomes less than $30,000; the percentage of individuals in the neighborhood who are black; and the percentage of families with children in a female-headed household. The research question was to determine the effect of these contextual variables on educational attainment, after controlling for a number of individual-level SES variables (family income, mother's education, mother's work status, and family structure). Duncan examined the results separately for white females, white males, black females, and black males. The results are summarized in Figure 4.6.

Not surprisingly, Duncan (1994: 47) found that "children growing up in affluent neighborhoods appear to do better than children in low-income neighborhoods." This finding held for all of the subgroups, except for black males. Generally this confirms the theories of collective norms and collective socialization, again except for black males, whose educational attainment is not affected by these SES neighborhood characteristics. In effect, black males do not benefit from growing up in an affluent-SES neighborhood, nor are they adversely affected by a low-SES

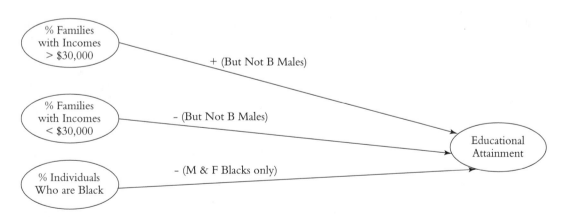

FIGURE 4.6   Neighborhood Effects on Educational Attainment, Controlling for Individual SES

Source: Greg J. Duncan, 1994. "Families and Neighbors as Sources of Disadvantage in the Schooling Decisions of White and Black Adolescents." *American Journal of Education* 103: 20–53.

Note: All neighborhood effects control for individual SES variables.

neighborhood. The only exception to this finding is that black males do benefit from an affluent neighborhood if and only if the affluent neighbors are themselves black. We call these type of findings interactions or specifications in which we have to specify that the effect is different for subgroups.

Duncan (1994: 48) also found that "both Black males and Black females did worse in neighborhoods with a greater concentration of Blacks, while the educational attainment for white males and white females was not significantly affected." Racial composition does not seem to influence the academic behavior of whites. This suggests that the academic achievement of blacks could be increased if they lived in more integrated neighborhoods, without reducing the attainment of white youth. Duncan (1994: 49) offers this caution however:

> Although some neighborhood effects proved important, family-level factors were generally much more powerful. Thus, policy efforts to influence individual families are likely to prove more successful than policies aimed at neighborhoods. Among the most potent family-level variables were economic status and mother's schooling.

Researchers have found stronger school and neighborhood effects on developmental outcomes. Rosenberg and Simmons (1972) demonstrated that a child's self-esteem was strongly influenced by the context of both school and neighborhood. For example, black self-esteem was significantly lower in predominantly white neighborhoods and predominantly white schools. Likewise, Rosenberg (1965) observed that self-esteem was negatively affected whenever an adolescent lived in a religious context that was dissonant.

This situation would exist, for example, for a Catholic living in a non-Catholic neighborhood.

◆ FAMILY STRUCTURE AS A CONTEXTUAL VARIABLE

An interesting variation on this can be obtained by examining family structure as a contextual variable in school. We have already determined that increasingly students grow up in single-parent families. This means that schools are increasingly populated by these students and that schools will vary in the degree to which the percentage of students live in single-parent families. Pong (1998) investigated this question using tenth graders in the NELS data. Specifically, she asked (Pong: 24), "Does a school's concentration of students from single-parent families affect school achievement for all children, above and beyond the effect of single parenthood on individual children?" Pong employed family structure as a contextual variable by computing the percentage of single-parent families in schools, which varied from zero to more than 50 percent. Moreover, she asked if the influence of family structure context in school could be explained by a mediating variable of parental-school network of social capital and school SES. Pong's model is depicted in Figure 4.7.

The notion of a school-based social capital is a simple extension of home-based social capital. Indeed, Coleman (1988b) recognized and emphasized the importance of social capital that existed (or was absent) in the neighborhood, the school, and all sorts of extracurricular activities that composed a web of relationships and networks that provided communal social capital to children. Pong assumed that in schools with a greater

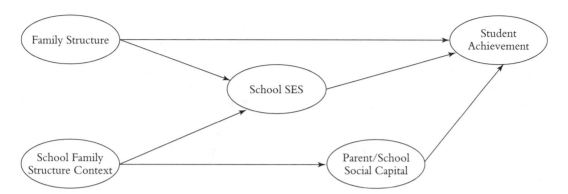

FIGURE 4.7   The Effect of School Family Structure Context on Student Achievement

Source: Suet-ling Pong, 1998. "The School Compositional Effect of Single-Parenthood on 10th Grade Achievement." *Sociology of Education* 71: 24–43.

concentration of students from single-parent homes, the schools would have fewer economic resources and fewer social capital resources (parents would have less time for involvement, meetings, special events, and so on). Although not shown in the model in Figure 4.7, Pong controlled for a full set of background variables at both the individual (SES, race) and school level (type of school, urbanicity).

The study obtained a significant school-level negative effect of school family structure, over and beyond the significant negative effect associated with family structure per se. On average, students in schools with higher levels of single-parent families scored significantly lower on both reading and mathematics tests than students attending schools with lower levels of students from single-parent families. Moreover, the analyses found that this negative effect of school family structure context can be fully explained. There is no arrow between school family structure context and achievement because the impact flows through the intervening explanatory variables of school SES and school social capital. "Together,

both the schools' economic status and social capital (in the form of parental involvement) completely explain the differences in mathematics or reading achievement between schools with low concentrations of students from single-parent families and schools with medium concentrations" (Pong, 1998: 38). This means that the academic disadvantage of attending schools with a large percentage of single-parent families (p. 23) "can be offset when social relations and networks among parents are strong." Of course, this would not be an easy task for teachers, school administrators, and parents.

◆ THE CONTEXT OF OPPORTUNITY STRUCTURES

A contextual variable can be formed within a community or a society simply on the basis of perceptions that people have of events. For example, if people perceive that the economy is in a recession, this becomes an active social context that may influence behavior. *Opportunity Structure Theory* argues that the perceptions that students and parents have about future educational and occupational opportunities condition their ongoing school performance (Baker et al., 2001; Mickelson, 1990; Ogbu, 1978). If students and their parents see an open and egalitarian system of schooling and occupations (one in which those who work hard can achieve whatever they want), then they will attempt to excel in school. If they perceive that the system is stratified in such a way as to favor one gender or one race over the other, then they will disengage and not invest as much in their education.

Recently, Baker et al. (2001: Abstract) demonstrated quite convincingly that "the stratification of likely future educational and workforce opportunities influence the effect of gender on school performance in school mathematics." They analyzed data from the Third International Mathematics and Science Study (TIMMS) using a multilevel model to determine the extent to which country-level variables measuring educational and occupational opportunities influence the relationship of gender to mathematics achievement. They found that generally the more egalitarian the country in terms of more opportunities for females, the smaller the difference between males and females on the mathematics test at the 8th and 12th grade levels.

❖ EFFECTIVE SCHOOLS MOVEMENT

The Coleman Report and the hundreds of studies that followed it painted a dim picture of the limits of schools in overcoming the inequalities that students bring with them to the schoolhouse door. These inequalities are fundamentally the result of differences in the social class (SES) home backgrounds of students

(especially as these differences are manifested in parental values, cultural and social capital, and parental involvement). Despite these findings, an "effective schools movement" arose in the 1970s (Edmonds, 1979; Austin and Garber, 1985; Brookover et al., 1979), led by educators and educational researchers who were both critical and supportive of the Coleman Report. Despite the consistent empirical evidence that schools were unable to reduce the influence of the home and had little independent effect on educational outcomes over and above the home, an overwhelming long-standing belief in the efficacy of good schools and good teachers persisted, as did a need to identify those characteristics of the school (as an organization) that *did* make a difference in student achievement.

Yet, another impetus for the further pursuit of school effects was methodological. The Coleman Report was subjected to numerous and exhaustive reanalyses (*Harvard Educational Review*, 1968; Mosteller and Moynihan, 1972). Although the findings generally withstood these extremely rigorous methodological critiques, reservations and qualifications did remain and were troubling, at least to some. A significant contribution, using data other than that of EEO, came from a study by Madaus et al. (1979). These researchers demonstrated that curriculum- or content-specific tests were more sensitive to between school differences and to what is actually taught in school than were the general standardized tests of the sort used by Coleman and his colleagues in EEO. Madaus et al. contend that the standardized measures tap such things as family influence, intelligence, and general experiences, whereas the curriculum-specific tests are more valid for measuring school effects per se. Hanushek (1989) noted that the problem was both conceptual and methodological—that is, correctly identifying and then measuring the relevant school characteristics. And, of course, there was clear evidence that the quality of schools did matter significantly for minority group students (see again Table 4.1).

One book that provided important insight into those factors about schools which do make a difference is *Fifteen Thousand Hours* (Rutter et al., 1979). The title refers to the amount of time that a student spends in British schools from the age of entry to the age of leaving school. The research was conducted in twelve secondary schools in inner-city London. The purpose was to examine the relationship between school inputs and educational outcomes.

Like so many previous studies, Rutter et al. found that the typical physical-facilities variables had little effect on school outcome measures of achievement (better student behavior, better attendance, higher test scores). Among the school characteristics that they did find to be related to achievement were higher teacher standards and expectations, better teacher preparation for class (not more credentials), greater overall academic emphasis in the school, and the establishment of clear goals and objectives by the entire staff of the school. The findings of *Fifteen Thousand Hours* served as a stimulus for the effective schools movement during the 1980s. Other ideas were the result of national "blue ribbon" commission reports and empirical studies such as Rutter et al., and some were essentially theoretical. In all of this, there still exist some differences as to what constitutes an effective school. Yet there are

some commonly agreed upon factors that can be identified (Purkey and Smith, 1983; Wilson and Corcoran, 1988):

1. strong administrative leadership;
2. clear goals, mutually articulated and agreed upon by all staff;
3. high academic ethos in the ambience of the school;
4. community (students, parents, teachers, neighborhood, district) support and involvement;
5. high degree of order, control, and discipline;
6. maximum time on learning tasks;
7. frequent evaluation of student performance;
8. school site management.

Wilson and Corcoran (1988) systematically examined 571 secondary schools that had been identified by the U.S. Department of Education as schools exemplifying success. These schools had been selected by the department in a nonscientific manner using a broad variety of input and output criteria. Although some of the input measures were, indeed, the attributes that we identified above, each school had been selected independently and in a more qualitative rather than quantitative manner. Thus, it was unknown to what extent the schools would reflect collectively the characteristics of effective schools. Certainly, it was strongly suspected and hoped that most of the characteristics would be found embedded in most of the schools. Wilson and Corcoran's empirical analysis confirmed that all of the 571 schools did possess most of the attributes.

One the most impressive studies within the tradition of the effective schools movement was conducted by Chubb and Moe (1990). Although the purpose of their book was to critique the existing democratically run public schools and advocate a policy of school choice (see discussion in Chapter 8), Chubb and Moe used the High School and Beyond survey to identify a set of effective schools. They identified four sets of organizational characteristics of schools: personnel, goals, leadership, and practice, which are all similar to the more qualitative goals identified above. They constructed measures of each subset from the data and built a composite index of effective school organization (from high to low) and demonstrated that this index was strongly related to sophomore to senior gains in achievement. One of the interesting results of their study was that they showed that the influence of good school organization is approximately equal to the influence of family characteristics. You will recall that most studies show family characteristics to be far stronger than the effects of schools. Here, however, Chubb and Moe loaded the deck, drawing solely on the effective school literature, which is grounded in the ten goals listed above, rather than in material resources. Once again, however, the absence of material resources in their index shows how relatively unimportant they are in the broad scheme of things.

❖ PUBLIC AND PRIVATE SCHOOLS

The idea that good schools could make a difference was viewed skeptically throughout the 1970s, largely as a result of the Coleman Report. Researchers turned to the mechanisms within schools, such as tracking, that affected achievement outcomes. Ironically, however, in 1980 Coleman was once again asked to study the effects of different types of schools.

Despite the previous difficulties associated with obtaining a "school effect" between types of schools, a view persisted that some schools (good schools) were more effective than other schools (bad schools). The lingering assumption was that private schools were more effective. It now seems surprising in retrospect that the effects of public versus private schools had not been investigated systematically at an earlier point. Over the past two decades, however, this omission has been rectified with dozens of studies.

Studies of public and private schools must address the issue of "selection bias"—the fact that students who attend private schools are more likely to come from high-SES homes than students from public schools. Moreover, students in Catholic school "choose" to be there, which is not the case for students attending public schools. As a result, the relationship between school type and achievement might prove to be spurious, resulting from the fact that the socioeconomic status of the home is a common cause of both school type and academic performance; that is, students from high-SES homes are more likely to attend private schools and to do better academically—not because of the school but rather because of the home. (This methodological issue was raised initially in Chapter 2; see in particular two models and the related discussion for Figures 2.5 and 2.6.)

Coleman's study went through several stages. First, he analyzed the base-year data from the High School and Beyond Survey, which was conducted in 1980 (Coleman, Hoffer, and Kilgore, 1982).

This contained seniors and sophomores in public, Catholic, and other private schools. Two years later, follow-up data on these students became available, allowing Coleman to examine the effects of public and private schooling on seniors in 1982 for whom previous test scores were available (these were the sophomores in 1980). During the second stage of the study, it was determined that there were too few other private schools in the sample and, therefore, the private sector was confined to Catholic schools only. In the final analysis, Coleman concluded that Catholic schools were more effective than public schools, that the effects were greatest among disadvantaged students, and that the effects of the school were due to (explained by) greater discipline and order in the schools as well as school policies such as tracking, coursework, and homework. Moreover, a later book (Coleman and Hoffer, 1987) argued that the effectiveness of Catholic schools was also due to the existence of a "functional" and "value" community both within the schools and between the schools and the families of students attending Catholic schools (for critiques, see *Sociology of Education*, 1982, 1983, 1985; *Harvard Educational Review*, 1981; Haertel, James, and Levin, 1987; for a later book supporting Coleman and Hoffer, see Bryk, Lee, and Holland, 1993; more recently, see Morgan and Sorenson, 1999; Carbonaro, 1999; Hallinan and Kubitschek, 1999).

Before turning to the substantive results of the study, we must first address the issue of "selection bias" and determine to what extent there is a school effect, after controlling for the possibility that better students may attend Catholic schools. This means that we need to examine the influence of school type on test results while controlling for home background variables. As a first step in that direction, Hoffer, Greeley, and Coleman (1987) began by controlling for the student's sophomore score, which is possibly the best variable in this data set for differentiating students in public and Catholic schools.[6] They posed the question: What was the difference in the average academic growth from sophomore to senior years in Catholic and public schools? The results of their analyses are shown in Table 4.2.

In Table 4.2, Hoffer, Greeley, and Coleman (1987) display the effect of school type on senior year test score outcomes as the difference in growth between Catholic and public schools, expressed as a one-year grade equivalent of growth. The first row of Table 4.2 shows the estimated Catholic sector increase in growth over and above the public school increase from the sophomore to the senior year in each subject area. One would expect that all students would gain 2 years of test score grade equivalency during this time, and in fact, students in public schools do gain about 2 years, but students in Catholic schools gain about 3 years. For example, on the vocabulary test, public school students, serving as the baseline, gain what amounted to a two-year increment on this test, whereas students in Catholic schools gain 2.8 years (.8 of a year more).

---

[6] Recall from Chapter 2 that in the ECLS-K data set with kindergarten children we were able to control for initial ability before students began school (or shortly thereafter). A major criticism of the Catholic-public secondary school studies is that 10th or 8th grade scores are inadequate to capture initial ability and thereby do not fully control for selection bias.

TABLE 4.2

THE EFFECTS OF SCHOOL TYPE (CATHOLIC/PUBLIC) EXPRESSED AS THE DIFFERENCE IN ACADEMIC GROWTH FROM 10TH TO 12TH GRADE (GRADE EQUIVALENT SCORES)

	Test		
	Vocabulary	**Reading**	**Mathematics**
Catholic-Public two-year growth	.8	1.3	1.7
Adjusted for Family Background	.8	1.1	1.1
Adding Explanatory Variables	.3	.7	0.0
Percent Explained by School Policy Variables	63%	36%	100%

Note: Explanatory Variables included academic program, hours of homework, coursework, attendance, disciplinary climate, and school social and academic composition.

Source: Adapted from Tables 2.1, 2.2, and 2.9 in Thomas B. Hoffer, Andrew A. Greeley, and James S. Coleman, 1985. "Achievement Growth in Public and Catholic Schools." *Sociology of Education* 58: 74–97.

The second row of Table 4.2 shows how the results in the first row are affected when an array of family background variables (SES and family structure, family functioning, race, and sex) are added for further control. Although the Catholic school effects are reduced slightly, the overall results remain essentially unchanged. This result is as expected since they had already controlled for initial sophomore test score in the first row of the table. The researchers also found the Catholic school advantage was greater for minorities and low-SES students, confirming the results discussed in Table 4.1 that school effects are larger for at-risk students. The Catholic school increment for whites is one-half or even one-third as great as the effects for blacks and Hispanics. And the same pattern is true for low-SES students compared to high-SES students but to a lesser degree. Thus, we note again that the strongest school effects occur among those students with the greatest degree of need.

The advantage of the HSB survey is that it does contain data on initial ability (sophomore test scores), and it does have good information regarding educational policies of the school, including the discipline, curriculum, coursework, and homework. A simplified version of the explanatory model using the HSB 1982 data is shown in Figure 4.8. The logic of the model is that there should be no direct effect between school type and senior-year test scores if the relationship is fully explained by the school policy variables.

Hoffer, Greeley, and Coleman began by establishing that a bivariate relationship existed between school type and senior test scores. They then controlled that relationship for home background and initial ability. At this point, any remaining difference between Catholic and public schools could be attributed to something about the

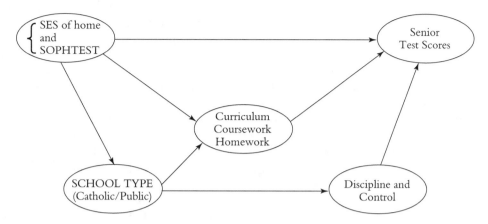

FIGURE 4.8   Modeling the Effects of School Type on Achievement

schools per se. Next they added school policies variables such as curriculum, coursework, homework, and the level of discipline and control in the schools. If the difference between the schools was reduced at this stage, it would be due to or explained by the school policy variables. These results are shown in Table 4.2.

After controlling for home **SES** background and initial test-score differences, the remaining school effect favoring Catholic schools was .8 in vocabulary, 1.1 in reading, and 1.1 in mathematics. These are grade equivalent advantages that accrue to students in Catholic schools in the last two years of high school, over and above the growth obtained in public schools and after controlling for home background variables. After adding the school policy explanatory variables, a considerable portion of the senior test score difference between students in Catholic and public schools had been explained by the model, as shown in Table 4.2 (the amount of explanation varies between 36 and 100 percent depending on the test). The policy implication is that students attending public schools would perform better on these outcomes if they had

access to greater discipline, more rigorous academic programs, more advanced coursework, and more homework.

Of course, another way to conceive the relative effectiveness of public and Catholic schools is to examine the equality of outcomes as opposed to quality. We raised this issue in Chapter 1 and discussed the results of a study by Bryk, Lee, and Holland (1993), which concerns the social distribution of achievement—namely, how the gap between whites and minorities is affected by attendance at either a Catholic or a public school. Bryk, Lee, and Holland demonstrate that the gap in achievement between white and minority students is decreased in Catholic schools whereas the gap is actually increased in public schools (see Table 1.2 in Chapter 1). Accordingly, these researchers conclude that the social distribution of achievement is more equitable in Catholic schools. Also, in a related study, Lee and Bryk (1988) show that track placement and course of study are the major explanatory factors that account for this equitable distribution of achievement (similar to the results we discussed above for the simple difference in achievement between the two sectors).

In addition to track placement, discipline, and course of study as explanatory factors, other variables have been identified. Coleman and Hoffer (1987) have argued that the key lies in the provision of functional communities between students, parents, and teachers. Riordan (1985, 1990) observed that a substantial number (42 percent) of Catholic secondary schools were single-sex schools and that there were no Catholic school effects among only coeducational institutions. Other explanations that have been offered are that Catholic school students wear uniforms, which reduce the salience of SES, and that Catholic school students feel a greater sense of commitment due to the financial sacrifice made by their parents to send them to Catholic schools.

In further work, Coleman and Hoffer (1987) and later Bryk, Lee, and Holland (1993) developed an explanatory model that centered on the idea of functional communities that tied schools, faculty, teachers, and students together. Underlying the theory was the fact that public schools were largely organized around residence while Catholic schools were organized around religious identity. This critical distinction makes possible a choice of schools and a sharing of values (both religious and educational). Notice that this also creates the problem of selection bias that we covered earlier, but that it also implies some advantages to schools of choice, which we will consider later (Chapter 8). And, of course, the idea is linked to the theory of social capital that we discussed in Chapter 3.

If the functional community is a valid explanation for why Catholic schools are more effective in producing higher achievement and more equality, the results should be conditioned by the degree to which students are integrated into the functional community. One would predict that students in Catholic schools who are Catholic and attend church often would do better than non-Catholic or non-churchgoers. In their analysis, Coleman and Hoffer (1987) show this to be true for both academic achievement and the propensity to not drop out of school.

Table 4.3 shows the results of the analysis for both mathematics and verbal achievement. Being Catholic in a Catholic school means being part of the functional community and these students make significant gains on both of these ability domains from sophomore to senior year. Being Catholic in a public school confers no significant advantage. Being Catholic and attending church frequently increases the Catholic school advantage (intensifying the degree of integration into the functional community) while greater attendance confers no significant gain for Catholic students in public schools. These results confirm that Catholic schools are most beneficial to students who are members of the Catholic community and support the functional-community hypothesis. Students with nonmembership in the community (non-Catholic or non-churchgoers) fare less well although they still outperform comparable students in public schools (though not significantly so). This latter finding is presumably due to the community effect even for those on the margins, along with the other factors such as coursework and homework and common curricula and discipline. Bryk, Lee, and Holland (1993) expand on this functional-community concept to include a more elaborate measure of the communitarian index than was employed by Coleman and Hoffer and conclude that this variable is the dominant

TABLE 4.3

PREDICTED ACHIEVEMENT GROWTH IN PUBLIC AND CATHOLIC SCHOOLS FOR CATHOLIC AND NON-CATHOLIC STUDENTS WHO ATTEND RELIGIOUS SERVICE FREQUENTLY AND INFREQUENTLY WITH BACKGROUND OTHERWISE EQUAL TO THE AVERAGE PUBLIC-SCHOOL STUDENT (EXPRESSED AS RAW SCORES)

	Sophomore to Senior Growth		Catholic Advantage
	Public	**Catholic**	
Verbal Achievement			
Catholic Religion	2.92	3.98	1.06*
Non-Catholic Religion	2.66	3.39	.73
Catholic Religion Students			
Attend Church Often	3.01	4.29	1.28*
Never Attend Church	2.82	3.53	.71
Mathematics Achievement			
Catholic Religion	1.61	2.37	.76*
Non-Catholic Religion	1.39	1.67	.28
Catholic Religion Students			
Attend Often	1.99	2.84	.85*
Never Attend	1.21	1.51	.30

Note: *Significant gain at $p < .05$; these are raw test scores.

Source: Adapted from Tables 5.9 and 5.10 in James S. Coleman and Thomas Hoffer, 1987. *Public and Private High Schools.* New York: Basic Books.

explanation for Catholic school's favorable effects.

There exists a large body of critical response to Coleman's studies of Catholic and public schooling. The criticism takes a variety of forms, including the difficulty of overcoming the influence of selection bias favoring Catholic schools, the influence of transfers and dropouts, the reliability and validity of the achievement measures, and the substantive importance of small effects (see *Sociology of Education*, 1982, 1983, 1885; *Harvard Educational Review*, 1981, Haertel, James, and Levin, 1987; Witte, 1992). Yet, the basic results for secondary schools

have remained robust throughout the criticism, as attested to by the recent reanalysis by Bryk, Lee, and Holland (1993), Hoffer (2000), and Morgan (2001).

Finally, however, it should be noted that during the period 1972 to 1992, there has been a dramatic transformation of the demographic composition of Catholic schools. Baker and Riordan (1998) examined the parental SES of students attending Catholic schools during this period using NLS (1972), HSB (1982), and NELS (1992). They found that whereas only 30 percent of students came from families in the highest SES quartile in

1972, this figure had risen to 46 percent by 1992. Similarly, in 1972, 12 percent of students attending Catholic schools were from the lowest SES quartile and this had dipped to only 6 percent by 1992. Since we have repeatedly demonstrated that Catholic schools are more effective for low-SES students, the implications of this demographic transformation are self-evident (see also, Riordan, 2000).

We have already noted in Chapter 1 that this Catholic school advantage is clearly not true for students in kindergarten. Here we are better able to control for initial ability at the very beginning of school and find no differences in yearly academic growth across the public and Catholic sectors (if anything there is a public school advantage). It is possible that the key is control for true initial ability and it is also possible that the effects are different across the sectors at different points in a student's educational career. In the final analysis, we do need to remember that the between schools effects are small by any comparison with effects associated with differences between homes or within schools, as shown in Chapters 5 and 6.

❖ SUMMARY

In this chapter, we have examined the Coleman Report of 1966 and its aftermath. The main finding of the report was that variation in the quality of schools was not related to variation in student achievement to any significant degree, on average. This finding, however, applied to whites and Asians only. Somehow, the fact that school quality has a much larger effect on achievement for all other racial groups was lost in the discourse of the report. This oversight becomes salient as we turn to more recent developments in Chapter 5. Throughout this chapter (and in Chapter 5), we discover that differences between schools do matter considerably for disadvantaged students, and that they matter much less so for middle-class students.

Since the difference between high- and low-performing students and between whites and blacks generally increases over the course of 12 years of schooling, it has appeared to many researchers that "schools played a role in creating and sustaining student differences in outcomes" (Hallinan, 2000: 76). But, later studies have shown that schools may play a much more benign role, and possibly even a remedial role, in reducing inequality. We examine this in Chapter 5.

Another conclusion of the report, quite controversial both then and now, is that home-family variables were the most important factors influencing academic achievement in school. This finding, fully consistent with Chapter 3 of this book, has passed through various interpretations with accompanying political-theoretical and policy implications over the years, including desegregation efforts, blaming the victim critiques, increased attention to private schools and school choice schools, and issues pertaining to possible social reproduction in the schools.

This chapter described the fallout of the Coleman report covering a period from the late 1960s to the late 1980s. We reviewed several developments that came about largely as a result of the Coleman Report: the controversial "culture of poverty" thesis, studies of contextual effects, and the effective school movement that eventuated in the standards and accountability movement. We have also examined the effects of Catholic and public schools, finding essentially the same results as in EEO; namely, very small school effects which are much larger for low-SES and otherwise disadvantaged students.

❖ KEY CONCEPTS

differences between schools
school effects
variation in student outcomes
  between and within schools
school quality
school resources
Coleman Report (EEO)
school effects and disadvantaged
  students
contextual variables
contextual effects
SES and racial context
classroom racial context
neighborhood context

school academic climate
integrated and segregated schools
opportunity structure theory
effective schools movement
Fifteen Thousand Hours
culture of poverty
blaming the victim
cultural differences
acting white (oppositional culture
  theory)
public and private schools
selection bias
explanations for the Catholic
  school effect

❖ KEY STUDIES

Coleman et al. (1966)
Dreeben (2000)
Fordham and Ogbu (1986)
Wilson (1959)
McDill and Rigsby (1973)
McPartland (1967)
Kahlenberg (2000)

Duncan (1994)
Pong (1998)
Baker et al. (2001)
Rutter et al. (1979)
Wilson and Corcorran (1988)
Chub and Moe (1990)
Hoffer, Greeley, and Coleman (1987)

❖ REVIEW QUESTIONS

1. Identify and describe three major findings of the 1966 Coleman Report (*Equality of Educational Opportunity*).

2. "At the end of school, the conditional probabilities of high achievement are even more conditional upon racial or ethnic background than they are at the beginning of school." What does Coleman mean to imply by this statement?

3. Discuss how the study by McDill and Rigsby demonstrated that the effects of SES context are "explained" or understood.

4. Discuss the implications of Coleman's findings on the influence of integrated schools with special attention to the limitations and the alternatives, and what the critics say.

5. Discuss the concept of contextual effects. Cite several studies covering SES, neighborhood, and racial context. Is SES context a proxy variable for academic climate established by educational policy?

6. Describe the consequences of the "no school effects" finding of the Coleman Report with regard to theories about the educational achievement of minority children. What does Table 4.1 contribute to this issue?

7. Describe McPartland's research on school integration. What are the implications?

8. Identify the problem of "selection bias" in the study of school effects. What problems does it cause? How is it controlled in research studies?

9. Summarize the research regarding the effects of school (Catholic/public) on academic achievement. How do race, SES, and initial ability condition these effects? How are these effects explained?

10. Contrast and compare the theories of cultural deprivation and cultural differences as they apply to school outcomes. How does each of these compare with the culture of poverty theory?

11. How can public school administrators utilize the knowledge obtained from the analyses of public and Catholic school effectiveness?

12. Describe Pong's research on family context within schools and the implications.

13. Describe Duncan's study of neighborhood context and the implications.

Chapter 5

DIFFERENCES BETWEEN SCHOOLS: THE CURRENT STUDIES

The achievement gap across social lines would be expected to widen over time for reasons having nothing at all to do with the schools.

KARL L. ALEXANDER, DORIS R. ENTWISLE, AND LINDA S. OLSON, 2001

Over the past decade, the thinking on school effects has changed somewhat as a result of new studies, prompted by new methodologies and a reconceptualization of the limits of school effects. A major problem with the early studies is that they overlooked the fact that students spend a sizable amount of each year at home during the summer. The small effect of school may be due to the fact that they are not open during the summer. Another avenue of research has been to reexamine the so-called "small school effects" across the full universe of studies using a technique called meta-analysis. Other studies have continued to pursue how much greater achievement money (per pupil expenditure) can buy. Still, other studies have asked how the school effects of class and school size influence achievement. Finally, new developments in multilevel modeling have been introduced.

Until recently, school effects studies were typically of two types. Some were longitudinal, in which measurements were made at the one grade level and then growth rates were computed based on achievement at the next grade level, as in the Catholic-public study in Chapter 4. Others were cross-sectional studies, where measures were made of different grades at a given point in time, as in the original Coleman Report, where they obtained achievement measures for grades 1, 3, 6, 9, and 12. All of these research designs are flawed in the sense that they assume that growth in school occurs over the course of the entire year when, in fact, this is obviously not the case. Students are in school for at best ten months of the year and at home for two months during the summer.

Also, until recently, students were assigned to schools solely according to their home residence. Concerns about school resources, especially per pupil expenditures, however, have spawned a new era of school choice with options for charter schools, vouchers, and privatization of the public schools. Driving this revolution is the persistent common belief (be it true or false) that school resources do make a difference and that schools in poor districts have fewer resources. For this reason, the

TABLE 5.1

SUMMARY OF ESTIMATED EXPENDITURE EFFECTS ON EDUCATIONAL OUTCOMES FROM 187 STUDIES OF EDUCATIONAL PRODUCTION FUNCTIONS

Input	Number of Studies	Statistically Significant		Statistically Insignificant		Unknown Sign
		+	−	+	−	
Teacher education	113	8	5	31	32	37
Teacher experience	140	40	10	44	31	15
Teacher salary	69	11	4	16	14	24
Per pupil expenditure	65	13	3	25	13	11

Source: Adapted from Eric A. Hanushek, "The Impact of Differential Expenditures on School Performance," *Educational Researcher 18* (1989): Table 3, p. 47.

fundamental question and the findings from the Coleman Report still remain salient and controversial today.

❖ STUDIES AND REFORMS IN SCHOOL FINANCE

In a recent review of two decades of research, Hanushek (1989: 45) confirms the findings of EEO. Hanushek conducted an exhaustive search of 187 "qualified studies" based upon thirty-eight separately published articles or books covering a period from 1967 to 1986.[1] For each

study, Hanushek categorized the results according to the independent variable (per pupil expenditure, teacher education, teacher experience, and so on) and the direction and statistical significance of the results. Table 5.1 displays some of these results.

Hanushek concluded that "variations in school expenditures are not systematically related to variations in student performance." The essential components of school expenditures are teacher salaries and class sizes—and salaries are determined largely by experience. This interpretation is based on the fact (shown in Table 5.1) that most studies *found insignificant or null results*. Note that Hanushek does not differentiate between the effects for minorities and nonminorities as per our discussion in Chapter 4 and this might increase the number of positive effects.

At the same time, he notes that a number of studies demonstrate the differential effectiveness of schools and teachers that can be found by simply comparing average student performance

[1] Hanushek defined a qualified study as one containing a production-function (input-output) analysis that (1) was published in a book or refereed journal, (2) related some objective measure of student outcome to characteristics of family *and* schools, and (3) provided information about the statistical significance of the relationships. Most of the articles and books provided a multiple set of "qualified studies" in the form of different independent and/or dependent variables.

across two or more classrooms or schools (while controlling for initial ability and home background).

> Enormous differences in teacher quality exist, but differences in teacher skill are not strongly related to educational backgrounds, amount of teaching experience, or teaching in small classes. . . . existing measures of characteristics of teachers and schools are seriously flawed and thus are poor indicators of the true effects of schools. (Hanushek, 1989: 45, 48)

In Chapter 6, we will examine this issue of teacher quality as a *within* school effect.

Several critics (Hedges, Laine, Greenwald, 1994; Baker, 1991) have disputed Hanushek's interpretation, pointing to the fact that among the significant results, the pattern points toward a positive effect for school expenditures (For an entirely separate analysis showing positive results, see Ferguson, 1991.) Moreover, Hedges et al. argue that the size of the effects in each of the studies should have been averaged in a meta-analysis.[2] In their 1994 analysis, these researchers show that "an increase of per pupil expenditure by $500 (this is approximately 10 percent of the national average and a spending increase that legislative bodies might be

willing to consider) would be associated with a 0.7 standard deviation increase in student outcomes" (p. 11). Achievement gains of this magnitude would amount to as much as two to four years of achievement in grade equivalency (see Jencks, 1985; Jencks and Brown, 1975). Although acknowledging the limitations of his "vote-counting" mode of analysis, Hanushek (1994) strongly affirms the validity of his findings.

In a fresh analysis, Greenwald, Hedges, and Laine (1996) acknowledge that the magnitude of some of the coefficients in the earlier study noted above may have been too large to be plausible. In this more recent paper, they report the results of a more comprehensive and exhaustive study that examines a larger universe of studies than any previously reported. Their findings revealed that the effect of a hypothetical $500 increase in per pupil expenditure (PPE) was considerably less than in the first article. Specifically, the effects in fractions of a standard deviation were .15 (for per pupil expenditure), .22 (for teacher education), .18 (for teacher experience), and .16 (for teacher salary). Greenwald, Hedges, and Laine (1996: 384) conclude "that school resources are systematically related to

[2] Hedges, Laine, and Greenwald (1994) argue that Hanushek's methodology of "vote counting" is flawed. Vote counting involves the sorting and counting of those studies with or without a statistically significant effect (and in which direction). Hedges et al. employ a technique called "meta-analysis" which allows for the estimation of an average magnitude of effect size for each independent variable. Vote counting does not allow for this, and there are other problems associated with vote counting (see Hedges and Olkin, 1980, as well as Hedges et al., 1994). Meta-analysis, however, must

contend with the problem of eliminating from consideration those studies that are significant and for which the direction of the effect was not reported. According to Hanushek (1994), this represents 30 to 40 percent of the studies confirmed in Table 5.1. The fact is that both methodologies have strengths and weaknesses and a fuller discussion is beyond the scope of this book. The interested reader can examine the 1994 exchange between the above parties and a more recent paper by Greenwald, Hedges, and Laine, 1996.

student achievement and that these relations are large enough to be educationally important."

The size of these effects is probably something less than a one-year grade equivalent in student achievement for a $500 PPE increase for a single year. In the Catholic-public school studies reviewed in Chapter 4, an effect size of .2 is approximately equivalent to a one-year gain in academic achievement for secondary school students. However, in elementary schools, students typically gain a full standard deviation from one year to the next so that an effect size of .15 to .22 would only be about one-sixth of a grade equivalent (see Jencks, 1985 for a discussion of effects sizes and grade equivalents at different grade levels). Since at least half of Greenwald, Hedges, and Laine's universe of studies were elementary school studies, the grade equivalent effect is likely to be somewhere between one-sixth and one whole grade equivalent gain for each $500 PPE. With this in mind, (along with the caveat in footnote 2), Hanushek's vote counting results do not differ appreciably from Greenwald et al. (1996), nor from the original Coleman et al. (1966) study. Thus, the matter remains unresolved at the research level. Obviously, the results depend partly on how the money is spent.

◆ State Government Funding of Schools

At the level of educational policy and reform, however, state governments are beginning to act as if expenditures do matter. Increasingly, impoverished communities have begun to take their case to the courts. Using a litigation strategy similar to that in *Brown v. Board of Education*, these communities (either small cities and towns or school districts) argue that

their relative lack of wealth and the unfair distribution of state school aid constrains them from being able to provide equality of education in terms of per pupil expenditures. Why should students in poor districts receive an education that costs half as much as students residing in affluent districts? They argue that the amount of money spent on each child in a state should be equal.

A recent report (The Education Trust, 2002) demonstrates that school districts with the higher number of poor students receive far less state and local tax money than school districts with fewer poor children. This report by the Education Trust, a nonpartisan group representing schools in urban school districts, found the average gap between poor and affluent school districts to be $966 in 1999–2000. The greatest disparity was in New York State, where schools with the highest percent of low-SES students received $2,153 less per student than schools with the lowest percent of low-SES students ($8,598 versus $6,445, on average). Comparisons of districts by race showed similar results with a gap of $2,034 between districts with the highest and lowest percent of minority students. It is a classic case of students with the greatest educational need receiving the smallest amount of per pupil expenditures from the state and local government.

The dilemma is that states provide about 47 percent of the cost of public school, local communities provide 47 percent, and the federal government provides the remaining 6 percent, on average (National Center for Education Statistics, 1992). Most of the local contributions are generated by local property taxes. The percentages of state and local contributions vary widely among communities within a state. Wealthy communities may operate with a 10/90 state-local split while poor cities may have an 80/20 state-local ratio. Citizens in a wealthy town might pay $6,000 in local taxes and receive $1,000 from the state on a per pupil basis. In a poverty-stricken city, on the other hand, citizens might provide $1,000 and receive only $3,000 from the state. The formula would allow poor communities to receive more income from the state if they spent an equal amount to the affluent communities, but they obviously cannot do this. The bottom line is that the money available per pupil in the above example is $7,000 for the affluent town versus $4,000 for the city.

Since property values are higher in suburban communities, local revenues for schools are greater, even at an equal tax rate. An affluent community with a high-property-tax base, therefore, will accumulate more revenue for schools than a poor community, and if necessary it will be better able to raise the tax rate. To exacerbate the situation, families in affluent communities also have higher incomes, allowing them to pay proportionately less of their income for higher school taxes. (And, of course, parents who pay these higher local taxes are able to write them off on their federal income taxes.) Typically, affluent communities have low-school-tax rates on high property values, which still ensures more funds for education than their counterparts in communities with low property values. The wealthier communities do not have the high tax burdens for municipal services such as police and fire. All of this has led to a demand to divorce education from property altogether or to provide radical reform of the types of formulas described above.

Complicating the issue even further is the fact that states reimburse local communities after the fact; that is, communities must first spend the money in a given tax year in order to be reimbursed in future years. (This gap is usually two full years due to time delays in legislative budget approval.) Poorer communities are simply without the financial resources to spend the money up front and thus are at a disadvantage to begin with.

States reimburse local communities according to a formula that normally takes into account property values, other measures of wealth such as income, the number of disadvantaged children, and special-needs children that are served. Typically, however, there are caps limiting the amount that a poor community can receive (regardless of its demonstrated needs) and setting a minimum as to what an affluent community can receive (regardless of its wealth). The caps are driven by the financial resources of a state and the demands on its budget that are made by other causes such as welfare, roads, and so on. In reality, a community that was designated to receive 80 percent of its actual spending as reimbursement from state funds might typically receive only 60 percent (Corrigan, 1994).

Over the past decade, thirty-one states have been sued for allegedly failing to provide equality of educational opportunity on these grounds. Although many cases have been dismissed in favor of the state (either on the grounds that education is not a fundamental right, or that school funding is not related to outcomes, or that the disparity between the rich and the poor was not enough to be judged unfair), recently the courts have more often ruled in favor of the disadvantaged school district (see Wise and Gendler, 1989). Note that some of these arguments by the state are not too far removed from the educational philosophy of Nozick reviewed in Chapter 1.

In Rhode Island, a court decision of this nature was linked to legislation to provide a Guaranteed Student Entitlement, which included a set of statewide reforms regarding performance assessment and standards, as well as state financing to ensure a uniform spending level per pupil (State of Rhode Island, 1994). The legislation was defeated in 1994. The most dramatic shift in school funding occurred in Michigan, where a sales and cigarette tax replaced the property tax to pay for schools (*Providence Journal Bulletin*, 1994). Kozol (1991) argues that schools should be financed entirely through federal taxes, but this is not likely to happen since the Tenth Amendment to the Constitution states that education is a state and local matter.

School choice is an alternative to reform of school finance. The impetus, however, is similar—existing gaps in inputs and outcomes associated with schools in affluent and in urban communities. The strategy is totally different. School choice relies on a strategy of incentives for both the suppliers and the consumers of education. The incentives for schools are attracting the best teachers and students possible; the incentives for students and parents are the ability to get into the best schools and remain there. Of course, these incentives already exist for schools and students in affluent communities. To whatever extent economically possible, parents "choose" a school by moving into the desired district or neighborhood. The problem, of course, is that the choice is limited to those who can afford to move. School choice reforms (and there are many options) are predicated on the same logic as school finance reforms—namely, that equality of educational opportunity is provided only when students are *not* constrained by residence to attend schools costing only half of what it costs to attend other schools.

❖ STUDIES OF SUMMER LEARNING

Throughout this book, we see that a major challenge in the sociology of education is separating the effects of the home from those of the school. When the influence of the school and the home can be teased apart, it becomes clear that schools are not responsible for SES or racial differences in educational outcomes. Studies of "summer learning" have been able to do this rather successfully. This research attempts to distinguish and compare test score gains that are made during the academic year and during the summer.

Cooper et al. (1996) conducted a meta-analysis of thirteen studies on summer learning that were done between 1975 and 1995. They found that summer losses in learning averaged at least one month of grade equivalent learning per year. Of course, this summer learning loss will vary according to race and social class, family structure and functioning, and possibly gender.

Figure 5.1 displays results from a 1966 study by Hayes and Grether (1969). Among students at the beginning of the second grade there was an average grade equivalent difference of about one-half (.5) between high- and low-SES students. By the end of the sixth grade, however, the difference had increased to 2.5. But as Figure 5.1 clearly reveals, virtually all of the increased difference is due to "losses" in reading achievement that are experienced in the summer months by

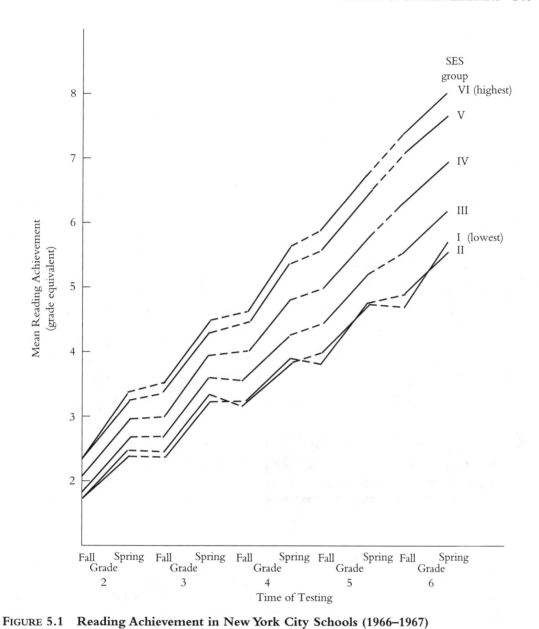

FIGURE 5.1   Reading Achievement in New York City Schools (1966–1967)

Source: Donald P. Hayes and Judith Grether, "The School Year and Vacations: When Do Students Learn?" (paper presented at the annual meeting of the Eastern Sociological Association, New York, 1969). Reprinted with permission.

low-SES students. During the school year, gains in reading achievement are approximately equal for each SES grouping, as evidenced by the parallel slopes during this time period. Heyns (1978) obtained similar results.

Entwisle and Alexander (1992) found a similar pattern of seasonal results among first and second grade students in a multivariate study where other confounding variables were controlled. These researchers used gain scores in mathematics as the outcome measure and compared gains that were made during the school year with the gains made during the summer over a two-year period. These results are shown in Table 5.2.

Consider the data controlling for family status. During the academic year, there is little difference in the average test score gains. During the summer period, however, students from single-parent

homes did not maintain their academic year growth. Without distinguishing between academic and summer gains and losses, it would appear that children from single-parent families do worse *in school* than children from two-parent families. The fact is, however, that children from single-parent families do worse only *in the summer*. Thus, these studies of summer learning strongly suggest that differences in cognitive development across racial/ethnic groups, class lines, and family structure are *not* the results of differential treatment in the schools.

In a later and more extensive study of these same students, Alexander and Entwisle (1995) report essentially the same results among the students covering the period from the beginning of school to the end of the sixth grade. In this report, the researchers used gain scores in both mathematics (CAT-M) and

TABLE 5.2

AVERAGE GAIN IN MATH TEST SCORES FOR STUDENTS WITH SELECTED CHARACTERISTICS BY SEASON AND RACIAL COMPOSITION OF SCHOOL: BALTIMORE CITY PUBLIC SCHOOLS, 1982–1984 (GRADES 1 AND 2)

Characteristic	Whites		African Americans	
	Academic Years (1982–83) (1983–84)	**Summer Years (1983) (1984)**	**Academic Years (1982–83) (1983–84)**	**Summer Years (1983) (1984)**
Family Status				
Father present	92.8	.5	90.3	−2.1
Father absent	95.7	−14.2	88.7	−10.3
Number of cases	209–229	193–224	255–313	237–266

Source: Adapted from Doris R. Entwisle and Karl L. Alexander, "Summer Setback: Race, Poverty, School Composition, and Mathematics Achievement in the First Two Years of School," *American Sociological Review 57* (1992): Table 2, p. 76.

TABLE 5.3

SCHOOL YEAR AND SUMMER CAT GAINS OVER THE ELEMENTARY SCHOOL YEARS BY SES LEVEL

SES Level	CAT-R			CAT-M		
	School Year Gain	Summer Gain	Total Gain	School Year Gain	Summer Gain	Total Gain
Low	193.3	.8	194.1	186.8	−7.9	178.9
High	190.9	46.5	237.4	186.3	24.9	211.2

Source: Adapted from Karl L. Alexander and Doris R. Entwisle, "Schools and Children at Risk," in *Family School Links: How Do They Affect Educational Outcomes?* eds. Allan Booth and Judith Dunn (Hillsdale, NJ: Laurence Erlbaum, 1995), Tables 1 and 2.

reading comprehension (CAT-R) as the outcome measures and compared gains that were made during the school year with the gains made during the summer over the full six-year period. These results are shown in Table 5.3 for both reading comprehension and mathematics.

Although average achievement rises for all students over time, inequality between students in the high- and low-SES groupings also increases over the six-year period. As Table 5.3 shows, however, this increasing gap between the low- and high-SES students does not occur as the result of learning during the school year. In fact, over the six-year period, the school year gains are virtually equal among the low- and high-SES students on both the mathematics (CAT-M) and reading comprehension (CAT-R) tests. Once again, we see that the gap is due entirely to "summer learning" or lack thereof. Looking at the total gains, we might incorrectly deduce that the inequalities of social class are "reproduced" in the school, when in fact, all of the social reproduction appears to result outside of the school.

In a cogent response to this study by Alexander and Entwisle, Gamoran (1995) raises certain key questions: Does schooling compensate for initial inequalities among students, or does it reinforce these inequalities? Or does it simply preserve though not magnify the differences that students bring with them to school? These questions, of course, are central to the sociology of education, as we have noted previously. At this point, we can directly confront the issue with data provided by Gamoran in his reworking of the Alexander and Entwisle (1995) data.

Gamoran plotted the gains in reading comprehension (CAT-R) that are implied by the separate gains observed during the school year and the summer. That is, he calculated the average monthly gain for the school year and the summer, and then plotted the twelve-month gain in each year based upon this school and home learning curve. Gamoran's analysis is depicted as Figure 5.2. The solid lines indicate the *actual gains* made over the course of elementary school for low- and high-SES students. The dotted lines

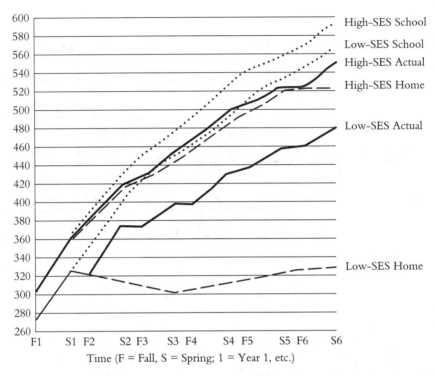

FIGURE 5.2   Compensatory Effects of Schooling on Reading Comprehension (CAT-R)

Source: Adapted from Adam Gamoran, "Effects of Schooling on Children and Families," in *Family-School Links: How Do They Affect Educational Outcomes?* eds. Allan Booth and Judith Dunn (Hillsdale, NJ: Laurence Erlbaum, 1995).

indicate *gains implied by schooling alone* (average monthly gains in school over a twelve-month period for six years). The dashed sequenced lines are the *gains implied by home* (six-year summer period) *alone*.

The actual average difference between high- and low-SES students is 68 points (third line from the top minus the fifth line from the top-right side of Figure 5.2). As noted previously in Table 5.3, 43 of the 68 points (237.4 minus 194.1) were the results of differential growth from the beginning of grade one through the end of grade six (there was a 25-point gap at the

outset). The two top lines (on the right side of Figure 5.2) show the difference that is implied if students remained in school for the full twelve months. This difference is about 23 points, or one-third less than the actual difference and exactly the amount of difference that existed at the beginning of school. The two remaining lines show the gap that is estimated by the summer learning curve. Here the difference is over 200 points. In the absence of school, therefore, the gap between the social classes increases dramatically. Clearly, school plays an important role in reducing the implied inequality that would result in the absence of schooling. On the other hand, as the top two lines suggest, schooling is unable to overcome and further reduce the inequalities that students bring with them in the first year of school.

In a more recent analysis using the same data, Alexander, Entwisle, and Olson (2001) show that the greatest high-SES gains and low-SES losses occur during the first two summers. You can actually see this in Figure 5.2 by examining the results for the actual low- and high-SES students during each summer.

It has been noted often that the benefits of a desegregated school context are greater for younger rather than older children (Schofield, 1989). Alexander, Entwisle, and Dauber (1994) have demonstrated that achievement outcomes in the first grade provide trajectories for children's later academic success and failure. Also, Jencks (1985) has argued that the potential for cognitive growth among younger children is much greater (perhaps ten times greater than it is for high school students). This suggests that research on children in early grades may be more important than in later grades.

Within this context, Entwisle and Alexander (1994) report the results of their research on the effects of racial integration among first and second grade children in Baltimore. During a two-year period, African American children in integrated schools made significantly greater achievement gains in reading comprehension. The results are shown in Table 5.4.

Entwistle and Alexander carefully controlled for the effects occurring during the formal school year from those effects occurring in the summer. Table 5.4

TABLE 5.4

AVERAGE GAIN IN READING COMPREHENSION SCORES (CAT) FOR AFRICAN-AMERICAN STUDENTS, BY SEASON AND RACIAL COMPOSITION OF THE SCHOOL: FIRST AND SECOND GRADE STUDENTS, 1982–1984

School Type	School Year 1982–83	Summer 1983	School Year 1983–84	Summer 1984	Total Two-Year Gain 1982–1984
Segregated	61.1	−13.4	54.1	−6.7	88.6
Integrated	48.3	14.2	35.2	4.3	104.3
Number of cases	(309)	(263)	(255)	(231)	(278)

Source: Adapted from Doris R. Entwisle and Karl L. Alexander, "Winter Setback: The Racial Composition of Schools and Learning to Read," *American Sociological Review* 59 (1994): Table 1.

Note: Multivariate repeated measures analyses of these results found that the differences between segregated and integrated schools was significant at $p < .05$ in each column. Note that the total two-year gain (1982–1984) is not simply the sum of the four separate seasons because a separate analysis was conducted for each season—that is, each seasonal analysis was based on a slightly different sample size.

depicts this seasonal breakdown of learning on the reading comprehension test for African American children. A close examination reveals an interesting interaction effect. Students in segregated schools learn significantly more than students in integrated schools while school is in session, *and* students who attend integrated schools learn significantly more than students in segregated schools during the summer (when the racial composition of the schools should not even matter). These effects hold even after a set of SES background controls have been added.

In a parallel analysis for mathematics achievement, Entwisle and Alexander (1992) found similar although insignificant results for African Americans—a total difference favoring students in integrated schools, a summer difference favoring students attending integrated schools, but no difference at all during the school year. Thus, considering both studies, the effects during the school year either are null or they favor segregated schools, and the summer effects (favoring students attending integrated schools) are what makes it appear as if integrated schools work. In fact, it appears that they work only when they are not in session!

The results suggest that the small positive effects of integrated schools for African Americans may be entirely spurious. Contrary to the conventional logic, these students may do better academically in segregated schools.[3] Entwisle and Alexander theorize that the acquisition of reading skills may be more difficult and inefficient in desegregated schools because language backgrounds differ. Another possibility, of course, is that the social climate in integrated schools is less hospitable to African American children. In any event, these results add to a growing sense of frustration and disappointment for educators, parents, and students alike regarding the promise of integrated schools. And more importantly, the results point up the importance of summer learning studies in disentangling the effectiveness of schools from the effects of the home.

These data seem to confirm the view that SES and racial differences between homes are strongly related to achievement differences that accrue to students over the course of their educational careers. The "summer learning" studies, in particular, suggest that schools seem to maintain whatever initial differences students bring with them from home. They are unable to overcome the disadvantages of birth, but they do not make matters worse. This suggests, contrary to other studies, that "social reproduction" is not an active process in the schools. Considering the potential effects of SES and race, the fact that school is able to free achievement from these influences is impressive.

Of course, other studies noted above, and others to be considered later, argue otherwise. Rist (1970), for example, found that inequalities are exacerbated by the school in the form of curriculum allocations as early as first grade. Rosenbaum (1976), Oakes (1985), and Pallas et al. (1994) report similar findings, pointing to the process by which nonwhites and low-SES students are more likely to be placed in low-ability groups (tracks) and that the permanence of these track placements exacerbates social reproduction within the school.

---

[3] Entwisle and Alexander found that the racial mix of the schools made little if any difference among white students, confirming previous findings since the Coleman Report.

❖ ADVANCES IN THE STUDY OF SCHOOL EFFECTS: FROM ECONOMIC PRODUCTION FUNCTIONS TO MULTILEVEL NESTED LAYER MODELING

Early studies of school effects employed what is referred to as an economic production function model. For example, Coleman et al. (1966) examined the extent to which student academic outcomes were a function of economic inputs such as expenditures, facilities, teacher credentials and so forth. This is often referred to as an input-output model.

> In this model, the school is an unopened black box. What goes on inside the school—the production process—is not observed. If the production process were straightforward and predictable, the input-output production function would be a sensible way to study the impact of school resources. Yet, the process of teaching and learning is complex and not fully routinized. (Gamoran et al., 2000: 38–39)

In our review of studies using this model, we have noted that the relationship between resources and outcomes is small and inconsistent. Over the course of time, researchers have realized the importance of opening up the black box to see how the resources are distributed. In effect, we now see that learning more about the effective use of resources is more important than simply looking at how average school resources influence average student outcomes. For example, school administrators might make decisions about the type of curriculum and the amount of allocated (mandated) minutes and this then allows teachers in the classroom to implement the material and promote learning. These are two separate actions—allocation of time and presentation of the curriculum. Each can be accomplished effectively or ineffectively (see Gamoran and Dreeban, 1986; Monk, 1992 for empirical illustrations). For example, Doyle (1992: 488) reviewed studies of the relationship of curricular allocation and concluded that "curriculum is a weak force for regulating teaching." In the United States, teachers vary widely on how they implement topics that are established in a formal curriculum and in the time spent on these topics and in the process of assessment. This may differ in countries other than the United States where the ideas of a centralized curriculum are more established (see Chapter 6 for further discussion of this).

Studies of school effects involve different levels of analysis "hierarchically nested" in layers of influence. Students are grouped in classrooms: We have variables describing the characteristics of students and variables describing the characteristics of classes. Some of the classroom variables may be aggregated student variables such as average socioeconomic status, but the classroom variables will also include characteristics of the teacher or the class *per se*, such as its subject matter or curriculum level. The classroom is part of the collection of classrooms within a school; the school is part of a district; the district is part of a state or region.

Within this complex system, several problems arise. We have noted earlier that the socioeconomic and racial context of schools are thought to influence achievement. The SES context of a school represents one of these multiple layers of influence. To create a contextual variable, individual student characteristics are combined (averaged) and this group variable is compared with the independent influence of the individual characteristics (see again Figures 4.3 and 4.4). The problem with this approach is that all students in the school get the same score on the contextual variable (school average). This produces a technical violation of the assumption of independence of observations, which is central to classical statistical techniques. In this case, each student's school-level variable is not independent but rather dependent upon school assignment or choice.

A second problem here is that relationships that are estimated from aggregated data have enhanced correlations. This occurs because much of the variation that occurs within units (classrooms or schools) is removed by aggregation. Consider that a group-level variable such as per pupil expenditures (PPE) has exactly the same effect on each student in the school; for example, students in a school with a PPE of $3,000 might have an average score of 40 while students in a school with a PPE of $5,000 might have an average score of 50. Among other things, the variability of the scores between schools is greatly constrained in contrast to the variability of the scores within a given school (which might range anywhere from 1 to 100). The school-level correlations to achievement will be higher than those estimated at the individual level. Robinson (1950) reported this "ecological fallacy" in a classic paper on the relationship of race and IQ.

A third problem is that the study of between school effects assumes that the influence of individual-level variables such as SES is the same across all the schools. In a single-level analysis of between school differences, the effect of home SES is assumed to be the same across all schools in the sample, and likewise, the effect of school type is assumed to be the same for students of all social class levels. Of course, this is simply not the case, as we have noted often in Chapters 1 and 4 where the effects of Catholic schools are greater among minority and disadvantaged students. (It is possible to minimize this problem at the simplest level by estimating the effects of SES for each school type, and the effects of school for each SES type, as shown in Table 1.2 of Chapter 1.) Beyond these simple three- and four-variable models, however, the use of aggregated school-level variables forces researchers to assume that all individuals within a school (or a classroom) are identically affected by school- (or classroom-) level variables. The fact is that the relationships between student, school, and classroom characteristics *and* student outcomes vary across schools. Even material resources at the school level are usually applied differentially to students (some students use more PPE than do others; see Madaus, Airasian, and Kellaghan, 1980).

What all of this amounts to is that studies in the tradition of the Coleman Report are attempting to measure the effects of schools without actually having measures of how the schools influence individuals within schools and classrooms. What is left out is the *process* that occurs within schools and classrooms (Barr and Dreeben, 1983; Bidwell and Kasarda, 1980; Burstein, 1980; Heyns, 1986; Gamoran et al., 2000). According to Murchan and Sloane (1994: 252), "[O]nly by documenting the process by which school-level resources are applied at the individual level could the process by which schools affect individuals possibly be measured and modeled."

In an attempt to overcome many of these problems, a new statistical technique called hierarchical linear modeling (HLM) has been developed (Bryk and Raudenbush, 1992). HLM involves a two-stage process of estimating the effects of schools. First, the influence of an individual-level variable on an outcome is estimated within each group (school). For example, the relationship of SES to achievement is examined within each school type (Catholic or public) to determine if the relationship is the same or if it differs, on average. These are referred to as random effects, treating each school as a random variable. Diagnostic tests then show the extent to which the effect of the student level variable varies across the schools. If there was no variation one could then proceed with a pooled or fixed effect analysis, which is how it was done in the Coleman Report. Assuming that the student-level effects do differ across or between schools, then the influence of the school-level variable on the within school individual-level effect is estimated. (An earlier version of the technique was first proposed by Burstein, 1980.) The procedure allows a clean separation of individual- and school-level effects, the determination of the between and within school variation on the outcome variable, and perhaps most importantly, the influence of the school-level variable on the individual-level effects. For example, we can see that in Catholic schools the influence of SES is smaller (the slope is flatter) than it is in public schools as we have noted on several occasions earlier in the book. As we discussed in Chapters 1 and 4, this allows the social organization of Catholic schools to increase the achievement of low-SES students.

The nested layer approach appears to have overcome some of the problems contained in the production function model. It allows us to estimate the effect of an individual variable such as SES within each school. This provides a more precise understanding of the process and the effect operating in each school. Technically, HLM overcomes the problem of violating the statistical independence assumption that occurs with the use of aggregated school-level data, since the estimates of student effects (level 1) are done within each individual school. In this process, the correct standard errors are obtained. Finally, in computing the within school (level 1) estimates, HLM weights down the estimates in schools with fewer cases because they would be less precise (see Bryk and Raudenbush, 1992).

❖ SCHOOLS AS LOOSELY COUPLED ORGANIZATIONS[4]

An entirely different response to the Coleman Report has been the development of an alternative model called "loose coupling" (Weick, 1976; Meyer and Rowen, 1977). While multilevel modeling has tried to reveal the complexity of the input-output model by identifying the connections between school resources, teaching practices, and student learning, loose coupling theory points out that these connections of school organization are actually loosely coupled and for this reason the input-output model is flawed. In a loosely coupled organization,

[4] In the following two sections, I draw heavily on a paper by Gamoran, Secada, and Marrett (2000).

decisions and rules that are made in one section of the system do not link easily and automatically to other sections of the organization. The inherent nature of schools and school systems and the entire training of teachers is such that decisions made at headquarters (the office of the superintendent or the Department of Education or by the principal) may have only little or even no effect on what actually transpires in the classroom. Classrooms are notoriously isolated work areas and teachers have relative autonomy over their classroom, and teaching practices are largely a result of teacher training and on-the-job socialization (often influenced by the powerful constraints of teacher unions).

Bearing this in mind, teaching practices are not likely to be strongly affected by certain school resources or policies, or administrative decisions at any level (Weick, 1982). Likewise, principals also operate in relative isolation. Although reform efforts have attempted to change some of this, the loosely coupled mode of social organization remains the norm. Metz (1989) provided empirical support for the loose coupling theory in a study of eight high schools. She noted that although the schools are tightly coupled symbolically in terms of adopting the same set of structures and routines such as time allocations, grading and evaluation policies, schedules, and the organization of grade levels, the actual experiences of teachers and students differed among both the school and the classroom (see also, Rowen and Miskel, 1999).

The loose coupling model provides a useful and fairly simple explanation for the inconsistent results obtained in the input-output model. Schools may look the same symbolically, especially when measured superficially such as in per pupil expenditures or number of books in the library or average teacher credentials. But what goes on in the classroom may be quite different. This is consistent with the findings that the little variability between schools and school variability is not related to variation in student outcomes (once again the Coleman Report and all subsequent studies). But there is substantial variability in classroom and teaching practices and student outcomes within schools (this is the focus of the next chapter). Loose coupling also explains why policy interventions at the federal, state, or local level often fail to reach the classroom. The problem with the loose coupling perspective, however, is the difficulty of operationalizing it into empirical, especially quantitative research. We can assert that the organization is loosely coupled, but can we find definitive support for the theory?

❖ BEYOND NESTED LAYERS: LOOSE COUPLING AND PRODUCTION FUNCTION MODELS

How then are we to conceptualize the processes whereby school structures and policies, teaching and classroom practices, curricula, and student outcomes are related? Fundamentally, the crux of the issue is the limitations of a one-way model between school resources via organizations and instructional practices and outcomes. Building on the loose coupling model, Gamoran, Secada, and Marrett (2000) have proposed a multidimensional model of the relationship of school organization and student learning

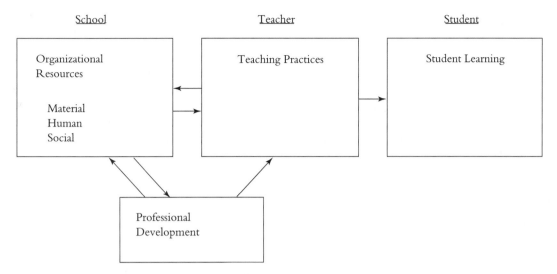

FIGURE 5.3   A Dynamic, Multidirectional Model of School Organization and Student Learning.

Source: Adam Gamoran, Walter G. Secada, and Cora B. Marrett. "The Organizational Context of Teaching and Learning," in Maureen T. Hallinan (ed.) *Handbook of the Sociology of Education.* New York: Kluwer Academic/Plenum Publishers, 2000, p. 46. Reprinted with permission.

(see Figure 5.3). They note first the importance of recognizing that the complexity of teaching requires a model that allows the connection between school organization, teaching practice, and learning to move in both directions, as depicted in the Figure 5.3. Second, they draw upon the research that clearly demonstrates the need for two-way paths in these relationships.

For example, Cohen et al. (1979) provide evidence from a sound longitudinal study showing that more complex teaching practices lead to more complex collaborative arrangements (classroom structures) to meet the new kind of instruction. The study is well summarized by Hall (1972: 163): "there is a strong tendency for organizations to become more complex as their own activi-ties and the environment around them become more complex." The study confirmed that, indeed, an increase in the complexity of instructional practice increased communication and team teaching among teachers, but that team teaching per se did not bring about more complex teaching.

A second study by Peterson, Mc-Carthy, and Elmore (1996) confirms the importance of professional development (teacher learning) to teaching practice (see this path in Figure 5.3). Using an in-depth set of case studies of three schools, these researchers reported that school structure (organizational resources) had little influence on teacher practice. Instead, instructional practices changed in response to teacher learning via professional development. The researchers concluded:

> Changing practice is primarily a problem of [teacher] learning, not a problem of organization. . . . School structures can provide opportunities for the learning of new teaching practices and new strategies for student learning, but structures, by themselves, do not cause [teacher] learning to occur. . . . School structures follow from good practice not vice versa.

Despite the value of applying loose coupling theory to our understanding of how schools work, Gamoran and his colleagues have concluded (2000: 46–47) that the

> Organizational context of teaching and learning . . . is more closely related to the nested layers model than to loose coupling. As in the nested layers view, and in contrast to loose coupling, we argue that student learning responds to instruction. This notion derives from research that documents the impact of variation in teaching on student learning, ranging from course-taking effects . . . to content coverage . . . to instructional coherence and teacher-student interaction. . . . Also, consistent with the nested layers view, we expect that organizational resources affect student learning, but only as they are applied by teachers in classrooms . . . resources matter for learning when teachers apply resources in their classroom teaching. However, our model moves beyond the nested layers view in that we recognize that school conditions and classroom teaching may work in both directions and may shift over time. School conditions may respond to teaching practices, and teaching practices may be constrained or encouraged by their organizational context, as causal effects flow in both directions. At the same time, our model draws from loose coupling the notion that teaching practices are influence by professional socialization and training.

Contrary to the typical jaundiced and skeptical view that most people, including teachers, have of professional development, Gamoran and his colleagues see professional development as a key mechanism for improving teaching and subsequently improving student learning. To do this, the process must be sustained, coherent, collaborative, and reflective. Done correctly, professional development can increase the human and social resources of a school. Moreover, when successful, it can increase material resources as well since principals react positively with supplies, equipment, and space when new teaching practices are sustained and collaborative (Dahl, 1997).

Finally, we should note that the model offered by Gamoran, Secada, and Marrett assumes that professional development would lead to something other than conventional teaching where isolation, recitation, lectures, and seatwork are the norms. The relationship between professional development and school organization and teaching practice are irrelevant in a scenario of conventional teaching.

❖ THE EFFECTS OF SCHOOL SIZE

Until recently, both theory and research on the effects of school size had been inconsistent (Boocock, 1980). Some studies have reported that students in small schools were more likely to participate in school activities (Barker and Gump, 1964; Morgan and Alwin, 1980; Lindsay, 1982, 1984). These studies infer that participation means involvement, which implies commitment and possibly higher achievement. By contrast, in their survey of 571 exemplary secondary schools in the United States, Wilson and Corcoran (1988: 47) discovered that these recognized effective schools had "larger enrollments than secondary schools in the nation as a whole." Likewise, Conant (1967) concluded in favor of large schools on the basis that they were better able to offer advanced placement and a wider variety of foreign language classes. In elementary schools, Fowler (1992) reported that the evidence in favor of small schools is entirely consistent.

The size of secondary schools has increased steadily since at least 1930. Guthrie (1979) reports that the average size of secondary schools in 1930 was about 100 and had increased to 550 by 1972. By 1987, the size of the average urban public high school was 1,097 students, while suburban schools averaged 1,027, and rural small city high schools averaged 543 students (National Center for Education Statistics, 1992). Thus, consolidation of schools has produced larger and larger schools at the secondary level.

The research on the effects of school size at the secondary level has been somewhat inconsistent. Part of this inconsistency is due to the fact that some studies have taken the variety of curricula offerings as an educational outcome measure. The availability of a larger variety of course offerings is not the appropriate measure to determine the educational benefits of school size. Moreover, it turns out that the advanced and alternative courses that are available in larger schools enroll only a small minority of students (Monk, 1987; Haller et al., 1990).

Fowler (1992) conducted an exhaustive review of the effects of secondary school size and four indicators of student outcomes. As secondary school size decreases, Fowler drew the following conclusions:

1. Students were more satisfied with school, more obligated and responsible, reported higher attendance, lower dropout rates, less frequent use of drugs and alcohol, and were less lonely.

2. The cognitive achievement, educational aspirations, and educational attainment of students was increased, especially among minority students and in rural schools; this is the least robust finding, there being several discordant studies.

3. There is greater student participation in a greater number and variety of curricula and extracurricular activities, especially for low-ability and low-SES students.

4. There are longer-term positive effects along the lines of continued educational achievement, participation, and community leadership.

Most people interpret these results in favor of small schools as being due to the fact that small schools are easier to control and manage. They are more personal and less anonymous, more likely to be homogeneous in student body representation, and better able to remain flexible to meet individual student and faculty needs. Some might argue that the effect is spurious since smaller schools are generally located in affluent communities, which may mean that the positive outcomes are due to the SES of the school (contextual effect) rather than to school size per se. Fowler and Walberg (1991), however, demonstrate that the effect of school size remains even after a number of other school and community characteristics have been controlled. They reported this in their study of 293 public secondary schools:

> District socioeconomic status and the percentage of students from low income families were the most influential and consistent factors related to outcomes. School size was the next most consistent and was negatively related to outcomes. (p. 189)

Some researchers argue that the most important benefit of small schools is that they are better able to counteract the influence of youth culture norms and deviant behavior in the schools. John Goodlad (1984) makes the point that the most effective schools are relatively small in *A Place Called School*, a study of thirty-eight schools. He notes that other studies support this conclusion across a variety of academic outcome areas, and that "it appears to be more difficult in small schools for the more extreme peer group values to take hold." McDill, Natriello, and Pallas (1986: 125) echo these sentiments by making the following claim:

> Of all the alterable characteristics of schools . . . school size is the one most emphasized. Researchers and practitioners are practically unanimous in asserting its importance. . . . Small schools of 300–400 students with a low student-adult ratio are viewed as having fewer disorders, higher achievement, higher rates of student participation in extracurricular activities, and feelings of satisfaction with school life.

These findings are not at all surprising since size is conceptualized as a basic structural feature of social groups and has been viewed "as the most important condition affecting the structure of organizations" (Blau and Shoenherr, 1971: 57). These results on school size are fully consistent with theory and research on organizational effects generally. Gooding

and Wagner (1985) examined ninety-five relations of size and outcomes in thirty-one field studies of schools, school districts, colleges, work groups, and manufacturing and service firms. The outcomes included academic achievement, employee output, and profitability. Productivity was inversely related to size—simply put, large organizations and large subunits of organizations are less efficient at generating high-quality outcomes.

Why are larger organizations so ineffective? Walberg and Walberg (1994: 20) summarize several theoretical explanations:

> In the language of organization theory, "coordination costs" among departments and administrative levels divert money, time, and attention away from avowed purposes. "Informational problems" prevent governing boards and chief executives from getting full information from subordinates several levels beneath them. "Bureaucracies" favor standard operating procedures over more productive and client satisfying innovations . . . "Agency problems" allow staff to work for their own (possibly self-interested) purposes. "Free riders" reap benefits of staff membership while evading costs of full effort. "Rent seekers" try to impose costs for unneeded or unperformed services, thereby reducing value in relation to consumer or public costs.

In a four-year study of school size in New York City, Stiefel, Berne, Iatarola, and Fruchter (2000) found that the cost to the city per graduate was equal in small and large academic high schools. Vocational schools and "last resort transfer" schools have the highest budgets per student regardless of size.

Despite all the empirical evidence and the theory confirming the beneficial effects of small schools, educators have been pursuing policies of school consolidation over the past half century. Coterminous with the increase in school size, Walberg and Walberg (1994) show that there has been a steady increase in the size of school districts and a corresponding increase in the percentage of total school costs that are paid by states, and that both of these variables, like school size, are negatively related to higher academic achievement. In view of these findings, a wide dissemination of the detrimental effects of large schools to educational policy makers seems in order.

Recently, many large schools have adopted the recommendations of the Carnegie Foundation (National Association of Secondary School Principals, 1996) in creating "schools-within-schools or houses" but there is little research that actually supports this strategy (for some research, see Fine, 1994). As a result of their study, Lee, Bryk, and Smith (1993: 189) cautioned that school size be "seen with a balance eyed. Schools should be neither too large to inhibit a strong sense of community nor too small to offer a full curriculum and adequate instructional facilities."

Lee and her associates (1993, 1997, 2000) have conducted several studies employing multilevel modeling, which we reviewed above. These studies are an excellent example of the need to use multilevel modeling. The size of a school is a school-level measure in contrast to student outcomes, which are measured at the individual level. Lee (2000) notes that school size clearly influences outcomes (high schools should be smaller than they are), but the mechanism by which school size influences student outcomes is unclear, and there are some surprising specifications. As shown in Figure 5.4, Lee (2000: 336)

reports that "students learn more... in medium sized high schools of 600–900 students compared to smaller and especially to larger schools." Moreover, and consistent with Fowler's (1992) review noted above, Lee finds (2000: 336) that "the effects of school size on learning were strongest in schools enrolling more students from lower SES families and more minority students." Her studies suggest that school size influences student outcomes both directly and indirectly through teachers' attitudes about their students (willingness to take responsibility for student learning).

In a recent study, Lee and Loeb (2000) conducted a multilevel study on the effects of school size in the public elementary schools of Chicago in the years 1996–1997. They examined nearly the entire population of students (22,599), teachers (4,495), and schools (264) in the sixth and eighth grades. Having already demonstrated that school size does influence student performance, this study was designed to specifically explore the mechanism (explanation) for how school size actually works. They hypothesized that size influenced teacher attitudes and specifically that teachers in small schools would be more willing to take responsibility for learning than those in either medium or larger size schools. The notion of the measure is that in a given school, teachers will vary in the degree to which they see student progress as mostly their responsibility, as opposed to a school where some teachers might tend to see student performance (or lack of it) as due to student motivation or family background. The choice of this concept of collective responsibility has received considerable attention in the school reform and restructuring movement (see Firestone and Herriot, 1982; Firestone

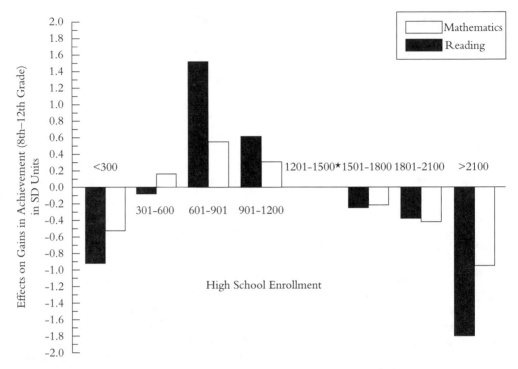

*1201–1500 students was used as the comparison group; thus by definition effect sizes are zero.

FIGURE 5.4   **Effects of High School Size on Achievement Gains in Mathematics and Reading.**

Source: Valerie E. Lee and Julia B. Smith, 1997. "High School Size: Which Works Best, and for Whom?" *Educational Evaluation and Policy Analysis 19:* 212. Copyright 1997 by the American Educational Research Association. Reprinted with permission.

and Wilson, 1985; Lieberman, 1992; Louis, Marks, and Kruse, 1996; Rowan, 1990) and is also closely linked to research demonstrating that high teacher expectations strongly influence student outcomes (see Rosenthal and Jacobson, 1968; Cooper and Tom, 1984; Firestone and Rosenblum, 1988). The underlying assumption is that teacher collaboration and cooperation and positive expectations for students are essential to influence student performance.

They employed a unique measure of teacher attitudes toward "collective responsibility" for student's learning (see Bilcer, 1997). To appreciate the meaning of this construct, the actual questions to teachers are shown below:

How many teachers in this school:
1. feel responsible when students in the school fail?
2. feel responsible to help each other do their best?
3. help maintain discipline in the entire school, not just their classroom?
4. take responsibility for improving the school?
5. feel responsible for helping students develop self-control?
6. set high standards for themselves?
7. feel responsible for all students to learn?

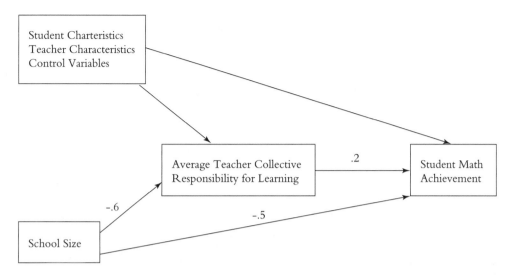

FIGURE 5.5   Empirical Model Relating School Size, Collective Responsibility, and Student Achievement in the Chicago Public Schools

Source: Adapted from Valerie E. Lee and Susanna Loeb. 2000. "School Size in Chicago Elementary Schools: Effects on Teachers' Attitudes and Students' Achievement." *American Educational Research Journal* 37: 3–31.

Note: Lee and Loeb actually computed two indirect effects: one for small versus medium schools (−.10) and one for small versus large schools (−.14). My coefficients are approximated from these results.

Lee and Loeb aggregated the teachers' responses on the above questions to the school level to obtain a school-level measure of "collective responsibility for learning" so that each school was assigned a value on this variable, just as it had a value for size.[5]

In their analysis, Lee and Loeb controlled for a large number of student-level variables (SES, race, previous test score), teacher variables (teaching experience, race, sex), background characteristics, and several school-level variables (percent minority and low income) as shown

in Figure 5.5. The focus, however, was on the relationships of school size, collective responsibility, and student achievement (mathematics). The results are presented as effect sizes, which make it possible for us to compare to other studies more easily. School size has large effect size influences on both collective responsibility of teachers (aggregated at the school level) and directly on student achievement. Collective responsibility has a small but significant effect on student achievement. All of this, of course, while controlling for all the other variables in

[5] Lee and Loeb actually employed this variable at both the teacher and the school level, but Figure 5.5 shows only the school level (aggregated collective responsibility) for simplicity. Also, Lee and Loeb broke school size down into

three categories (small, medium, and large), which produced two effects of school size for each dependent variable whereas I have shown only the average effect again for simplicity, and without any distortion of the results.

the model. Teachers' collective responsibility increases dramatically in smaller schools and has a positive influence on student performance. The indirect (explanatory) effect is $(-.6)(.2)$ or $-.12$ which turns out to be about 20 percent of the overall total effect $(-.62)$ of school size on student achievement. Note that a large direct effect of school size on achievement $(-.5)$ remains unexplained. What other factors can you identify that could serve as an explanatory mechanism? What other outcomes might be favorably affected by smaller school size besides academic achievement?

It should be noted that this study of elementary schools by Lee and Loeb does slightly contradict earlier findings on a different data set by Lee and Smith (1997) where they found that medium size high schools were more effective than either smaller or larger schools (see Figure 5.4), but there is certainly consistency in that smaller schools in general are clearly better than larger schools, across both studies. Although not a focus of their study, Lee and Loeb did discover that collective responsibility was negatively related to teaching experience—that is, more experience is actually negatively related to collective responsibility. Lee and Smith (1997) caution that the results of their study showing that high schools can be too small should constrain educational policy makers from moving ahead blindly to create small schools. Unfortunately, educational policy is impatient and does not wait for further research but rather responds to trends, as demonstrated in New York City with an effort to open forty-six experimental small high schools in the range of 110–660 student range (see Dillon and Berger, 1995; Gonzales, 1995).

But the issue of school size is not quite as simple as the studies might imply. Ingersoll (1999, 2001b) has found that small schools (both public and private) suffer from greater staffing problems, including more teacher turnover and more underqualified teachers. Ingersoll argues that these factors are likely to decrease student achievement (see Chapter 6 for a detailed discussion of Ingersoll's research). In addition, a survey by the Public Agenda (2001) found that teachers and parents held both positive and negative attitudes toward small schools. On the one hand, they found that parents and teachers thought it was easier to "spot troubled students" and easier to "tailor instruction to individual needs." But on the other hand, teachers and parents indicated that small schools would have "less money for things like labs, elective courses, and school equipment" and that it would be "tougher for a student to switch out of a class if they were having a hard time with a teacher."

❖ THE EFFECTS OF CLASS SIZE

Class size is both a between and within school variable. More commonly, however, it is considered a between school or between system variable. The size of classes in a school or in a community is relatively uniform, largely resulting from contractual agreements between teacher unions and school boards. Similarly, the average class size in a national school system is relatively uniform. There may be differences across various sectors (public, religious, private) within each country. Of course, there will be some variation within schools, especially with regard to different types of classes. Handicapped and special education classes are normally smaller than regular classes. In any event, most of the research on this topic has compared differences in class size between schools or systems.

We have noted previously that class size is a basic component of instructional expenditures and that "there is no strong or systematic relationship between school expenditures and student performance" (Hanushek, 1989: 47). In his review, Hanushek examined 152 "qualified studies" of class size and found an equal number of studies reporting positive and negative outcomes. Nonetheless, educators and researchers have been reluctant (almost recalcitrant) to forsake the hypothesis that small classes are related to higher student achievement. Greenwald, Hedges, and Laine (1996), for example, conducted their own meta-analysis and concluded that the magnitude of the effect sizes for small classes is at least moderate.

In 1988, Tommy Tomlinson was asked by the U.S. Department of Education to re-view the empirical evidence on class size and student achievement and its history. The following discussion draws heavily on his report. There are three comparable, although different, indicators of class size: (1) number of students per teacher or student-teacher ratio, (2) number of students per class, and (3) number of students taught per teacher per day. Although each of these measures represents a somewhat different view of the same event, we will use the term "class size" as a general descriptor for all three. In fact, the total number of students taught per day is perhaps the most accurate measure, since classes in urban schools with high teacher-pupil ratios are probably smaller than those ratios due to lower attendance rates.

Figure 5.6 shows clearly that pupil-teacher ratios have been decreasing—

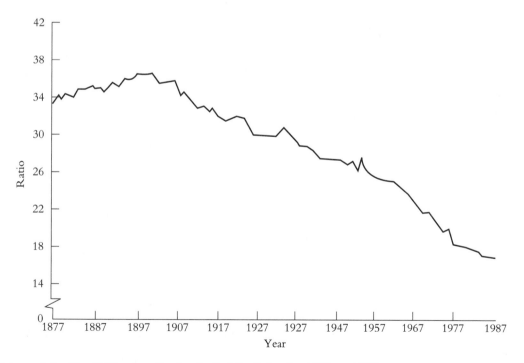

FIGURE 5.6   Pupil–Teacher Ratios in Public Schools: 1877 to 1987

Source: Tommy M. Tomlinson, *Class Size and Public Policy* (Washington: U.S. Department of Education, 1988). See Tomlinson for specific statistical references used in the figure.

from a peak of about 37 at the turn of the century to about 18 in 1987. In contrast, pupils per class is invariably higher and widely held to be the more valid measure of actual class size. Figure 5.7 indicates that average class size in public elementary schools has dropped from about thirty in 1960 to twenty-five in 1985; for public secondary schools, the figures are about twenty-seven in 1960 and twenty-two in 1985. Needless to say, reductions in class size have been due in large part to the demands of teachers in contract negotiations as they have sought to reduce their workload. This effort has been supported by the National Education Association, which adopted a position advocating an optimal class size of 15 as early as 1969 (National Education Association Resolution, 1986). During the past decade in the context of widespread school reform, numerous states have developed legislative packages designed to reduce class size at substantial costs to the taxpaying public. Interestingly, "the Mississippi legislature has recommended allowing class sizes to increase as a means of saving money" (Tomlinson, 1988: 4).

What is the best available evidence of class size effects on student achievement?

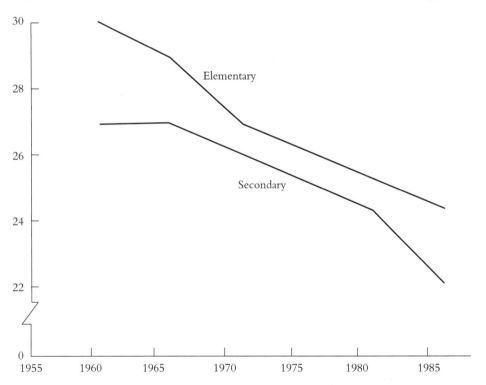

FIGURE 5.7 **Median Class Size in Public Elementary and Secondary Schools: 1961–1986**

Note: "Year" denotes spring of school year.

Source: National Education Association, *Status of the Public American School Teacher, 1985–1986* (Washington: National Education Association, 1987).

What is the basis for the NEA recommendation of a class size of fifteen students? The most often cited research on this matter was conducted by Gene Glass and Mary Lee Smith (1978, 1979). Glass and Smith used a technique called "meta-analysis" that closely examines many studies simultaneously. They reviewed over eighty studies that had been reported since 1900, but decided to limit their main analysis to the fourteen "best" studies that were available after 1950. The effects of class size in these fourteen studies are displayed in Figure 5.8. Several features of the resulting curve stand out. First, for class sizes in the range of twenty to forty students, the effects are minimal. Second, significant improvement in student achievement does not occur until class sizes are in the range of fifteen students or below.

Problems have subsequently emerged with regard to these findings. First, there has been strong criticism of the study. Some critics have argued that the results of class size are greatly exaggerated since the impact of many key variables was overlooked in most of the fourteen "best" studies used by Glass and Smith. Second, Slavin (1989) makes the disquieting note that among the fourteen best studies, the one having the highest class size effect was a study of tennis, with "achievement" being measured by the number of times a tennis ball was hit into a wall in thirty seconds. Slavin conducted his own "meta-analysis" using only eight studies meeting his criteria and concluded that

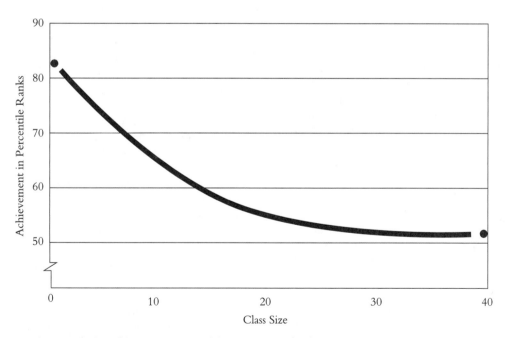

FIGURE 5.8 **Relationship Between Achievement and Class Size**

Source: Gene V. Glass and Mary Lee Smith, *Meta-Analysis of Research on the Relationship of Class Size and Achievement* (San Francisco: Far West Laboratory of Educational Research and Development, 1978).

"substantial reductions in class size (from about twenty-seven to sixteen) do generally have a positive effect upon student achievement, but the effects tend to be small" (p. 251). Critics have also argued that most class size studies lack both external validity (small experiments may not generalize to other settings) and internal validity (it is difficult to know in survey studies whether students are assigned to small classes because their achievement is low or if small classes cause achievement to vary).

More recently, however, a large-scale experiment that confirms the Glass and Smith (1979) meta-analysis has been conducted in Tennessee. This statewide experiment reports significant benefits to kindergarten students who were randomly assigned to one of three treatment groups: (1) classes of 13 to 17 pupils (small); (2) classes of 22 to 25 pupils with one teacher; and (3) classes of 22 to 25 pupils with one teacher and one full-time aide. The sample contained 128 small classes, 101 regular classes, and 99 regular classes with teacher aides. In all, 6,400 students participated in the study (Finn and Achilles, 1990; there are some discrepancies on these numbers due to attrition, see Nye, Hedges, and Konstantopoulos, 2000). The assignment to each class was random within each school, ensuring that any effect would be due to class size. Students remained in these same size classes for four years, and students in the small classes outperformed pupils in the other two types of classes on every outcome measure (see discussion of this study in Chapter 2 for further details on procedural variations). Finn and Achilles offered this summary:

> The results are definitive: (a) a significant benefit accrues to students in

reduced-size classes in both subject (reading and mathematics) areas and (b) there is evidence that minority students in particular benefit from the smaller class environment, especially when curriculum-based tests are used as the learning criteria.

Thus, the results are unequivocal in this Tennessee study. Class size effects occur only when class size is reduced to about fifteen students. Yet, the results are significant, long-term, and of greatest benefit to disadvantaged and minority students. Moreover, follow-up studies have now determined that the positive effects of the smaller classes are actually sustained even when students were moved to larger classrooms in later schools years (see Nye et al., 1994; Mosteller, 1995). Mosteller emphasizes the integrity of the research design and the validity of the findings. In his analysis, he found that the long-term enduring effects (over a nine-year period) of small class size for minorities are about double the effects for whites (which are also significant and substantial).

Finally, researchers have subjected the Tennessee data to a multilevel complex analysis, which adjusts for issues pertaining to the fidelity of implementation (variation in the actual size of the class within a treatment condition), attrition of students from the study, switching of students from one treatment group to another, level 1 student controls and level 2 school controls.[6] Despite these cautions,

---

[6] Hoxby (2000) cautions that field experiments may suffer from other sources of internal invalidity. Specifically, (1) participants (parents, teachers, and policy makers) may become aware of the experiment and not wish it to fail since that would jeopardize its broader

(continued)

Nye, Hedges, and Konstantopoulos (2000, 2001) have concluded:

> These results demonstrate that, across all schools . . . the average effect of small classes is significant and positive in both mathematics and reading at every grade level, ranging from .15 to .30 SD units. . . . At every grade, the effects of small classes are greater for more years spent in small classes (2000: 143, 146). . . . Class size effects persisted for at least 6 years and remained large enough to be important for educational policy . . . small classes in early grades have lasting benefits and those benefits are greater for minority students than for white students (2001: 245).

In view of this, the question of using class size as a mode of school reform must be evaluated in terms of the costs of implementing class size reduction from the current average nationwide of about twenty-three to fifteen. Tomlinson (1988: 11) concludes as follows:

> The immense costs make classes smaller than 15 utterly out of the question. In 1986, for example, a reduction of the national average for regularly convened classes from 24 to 23 pupils would have required almost 73,000 more teachers and 5 billion additional dollars, not

---

implementation, thereby altering the incentives; (2) some individuals (students and parents) will temporarily increase their productivity when they know they are being evaluated—a phenomenon widely known as the "Hawthorne Effect"; some individuals will try to alter the randomness of the experiment which happened in this case when some parents complained that their children were being denied the opportunity to be in the smaller classes and some adjustments were made.

counting the expenses of building more classrooms. Reducing the average class to 20 students would require over 335,000 more teachers at an added $22.8 billion. At 15 students, 1 million extra classroom teachers would be needed and added costs close to $69 billion.

Thus, costs alone seem to make the optimal class size of fifteen impracticable. In contrast, the cost associated with operating smaller schools would be minuscule. Tomlinson (1988: 1–2) comments further on the issue:

> Unless the number of pupils per class is reduced substantially below 20 . . . little improvement in student achievement may be expected. . . . Smaller classes will worsen the shortage of both teachers and classrooms, a result that is contrary to the goals of school improvement and higher student achievement. . . . By itself, reducing class size is a very costly "reform."

The researchers associated with the Tennessee study, however, argue that it actually costs more to ameliorate the problems that arise when students are repeating grades, dropping out of school, and not learning efficiently.

Finally, Pong and Pallas (2001) report an interesting study examining the effects of class size on eighth grade mathematics achievement across nine different countries using the Third International Math and Science Study (TIMMS). The researchers were particularly interested in the manner in which school governance might influence the relationship between class size and achievement. They offered several contrasting hypotheses: curricula coverage would be fairly uniform in centralized systems, negating the effect of smaller classes; teaching practices might vary in smaller classes allowing more personalized attention, even in centralized systems. They chose countries that ranged from the most decentralized (United States, Canada, and Australia) to the most centralized (Singapore, Hong Kong, and Korea) with three countries (France, Germany, and Iceland) lying in between these two extremes. They found that eighth grade class size varied according to the system of educational governance with centralized systems having larger classes. Moreover, math achievement is greater in countries with the larger classes (in 8 of the 9 countries, higher math achievement is positively related to large class size). Only in the United States was math achievement related to smaller classes (although the effect was not statistically significant), after controlling for the effects of teacher, school, and other classroom variables. There was "no evidence to support the achievement benefits of small classes in most countries" (Pong and Pallas: 270). This casts caution on the perils of generalizing about class size beyond the United States. Moreover, it raises questions as to why this expensive reform of class size reduction is necessary in the United States though not in other countries that generally outperform the United States in student achievement (with the exception of Iceland).

Interestingly, as is the case with school size and with school expenditures, educational policy is again out in front of the research on class size. Over the past decade, states and the federal government have invested billions of dollars for initiatives to reduce class size, especially in the early grades (Jacobson, 2001). Most of these programs are aimed at reducing class size to twenty students, and most assume that simply reducing class size is sufficient to bring about positive results. Virtually no funds have been set aside to evaluate the state and federal programs. In Nevada, for example, $500 million has been spent to reduce class size to twenty while only $374,000 was set aside to evaluate the results of the policy (Jacobson, 2001). Several problems are obvious: (1) the research shows that positive effects require reductions to a class size of 15 students, but this is confined to the United States; (2) the ratio of costs and benefits of the policy have been ignored; and (3) further research and training are needed to determine what changes teachers must make to operate effectively with small classes.

❖ SCHOOL EFFECTS AND SCHOOL REFORM

What are the implications of our knowledge of between school effects and educational reform? How does the school effects research affect our thinking about the dualities of quality and equality, and of state versus family control? What should be the criteria for identifying an effective school? Is greater equality a legitimate criterion? And should equality or quality receive greater weight? What is a reasonable standard that schools should be held to with regard to the achievement gap between the rich and poor, blacks and whites?

There is ample evidence that children arrive at the schoolhouse door in kindergarten with preexisting differences between homes. We see this repeatedly in the book (see Table 2.1; Figure 3.7; Figure 5.2). Moreover, studies in the tradition of the Coleman Report have demonstrated that the gap between at-risk students and advantaged students increases with each year of school (see also, Jencks and Phillips, 1998). Given the latter finding, it might appear that the process of social reproduction was active in both the home and in the school. But, the summer learning studies provide an entirely new gloss on this perplexing issue.

Coleman took the view that schools should be challenged to free students from the trapping of their status origins by which he meant that schools should reduce the relationship between race and social class and achievement to reduce the gap.

> Schools are successful only insofar as they reduce the dependence of a child's opportunities upon his social origins. . . . The effectiveness of the schools consists, in part, of making the conditional probabilities less conditional— that is, less dependent upon social origins. Thus, equality of educational opportunity implies not merely "equal" schools but equally effective schools, whose influence will overcome the differences in starting point of children from different social groups. (Coleman, 1966: 71)

Of course, a school that produces greater equality but very low quality of academic performance will not be an effective school. Moreover, what about the needs of bright children? Are they not entitled to a school environment that matches their ability? And are schools not responsible for the fullest development of talent to meet the needs of society? And, given the constant influence of the home as a force in social reproduction, is Coleman's challenge too great? Perhaps the standard should be that schools demonstrate simply that social reproduction does not

increase during school time, as is reflected in the summer learning studies.

> Alexander, Entwisle, and Olson (2001: 174, 183) sum it all up as follows: Practically the entire gap across socioeconomic lines traces to summer learning differentials. . . . The seasonal pattern of learning . . . undercuts some long standing but mistaken ideas about schools and social inequality: that schools are ineffectual and unable to equalize educational opportunity, or worse still that they actively handicap disadvantaged children. . . . Schools *do matter*, and they matter most when support for academic learning outside school is weak.

One finding that has persisted throughout the book is that the educational performance of disadvantaged students *is affected by* the differences between a high- and low-quality school. Conversely, the performance of middle-class students is relatively *unaffected* by school type, school quality, school size, or class size. We saw this initially in the original Coleman Report (see Table 4.1) and later for the effects of "summer learning" and finally for the effects of both school and class size. Being out of school in the summer has very little negative effect on the cognitive development of middle-class youngsters, who in some cases, seem to learn as much during the summer as they do in school.

One explanation is that middle-class students attend summer enrichment programs that low-income families cannot afford. A more plausible explanation is that middle-class students have access to an educational environment in their homes that is not very different from that provided in schools. Among low-SES students, as well as those coming from dysfunctional families, however, being out of school in the summer is a disaster. It is the only time that they experience significant losses in cognitive development relative to their middle-class counterparts. Here is a clear-cut example of a real "school effect" par excellence—not between a rich or poor school, a Catholic or public school, a small or large school, but rather between school and no school (see also Alexander, Natriello, and Pallas, 1985).

If we accept the goal of equality as a legitimate one for educational institutions, the challenge is to get *all* students into a good school and keep them there for as long as possible each day and each year. More importantly, however, is to assure that disadvantaged and at-risk students be provided with extended schooling beginning in preschool and then with full-time kindergarten. This should be followed by after-school enrichment experiences and summer programs. All of these programs should have a strong emphasis on reading and they should not be limited to traditional academics. They should involve the kind of cultural and human capital experiences that middle-class children receive every day, including but not limited to libraries, museums, swimming and music lessons, and organized sports where they have the opportunity to engage in complex rule systems and decision making and to have fun in doing so (Alexander, Entwisle, Olson, 2001).

One path is for the state and federal government to provide greater financial aid to poverty-stricken school districts. This would allow these school districts to hire more teachers and have smaller classes, to reorganize the physical plants to operate with smaller schools, and to generally raise the quality of schools and teachers. This path would maximize state control and minimize family control, and it would reduce inequality of educational opportunity and educational outcomes. It would not produce equality of educational opportunity or equality of outcomes. As Kozol (1991) states, "Equity, after all, does not mean simply equal funding. Equal funding for unequal needs is not equality" (Kozol, 1991: 54).

Another avenue of reform is school choice. Under such a plan (and there are many varieties) parents would be able to choose which school their children would attend. In some cases the choice would be limited to the district, in others it would be limited to public schools, and in yet others, there would be hardly any constraints, except that schools could not be out of racial balance proportionate with the district or state. On the face of it, school choice offers greater opportunity for disadvantaged children to attend better quality schools. However, the plan maximizes family control and minimizes state control. As a result, there is concern that high-SES students will get first choice of the better schools, thus confirming the theory of social reproduction. Not surprisingly, proposals from school choice receive less public resistance than plans for state finance reform.

Efforts to redistribute state funds to the benefit of low-SES communities elicit quick and strong protests from the more affluent school districts (see Celis, 1992a; McVicar, 1993). School officials in these districts cry out that they will be unable to operate their schools without raising taxes. What this means is that they will be unable to operate in an "advantaged" fashion without raising taxes.

❖ SUMMARY

In this chapter, we have extended our review of studies that investigate the effects of between school differences. In particular, studies of school resources, summer learning, school size, class size, and multilevel modeling have been considered. Following the initial findings of the Coleman Report, studies of school resources show mixed results at best. The summer learning studies reveal that all students learn at about the same pace when they are actually in school. During the summer, low-SES students, black students, as well as students from single-parent families learn significantly less than high-SES students, whites, and students from intact families. The result is the historical "mismatch" between so-called disadvantaged students and the schools (Cuban and Tyack, 1992).

The summer learning studies are particularly supportive of the conflict and social reproduction theories. They show, more convincingly than any other study, the overwhelming influence of social class (whatever might be the processes and mechanisms). Gamoran's (1995) reanalysis of the Alexander and Entwistle (1995) study shows that family background is clearly the major determinant of differential educational outcomes. Schools cannot overcome the probative impact of social class differences. Even if school were to operate on a year-round basis, Gamoran demonstrates that the initial social class differences would remain (see again, Figure 5.2). Although it appears that schooling serves to preserve rather than exacerbate initial social class differences, there are also some hints

here that school may be involved in the social reproduction process. We will pursue this possibility further in Chapter 6.

This is a much more reasonable and consistent view of the process of social reproduction, which locates it primarily in the home and not in the school. Supporting this notion of schools as egalitarian institutions is the fact that small classes and small schools are of greatest value to low-SES and nonwhite students. Although these better-quality schools and classrooms are more available to advantaged youth, they actually benefit disadvantaged students whenever and wherever they do exist. To a large degree these findings free the schools and teachers of the charges that they are not actively involved in providing equal educational opportunities.

At the same time, however, we must be vigilant about what is going on in schools and classrooms. Even if differences in school quality (be it financial, social, physical, or governance) do not lead to differences in academic outcomes, it is entirely possible that difference within schools may exacerbate existing racial and social class differences. Indeed, "over 80 percent of the variation in student learning occurs within schools, not between schools" (Gamoran et al., 2000: 38). All of this has led to an increased concern for how all schools differ internally. The question now arises as to whether similar effects will be found for students assigned to a high- or low-quality classroom or track *within* a school. In Chapter 6, we focus on the topic of within school differences and their effects.

❖ KEY CONCEPTS

production functions
per pupil expenditures
school finance reform
vote counting
meta-analysis
effect sizes
school choice
summer learning effects
multilevel modeling

nested layers
ecological fallacy
violation of statistical independence
loosely coupled institutions
two-way causality
the effects of school size
the effects of class size
school effects and school reform

❖ KEY STUDIES

Hanushek (1989)
Greenwald, Hedges, and Laine (1996)
Hayes and Grether (1969)
Entwisle and Alexander (1992)
Alexander and Entwisle (1995)
Gamoran (1995)
Entwisle and Alexander (1994)
Bryk and Raudenbush (1992)
Bryk, Lee, and Holland (1993)
Gamoran, Secada, and Marrett
   (2000)

Peterson, McCarthy, and Elmore (1996)
Fowler (1992)
Lee and Smith (1997)
Lee and Loeb (2000)
Tomlinson (1988)
Glass and Smith (1979)
Finn and Achilles (1990)
Nye, Hedges, and Konstantopoulos
   (2000, 2001)
Hoxby (2000)
Pong and Pallas (2001)

❖ REVIEW QUESTIONS

1. Describe the results of Hanushek's review of school-quality studies over the past two decades, noting especially his view of existing measures.

2. Describe the results found by Greenwald, Hedges, and Laine (1996) and discuss how and why these findings differ from Hanushek.

3. Describe the summer learning studies and their implications for the study of school effects. Drawing specifically upon Gamoran's analysis, summarize the quantitative results of summer learning.

4. In view of the summer-learning studies, discuss the likelihood of social reproduction occurring within the schools.

5. How does multileveling modeling help to understand the effects of schools and homes on student achievement?

6. Describe the theory of loose coupling and how it applies to schools.

7. Employing the study by Peterson, McCarthy, and Elmore (1996), demonstrate the importance of consideration of reciprocal causation in the study of school effects.

8. Drawing upon Figures 5.4 and 5.5, summarize the findings of Lee and her associates regarding school size.

9. Summarize the results of the research on the effects of school size.

10. Summarize the results of the research on the effects of class size. To what extent is smaller class size a valid and practical school reform? Be specific with regard to the size of classes that are necessary for differential effectiveness.

Chapter 6

DIFFERENCES
WITHIN SCHOOLS

There is far more variation in educational attainment between different students in the same school than between the average student in one school and the average student in another school.

CHRISTOPHER JENCKS (1972: 156)

O f all the factors influencing the educational outcomes discussed in this book, the differences that exist within classrooms are the most concrete. All of us have experienced the effects of differences in the schools we attended. Research confirms that even young children are fully aware of the variety of grouping and teaching practices in their schools. Certainly, we can all recall those students (regardless of whether they were grouped or not) who were the brightest and those who were the troublemakers. By contrast, most of us have experienced only a limited number of homes and types of schools. For this reason, the study of the effects of different homes and different schools can be elusive, as perhaps it was in the previous chapters. In any event, this chapter will focus on the more tangible differences within schools.

Barbara Heyns (1974: 1435) has identified the importance of *within* school effects:

Tracking and assignment policies typically segregate students within schools and define an academic hierarchy through which certain rewards may be allocated. The general conclusion that resources do not determine achievement differentials between schools . . . ignores stratification patterns and access to resources within schools and necessarily understates the effects of such resources. If access to better teachers, counseling, and highly motivated, academically oriented peers affect achievement to any degree, such resources should operate between curricula within schools as well.

This is not to say that studies of tracking were new in 1974. The rationales and the consequences of ability grouping have been documented since at least 1932 (Billet, 1932; Ekstrom, 1959; for reviews of the studies, see Findley and Bryan, 1971).

Functional theory has long argued that curriculum differentiation is the major mechanism by which schools perform their "functions" of selecting and allocating youth to adult roles (Parsons, 1959). Accordingly, schools select and channel those students deemed to be best qualified for functionally important adult roles into more demanding academic curricula (see Chapter 1 for a review). In contrast, conflict theory argues that track placement is often based on irrelevant ascriptive status characteristics, and that it is a key mechanism by which schools assist in reproducing inequalities. In contrast to the conclusions reached in the last chapter, we now rekindle interest in the role of the school in the process of social reproduction.

Student outcomes vary considerably as a result of the policies, decisions, structures, and processes that take place *within* schools and classrooms. Virtually every school groups and tracks students into curricula (Oakes, Gamoran, and Page, 1992). At the classroom level (regardless of track), resources may be allocated differentially according to sex, class, race, ability, or other factors. Research has consistently shown that within school resources, especially curricula, are differentially distributed by gender, race, and social class, and that a portion of the status origin to school outcome relationship arises from these disparities.

And related to curriculum differences are differences in the quality of teachers. In virtually every school, there are high-quality and low-quality teachers. The effects of teachers (including teacher quality and teacher expectations) operate mainly as differences within the school, being related to tracking and student quality. Somehow, good teachers prefer good students, and vice versa; and more often than not, both good teachers and good students are located together in higher-level (college) tracks (see Oakes, 1985; Choy and Bobbitt, 1993). Note that this relationship may result, in part, from the policy of tracking (rather than from teacher training or motivation); that is, assignment to lower-track classes may lead to a poorer quality of classroom teaching.[1]

Differences within junior and senior high schools are essentially differences between classes within schools—that is, differences between tracks.

> Originally, secondary school students were assigned to academic, general, or vocational tracks, with the courses within those tracks designed to prepare students for postsecondary education or careers. More recently, these track categories have been replaced by course levels, with students typically being assigned to advanced, honors, regular, or basic courses. These courses continue to be referred to as tracks. (Hallinan, 1994)

In elementary schools, these differences exist as within class ability groups (Hallinan, 1992).

Some factors discussed in previous chapters as between school variables may also operate within schools. For example, classroom size, physical resources, and the degree of racial diversity will vary within schools according to classroom. Indeed, the effectiveness of racial integration is most pronounced when integration exists at the classroom level (McPartland, 1967). In fact, between school differences can be deceiving if there is large variation on a particular characteristic within schools. This would occur, for example, if

---

[1] This relationship appears to exist despite the fact that administrators are increasingly dividing teacher assignments equally to high-track and low-track classes within a department at a school. Moreover, wherever assignment is by teacher choice, it is probably senior teachers who will get the higher-track classes. As noted in Chapter 5, research is quite equivocal regarding the relationship of seniority and teacher quality.

some classes in a seemingly "more effective" school were of exceedingly high quality, while others were of low quality. In such a case, the average quality of the school might appear to be greater than other schools. This is less likely to be the case with regard to the physical resources of a school and more likely to be true with regard to the contextual characteristics and the curriculum content of classrooms. Some people argue that this is exactly the case with regard to the effects of racial integration. Thus, one of the assumptions of "between school" studies is that the quality of a school is uniformly distributed within the school. As we shall see, this is certainly not true with regard to the allocation of curriculum resources in the United States. In any event, in this chapter we consider only those features of school that most clearly operate *within* rather than *between* schools, focusing specifically on the organization of the curriculum and the quality of instruction.

❖ THE CURRICULUM AND THE OPPORTUNITY TO LEARN

In most countries, and certainly in the United States, the curriculum is the most important difference operating within the school. Curriculum is a broad and often misconstrued concept. It is the sum of all experiences under the auspices of the school. Defined more specifically in terms of purely academic matters, curriculum refers to the contents of a set of courses available to students and the process or sequencing by which these courses are taught. A school curriculum may be specialized and selective, or it may be common and uniform. It may be unique to a given school, district, state, or country, or it may be required and nationalized throughout a country. Often, the curriculum in a given school is a bit of everything. For example, middle schools and high schools in the United States will frequently offer distinctively different curriculum tracks for students in English and mathematics but require a more uniform and integrated (as opposed to selective) curriculum in other subjects. This makes the study of track allocation and track effects more complicated. Research has demonstrated, however, that by the eighth grade, track placement is relatively permanent (Oakes, 1985; Rosenbaum, 1976).

In the United States, curriculum reform is widespread due largely to the problems described in this chapter and elsewhere in the book; namely, the underperformance of low-SES and nonwhite students and the low performance of American students to their counterparts in other countries. Curriculum reform takes a variety of forms ranging from comprehensive or whole school reform to subject matter reform such as in reading, mathematics, or science. Subject matter reform centers on what is taught (content) and how it is taught (pedagogy). With regard to subject area curricula reforms, the debate has risen to an acrimonious level described by some commentators as the "reading wars" and the "math wars" (Ravitch, 1999; Shouse, 1999). Although some of these subject matter reforms emphasize uniform or inclusive curriculum for all students at a specific grade level, the programs are still experimental and do not represent the mainstream of broad curriculum implementation at the school level, which remains largely noninclusive or tracked. Much of this chapter is limited to this latter issue.

In many countries, there are wide discrepancies between the *intended* and the *implemented* curriculum (Westbury, 1989). The intended curriculum is established largely by curriculum specialists and policy makers (administrators). Teachers, of course, implement the curriculum in the classroom. Discrepancies between the intended and the implemented curriculum are less likely to occur in countries in which the curriculum is controlled and monitored at the national level (Stevenson and Baker, 1991). In the United States, where local control is the norm, differences between the intended and the implemented curriculum are likely to occur. In addition, there is of course the *achieved* curriculum, which is how much of the implemented curriculum is actually learned by students. This relationship is extremely important since it bears on the efficiency of the class and the teacher among many other things.

Closely associated with the idea of curriculum is the notion of opportunity-to-learn (OTL). A basic and obvious principle of learning is that students cannot learn unless they are provided with the opportunity to do so. Opportunity-to-learn is thus defined as the amount of potential curriculum content that has been made available to students. OTL is more broadly conceived than the amount of time spent on learning tasks. Students may be provided an OTL on a topic, but the time on task may vary from class to class and school to school. OTL is measured by the extent of exposure to the "intended" curriculum—that is, by the percentage of the intended curriculum that was implemented or exposed to a set of students. Thus, OTL *is* the implemented curriculum. OTL is determined primarily by school policy, by class composition or

track level, and by the classroom teacher. International studies have shown that OTL varies considerably from country to country. When a common curriculum is provided uniformly to all students, everyone is likely to have the same (equal) OTL. Even here, however, OTL may vary from classroom to classroom as teachers implement the intended curriculum in different ways and to different degrees. And certainly time on task may vary considerably.

❖ CURRICULUM AND TRACKING

The term *tracking* refers to the process of assigning students to groups or classes on the basis of ability. If tracks differ in content and style, we can assume that tracking influences a student's opportunity to learn. Several things are known about OTL and tracking. First, we know from the international studies (SIMS and TIMMS) that OTL varies according to country and, not surprisingly, that it is closely related to achievement. In Japan, for example, OTL ratings on mathematics instruction are among the highest of any country (more students have greater OTL). Second, differences in OTL vary according to personal characteristics of students such as race, gender, and socioeconomic status. Thus, there are between school differences and between home differences in the *allocation* of OTL. Third, there are important OTL differences within schools according to curriculum (track) allocation or selection.

Curriculum, taken in the larger sense of including policies that determine types of classes as well as what will be studied in each type of class, serves the social function of distributing opportunities to learn. . . . The curriculum adopted for a given class sets boundaries on the attainments of individual students by determining the content to which they will be exposed and therefore the learning opportunities afforded them. (McKnight et al., 1987: 103)

Thus, OTL, curriculum differentiation, and tracking are all part of the same processes.

Within this context, many questions arise.

1. What are the pedagogical bases for the use of tracking as a mode of school organization?
2. Who makes the decisions regarding track placement?
3. What are the differences between tracks in terms of educational contents and processes?
4. How pervasive is tracking and when does it begin?
5. Is track placement permanent or temporary in the educational career of a student?
6. Is track placement meritocratic or class, race, and gender biased? Does homogeneous grouping create groups that are truly homogeneous in ability?
7. What are the short- and long-term consequences of track placement in terms of academic achievement, in terms of social identity and social behavior? Does tracking increase overall achievement in schools or school systems relative to untracked schools or systems? Does tracking increase inequality between students relative to untracked schools or systems?
8. Is tracking as a mode of school organization constitutionally legitimate?

9. Is tracking relatively universal among other countries?

In the next several sections, we examine each of these questions in turn.

◆ 1. What Are the Pedagogical Bases for the Use of Tracking as a Mode of School Organization?

The intended purpose of tracking is to increase the efficiency and the quality of instruction for all students. According to Oakes (1985), all of the following rationales have been advanced in favor of tracking at one time or another:

1. Tracking is only temporary.
2. Students learn better in groups with others like themselves.
3. Tracking is in the best interests of all students.
4. Slower students develop more positive attitudes about themselves in schools where they are not mixed with more capable students.
5. Track placement is accurate and fair and reflects past achievements and natural ability.
6. Tracking allows teachers to meet the individual needs of students more effectively.
7. Students or parents select whichever track they prefer.
8. Groups of similar students are easier to teach.

Of these, only the last is generally accepted as true, but Oakes (1985: 14) argues that it cannot be justified in view of the educational and social costs that accrue to low-track students. All of the remaining rationales are generally viewed as controversial and problematic, and the pros and cons of these other rationales are discussed under one or more of the questions that follow.

◆ 2. WHO MAKES THE DECISIONS REGARDING TRACK PLACEMENT?

To suggest that students or parents choose their track is disingenuous. Quite obviously, it directly contradicts the rationale that track placement is based on past achievement and ability, and that it is accurate and fair. If parents and students had their choice, most would prefer the higher-track courses and classes (this holds more so for parents than for students, and to whatever extent possible, parents would make this choice for their children). But talent is normally distributed with most people in the middle and only smaller percentages in the top and bottom. As a result, teachers and guidance counselors observe and record this variation in achievement and assign students to tracked courses accordingly (Oakes, 1985; Rosenbaum, 1976; Oakes, Gamoran, and Page, 1992).

To be sure, students are asked which tracks (courses, classes, careers, and so on) they would prefer, but in the end, schools make the decisions about track placement, and appropriately so. Rosenbaum (1976) has demonstrated that schools (teachers, administrators, and counselors alike) provide an illusion to students and parents that they do have a choice when, in fact, they do not. The illusion is based upon misinformation and miscommunication by school officials (Rosenbaum, 1976, 1980; Fennessey et al., 1981). Moreover, and perhaps to a lesser extent today, earlier research has demonstrated that ability grouping and track placement have been often based on nonrelevant ascriptive

factors (Rist, 1970; Cicourel and Kituse, 1963; Erickson, 1975). In these reports, tracking decisions by teachers and counselors were strongly affected by race and class.

◆ 3. WHAT ARE THE DIFFERENCES BETWEEN TRACKS IN TERMS OF EDUCATIONAL CONTENTS AND PROCESSES?

Most studies have shown that more learning occurs in higher tracks (Rosenbaum, 1976; Metz, 1978; Oakes, 1985; Natriello, Pallas, and Alexander, 1989). Generally, this has been shown to be true after controlling for initial ability and various home background variables including gender, race, and socioeconomic status (for a review, see Gamoran and Berends, 1987; for several exceptions to the rule, see Jencks and Brown, 1975; Alexander and Cook, 1982).

Oakes (1985) has described in rich detail the distribution of knowledge that is made available to students in high- and low-track classes. Her study of twenty-five schools in the United States found enormous differences between the tracks in English and mathematics classes from the elementary through the high school levels. Low-track classes provide only a small amount of the curricula content that is found in high-track classes. The course content of high-track classes contains knowledge that involves critical thinking and problem solving and information useful to high-status occupations. The course content of low-track classes is generally limited to simple memory tasks and to elementary knowledge of low-status occupations. Teachers of low-track classes emphasize the importance of conformity, punctuality, and getting along with other people. Teachers of high-track classes, on the other hand, emphasize self-direction, creativity, and critical thinking. Oakes (1985: 79–92) terms these latter differences "learning beyond content."

Oakes also examined the differences between tracks from the perspective of the opportunity to learn concept. On the bases of both classroom observations and interviews, she found that students in high-track classes spent more time on "learning" while their counterparts in low-track classes spent as much time on other things (like daily routines and behavioral disruptions) as on learning. In addition, high-track students were provided with better quality of instruction and were assigned more homework than low-track students (Rosenbaum, 1976, Finley, 1984; Oakes, 1985).[2] In effect, the data show that low-track classes are provided fewer opportunities to learn. Thus, the quality and the quantity of instruction increases from low- to high-track classes.

Not surprisingly, Oakes confirms the underlying principle of tracking—tracks differ in curriculum content and in other critical ways. She speculates on the implications of this. Students in low-track classes are presumably those with the greatest academic needs. Yet in a tracked system these students receive lower levels of knowledge, fewer opportunities to learn, and poorer quality of instruction. Why is this so? Oakes argues convincingly that schools fail to distinguish those students who have a hard time behaving from those who have a hard time learning. Low-track classes are structured to "educate" those students who have a hard time behaving. Hence, the great emphasis on conformity and appropriate behavior and the low levels of knowledge and homework. According to Oakes (1985: 90), "We may saddle those who find it hard to learn with those who find it hard to behave." In so doing we create a classic mismatch between the needs of students and the resources that schools have to offer these students.

We can turn to data from the Second International Study of Mathematics (SIMS) study for direct evidence of curriculum differentiation in the United States (see McKnight et al., 1987, especially pp. 104–106).[3] On the basis of teacher data and the types of textbooks that were used, four distinct eighth grade curricula were identified: remedial, typical, enriched, and algebra.

Not surprisingly, there is a relationship between OTL and academic achievement. Figure 6.1 shows a large difference in achievement between classes (curriculum tracks), which corresponds with large differences in OTL. There are several important points to note here. First, there do exist clear differences in ability or "knowledge" at the beginning of the eighth grade. For whatever reason, students are unequal at the outset and this fact is part of the rationale for providing differential curricula. Second, the remedial and typical classes learn less than 25 percent of the "new" subject matter that is presented over the course of the year. The enriched and algebra classes, on the other hand, demonstrate a more

---

[2] For judging the quality of instruction, Oakes relies on a set of criteria developed by Rosenshine and Furst (1971). These include clarity of presentation, variability of activities, teacher enthusiasm, high task orientation, and a lack of strong student criticism.

[3] Essentially the same results have been reported for the TIMSS study of mathematics and science in the 1990s (see Cogan, Schmidt, and Wiley, 2001; Schmidt et al., 2001). But the SIMS results are displayed more simply.

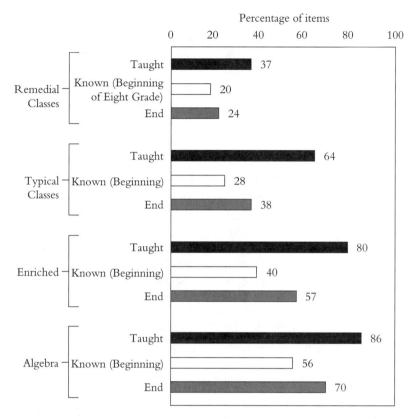

FIGURE 6.1   Eighth Grade Mathematics Curriculum Taught, Known Previously, and Learned by Type of Mathematics Program

Note: Four different class types are found in eighth grade mathematics in the United States, each with a different mathematics curriculum. In this graph, the amount of algebra taught and learned by students in each class type is shown. Students in the remedial classes were taught only about one-third of the algebra on the international test, and very little algebra was learned during the year. On the other hand, students in the algebra classes were taught almost all of the algebra on the test, and a great deal was learned. More extensive tracking was found at this level in the United States than in any other country in the study.

Source: McKnight et al. *The Underachieving Curriculum: Assessing U.S. School Mathematics from an International Perspective* (Champaign, IL: Stipes Publishing Company, 1987): 106.

effective learning curve, mastering nearly 50 percent of the new knowledge. Third, the amount of new work that was implemented varies by track. Specifically, the new material provided to the three upper-track classes is twice as great as that provided to the remedial-track classes.

The initial difference in ability among students is obviously due in large part to the effects of tracking that have occurred in the previous eight (K-7) years of school. Even assuming perfect equality at the outset of schooling, the results of Figure 6.1 imply that achievement differences will occur because of tracking.

Even assuming real differences at the outset of schooling, the fairness of the OTL differences is questionable in terms of inequality of exposure and the learning curve. Oakes (1985) has argued that lower-performing students obviously need more rather than less instruction.

Thus, tracks do differ in the quantity, quality, and the pace of instruction (in addition to the above, see Gamoran, 1984, 1986; Dreeban and Barr, 1988; Pallas et al., 1994). In addition, there are at least two other ways in which the structure and processes of tracking may differ. First, tracking may influence children's expectations of their own performance and their self-concepts. High-track students develop high expectations for their performance potential, thus generating a self-fulfilling effect independent of the actual content and pace of instruction (see Persell, 1977; Eder, 1981; Rosenbaum, 1980; Schwartz, 1981; Metz, 1978; Eckert, 1989; Rosenthal and Jacobson, 1968).

Second, tracks may differ because of the institutional norms associated with them and in the expectations of parents and teachers. Guidance counselors are implicated in this institutional process as well, having been observed to communicate more positive academic expectations to higher-track students (Cicourel and Kituse, 1963; Rosenbaum, 1976; Rosenthal and Jacobson, 1968; Oakes, 1985). Pallas et al. (1994) tested the plausibility of all of the mechanisms by which tracks differ and found support only for quantity, quality, and pace of instruction.

◆ 4. HOW PERVASIVE IS TRACKING AND WHEN DOES IT BEGIN?

Until recently, tracking was deeply entrenched in the fabric of American schools. Oakes (1985) concluded that one-third of all classes were tracked in the schools she studied. Among eight subject areas, Oakes noted that an average of six were tracked, and nearly all students remained in the same track year after year (see also, Goodlad, 1984). Some researchers have noted that the lack of tracking in some nonacademic areas merely deludes students and parents into thinking that the school is not entirely tracked (Rosenbaum, 1976). Lucas (1999: 6) makes the point that during the period 1965–1975, most schools dismantled the overarching tracking programs and implemented individual subject matter track levels; "But, the foundational element of tracking, the differential curriculum, remained."

Goodlad (1984: 141) explains tracking this way:

> Organizing early elementary classes into instructional groups for reading and mathematics is about as common as a daily recess in school. These grouping decisions are made during the first few weeks of the first grade. Teachers make them on the basis of their own judgement, sometimes with the assistance of test scores. Usually, they set up three groups in each subject; two are more common in mathematics than in reading, and four are more common in reading than in mathematics. More regrouping occurs during the first few months of the first grade than thereafter. Indeed shifts later on are relatively rare.

The results shown above from the SIMS study confirm that differentiated tracks in mathematics were clearly and deeply in place in the 1980s (McKnight et al., 1987).

Recent reports from the Third International Mathematics and Science Study (TIMMS) show that tracking in mathematics in the eighth grade is still the norm. The TIMMS data show that 75 percent of eighth graders in the United States were provided with two or more distinct types of mathematics classes (Schmidt and McKnight, 1998), compared to 10 to 20 percent for Canada, England, and Germany, and 0 to 1 percent for France, Korea, and Japan. Clearly, tracking is deeply embedded in the structure of American schools.

A recent report (Manlove and Baker, 1995) of 912 public secondary schools, however, notes that 85 percent of schools today have policies of open student choice. Manlove and Baker found evidence that schools seem to have begun to uncouple the rigid tracking system described above. Based upon the reports of principals at these schools, they observed that many schools now offer untracked classes along with tracked classes and are more likely to allow movement from an untracked class to a tracked class and vice versa. Such student choice, however, is only allowed with the proviso that students have taken the required course prerequisites. Many critics would view this as a large constraint toward maintaining a rigid tracking system.

Ability grouping actually begins in kindergarten in the United States. Data from the kindergarten cohort of the Early Childhood Longitudinal Survey (ECLS-K) provides excellent evidence of these early tracking patterns. By the end of kindergarten in 1999, fully 37 percent of teachers reported that they divided their classes into reading groups at least three or four times per week (20 percent did so every day), and 26 percent divided their classes into math groups at least three or four times per week. Only 30 percent of kindergarten teachers never grouped in reading and only 45 percent never grouped in mathematics (author's computations from base year ECLS-K).

◆ 5. Is Track Placement Permanent or Temporary in the Educational Career of a Student?

In principle, track placement is temporary. In practice, it is quite permanent.

> One of the reasons for this stability in group membership is that the work of upper and lower groups becomes more sharply differentiated with each passing day. . . . It is not uncommon for a child in the advanced group to have progressed five times as fast as a child in the least advanced group over the course of a year. . . . By the fourth grade, children at the top and bottom differ in overall scholastic achievement, as measured by tests, by the equivalent of four full grades. In reading, this spread is often as much as six grades. (Goodlad, 1984: 141)

Another look at Figure 6.1 demonstrates the difficulty of a student moving up even a single level among the four class types of eighth grade mathematics in the United States.

With each year, the gap in the knowledge base between each track widens. Students in the eighth grade typical class could hardly be expected to perform successfully in a ninth grade class made up mostly of students from the eighth grade enriched class. This knowledge base quickly translates into sequential course taking—that is, students who have completed algebra in the eighth grade can take geometry in the ninth grade. Stevenson et al. (1994) show that the pattern of course taking locks students into a sequence of opportunities to learn that influences their educational outcomes. Recently, however, Hallinan (1996) has reported evidence showing that a considerable degree of track mobility does exist. In a longitudinal study of 2,000 students in seven high schools, Hallinan found that fully 30 percent of students changed track in English and 11 percent changed track in mathematics, from the ninth to the twelfth grades (see also, Lucas, 1999). Thus, the matter is not an open and shut case.

◆ 6. IS TRACK PLACEMENT MERITOCRATIC OR CLASS AND RACE BIASED?

A fundamental assumption of tracking is that the students in a given track have the same level of cognitive ability. The reader will recall that one of the pedagogical bases of tracking is that track placement is accurate and fair, that it reflects past achievements and natural ability. Given this assumption, students in tracked classes should be relatively homogeneous in ability.

To what degree is this true? To what degree is track placement meritocratic? This is a complicated question for several reasons. First, there is the possibility that measured ability may be biased by class, race, or gender considerations. For example, a black student might score lower on a test and be placed in a lower track, but the test might be invalid or biased. Second, placement might be affected by teacher or counselor bias irrespective of cognitive ability. Third, and perhaps most importantly, track placement is highly dependent on past placement, as noted in Figure 6.1. This means that answers to the above questions are difficult to come by unless we examine children in the first grade. Fortunately, such data is available.

Pallas et al. (1994) reported a study of first grade students in Baltimore who were then followed in subsequent years. Students were selected in a two-stage sampling process with schools as the first-stage unit and students within the schools as the second-stage. The research project collected extensive data from parents, students, teachers, and school records. Information on reading group placement was obtained from the teacher's report of assignments that were made prior to the issuing of the first report card.

For each child, the teacher was asked to rank the reading group placement from highest to lowest. Since the classroom differed in the number of reading groups, it was necessary to develop a ranking system that would preserve each student's relative placement in an appropriate manner. To do this, Pallas et al. utilized a system whereby all students were ranked according to deciles—that is, the group rank of each student was recomputed so that it reflected where the student would be if the class had ten groups. Thus, a student in a high-level reading group would obtain an estimated score of 8 or 9 whereas a student in a middle-level group would get a score around 5. This standardization allowed comparisons across classrooms. Having done this, the researchers could examine the relationship of reading group placement to a student's test score based upon the reading comprehension subtest of the California Achievement Test (CAT), which was given at the beginning of school. Figure 6.2 displays a plot of this relationship for a typical school.

In this school, the range of CAT scores for the top group (just below 9 on the scale) was 175 to 340 while the range for the lowest group (just above 1 on the scale) was 175 to 300. There is little homogeneity of ability in these reading ability groupings (see also Dreeben and Barr, 1988). In their multivariate analysis of the data, Pallas et al. (1994) found that track placement was not linked to academic potential as measured by the CAT. They concluded that "children with

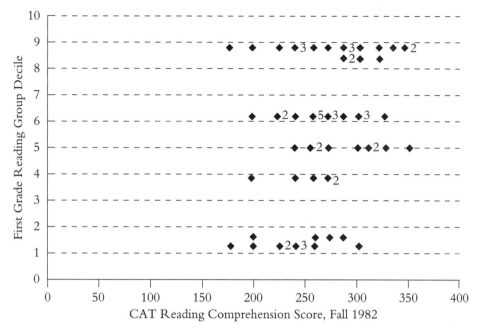

FIGURE 6.2   Plot of Reading-Group Placement by Fall 1982 CAT Reading Comprehension Subtest: School Number 1

Source: Pallas et al. "Ability Group Effects: Instructional, Social, or Institutional?" *Sociology of Education 67* (1994): Fig. 1, p. 36. Reprinted with permission.

comparable levels of measured academic performance and social backgrounds are often placed in reading groups that rank them anywhere from near the top of their class to near the bottom" (p. 43).

Although Pallas et al. found that race and class did not influence track placement, a considerable body of other research has demonstrated otherwise.[4] Some research has shown emphatic and direct influence of class and race on group or track placement. For example,

[4] Quite possibly, the null results obtained for race and class may be due to the nature of the sample. This study was conducted in a large city (Baltimore) which is 75 percent African American in population. This may obscure some typical relationships between class and race and educational outcomes.

Rist (1970) reported that kindergarten reading group assignments were made during the first few days of school and that these placements were based to a large degree on socioeconomic characteristics of the students—that is, dress style, racial differences, parental work patterns. The interesting thing about this study is that it was an all-black class with a black teacher, thus in effect providing control for race (racial differences were made on the basis of the darkness of skin color). One would assume that if race and class differences operate in an all-black setting, they would surely be activated in a mixed race and class situation. In fact, Rosenbaum (1976, 1980) and Lucas (1999) demonstrate that low-SES and minority students are more likely than high-SES and white students to be

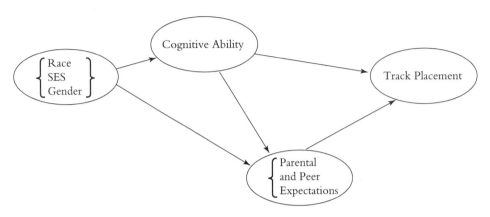

FIGURE 6.3   **Model of the Determinants of Curriculum Placement**

assigned to low-track class in high school, even after ability is held constant (see also Oakes, 1985). Hallinan (1996) found that even track mobility is conditioned by SES, race, and gender.

Several analysts have demonstrated that verbal achievement scores and the expectations and guidance of others (parents, teachers, guidance counselors, and peers) are influenced by class and race, and that these mediating variables then influence track placement (Cicourel and Kituse, 1963; Rosenbaum, 1976; Erickson, 1975). There are two ways in which class and race differences in track placement can come about. It is possible that initial poor student performance may be caused by low SES or minority status and this leads to low-track placement. It is also possible that these differences in curriculum allocation within schools are caused by teacher or counselor discrimination based on SES (and race and gender), irrespective of abilities. This is a critical distinction.

Alexander, Cook, and McDill (1978) reported substantial influence of status origin variables (SES, race, and gender) even after controls for ability. They examined the determinants of high school track placement while controlling for a set of typical home background variables (SES, race, and gender), junior high school cognitive achievement, and junior high school parental and peer expectations for the student. This model is shown in Figure 6.3. Alexander et al. (1978) found that the effects of ability and peer expectations greatly exceed the effects of the home variables. "Our results suggest that the socioeconomic characteristics of students do affect their curriculum enrollment but do so almost entirely through their influence upon achievements, goals, and encouragements by others in junior high school" (p. 62).

◆ 7. WHAT ARE THE SHORT- AND LONG-TERM CONSEQUENCES OF TRACK PLACEMENT IN TERMS OF ACADEMIC ACHIEVEMENT, IN TERMS OF SOCIAL IDENTITY AND SOCIAL BEHAVIOR, AND EQUALITY?

With only a few exceptions (Jencks and Brown, 1975; Alexander and Cook, 1982), track placement has been shown to have significant and substantial effects on virtually every conceivable academic and educational outcome. This is true after controlling for the full array of home background variables, between school influences, and other within school factors such as teacher quality. Students in high tracks obtain high test score achievement (Gamoran and Mare, 1989), and they are more likely to expect to go to college (Alexander et al., 1976, 1978; Heyns, 1974; Rosenbaum, 1980; Vanfossen, Jones, and Spade, 1987). Students in high tracks are more likely to actually attend college (Alexander and Eckland, 1974, 1975; Jencks and Brown, 1975; Rehberg and Rosenthal, 1978; Hauser, Sewell, and Alwin, 1976; Thomas, Alexander, and Eckland, 1979) and to graduate from college (Alexander et al., 1982, 1987; Velez, 1985; Wolfle, 1985).

Theoretically, we might expect that developmental and affective outcomes would also be related to track placement. Research results in this area, however, have been inconsistent. Although earlier cross-sectional studies found that high-track students had more positive attitudes toward themselves (Schafer and Olexa, 1971; Schafer and Polk, 1972; Oakes, 1985), later studies using longitudinal designs have obtained null findings. For example, Waitrowski et al. (1982) found no effects of tracking on self-esteem, positive attachment to school, or delinquent behavior. Vanfossen, Jones, and Spade (1987) obtained only a small positive effect of track on self-esteem after controlling for an earlier measure of self-esteem. The lack of positive results on these developmental outcomes is surprising and may reflect measurement problems that have always been associated with affective concepts such as self-esteem. Of course, it should also be noted that the pedagogical theory of tracking argues that the self-esteem of students in

low tracks is not damaged as a result of the absence of invidious comparisons with more academically able students. This would account for the fact that students in different tracks have similar levels of self-esteem and other related developmental attitudes and behaviors.

Ethnographic research, however, finds that tracking does affect the social identities and self-concepts of students as a result of the labeling process at the peer group level (for a review, see Gamoran and Berends, 1987). For example, Schwartz (1981) noted that students constantly refer to themselves and others as "smart," "dumb," "stupid," "slow," "bright," and so on (see also, Metz, 1978; Oakes, 1985; Rosenbaum, 1976). Teachers and parents contribute to this stereotyping (Rosenbaum, 1976; Finley, 1984). This creates polarization in peer interaction, and most importantly, a sense of despair and bitterness toward school on the part of low-track students. Willis (1977) has written extensively on the antischool attitudes and behaviors that are adopted by lower-class boys in low tracks as a way of dignifying and valorizing their nonacademic identities.

Does tracking increase overall achievement in schools or school systems relative to untracked schools or systems? Does tracking increase inequality between students relative to untracked schools or systems? Not surprisingly, most research demonstrates that grouping and tracking widens the gap between students in the high and low tracks, thereby creating more inequality of educational results (see Alexander, Cook, and McDill, 1978; Alexander and McDill, 1976; Gamoran, 1987b; Heyns, 1974).

Tracking may also influence a school's average level of achievement. The degree of inequality among students within a school may or may not increase, but the average student growth in a school (practicing a certain form of tracking) may be smaller or larger than students attending another type of school. That is, "a more productive system must have a greater positive effect for high track students, or less negative impact for students in low tracks, or some combination" (Gamoran, 1992). Some forms of tracking may be more productive than other forms. If this is true, then variation in forms of tracking would create a *between school effect*.

Building on the earlier work of Sorensen (1970), Gamoran (1992) has demonstrated that the effects of tracking depend to some degree on the structural characteristics of the tracking system. Gamoran identified four distinct structural dimensions of all tracking systems:

1. *Selectivity*—the degree of homogeneity within tracks;
2. *Electivity*—the degree to which students choose their track;
3. *Inclusivity*—the proportion of students in an academic track;
4. *Scope*—the pervasiveness and flexibility of the track assignment.

Gamoran found that "schools with less mobility [pervasive and inflexible] . . . have greater between-track inequality in both subjects [math and verbal], and they have lower overall math scores" (p. 825). Thus, this type of structure produces high inequality and lower overall achievement. Gamoran also found that average math and verbal scores were higher in schools that have more inclusive tracking systems. The effects of selectivity and electivity were null—these factors did not influence the effect that tracking had as a whole. In general, assignment to an aca-

demic track is beneficial to individual achievement even though this occurs at the expense of those who are excluded (greater inequality). However, this increase in inequality is not the same in all schools. According to Gamoran (1992), "The academic track advantage is less in schools with more flexibility and (for math) moderately inclusive tracking" (p. 825). Moreover, overall achievement increases in schools with more inclusive tracking systems.

♦ 8. IS TRACKING AS A MODE OF SCHOOL ORGANIZATION CONSTITUTIONALLY LEGITIMATE?

In view of laws passed over the past forty years emphasizing the equal protection clause of the Fourteenth Amendment, the question arises as to whether it is legal to separate students into different tracks. It is fairly clear that students in these different tracks receive an unequal educational opportunity. In this regard, is tracking not similar to policies, now deemed illegal, holding that schools can be separate and equal? In the case of race, this law/policy was struck down by the 1954 Supreme Court decision of *Brown v. the Board of Education of Topeka, Kansas*. In the case of gender, Title IX of the Educational Amendments of 1972 requires that "no person in the United States shall, on the basis of sex, be excluded from participation in, be denied the benefits of, or be subjected to discrimination under any educational program or activity receiving Federal financial assistance" (Section 901a of the Educational Amendment of 1972). Tracking, in the same way as separate schools or the exclusion of females from certain educational programs, might be conceived as a barrier to educational equality. On the face of things, it seems to provide unequal educational opportunity *within* rather than *between* types of schools (see Oakes, 1985, ch. 9).

◆ 9. IS TRACKING RELATIVELY UNIVERSAL AMONG VARIOUS COUNTRIES?

How does the United States compare with other countries with regard to tracking? Do other countries follow the U.S. model? How is tracking related to achievement differences across countries? Since tracking is so pervasive in America, the impact of tracking (as opposed to less or no tracking) can only be assessed if there are other educational systems in other countries with less tracking than in the United States. A key question therefore arises: How do other countries organize instruction? Perhaps tracking is universal, since arguments can be made that curriculum differentiation may be essential to efficient classroom instruction and for enhancing the development of each individual to the maximum.

It turns out that this matter is difficult to assess, even with the data from the second IEA mathematics study (SIMS). There are great differences between the curriculum that systems "intend" and the curriculum that is actually "implemented." Westbury (1989) examined variation in the distribution of the implemented curriculum across eight countries. The results of this analysis are shown in Figure 6.4. Westbury compared variation in the algebra coverage (OTL) among students in the third highest quartile with those in the lowest (first) quartile. The data shown are drawn from teacher reports (of classes) of items covered on the algebra section of SIMS. The average level of coverage in the third quartile is represented by the top of each vertical line in the figure and the average level of coverage for the bottom quartile is indicated by the bottom of the vertical line. As you can see,

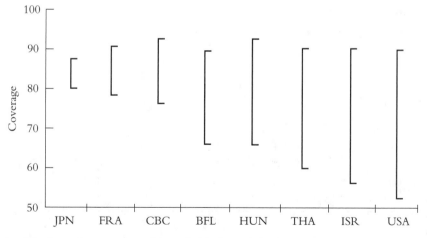

FIGURE 6.4   **Algebra: Coverage at Q3 and Q1 for High-Coverage Systems**

Source: Ian Westbury, "The Problems of Comparing Curriculums Across Educational Systems," in *International Comparisons and Educational Reform,* ed. Alan C. Purves (Alexandria, VA: Association for Supervision and Curriculum, 1989): 24. Reprinted with permission.

there is little variation in OTL across countries for classes providing high coverage. In these high-coverage (high-track) classes, teachers report that their students covered more than 85 percent of the questions contained in the SIMS item pool. A distinctly different pattern exists when we look at the low-coverage classes. Westbury (1989: 23)

> In Japan, low-coverage classes experience a curriculum that is virtually the same as the curriculum of the highest-coverage classes. Substantial equity in coverage exists across all classrooms in the system. In the U.S., on the other hand, curricula are extremely diverse, and a substantial difference in the levels of coverage exists . . . between the high- and low-coverage classes. U.S. teachers of high coverage classes report teaching about 90 percent of the content represented by the SIMS algebra pool,

whereas teachers of low-coverage classes report teaching only about 55 percent.

The inference to be derived from this analysis is that school systems scoring highest on the Second IEA math test (Japan, France, Canada, and to a lesser extent Belgium Flemish, as shown in Figure 6.5) demonstrate the least variability in OTL. This suggests that curricula differentiation or tracking may not be efficacious for generating high achievement. In the high-performing systems, there is much more homogeneity of OTL, with students of all ability levels being exposed to the same level of curriculum content.

The comparisons between Japan and America are particularly revealing. Japan demonstrates the least variability in curriculum and the highest level of mathematics achievement. The United States shows the greatest degree of curriculum

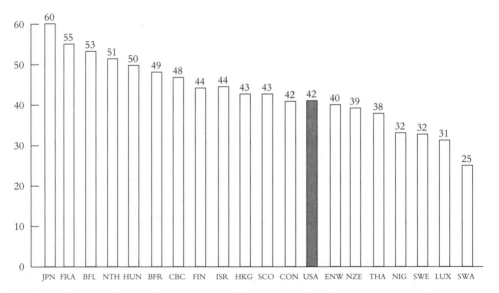

FIGURE 6.5   Algebra (Population A): Mean Percentage Correct

Source: Ian Westbury, "The Problems of Comparing Curriculums Across Educational Systems," in *International Comparisons and Educational Reform,* ed. Alan C. Purves (Alexandria, VA: Association for Supervision and Curriculum, 1989): 20. Reprinted with permission.

differentiation and a low level (below the mean) of achievement in mathematics. It would perhaps be helpful to reexamine Figure 1.3 in Chapter 1, which shows a pattern of test score results in Japan with both greater achievement and greater equality (than the United States). This is entirely consistent and predictable from the pattern of curriculum distribution and achievement shown in Figures 6.4 and 6.5. Given these results for SIMS, it is not surprising that the results ten years later for TIMSS are pretty much the same with Japan, France, Canada, and Belgium Flemish all scoring among the highest in eighth grade in mathematics, and significantly higher than the United States (NCES, 1999; Schmidt et al., 2001).

❖ IMPROVING TRACKING OR DETRACKING: WHICH COURSE FOR THE FUTURE?

Reacting to the many criticisms of tracking that we have reviewed above, Oakes (1994) and others have proposed that tracking be abolished. This form of organization for learning has come to be labeled "detracking." It promotes heterogeneous grouping—that is, students are taught in groups in which there is a wide range of abilities and motivations. The fundamental rationale for detracking (in addition to addressing the shortcomings of tracking) is the idea that cognitive diversity provides an effective atmosphere for learning.

Proponents of detracking argue that tracking cannot be understood and conceptualized as a neutral form of school classroom organization, apart from the normative and political context in which it is imbedded. Tracking is both "a cause and an effect of a social climate of discrimination and inequality" (Oakes, 1994: 91). Tracking is not simply intended to facilitate learning as some educators have assumed. Rather, according to Oakes, it is as much about meeting the social and workforce needs of society as it is in meeting the cognitive needs of students. Since its emergence at the turn of the century, tracking has ensured the availability of an ample supply of low-skilled and "efficient" workers for low-paying occupations. Viewed in this manner, tracking is an institutionalized mechanism for ensuring the generational transfer of social, economic, and political power and privilege, that is, for ensuring social reproduction. Moreover, tracking promotes a climate of tolerance for racism and elitism. The process of labeling some students as "academic" and other as "nonacademic" creates a divisive and unjust social climate. Within this broader normative and political context, the modifications to improve tracking are seen as supercilious by many educators. Several recent studies of detracked schools report positive results (Oakes and Lipton, 1992). Manlove and Baker (1995) report that at least some "untracked" schools do report teaching the same curricula to 90 percent of students in the tenth grade.[5] This study provides no data, however, on the results of these endeavors or how the classes are conducted in the classroom.

In response to proposals to detrack the schools, Hallinan (1994) counters that

---

[5] Manlove and Baker (1995) note also that this shift in the curricula may have serious implications for children with lower levels of parental involvement. To the extent that schools are changing and are not uniform in their curriculum structure, it is even more difficult for parents to navigate the curricula and make choices for their children.

many studies of detracking have been conducted in schools that possess a positive normative social and political climate and an elaborate support structure including the employment of teacher aides and special programs to meet the needs of lower-ability students. She argues that "this normative climate and support structure, rather than heterogeneous grouping, is responsible for the success of detracked schools" (p. 90)—that is, that the effect of detracking may be spurious.

This implies that a system of tracking could be equally effective in a context of favorable institutional supports. According to Hallinan, there is insufficient evidence available regarding the relationship between tracking/detracking and this positive institutional environment. Detracked schools *may not* always be accompanied by positive structural support, and it *may be* possible to establish tracked schools that do have these supports. Thus, Hallinan (1994) notes that "changing a school climate may eliminate the need to abandon tracking" (p. 91). In contrast to the detracking movement, Hallinan and others have argued that tracking should be improved rather than eliminated. According to Hallinan (1994: 84),

> [T]racking facilitates instruction and learning. The many teachers who favor tracking have concluded, from pedagogical experience, that teaching heterogeneously grouped students without additional resources, such as teacher aides and supplementary material, is a formidable task. Moreover, the outcomes of detracking in less-than-ideal circumstances may be as unsatisfactory as that of tracking that is not practiced according to principle.

Hallinan identifies the many problems of tracking as unintended consequences resulting not from the organizational technique itself but rather from the way that tracking is currently practiced. If educators were to correctly administer tracking, the unintended results could be eliminated and the intended results would benefit all students in each track. To do this would require serious effort on the part of teachers and administrators. At a minimum, it would be necessary to (1) apply more objective criteria in the track assignment process to ensure that the tracks were truly homogeneous (that is, fair and accurate placement); (2) monitor student learning more carefully so as to allow and encourage track reassignment more frequently; (3) provide special attention to students in low-track classes so as to ensure a higher quality of instruction for these students; (4) provide special programming to ensure support and rewards for students in low-track classes to protect against negative psychological effects from their low-status assignment; and finally (5) ensure that all students spend a large part of their day in integrated settings to counteract the negative effects of segregation by track. Hallinan implies that the cost of these improvements is no greater than the cost of detracking. "A tracked school's failure to provide students with equal opportunities to learn is not due to tracking, but to the absence of the school's commitment to equality" (Hallinan, 1994: 90). Recent research (Gamoran et al., 1995: 708) confirms Hallinan's view by concluding "that achievement inequality could be reduced by raising the caliber of both instructional content and instructional discourse in regular and remedial classes."

In many respects, detracking and tracking resemble the policies of integrated and segregated schooling. In *Brown v. Board of Education* (1954), the Supreme Court ruled that separate schools are *inherently* unequal. The Court contended that the policy of separatism prohibited a climate of equality. In much the same way, we could argue that the current policy of tracking prohibits the improvements that Hallinan claims are necessary for it to operate without its unintended negative consequences (see Oakes, 1994). On the other hand, as noted in Chapter 4, fifty years of integrated schools have failed to produce consistently positive results, and critics of desegregation are now demanding that financial resources formerly given over to integration (such as money for busses and extra teachers) now be given directly to the schools, be they integrated or segregated. Thus, a middle ground to the issues of tracking and detracking (or segregation and desegregation) might be that students in low-track classes would receive additional funding that might be used to provide surrogate parental tutoring after school or technological support perhaps in the form of a personal computer, or incentives to attend summer school. Conceivably, this strategy might prevent what some fear will be "bright flight" from detracked classes similar to "white flight" from desegregated schools.

❖ SPECIAL EDUCATION PLACEMENT AND TRACKING

Richardson (2000) introduces the successful policy of inclusion of special education programs to researchers in the sociology of education. He demonstrates that tracking and special education placement share many features in common and that the advances in special education can provide a model for understanding the recalcitrance of tracking. Each of these forms of school organization is subject to the influence of irrelevant status char-

acteristics and the erroneous misclassification of students. Moreover, the legal history of each has followed the same paths. Yet, despite the similarities, special education has broken through the legal and bureaucratic obstacles and achieved unification and full inclusion in most respects. The key to this success lies in a crisis in school psychology as a profession and establishing exclusion as a moral problem as opposed to the simple publication of research.

Tracking and special education programs share many characteristics: both involve selection and placement requiring some form of decision making and testing; the accuracy of placement based on testing is questionable; the process leads to a series of largely negative consequences associated with exclusion as documented above for tracking; and legal challenges have been made to each of these forms of school organization. Richardson argues, however, that special education has been able to capitalize on the legal rulings to establish a moral outrage among parents and educators leading to the current policy of inclusion, wherever possible. In addition, special education benefited from the emergence of the field of school psychology that used the issue as a basis to secure legitimacy as a true subfield in education. Richardson argues that tracking has been unable to extend legal rulings favoring detracking into broad educational policy. One area that Richardson overlooks is that the moral concerns about excluding special needs children from the full array of educational resources did not create a backlash among parents of non-special needs children, quite understandably. Detracking, however, is steadfastly opposed by middle-class parents who say "not for my kid" (Kohn, 1998).

❖ STATUS ATTAINMENT: SOCIALIZATION OR ALLOCATION?

A broader sociological issue of the tracking controversies is the question of the role played by curriculum placement in the process of occupation (or status) attainment. Recall once again that there are two contrasting views on how this works. Functional theory views schools as sorting institutions that select and channel the most able students into the most demanding courses, which in turn prepare them for the most demanding and functionally important jobs in a society. Functionalists see this process as not only necessary (in order that the jobs get done by the most qualified people) but also entirely just and fair since the selection process is based upon merit. Conflict and social reproduction theorists, however, argue that the selection process is always influenced by nonrelevant variables of status origin (SES, race, ethnicity, religion, gender). To the extent that this is true, the process is unfair, biased, and dysfunctional.

In a classic paper, Kerckhoff (1976) differentiated between a school process model of "socialization" and one of "allocation." He observed that most status attainment research until that time had generally neglected the structural and organizational arrangements of school that might enhance or constrain educational opportunities. This earlier theory, often referred to as the "Wisconsin" model (Sewell et al., 1969, 1970), focused on the process of socialization and especially on the influence of peers and parents in shaping the motivations of children. The basic idea was that the influence of status origin variables such as social class and race on educational

and occupational attainment was mediated by the expectations of teachers, parents, and peers. Kerckhoff (1976) argued that the Wisconsin model overlooked important structural factors, such as curriculum placement, which may influence status attainment independent of the other variables. Our review of the effects of tracking attests rather well to the importance of Kerckhoff's allocation model.

To what degree is status attainment structurally constrained by tracking allocation as a fundamental form of school organization? The research provides some support for both a socialization (or functional) model and an allocation (or conflict) model. Alexander, Cook, and McDill captured this double-edged reality quite nicely. In their longitudinal study of students tested initially in the ninth grade and followed to the senior year, they found that the effects of home background are entirely indirect, influencing a number of ninth grade variables which in turn determine track placement.

> The major determinants of curriculum assignment *are* ability, junior high school achievement, and curriculum and educational aspirations in the ninth grade.... However, there is actually considerable slippage in the process of curriculum sorting. Factors entirely unrelated to objectively assessed performance and potential are important determinants of track placement.... Two students of equal ability, motivation and past performance can be, and often are, assigned to different curricular! (Alexander, Cook, and McDill, 1978: 64–65)

This finding is similar to that obtained by Pallas et al. (1994) and discussed earlier regarding the inaccuracy of track placement and the likely influence of other factors. In any event, Alexander et al. (1978)

do conclude that track placement, whatever its determinants may be, substantially affects later educational and occupational attainments. The net result is that track allocation plays a prominent role in the status attainment process and the determinants of track placement are a little bit of everything (ability, home background factors, and several things that we are not able to identify at this time).

❖ TEACHER QUALITY

In Chapters 4 and 5, we concluded that teacher characteristics such as credentials and years of experience have been found to be unrelated to student achievement. This was reported initially in the Coleman Report (EEO) and later confirmed in Hanushek's (1989) review of 187 studies (see Table 5.1 in Chapter 5). In his review, however, Hanushek cautions that current measures of teacher characteristics are flawed and that "enormous differences in teacher quality exist" (p. 45).

There is voluminous literature surrounding the topic of teacher quality. In fact, there are at least three different literatures. This is, of course, understandable since aside from the sociological context of homes and school as groups and organizations, teacher characteristics are thought to be key to educational outcomes. First, there is a teacher training and reform literature that is primarily concerned with the "professionalization" of teaching. Although it draws upon sound research, its goal is to sustain and protect teaching as a profession (Darling-Hammond, 2001; Darling-Hammond, Wise, and Klein, 1995; McLaughlin and Oberman, 1996). Second, there is an edu-

cational research literature that is based largely on classroom observations and experimental analyses (for reviews, see Walberg, 1986; Kash and Borich, 1982). Third, there is a small literature in the sociology of education (Coleman et al., 1966; Rutter et al., 1979; Fuller, 1986; Hanushek, 1989; Greenwald, Hedges, and Laine, 1996; Goldhaber and Brewer, 2000; Ingersoll, 1999).

But the issue of teacher quality is highly controversial. Several recent studies have concluded that fully certified teachers are simply no more effective than those who are not (see www.abell.org along with a response from www.nctaf.org). On these two web sites, Kate Walsh of the Abell Foundation argues that a review of studies shows that certified teachers are no more effective than uncertified teachers, and Linda Darling-Hammond of the National Commission on Teaching and America's Future, argues otherwise. Monk (1994) shows that the number of courses that teachers complete in content areas (such as science) correlated positively with student achievement in that area. Goldhaber and Brewer (2000) demonstrate that student achievement is not affected by whether or not teachers have standard credentials in science. But the relationship did hold up in mathematics. They compared those with standard certifications with teachers who had been given emergency "licenses" without certification. Darling-Hammond (2001) reviews the entire set of available studies and concludes that certification policies are crude indicators of subject matter knowledge and knowledge of teaching, and that historically, they may have been flawed. But the implications of a teaching profession without certification and qualifications are an anathema to Darling-Hammond and others in the debate.

Characteristic   Findings

A. Teacher quality
    1. Preservice training   No consistent + effect
    2. Experience as teacher   Mixed effect
    3. Verbal ability   Positive effect
    4. Salary   No consistent + effect

B. Classroom structure teaching process
    1. Classroom time on task   Positive effect
    2. Homework   Positive effect
    3. Cooperative instructional tasks   Mixed effects
    4. High teacher expectations   Positive effect
    5. Active teaching and learning roles   Positive effect
    6. Tight evaluation of student achievement   Positive effect
    7. Clarity of teacher's presentation   Positive effect
    8. Individualized instruction   Mixed effects

FIGURE 6.6   **Teacher Quality and Student Achievement: Review of Research in the United States and Western Europe**

Source: Adapted from Bruce Fuller, "Defining School Quality," in *The Contributions of the Social Sciences to Educational Policy and Practice: 1965–1985,* eds. Jane Hannaway and Marlaine E. Lockheed (Berkeley, CA: McCutchan Company, 1986).

Most people on both sides do agree that teachers' basic knowledge in verbal ability and content skill areas are the best indicators of good teaching. Ferguson (1991) in a Texas study found that teachers' standardized scores on basic skills had the largest influence on student achievement, followed by teacher experience, class size, and teacher qualifications, in that order. By far the major obstacle in this research is the vested interests that people on both sides have, and the need for third-party studies is a priority. Currently, a project titled The Study of Instructional Improvement is under way at the Consortium for Policy Research at the University of Michigan, examining cohorts of students and teachers ninety times per year to determine the critical elements of instruction that influence student achievement (Archer, 2002a).

One of the best reviews of the overall research was conducted by Fuller (1986).[6] In his analysis, Fuller considered the work of all three of the above-mentioned groups and examined both empirical studies and existing reviews covering the period 1971 to 1984. Most of the studies were grounded in the educational productivity model, which has been emphasized throughout this book. Fuller's results are summarized in Figure 6.6. Several findings stand out, the most notable being that Fuller found no consistent positive effects for preservice training (that is,

[6] There are certainly many other best reviews, including *What Works* (1987); Kash and Borich (1982); Walberg (1986); and Glass (2002). In addition, Fuller (1987) and Fuller and Clarke (1994) have conducted reviews pertaining only to education in the Third World.

traditional teacher education), teacher experience, or teacher salary. These findings were obtained in the EEO study (Coleman et al., 1966), and by Hanushek (1989) and Rutter et al. (1979). The latter study specifically found that better teacher preparation (not more credentials) was related to higher student achievement (see discussion in Chapters 4 and 5).

These findings are consistent with the *emergent* models of the teacher training and reform literature (see Darling-Hammond et al., 1995). During the past decade of school reform, the professional development of teachers has undergone considerable revision. Leaders in the field (Darling-Hammond et al., 1995; McLaughlin and Oberman, 1996; Lieberman, 1995) have pronounced that the old models of "preservice" and "inservice" training must be discarded. The complexities of subject matter, the diversity of students, the transformations in the family and in the corporation have all led to a revolution in teacher training and lifelong learning.

Returning to Figure 6.6, we can observe that time on task in the classroom is one of the factors with positive results. This is one of the most consistent findings in all studies of teacher effectiveness. It is strongly similar to findings on summer learning, both of which lead to the following conclusion: School quality increases as time in school and time spent on learning increases. This certainly seems rather obvious. But, nonteachers should note that there is ample evidence that classrooms are often characterized by *time off from learning* (see Jackson, 1968; Oakes, 1985).

We had several occasions earlier in this chapter to note that low-track students are provided less opportunity to learn in terms of differential content and time on task. In addition, Oakes (1985: 110–111) reported the following:

> The instructional environments of high-track classes were more characterized by a whole set of teacher behaviors thought to promote learning than were those of low-track classes. . . . more time set aside for learning by teachers, more actual class time observed to be taken up with learning activities, more time expected to be spent on homework, fewer students observed off-task, students' perceptions of learning as the thing they do most in class, and more of the kind of instructional practice that is likely to motivate students to learn and decrease the time needed to do so.

All of these teacher characteristics identified by Oakes appear on Fuller's list of behavior characteristics of high teacher quality.

Oakes notes that factors such as clarity and task orientation would especially affect the time that students need to learn. When teachers lack clarity or task orientation, students will need more time to learn. And since that time is usually greater in low-track classes, equality of educational opportunity for these students has been compromised. Recall from our earlier discussion that students in low-track classes actually receive less time to learn anyway, regardless of the quality of instruction. Thus, we observe that those teacher behaviors that have been shown to increase achievement are differentially allocated to students within the school.

Recent research confirms Fuller's meta-analysis of the characteristics of teacher quality. Wenglinsky (2000) examined the math and science NAEP scores for students and their classroom teachers.

Using responses from teachers and principals, the research investigated the relationship of teacher credentials and practices to classroom mean student outcomes, controlling for student socioeconomic status and class size. Although there are some differences in the results for mathematics and science, several findings stand out across the two tests. Student scores were significantly higher (in some cases as great as 50 percent higher) when teachers held a major or a minor in the subject matter, provided hands-on learning, gave frequent tests, and possessed professional development in working with diverse student populations and in classroom management. These findings by Wenglinsky are consistent with those provided by Fuller in Figure 6.6. Note also the importance of a teacher possessing either a major or a minor in the subject matter because we turn now to examine this latter issue in considerable detail.

❖ THE PROBLEM OF UNDERQUALIFIED TEACHERS IN AMERICAN SECONDARY SCHOOLS

Over the past two decades, the question of teacher qualifications has received increased attention. National commission reports such as *A Nation at Risk* (National Commission on Excellence in Education, 1983) have spawned an era of reform that includes state initiatives for stronger teacher education and certification standards for teachers. These reports have argued that schools are not able to adequately staff classrooms with fully qualified teachers and that this is due largely to an increase in student enrollments together with increasing teacher attrition

due to retirements. The net result is an alarming shortage of qualified teachers (see Darling-Hammond, 1984; National Commission on Teaching and America's Future, 1997; Ingersoll, 1999, 2001b).

Of course, there has always existed concern on the part of school boards, parents, and the teaching profession to upgrade the quality of teaching. Despite the mixed findings regarding the relationship between teacher credentials and student achievement (see above and Chapter 5), teacher quality is still held to be one of the important factors that influence student learning. Moreover, teacher compensation is the largest component of the cost of education, causing all parties to assess the credentials of teachers. The notion that underqualified teachers could possibly be as effective as qualified teachers is counterintuitive and perhaps counterfactual.

One might think that under this type of scrutiny, the vast majority of teachers would be qualified to teach the courses that they are hired to teach. In actuality, however, this does not turn out to be true. Ingersoll (1999) has examined the problem of out-of-field teaching in depth using national data from the Schools and Staffing Surveys (SASS). These surveys have been conducted by the National Center for Education Statistics over the past decade on an every-other-year basis. Each survey contains a sample of about 5,000 school districts, 11,000 schools, and 55,000 teachers.

Prior to the SASS, studies of out-of-field teaching had at least two serious difficulties regarding the validity of the data. First, out-of-field teaching is a politically sensitive issue since it can directly and adversely effect school accreditation. For this reason, researchers have been skeptical of data and analysis that has been conducted by local or state school officials (Haggstrom, Darling-Hammond, and Grissmer, 1988; Robinson, 1985). One of the strengths of the SASS data on out-of-field teaching is that it is not obtained directly from school officials or from teachers by asking them about their out-of-field teaching assignments. Rather, the data are collected indirectly by asking teachers about daily schedules, along with questions regarding their training, education, and certification. Ingersoll independently computed the out-of-field assignments by comparing the teacher assignments and training.

Another problem is how to define out-of-field teaching. Typically, the standard indicator is a certification or license to teach a particular subject which all teachers must possess. The problem with this is that the standards for certification

in teacher training programs vary widely across the country (Tryneski, 1997). Ingersoll (1999: 27) resolved this issue by adopting a minimal definition of a qualified teacher at the secondary level—the possession of either a minor or a major in his or her current teaching field.

Table 6.1 shows the extent to which out-of-field teaching exists across seven different subject fields in the public schools, broken down by school size, school poverty level, and the presence or absence of teacher unions. There is substantial out-of-field teaching across all subject areas in secondary schools for the United States as a whole, ranging from 20 percent in social studies to 57 percent in physical science. Ingersoll argues that the consequences of out-of-field teaching are negative and multidimensional: low student achievement, narrow textbook

TABLE 6.1

PERCENTAGE OF SECONDARY SCHOOL (GRADES 7–12) TEACHERS IN EACH FIELD WITHOUT A MAJOR OR A MINOR IN THAT FIELD

	English	Math	Science	Life Science	Physical Science	Social Studies	History
U.S. total	24.3	33.1	20.3	33.1	56.5	19.9	53.1
Public total	24.1	31.4	19.9	32.9	56.9	19.3	53.1
School poverty level							
Low poverty	20.1	26.8	17.5	29.2	51.3	15.8	46.4
High poverty	25.7	42.8	27.8	40.1	65.1	25.1	60.0
School size							
Small	30.4	41.2	25.5	38.1	64.5	25.5	62.8
Large	22.4	27.5	17.6	30.1	53.7	17.2	48.1
Teacher union							
Member	24.3	31.2	19.1	32.0	55.7	18.5	52.9
Nonmember	23.3	32.1	23.1	36.3	61.7	22.1	53.9

Source: Adapted from Richard M. Ingersoll, 1999. "The Problem of Underqualified Teachers in American Secondary Schools." *Educational Researcher 28,* #2 (March): 26–37. Reprinted with permission.

teaching, and broad negative effects on students in other classes of the teacher resulting from extra time given over to the out-of-field class. Recently released data shows that very little improvement has been made to change these results from 1987 to 1999 (NCES, 2002; Gewertz, 2002; Education Week, 2003).

In any event, Table 6.1 shows that high-poverty schools are more likely to have teachers in out-of-field assignments than low-poverty schools, and teachers in small schools are more likely to be out-of-field than in large schools. Note carefully that Ingersoll's analysis is limited to the question of whether teacher quality differs between and within schools and that he assumes that teacher quality is related to student achievement. Thus, he does not empirically address the question of the actual effects of teacher quality. Here we see that high poverty and small schools have more out-of-field teachers, implying less teacher quality. It is certainly reasonable that small schools would have to rely on more out-of-field teaching to solve their staffing problems. Note that the presence or absence of teacher unions in the schools made no difference in the practice of out-of-field teaching.

The Coleman Report, among many previous studies, found that differences between schools in teacher quality were very small or zero. But we noted in our review of this study that the measures were fairly crude. Ingersoll's study improves on the measurement of teacher quality, showing that the difference results from the misassignment of teachers to classes for which they are not qualified. This could not have been observed in the many other studies of teacher quality that simply measure the level of teacher educational credentials, or training per se. This refinement of the mea-surement of teacher quality is a critical contribution of Ingersoll's research, over and above the substantive results.

Not surprisingly, there also exist substantial differences within schools in terms of students who are taught by out-of-field teachers. Ingersoll found that low-track students in all subject areas (except social studies and history) were more likely to be taught by a teacher without either a minor or a major in the subject area (see Table 6.2). Specifically, the within school differences (in track) are approximately as great as the between school differences shown in Table 6.1 for school poverty level and school size. It was not possible in these data to ascertain the amount of variation that was within rather than between schools, but the differences in both cases were substantial.

These data raise the question as to why so many teachers are teaching subjects for which they have little or no training. Ingersoll (1999) noted that there are three commonly employed, but flawed explanations for the phenomenon of out-of-field teaching. The first of these is the inadequate training of teachers. In fact, 99 percent of public school teachers have a bachelor's degree, and almost 50 percent have a graduate degree as well (Ingersoll, 2002). Over the past two decades, reform efforts have focused on requiring substantial work in an academic discipline (a subject area such as mathematics) in addition to the typical required courses in educational methods. Also, teachers are increasingly provided with opportunities for professional development in subject areas. But the problem is not training in the subject matter area; rather it lies in the assignment to teach in another area in which one has not been trained.

TABLE **6.2**

PERCENTAGE OF SECONDARY SCHOOL (GRADES 7–12) STUDENTS IN EACH FIELD TAUGHT BY TEACHERS WITHOUT A MAJOR OR A MINOR IN THAT FIELD

	English	Math	Science	Life Science	Physical Science	Social Studies	History
Track of class							
Low-track	24.7	33.5	20.4	42.3	66.8	14.3	55.1
Medium-track	11.8	15.7	9.2	31.4	42.8	8.9	44.9
High-track	11.2	20.4	7.2	20.7	43.0	11.2	51.1

Source: Adapted from Richard M. Ingersoll, 1999. "The Problem of Underqualified Teachers in American Secondary Schools." *Educational Researcher 28,* #2 (March): 26–37. Reprinted with permission.

A second explanation for out-of-field teaching blames teacher unions. The argument is that unions dictate a mandate of "last-hired, first-fired" policy, which works to protect veteran teachers (Toch, 1996). In this type of seniority rules scenario, experienced teachers are given priority in assignment regardless of competence, especially during times of teacher oversupply. The data, however, do not support this explanation as schools with unions actually display less, rather than more, out-of-field teachers (see Table 6.1). Other research (Steelman, Powell, and Carini, 2000) confirms that the existence of teacher unions, contrary to widespread belief, do not deter instructional reform or student achievement.

The most popular explanation for the staffing problems created by out-of-field teaching is teacher shortages in the country. The argument is that there is an increase in student enrollments and an increase in teacher retirements. According to Ingersoll (1999), there is some degree of support for this contention, but it is limited. There has been an increased demand for teachers since the mid-1980s and student enrollments have increased by about 15 percent, and there are teacher vacancies each year since the mid-1980s. Ingersoll shows, however, that these vacancies are not due mostly to increasing enrollments or teacher retirements, but rather the teacher shortages result mostly from teachers leaving their jobs (teacher turnover). As Figure 6.7 shows, less than one-fifth of the total turnover of teachers in the 1994–1995 school year was due to retirements. Instead, teacher turnover is more often due to either dissatisfaction (30 percent), pursuit of another career (24 percent), or family or personal issues (47 percent). Thus, the data suggest that the cause of teacher shortages and the demand for new teachers is the result of too many teachers who are leaving teaching. In a multivariate analysis, Ingersoll (1999: 33) demonstrated that the high rate of teacher turnover is due primarily to "low salaries, inadequate support from administrators, rampant student discipline problems, and little faculty input into school decision-making."

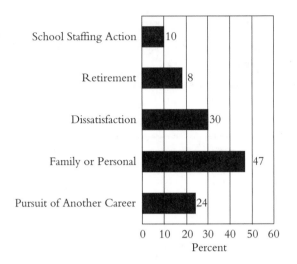

FIGURE 6.7 **Percentage Teachers Giving Various Reasons for Turnover.**
Source: Richard M. Ingersoll, 1999. "The Problem of Underqualified Teachers in American Secondary Schools." *Educational Researcher 28,* #2 (March): 26–37. Reprinted with permission.

❖ SCHOOL STAFFING PROBLEMS

Out-of-school teaching is only one indicator of the larger concept of school staffing problems. The problem, as Ingersoll sees it, is not teacher shortages, or increasing enrollments, or retiring faculty. Rather, the problem is that teaching is considered low-status work and teachers are considered semiskilled workers. Since the turn of the twentieth century, "American educators have sought to promote the view that the teaching, like other professions, is a highly complex kind of work, requiring specialized knowledge and skill and, like other professions, deserves commensurate prestige, authority, and compensation" (Ingersoll, 1999: 33). By and large, these efforts have not been successful. Teachers have only limited authority over workplace decisions, including what they teach and when they teach.

Teacher compensation remains just on the high end of any typical blue-collar working-class job. The evidence on out-of-field teaching shows that the notion of the profession having access to specialized and complex knowledge has not been accepted.

In further work using the same data set, Ingersoll (2001b) pursues the question of teacher staffing problems. Beyond the problems identified earlier concerning teacher qualifications, teacher shortages are widely believed to have reached epic proportions. Some American school systems are now importing teachers from as far away as the Philippines to fill vacant teaching positions (Coleman, 2002). Teacher turnover is highest among beginning teachers (and, of course, older teachers who are retiring) and among those teaching special education, science, and mathematics (Grissmer and Kirby, 1997; Murnane, 1987; Boe et al., 1998).

Ingersoll identifies two different types of teacher turnover. First, there are teachers who leave the system entirely, either retiring or moving to an alternative occupation. Second, there is turnover that results from teachers who move from one school or school system to another. Moving jobs as a form of turnover is just as common as leaving, at least among public school teachers, and results largely from the fact that many teachers are unhappy in positions in distressed schools and are prepared to move to an improved situation whenever possible (Ingersoll, 2001b).

Teacher turnover is slightly higher (13.2 percent) compared to all other occupations (11 percent). Private school turnover is significantly larger than for the public schools, and this is especially true in small private schools. Among public schools teachers, turnover is greatest in high-poverty and urban schools. Note that among public school teachers, school size makes little difference, but that private school teachers in small schools are the most likely of all categories to leave (22.8 percent).

Considering these results for teacher turnover and out-of-field teaching, Ingersoll examined the relationship of teacher turnover to school staffing problems. A common argument is that school staffing problems (which in turn lead to decreases in student performance) are caused by teacher shortages, which in turn are caused by student enrollment increases and teacher retirement increases. This is shown in Figure 6.8 as the Contemporary Education Theory. By contrast, Ingersoll proposes that school staffing problems are caused by teacher turnover which is the result of negative organizational conditions.

Using the SASS data once again, Ingersoll conducted a multivariate analysis showing that the organizational model is supported. School staffing problems are due in part to enrollment increases and to

Contemporary Education Theory

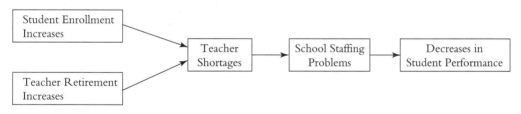

An Organizational Perspective

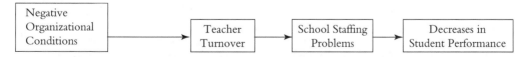

FIGURE 6.8   Two Perspectives on the Causes and Consequences of School
                    Staffing Problems

Source: Richard M. Ingersoll, 2001b. "Teacher Turnover and Teacher Shortages: An Organizational Analysis." *American Educational Research Journal 37:* 499–534. Reprinted with permission.

teacher retirements, but the largest influence on school staffing problems (defined as teacher turnover here, but clearly applicable to broader problems such as out-of-field teaching) are a set of negative organizational conditions. Ingersoll examined the influence of teacher and school characteristics on rates of teacher turnover. But he also constructed four organizational variables that reflected the degree of teacher satisfaction with the social organization of the school. These organizational variables were: salary scale, administrative support, student discipline problems, and faculty influence. The teacher and school type variables continue to influence teacher turnover even after controlling for the organizational factors. That is, turnover was consistently higher in low-poverty schools and among very young and older teachers. In support of his theory, however, Ingersoll found that three of his four organizational variables were significantly related to teacher turnover: specifically, turnover was lower with greater administrative support, higher levels of student discipline, and lower levels of student discipline problems.

Ingersoll concluded that school staffing problems are more likely to be due to teacher turnover than to teacher shortages (meaning a lack of supply). And that turnover was caused largely by a set of negative organizational conditions. Figure 6.7 demonstrates that turnover is not largely due to retirements (only 18 percent) and is far more likely to result from dissatisfaction or the desire to pursue another occupation. And younger teachers (under thirty years of age) are more likely to leave. In his multivariate analysis, Ingersoll determined that the odds of younger teachers leaving the profession are 171 percent higher than for middle-aged teachers. But the force be-

hind the turnover of younger teachers is fundamentally dissatisfaction (he notes that middle-aged teachers settle in and accept the status quo). This manifests itself in the larger organizational analysis in which teachers identify the poor organizational conditions of their school as to why they have left the profession. The entire analysis fits together into a compelling argument that few would disagree with, and yet no one knows how to truly intervene to correct the problem. The analysis is not foolproof as Ingersoll does not demonstrate that out-of-field teaching or teacher turnover does indeed result in lower student academic performance (see critique by Friedman, 2000 and rejoinder by Ingersoll, 2001a). Of course, as we have noted above, the research of Greenwald, Hedges, and Laine (1996) and Wenglinsky (2000) demonstrates the consistent positive influence of teacher education, experience, and ability on student achievement, which is consistent with Ingersoll's argument.

Despite the lack of consistent empirical verification, there is an intuitive sense that teacher quality is related to student outcomes and there are studies that do confirm this as noted earlier (see especially, Greenwald, Hedges, and Laine, 1996). Ingersoll argues (in response to Friedman, 2000) that no one questions credentials in the other professions; that is, no one would consider going to a doctor, dentist, attorney, or architect that lacked the appropriate credentials. In these higher-status occupations, Ingersoll argues, there is no one questioning the lack of research demonstrating that these "qualified" professionals are more effective than "underqualified" people. The only reason that this is an issue with teacher quality is the low status that the profession is regarded.

Recent evidence confirms Ingersoll's contentions. Hanushek, Kain, and Rivkin (2001) report a study of 375,000 teachers in Texas during the years 1993 to 1996. The study was designed to determine why teachers change schools or exit the school, and especially, if they did so for financial reasons. If the teachers did change for economic reasons, the notion of providing a bonus salary to teachers for working in high-poverty schools might be a viable intervention. Unfortunately, the researchers discovered that teachers seek better working conditions by switching to schools with fewer minority students, higher test scores, and a smaller percentage of low-SES students. They concluded that teacher mobility is much more strongly related to characteristics of the students, particularly race and achievement, than to salary, although salary was a secondary consideration. The findings suggest that more attention should be given to the existing working conditions in schools rather than to paying teachers more to work in tougher schools.

❖ CLASSROOM STRUCTURE AND INTERACTION

An important element of teacher quality is the capacity to structure student interaction in the classroom in a manner that promotes achievement and equality for all students. The structure of a classroom and the various possibilities for social processes within classrooms is a large topic that has received considerable attention (Jackson, 1968; Goodlad, 1984; Dreeben, 1968; Barr and Dreeben, 1983; Flanders, 1970; Parsons, 1959; Boocock, 1980; Ballantine, 1993).

One of the most basic concepts in sociology is status—a position in the social structure which consists of a set of norms or rules for behavior. (The social structure could be as large as the society or as small as a family.) Generally, normal human behavior involves conformity to the norms associated with status positions.[7] Although we hate to think of ourselves as conformists, sociology (and all the social sciences) is based upon the premise that typical behavior *is* in accordance with the norms and obligations of status positions. Status positions can be ascribed or achieved, active or dormant, equal or unequal, and relevant or irrelevant (Berger, Connor, and Fisek, 1974).

Since all of us occupy hundreds of status positions, most remain dormant at any given time. In a typical classroom situation, the only status positions that should be active are teacher and student; for example, the status characteristics of race or gender would be irrelevant to the interaction. It is possible (and likely), however, that these ascribed characteristics of gender and race may become active, thereby resulting in manifestations

[7] Obviously, there are limits to the scope of this model of human behavior, and this is the source of considerable debate within the discipline. People do not always play their role with sincerity and sometimes they refuse to play at all (Goffman, 1959). Indeed, there is a whole literature documenting how this process works itself out in schools, usually to the detriment of all concerned (Willis, 1977). These studies complement the work described in this section and are applicable over and above this discussion. That is to say, this discussion is limited in scope, but it is not invalidated by the existence of alternative frames of reference.

of sexism or racism that are clearly irrelevant to the task at hand. This classification system is a useful way to identify racism and sexism that are sometimes used indiscriminately.

Research has shown that small task groups, such as the typical classroom, exhibit status hierarchies where some group members are more active, influential, and powerful than others (Berger and Zelditch, 1985). These unequal status positions occur in groups in which participants have been carefully matched according to various irrelevant status characteristics such as race, gender, age, height, educational level, and occupational attainment. This process has been termed status generalization (Berger et al., 1974). Status generalization is a basic component of "expectation states" theory—the idea that behavior follows from expectations associated with status positions.

If dominance and inequality emerge in groups with people who are otherwise equal in societal status, it is not surprising to learn that this occurs even more predictably when group members differ in status characteristics that are viewed as unequal. Thus, since gender and race have historically been defined as unequal (males and whites having higher status in society), expectation states theory predicts that whites and/or males will assume high-status positions in classrooms. Attractiveness also acts as an irrelevant status characteristic (Webster and Driskell, 1983).

In addition, students hold unequal standing in the classroom based upon previous academic performance. Students hold relatively clear expectations for each other as to academic competence at various tasks (Cohen, 1984, 1994; Cohen and Lotan, 1995; Rosenholz, 1985; Tammivaara, 1982). Furthermore, the research demonstrates that group members who assume and are accorded high status in one area of expertise, such as reading, are expected to be more competent and influential in other nonrelated tasks as well, academic and nonacademic. What this means for classrooms is that some students are seen as having the best ideas in specific tasks such as reading ability, but also in most other tasks as well, however irrelevant they may be to reading (Rosenholz, 1985).

A landmark study using expectation states theory was conducted by Elizabeth Cohen and her colleagues at Stanford University (1972). In Cohen's study, and several replications, it was found that simply placing black students and white students in what appeared to be an equal-status problem-solving situation was *insufficient* to guarantee equal-status outcomes. In fact, the studies have documented and reported relatively extreme manifestations of racism—that is, white dominance. Moreover, in these studies extensive efforts were made to alter the interaction pattern of white dominance with little success, except under one condition in which the black students were literally allocated to a dominant role *vis a vis* the white students who were allocated a submissive role. These results led Cohen and Roper (1972) to this conclusion:

> The oft made assumption that one has only to join Blacks and Whites on an officially "equal" footing in the same building for "equal status" relations to develop is not sound. . . . Belief systems concerning race and other status characteristics are so powerful that they will likely reinforce rather than damage stereotypical beliefs. (pp. 645, 657)

The Cohen and Roper experiment was part of a large research program in expectational states theory that conducted many other studies using what has come to be known as a "standard" research situation. In this experimental situation (both in the laboratory and in the field) subjects find themselves in either an equal or unequal interaction. An example of an equal-status interaction would be a group of two to four people who are white, female, eighteen-year-old college students, matched according to height, grades, aspirations, and social class. An example of an unequal status interaction would occur if one of the participants was white while the other was black, or if one was male and the other female. The group is asked to work on a problem-solving task, and observations are made regarding the manifestations of power, influence, and leadership.

The results of Cohen's analyses are clear: Mixed-race interaction is characterized by white dominance unless strenuous efforts are made to intervene. Moreover, it seems insufficient to merely "equate" the conditions since white dominance remains. Only by providing some form of black expectancy advantage are we able to consistently obtain equal-status interaction. The same findings have been reported consistently and persistently for the status characteristics of gender, age, expert status, academic status, and peer status. This has been shown in the laboratory and in the classroom.

The greater portion of this chapter has addressed the *structural* sources of inequality that may exist within schools as a result of tracking. This perspective, valuable as it may be, ignores the theory and research that describes the *processes* of stratification that may arise in hetero-geneous or untracked classes. Cooperative learning is a widely recommended technique for establishing greater equality in heterogeneous classrooms (Slavin, 1983). Although cooperative learning can

imply many different things, Cohen (1994) argues that used correctly, cooperative learning can be a tool to overcome the effects of status generalization that we have described above. In a properly prepared cooperative learning classroom, students can come to learn new norms that stress and establish the idea that the contributions of all students are necessary to complete the tasks and the goals of the classroom.

Cohen and her colleagues have documented the difficulties of working in heterogenous groups (Cohen and Lotan, 1997; Cohen, 1994). Summarizing this work, Cohen (2000) examines the junction of equality of educational opportunity as it occurs at the classroom level. Notwithstanding the fact that macro-inequalities in the larger society interpenetrate the social system of the school, it is classroom experiences that are the proximate causes of educational success and failure. Cohen (2000: 266) argues that within school process such as "tracking and ability grouping lead to unequal treatment in instruction, unequal access to peers who represent resources of academic achievement, and status orders that arise in the classroom and lead to unequal status interaction among peers." The most important aspects of Cohen's work are her own attempts to modify the social system of classroom in order to (p. 267) "defeat the process by which educational outcomes mirror the social inequalities among individuals."

Unlike other researchers and practitioners, Cohen emphasizes the persistent emergence of inequality in the classroom. As we have noted, a great deal of classroom inequality originates in the larger society and in the home in the form of SES, race, gender effects, and other family structure advantages and disadvantages. And when tracking is used to organize classrooms, this organizational inequality overlays the existing individual inequalities. But, even within heterogeneously grouped untracked classrooms working in cooperative learning, Cohen and Lotan (1997: 7–8) observe that

> [T]he task and evaluation practices of the classroom help to build inequalities through a process of social comparison by which students see each other arrayed along a single dimension of ability in schoolwork. . . . Students compare themselves to each other as they complete tasks and when they hear teachers make public evaluations. Standardized tasks encourage a process of social comparison in which students evaluate how well they are doing in completing assignments rapidly and successfully. Emphasis on marking and grading has the same effect, giving students objective grounds for deciding where each person stands on academic ability and achievement. The net result of this process of social comparison is an agreed-upon rank order by teachers and students on the "relative" smartness of each member of the class.

This process, so familiar to everyone, teachers, parents, and students, is a major source of inequality in the classroom. Expectations for competence are established on the basis of student action and teacher and peer response, they form the basis for general expectations across other tasks both in and out of the classroom, and they generate differential effort and performance on the part of those students who hold high status on academic rank and those who hold low status. The process itself becomes the basis for a self-fulfilling prophecy about student performance and eventually can become the basis for placement into low-track or special education class (Mercer, Iadacola, and Moore, 1980).

Cohen's work is pivotal as we consider the possibilities of untracking in classrooms. The elimination of tracking and special education classes leads directly to an increase in heterogeneous fully inclusive classrooms. Creating an equitable classroom under these conditions is challenging for teachers because of the ongoing process of academic and peer status generalization as described above. This has led Cohen and her associates to develop a program for overcoming status differentiation as it emerges in heterogeneous classes (Cohen, 1994, 2000; Cohen and Lotan, 1997).

Using Expectation States Theory as a foundation, creating an equal-status classroom in a heterogeneous setting requires modification of the learning tasks and the evaluation structure and changing the curriculum, as well as direct treatment by the teacher of status problems as they exist and emerge (see Cohen, 1994; and a meta-analysis conducted by Lockheed, 1985). First, the task must change from a unidimensional (only one way to solve math problems) to a multidimensional approach in which there are fewer opportunities for a invidious comparison among students and more opportunities for innovation in group work. Without neglecting the basic content of the curriculum, one can broaden it so that a wider variety of skills and abilities become relevant to completing the tasks. This makes available a variety of paths for student contributions.

Cohen (2000) calls this the "Multiple Ability Treatment" component of creating equal status in the classroom. Teachers must convince students via the curriculum and the nature of the tasks that many different types of intellectual ability are required. Moreover, that no students will excel in all of these abilities and that some will excel on some of the abilities. In her research, however, she and her colleagues have discovered that this Multiple Ability Treatment is a necessary but not sufficient condition for obtaining equal status. What happens is that regardless of how many skills and abilities are required by the curriculum, the process of status generalization persists, whereby some students perform well on some of the abilities and this is then generalized to other abilities that are manifested in the classroom (see Cohen and Lotan, 1995, 1997).

The necessary and complimentary condition is called Assigning Competence to Low Status Students and requires teachers to carefully monitor low-status children as they work on multiple ability tasks, looking for opportunities to comment on a contribution that a low-status student makes, which demonstrated some intellectual skill or ability. "The teacher publicly comments on the ability or skill that has been demonstrated by the low-status student, making sure the other students understand that the low-status student has shown an important ability" (Cohen, 2000: 277). The teacher uses her or his authority as an evaluator of these tasks to assign a high level of competence to the low-status students and demonstrates how it is relevant to the successful completion of the task. Cohen provides ample empirical data to support the success of these interventions.

❖ STUDENT ACHIEVEMENT IN JAPAN AND THE UNITED STATES

In this chapter and in Chapter 1, we presented comparisons of student achievement in Japan and the United States (see again Figures 1.3 and 6.5). Are the data

favoring Japan due to differences that operate *between* the two educational systems or are they due to elements that operate *within* schools in each system? Or are they due to differences between homes in Japan and in the United States? In fact, the latter is most likely the case. Numerous studies have documented the differences in family structure and functioning variables between the United States and Japan (Stevenson and Baker, 1992; O'Kelly and Carney, 1986). Unfortunately, IEA data do not contain adequate information on family structure and functioning to test the influence of these variables. Consequently, the following discussion is confined to a comparison of between school (system) and within school (system) effects.

◆ BETWEEN SYSTEM EFFECTS

Are differences in achievement between students in Japan and the United States explained by differences between the two types of school systems? Many researchers have explored this question. Schaub and Baker (1991) reviewed nine studies that tested eight hypotheses regarding the likelihood that differences between the two educational systems might explain the differences in mathematics achievement. Table 6.3 summarizes of the results of these studies. None of the eight hypotheses are supported consistently. Achievement differences between Japan and the United States are *not* due to class size, teacher salaries, teacher training, teacher experience, selection bias, student body characteristics, amount of instructional time, per pupil expenditures, or student IQ. In some cases, there are inconsistent findings from several studies, but there are no consistent findings that support any of these between system explanations.

TABLE 6.3

TEST OF ONE-VARIABLE HYPOTHESES OF MATHEMATICS ACHIEVEMENT DIFFERENCES BETWEEN JAPANESE AND U.S. MIDDLE GRADE STUDENTS

Hypothesis	Hypothesis Supported
1. Japan has smaller teacher/student ratio.	No
2. Japan has better paid teachers.	No
3. Japanese teachers receive more training and are more experienced.	Mixed
4. Japanese students receive more instructional time.	Mixed
5. Japanese schools have a more select student population.	No
6. Japanese students are more homogeneous at the classroom level.	Mixed
7. Japan spends more resources on education.	Mixed
8. Japanese students are more intelligent.	No

Source: Adapted from Table 1 in Maryellen Schaub and David P. Baker, "Solving the Math Problem: Exploring Mathematics Achievement in Japanese and American Middle Schools," American Journal of Education 99 (1991): 623–642; see original study for specific references regarding the research for each hypothesis.

For example, Schaub and Baker note that there are inconsistent findings regarding the amount of instructional time. Although the Japanese students spend more time in school (days), they do not receive more mathematics instruction at this grade level.

In view of these null results, Schaub and Baker (1991) conducted an analysis using classroom-level variables.[8] They hypothesized that achievement differences may be explained by variations in the management of class time and instructional methods. Using the Second International Mathematics Survey (SIMS), Schaub and Baker found that teachers in the United States spend less time preparing for class, review older material more, and spend more time keeping order and doing administrative tasks than their counterparts in Japan. Japanese teachers spend more time explaining new material and lecturing to the entire class. U.S. teachers are more likely to ask their students to work alone at their desks or to work in groups, and they administer tests more frequently. How are these classroom differences related to differences in mathematics achievement?

Schaub and Baker regressed achievement on these classroom variables and found that "the pattern of teaching that is more evident in Japan increases class mathematics achievement, while the pattern that is more evident in the United States decreases class achievement" (1991: 635). These results are depicted in Table 6.4. The positive and negative signs in the table refer to increases or decreases

[8] Schaub and Baker aggregate all variables at the classroom level—that is, mean scores for student achievement, teacher instructional time, and so on.

TABLE 6.4

CONTROLLED REGRESSION EFFECTS OF MANAGEMENT OF CLASS TIME AND METHODS OF INSTRUCTION IN JAPAN AND THE UNITED STATES

Predictor Variable	Direction of Effect
Management of class time	
Preparing for class (Japan > U.S.)	No significant effect
Explaining new material (Japan > U.S.)	+
Reviewing old material (U.S. > Japan)	−
Doing administrative tasks (U.S. > Japan)	+
Spending time keeping order (U.S. > Japan)	−
Instructional methods	
Lecturing to the entire class (Japan > U.S.)	+
Having students work alone at their desks (U.S. > Japan)	−
Having students work in groups (U.S. > Japan)	−
Taking tests (U.S. > Japan)	No significant effect
Total R^2 (percentage variation explained for between country difference in mathematics achievement	.44

Source: Adapted from Tables 4 and 5 in Maryellen Schaub and David P. Baker, "Solving the Math Problem: Exploring Mathematics Achievement in Japanese and American Middle Schools," *American Journal of Education* 99 (1991): 623–642.

for the average classroom score on the mathematics test as a result of increases in the predictor variable—that is, the more time spent on keeping order in the classroom, the lower the achievement. Note that the time spent on "keeping order" is not at all the same as "having order" in the classroom, which we have already noted repeatedly is positively related to achievement (see Chapter 4).

Thus, Schaub and Baker (1991: 635) conclude that "time spent on explaining new material and lecturing to the whole class raises posttest means (Japan does more of this than the United States), while reviewing older material, keeping order, and having students work alone or in small groups lowers achievement (U.S. does more of this than Japan)." There is

no simple explanation for why doing administrative tasks increases achievement, but in general, the implications for American schools and educators are rather obvious. Differences between the two school systems in the management of class time and instructional methods do appear to be related to differences in achievement.

♦ WITHIN SYSTEM EFFECTS

Can tracking explain the Japanese achievement advantage? Westbury (1992) raises the possibility that the difference in achievement can be explained by considering the difference in the opportunities to learn that exist within each educational system. He proposes that Japanese

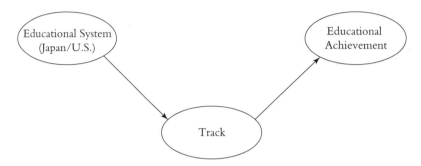

FIGURE 6.9   **Westbury's Theoretical Model**

students do better because on average they have greater OTL. This is made possible by a uniform curriculum that is taught to nearly all students in each grade (see again Figure 6.4). By contrast, as we have noted earlier, U.S. students are tracked, thereby receiving a differentiated curriculum. In effect, Westbury hypothesized that the difference between the two educational systems would disappear if we compared only students who received the same curriculum (OTL).

To do this, Westbury examined the relationship of educational system to mathematics achievement controlling for track among both eighth and twelfth grade students in the Second International Mathematics Survey (SIMS). Westbury's theoretical model is displayed in Figure 6.9. The strategy of this analysis is quite similar to that reviewed in Chapter 4 regarding differences between Catholic and public schools in America.

The results of Westbury's analysis for the eighth grade students are shown in Table 6.5 and Figure 6.10.[9] The results are

quite illuminating. For each question on the mathematics test, teachers were asked to indicate whether the material was covered during the eighth grade (seventh grade in Japan). In the table, Westbury shows that 82 percent of the items were covered in Japanese classrooms, on average. For the two highest U.S. tracks, the coverage was similar (88 percent in the algebra track and 78 percent in the enriched track). The coverage, which measures OTL, drops severely in the two lower U.S. tracks (64 in the typical courses and 34 percent in the remedial classes).

Comparing achievement for students in the two highest tracks (algebra and enriched) for the United States with students in Japan, there is no difference, as shown in the boxplot of Figure 6.10. The Japan-U.S. achievement difference in mathematics occurs only when we compare the two lowest U.S. tracks (remedial and typical) with their counterparts in Japan. It is a clear case of a specification effect: "When the curricula of the two countries are similar, there is essentially

---

[9] Westbury also aggregated the variables at the classroom level. In Japan, SIMS tested seventh grade students because the curriculum was a better match overall—that is, eighth grade stu-

dents in Japan receive a more advanced curriculum than eighth grade students in the United States and in all other countries worldwide.

TABLE 6.5

U.S. EIGHTH GRADE COURSE TYPES AND TEACHER-REPORTED COVERAGE OF ALGEBRA ITEMS ON THE SIMS COGNITIVE TESTS

Course Type	Number of Classrooms N	Percentage of Sample	Coverage (%)
United States			
Remedial	30	11	37
Typical	174	64	64
Enriched	31	11	78
Algebra	38	14	88
All classes	273	100	66
Japan	213	100	82

Source: Ian Westbury, "Comparing American and Japanese Achievement: Is the United States Really a Low Achiever?" *Educational Researcher 21* (June–July 1992): 18–24. Copyright (1992) by the American Educational Research Association. Reprinted by permission of the publisher.

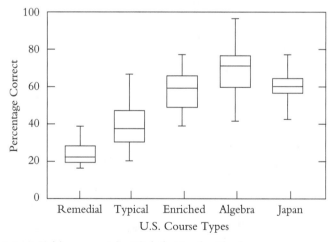

FIGURE 6.10   Post-test Achievement in Eighth Grade Algebra

Note: In a boxplot, the length of the box represents the proportion of the distribution that falls between the twenty-fifth and seventy-fifth percentiles. The line across the box represents the median. The length of the "whiskers" represents the minimum and the maximum or the adjacent outermost value.

Source: "Comparing American and Japanese Achievement: Is the United States Really a Low Achiever?" *Educational Researcher 21* (June–July 1992): 18–24. Copyright 1992 by the American Educational Research Association. Reprinted by permission of the publisher.

no difference in the performance of U.S. and Japanese students" (Westbury, 1992: 21). The difference in performance occurs only when the curricula are different. The results for the twelfth grade students were remarkably similar.

Westbury (1992: 23) concludes "that the difference between Japanese and U.S. achievement can be seen as a consequence of different curricula." There are several important implications in this statement. First, it suggests that efforts to explain the seemingly higher Japanese achievement by cultural variables (commitment to education, excessive television viewing, family structure and functioning, and so on) is unnecessary. Second, the results suggest that ongoing reforms directed at teacher training or national competency testing may be ill-advised. Third, the results reaffirm the salience of curriculum as the fundamental variable in explaining differences in achievement.

As we noted repeatedly in this chapter, recent studies in the United States have shown convincingly that curricula differentiation mediates the effects of the between home (race, SES) and between school (Catholic/public) effects. "The curriculum is, from this perspective, a fundamental component of the structured process of *schooling*, and it is the ways in which the experience it offers students, and the ways in which those experiences are distributed that actually 'produces' the *effects of schools*" (Westbury, 1992: 23).

Baker (1993) takes issue with Westbury's analysis and conclusions, presenting a critique that involves a more precise measurement of how well students in each system learn the material that they have been exposed to. Whereas Westbury simply describes the average coverage in all the Japanese classrooms and the four

U.S. tracked classrooms, Baker calculates students' test scores given the material that is taught within each classroom. Thus, for each student, a score (percentage correct) is computed given a certain number of items that were taught in that classroom. (By contrast, Westbury computed the average number of items that were taught in each track grouping—that is, the average number of items taught in the sixty-four U.S. classrooms with a typical curriculum.) In contrast to Westbury, Baker finds that considerable difference in mathematics achievement remains, even after controlling for track or opportunity to learn. Not surprisingly, Baker attributes this between system achievement difference to classroom management, instructional methods (see Schaub and Baker above), and home background.

Which findings are correct? It is probably a little bit of both. Baker is undoubtedly correct in providing a more accurate measure of OTL as a control in the analysis. However, this may actually overcontrol for track. Baker computes a test score, controlling for the OTL in each specific classroom in the United States and Japan (unlike Westbury who computed scores within each type of classroom). In this process, the effect of the large number of typical classrooms in the United States (174 of 278 classrooms) outweighs the results from the enriched and algebra classes. In placing all American students together in the analysis, Baker obscures the differential learning curve that exists between high and low tracks. High-track students learn at a rate that is nearly double that of low-track students (see again Figure 6.1 and the related discussion). Thus, Baker's analysis overlooks the specification finding that appears in Westbury's analysis. The percentage correct for United States students, in effect, is skewed downward by the students in the typical track who only get around 40 percent correct, as was shown in Figure 6.10. It may have been preferable to have combined the two studies showing the percentage correct of those items taught within the track designations that Westbury relied upon (algebra, enriched, and so on). Conceivably, this might show less explanation due to track than found by Westbury, and less achievement difference remaining after controlling for opportunity to learn as reported by Baker.

❖ SUMMARY

This chapter has focused on a wide range of organizational issues that primarily operate within schools. The structure and the processes associated with tracking are clearly the dominant organizational forces in schools in the United States. The influence of tracking upon achievement is significant and substantial. Typically, tracking also increases inequality among students within a school, but this can vary from school to school. The major concerns with tracking focus on the issue of equality of educational opportunity. These same concerns are part of the discussion of teacher quality and the structure of classrooms. How can schools and classrooms be staffed and structured so as to obtain greater academic achievement and greater equality of outcomes?

❖ KEY CONCEPTS

differences within schools
curriculum
opportunity-to-learn (OTL)
intended and implemented curriculum
tracking, ability grouping, curriculum
   differentiation
pedagogical basis of tracking
tracking decisions
meritocracy of tracking
effects of race and social class on
   tracking

constitutionality of tracking
universality of tracking
educational contents and processes in
   different tracks
detracking
characteristics of teacher quality
out-of-field teaching
teacher turnover and teacher shortages
expectation states theory
status generalization
cooperative learning

❖ KEY STUDIES

Oakes (1985, 1994)
Rosenbaum (1976)
Stevenson and Baker (1991)

McKnight et al. (1987)
Goodlad (1984)
Hallinan (1994, 1996)

Pallas et al. (1994)
Richardson (2000)
Westbury (1989, 1992)
Kerkhoff (1976)
Alexander et al. (1978)
Gamoran (1992)

Fuller (1986)
Wenglinsky (2000)
Ingersoll (1999, 2001b)
Cohen (1994, 2000)
Cohen and Roper (1972)
Schaub and Baker (1991)

❖ REVIEW QUESTIONS

1. Discuss the relationship between OTL and tracking. Use results from the analysis of the SIMS data to support your discussion. Specifically, cite several facts derived from Figure 6.1 showing the relationships of track, OTL, and math achievement.

2. Summarize Westbury's study of algebra coverage in quartiles 3 and 1 of eight countries in the Second IEA Mathematics Study. How is this variation in algebra coverage related to mathematics achievement in SIMS?

3. Identify, describe, and critique five rationales often raised by educators in defense of tracking.

4. According to Cohen and Roper (1972), "In the classroom it is impossible to compose groups where all the members have equal status." Why is this the case?

5. Contrast and compare the curricula content and opportunities to learn that are provided by high- and low-track classes, according to Oakes.

6. Oakes points out that a mismatch exists between the *needs* of poor and minority children and tracking. Explain.

7. Drawing upon the empirical data reviewed in the chapter, discuss the problems of accuracy and fairness in track placement.

8. Describe the Pallas et al. (1994) study of the relationship of reading group placement and the CAT reading subtest. What are the implications?

9. How does the scope, inclusivity, electivity, and selectivity of tracks (Gamoran) affect achievement and equality in schools?

10. According to Schaub and Baker (1991), Japan-U.S. differences in achievement can be explained with references to instructional and organizational differences. Discuss.

11. According to Westbury (1992), Japan-U.S. differences in achievement can be explained by tracking policies. Describe his model and data results.

12. Identify the relationships between teacher quality and teaching practices as they are associated with student achievement (Fuller).

13. Describe the extent of out-of-field teaching and its relationship to the characteristics of schools. What are the causes of teacher turnover and out-of-field teaching?

14. Summarize more recent studies regarding the effect of teacher quality drawing upon Darling-Hammond (2001) and Archer (2002a).

Chapter 7

PEER GROUP DIFFERENCES

Teacher and pupil confront each other with attitudes from which the underlying hostility can never be altogether removed.

(WALLER, 1932: 195)

Student cultures play a key mediating role in the production of student outcomes, and such cultures are not a simple response to practices either within or outside the schools. Student cultures are, rather, semi-autonomous and, as such, cannot be controlled easily or directly.

(WEIS, 1985: 219)

In Chapter 1, we focused on the conflicting goals of equality and productivity that centered in our schools. In this chapter, we consider another manifestation of conflict: Schools and students are at serious odds with one another in today's society. First, we compare the cultural values of schools and youth, and we show that conflict does indeed exist. Drawing from the school effects model discussed throughout this book, we examine the relative impact of peer groups and schools on educational outcomes. Also, we consider the role of extracurricular activities and the problem of peer sexual harassment. It is, of course, impossible to examine the influence of peer group differences on achievement and development without taking the variables of family background and school relationships into account.

❖ THE CULTURE OF SCHOOLS: ACADEMIC OR ADOLESCENT?

During the past century, American education has wrestled with duplicity. Since 1893, when the Committee of Ten (Sizer, 1964) advocated a more demanding classic education for all students, a variety of social forces has created a system of schooling that remains patently anti-intellectual. Powell, Farrar, and Cohen (1985) document this process in *The Shopping Mall High School*. They show how high school attendance expanded at the turn of the century largely because of economic and technological changes, *not* because of a youthful hunger for academic learning.

Mass schooling was created as a result of a reduced need for adolescents to work. In 1900, only 11 percent of American high school–age youth were in high school; by 1930, the proportion had jumped to 70 percent (Trow, 1961); today the figure is over 90 percent. Child labor and compulsory attendance laws stimulated this growth, as did major transformations that occurred in the economy, the family, and the household. As Coleman (1987) notes, the expansion of schooling was accompanied and perhaps precipitated by a shift in the dominant work locations of men and women from the household to the corporation, office, or factory. Thus, from the turn of the century onward, increasing numbers of young people attended schools. Displaced from the labor force and facing empty homes, adolescents turned to each other.

Historically, therefore, students rarely attended schools primarily for educational benefits and opportunities. Rather, as the Lynds (1929) and Hollingshead (1949) observed from their community studies, extracurricular activities, sports, and socializing were the primary attractions. Schools, in effect, created what came to be termed the adolescent or youth subculture (Coleman, 1961). According to Powell et al. (1985: 239), "most students seemed not to have wanted a heavy academic diet, and in general they got what they wanted." Powerless to do otherwise, teachers have reluctantly adjusted to this state of affairs in the form of "bargains" and "treaties" that are worked out with students in the classroom, leading at best to a mediocre system of education. Sizer (1984) describes this process whereby students and teachers enter into implicit compacts:

> He signaled to the students what the minima, the few questions for a test were: all tenth- and eleventh-graders

could master these with absurdly little difficulty. The youngsters picked up the signal and kept their part of the bargain by being friendly and orderly. They did not push Brady and he did not push them . . . Brady's room was quiet, and his students liked him. No wonder he had the esteem of the principal who valued orderliness and good rapport between students and staff. Brady and his class had an agreement all right, agreement that reduced the efforts of both student and teacher to an irreducible and pathetic minimum.

Perhaps there was a time when the goals of educators were congruent with the goals of parents and students; perhaps there was not. At any rate, over the past century we have witnessed something less than a golden age of schooling (Powell et al., 1985; Sedlak et al., 1986). During this time, educators have assumed that their major objective was academic learning; students have assumed otherwise. This seemingly bold conclusion is well founded, though not openly acknowledged. Goodlad (1984: 39), for example, found that high school teachers were twice as likely as their students to prefer intellectual goals over social, personal, and vocational goals. He also reports that parents are at least reasonably satisfied with the schools just as they are.

Educators have consistently regarded the schools as substandard. A report by the Twentieth Century Fund (1983: 3) unabashedly summarized the situation: "By almost every measure—the commitment and competency of teachers, student test scores, truancy and dropout rates, crimes of violence—the performance of our schools falls far short of our expectations." This view is shared by more than thirty commissions, task forces, and individuals who have produced reports on the state of American education since 1980. These critiques identify the absence of academic excellence and productivity as the central problem facing American education today. Over the past twenty-five years, measured teacher satisfaction has exhibited an alarming drop. According to membership polls conducted every five years by the National Education Association, 50 percent of all teachers in 1961 said they would certainly choose to become teachers if they had to do it again; by 1986, the figure had decreased to 23 percent (Webb and Sherman, 1989: 203). Such dissatisfaction has generated numerous proposals at the national, state, and local levels for enhancing academic standards in the schools. Yet by most accounts little progress or change has occurred, especially in lower-tiered schools (Devine, 1996).

❖ THE ADOLESCENT SUBCULTURE

Secondary schools are composed of and affected by an adolescent subculture. As early as the 1920s and 1930s, the Lynds (1929) found that high school students in Middletown had little interest in academic work; only a few students saw academics as the primary or even the secondary reason for attending school. Hollingshead (1949) found the same pattern of student disengagement from learning in his 1941 study, *Elmtown's Youth*. These early community studies provided the first empirical evidence of the adolescent subculture operating in the schools. Coupled with our theoretical understanding of the economic impetus

underlying the growth of schooling, such studies support the notion that the development of this subculture paralleled the expansion of schools.

The existence of a distinct adolescent subculture has been discussed by several theorists in sociology. Eisenstadt (1956), drawing upon the concepts of Parsons and Shils (1951), theorized that major problems for youth arise in modern society because of shifts in role allocation from *ascription to achievement* and from *particularism* to *universalism*. In earlier societies, the roles of children and adults were characterized by ascription and situational particulars, and hence, the transition from childhood to adulthood was not problematic. One's destiny in terms of educational or occupational status was determined at birth, and it was unquestioned in this type of social context. This might be labeled as the penultimate form of social reproduction.

In modern societies, however, according to Eisenstadt, childhood roles remain particularistic and ascriptive, but adult roles are mostly based upon universalistic and achievement criteria. This creates problems in the transition from childhood to adulthood. And it is here that the "adolescent subculture" arises, serving as a conduit between the family and adult institutions. Eisenstadt saw the adolescent subculture as providing positive social functions, essentially allowing the continuation of particularistic and ascriptive roles (that is, hierarchies based on age, gender, and physical prowess) while simultaneously beginning to recognize some roles that are universalistic and achievement based (that is, recognition of achievements and leadership ability of younger members, perhaps in the marketplace of street hustling, and so on).

In contrast to Eisenstadt, most theorists have viewed the adolescent subculture as being more dysfunctional than functional. Parsons (1964), for example, argued that youth cultures provided a psychological and physical outlet for the tension that was caused by the problems of transition noted above. Although the subculture serves a functional purpose as an outlet for frustration, it leads to an excessive emphasis on athletics and nonintellectual interests. In this regard, it is counterproductive to the goals of schools. Urie Bronfenbrenner (1970) is among a large group of theorists who see the adolescent peer group in the United States almost entirely as an antisocial and antischool force (see also Coleman, 1961, 1965; Eve, 1975; Weis, 1985).

Some social theorists have argued that the real villain is society, not the adolescent. The classic statement from this perspective is perhaps found in Paul Goodman's *Growing Up Absurd* (1962), a book that romanticizes the value of the adolescent subculture (in terms of providing a context for the development of such traits as honesty, bravery, courage, and so on). Goodman pessimistically predicted, however, that this rich and vital youth culture was destined for destruction by the vicissitudes of modern society, which would no longer tolerate these character traits (see also Friedenberg, 1959, 1963; Henry, 1963).

Following these early reports, there have been many excellent quantitative studies further documenting the existence and the effects of the adolescent subculture. Remmers and Radler (1957) asked American teenagers to identify "the most important thing young people should get out of high school." Only 14 percent of the respondents listed "academics" as their answer. Thirty years

TABLE 7.1

STUDENT OPINIONS OF THE ONE BEST THING ABOUT SCHOOL

Response	Percentage
My friends	35
Sports	13
Positive student attitudes	11
Nothing	8
Classes I'm taking	7
Teachers	4
Other	22

Source: John Goodlad, *A Place Called School* (New York: McGraw-Hill, 1984), 76–77.

later, John Goodlad (1984) asked his sample of high school students, "What is the one best thing about this school?" The responses, shown in Table 7.1, dramatize the inconsequential place of academic learning in the lives of students.

If students had more to say about it, there would be even less academic emphasis than currently exists. In a study of thirty-eight schools, Goodlad (1984: 64) asked 8,624 parents, 1,350 teachers, and 17,163 students to cite the one goal that the schools seem to emphasize most. The choices were intellectual, social, personal, and vocational goals. He also asked members of each group to identify which goal they would *prefer* if they had their choice. Figure 7.1 displays Goodlad's results. Among high school students, 63 percent said that intellectual goals were most emphasized, but only 27 percent would prefer this state of affairs. Of course, it would be naive to envision students wanting more rather than less academic work. The real problem is whether student preferences adversely interfere with

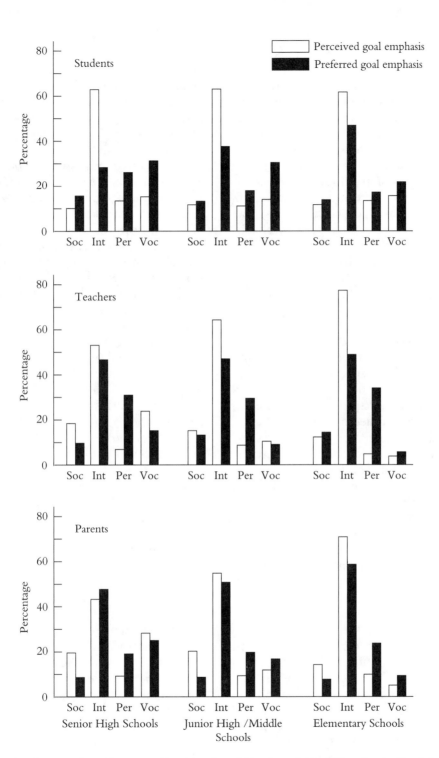

FIGURE 7.1 Comparison Between Perceived and Preferred Goal Emphasis (Social, Intellectual, Personal, and Vocational) for Students, Teachers, and Parents

Source: John Goodlad, *A Place Called School* (New York: McGraw-Hill, 1984), 64. Reprinted with permission.

academic work, and whether teacher preferences are compromised, and the extent to which these perceptions and references are in conflict.

Figure 7.1 also shows that at the high school level there is very little gap for either teachers or parents between their perceived and preferred emphasis on intellectual goals. For both groups, the perceived *and* the preferred emphasis hovers at about 50 percent. This figure is incongruent with either the perceived (63 percent) or the preferred (27 percent) emphasis for students. What can be made of this? Students believe that the school has a considerably *greater* academic emphasis than either teachers or parents perceive or prefer that it should have. Students see school as overly academic, and this is obviously an area of conflict. It is perhaps more significant to note that students would actually *prefer* that the academic emphasis be substantially *less* than teachers and parents either perceive or prefer. This may be an even greater area of conflict. The whole thing strongly suggests groups of "unhappy campers."

Contrast this state of affairs at the high school level with the situation that exists at the elementary school level. Here we see that both students and teachers agree that the preferred degree of intellectual emphasis should be about 50 percent. And the perceived emphasis is actually the reverse of the high school data. Whereas in high school, the perceived emphasis of intellectual goals for students (63 percent) is higher than that of teachers (54 percent); in elementary school, the perceived intellectual emphasis of teachers (78 percent) is higher than that of students (63 percent). Note especially that the perceived-preferred difference is much *smaller* for students in

elementary than in high school. In elementary school, the perceived-preferred gap is only 10 percentage points while in high school it is 35 percentage points.

Figure 7.1 shows a number of other interesting patterns. Among students, the gap between perceived and preferred intellectual goal emphasis increases from elementary school to high school. Among teachers, however, the reverse pattern is found. Teachers perceive the elementary school to be more academic than they would prefer, whereas at the high school level, they believe that intellectual goals are less emphasized, more in line with their preference.

Students perceive no change in the intellectual goal emphasis over their entire educational career, whereas teachers perceive that the intellectual goal emphasis declines in the school at higher levels. Parents tend to see it in a similar manner to teachers, more or less. What can we make of this? *The findings seem to suggest that over time students increasingly prefer to reject the intellectual goals of school and that over time teachers accommodate to this student preference by reducing the emphasis upon this goal.* From the point of view of teachers, schools become less intellectual. Yet, students do not perceive this decrease.

In analyses not depicted in Figure 7.1, Goodlad (1984: 65) also discovered that the degree of congruence between *preferred* goals and *perceived* goals decreased substantially from elementary to high school among students, teachers, and parents. In high school, Goodlad's data show that there is clearly more incongruence than congruence for everyone involved in terms of the goals that are desired and the goals that are perceived to exist. In this analysis, Goodlad considers all four goals depicted in Figure 7.1. In other words, on average, more people (students, teachers, and parents) experience goal conflict at the high school level than at any other time.

The classic and probative study of youth subcultures was conducted by James Coleman (1961) and published as *The Adolescent Society*. Coleman did not simply confirm the salience of an adolescent subculture in the schools; more importantly, he demonstrated the relationship between a strong youth culture and poor academic outcomes. Coleman asked students to identify whose disapproval (of a school activity) would be most difficult to accept—that of a parent, teacher, or friend. Only 3 percent were concerned with a teacher's disapproval; 54 percent and 43 percent, respectively, were concerned about disapproval by parents and friends.

Coleman asked students how they would best like to be remembered. Overwhelmingly, boys wanted to be remembered as an athletic star and girls as either the most popular or as an activities leader. Neither sex indicated any interest in being remembered as a brilliant student. Coleman also asked the students to speculate about their parents' preferences for their success in school. Their responses were patently supportive of the values of the adolescent subculture, leading Coleman to conclude that "even the rewards a child gains from his parents may help reinforce the values of the adolescent culture" (1961: 34). This latter finding has often been replicated, although it has been argued that the values of students, parents, and teachers do *not* differ as much as is implied by Coleman and by Goodlad (see Eve, 1975; Braddock, 1979; Clark and Trow, 1966). Eve's study, however, is particularly revealing, showing some degree of similarity between teachers and students (as

one might expect) but distinct differences on dimensions reflecting antiadult and antisocial values.

The adolescent subculture concerns *informal*, student-generated norms dictating behavior antithetical to the formal norms of the school. The adolescent subculture centers on youth values— athletics, physical appearance, popularity, social life, and negative attitudes toward academic activities. Among males, the focal concern is a cult of masculinity (being tough, cool, and athletic). Among females, the focal concern, even today, is a cult of attractiveness, romance, and domesticity (see Adler, Kless, and Adler, 1992). Youth cultures vary from the worst possible scenarios involving drugs, violence, and crime to a less threatening middle-class style. One way in which this is manifested is in the level of disciplinary problems that exist in schools. In schools where students frequently cut class, disobey, or talk back to teachers, it is reasonable to assume that a strong youth culture is present. Likewise, in schools where student values emphasize athletics and social life over that of academics, a strong youth culture exists.

A recent survey on student victimization in schools demonstrates the prevalence of youth cultures at the extreme levels. Students in grades six through twelve were studied in the 1993 National Household Education Survey (Nolin et al., 1995). Figure 7.2 shows that fully 42 percent of students in these grades had witnessed bullying and 8 percent had experienced being bullied. Thirty-three percent had witnessed a physical attack and 4 percent had been attacked. These data are only incidents that occurred in school or at school-related events. Interestingly, boys were nearly

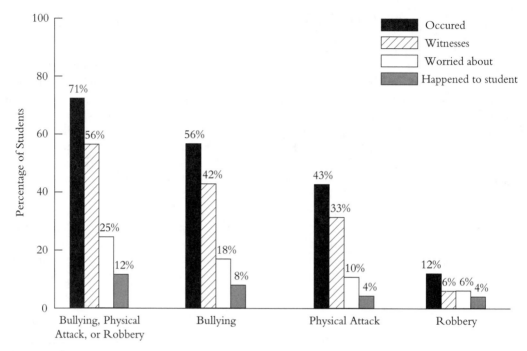

Figure 7.2   Sixth- Through Twelfth-Graders' Reports of Selected Incidents in 1993*

*Students who reported more than one type of incident are included in the overall victimization percentages only one time.

Source: Mary Jo Nolin, Elizabeth Davies, Westat, Inc., Kathryn Chandler, *Student Victimization at School* (Washington: National Center for Education Statistics, 1995).

twice as likely as girls to have been bullied, robbed, or assaulted.

❖ THE EFFECT OF THE ADOLESCENT SUBCULTURE ON ACHIEVEMENT

Of course, the existence of an adolescent subculture does not necessarily mean the demise of academic learning. Or does it? For each of the ten schools in his sample, Coleman computed a school "value climate" reflecting the relative importance of academics, sports, and social activities to students in the school. Although

nonacademic values were dominant in all schools (as noted above), Coleman ranked each school in terms of its relative emphasis upon the adolescent value system. This made it possible to examine the influence of the adolescent subculture on academic achievement. Coleman found that the adolescent climate was *negatively* related to educational aspirations and homework, even though each of these depends to a greater degree upon family background and on the amount of homework assigned by teachers. A model of these findings is depicted in Figure 7.3.

Comparing schools where the adolescent value climate was weakest (that is, where more people valued good grades

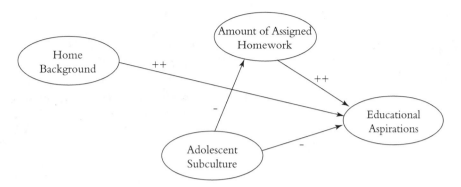

FIGURE 7.3   Model Showing the Influence of Adolescent Subculture

Note: Double plus signs indicate that the strength of the relationship is greater than a single plus or a single minus sign. A strong (high) adolescent subculture is conceived to have an inverse (negative) effect on academic outcomes.

Source: James S. Coleman, *The Adolescent Society* (New York: Free Press, 1961).

and brilliant students) with those where it was strongest, Coleman found that the IQ scores of students with good grades were higher in the former situation. Coleman (1961: 260) accounts for this somewhat perplexing finding by noting that "highly rewarded" activities breed widespread competition, which makes the most able participants likely to become the strongest achievers. When activities like academic learning go relatively unrewarded, however, the most able may be less motivated to compete, thus allowing their less able counterparts to exhibit the highest levels of achievement.

Thus, Coleman concludes that the presence of a strong adolescent value system in school "exerts a rather strong deterrent to academic achievement" (1961: 265). Under these conditions, the functional theory of stratification unravels. Recall that this theory argues that schools select and sort students according to ability and motivation, and then channel the "best" students into the most challenging and important occupational

positions in society. In the scenario reported by Coleman, it is the less able (in terms of IQ) who rise to the top (in terms of grades and subsequent opportunities). This is a sobering thought even for those with little faith in functional theory. On the other hand, it suggests that greater equality of opportunity (but probably lower overall achievement) might emerge in schools with more intense youth cultures. In effect, it presents a paradox.

We can examine the influence of the adolescent subculture using the High School and Beyond (HSB) survey, which involved strenuous efforts to obtain data on the adolescent subculture. The following school-level questions were asked of students and can be used to generate a measure of the adolescent subculture, aggregated to the school level.[1]

---

[1] Students answered questions 1 and 2 as either true or false, and questions 3 to 7 as follows: often happens, sometimes happens, rarely or never happens.

TABLE 7.2

THE EFFECT OF YOUTH SUBCULTURE ON SELECTED VARIABLES (PERCENTAGE)

Youth Culture	More Than 5 Hours/Week Homework	More Than 3 Hours/Day Television	Higher Than 50th Percentile on Sophomore Test	Higher Than 50th Percentile on Senior Test
Low	53	50	63	64
Medium	43	58	49	49
High	42	59	41	43
	D = 10	D = 9	D = 22	D = 21

Source: Estimates were computed by the author from the High School and Beyond (HSB) Sophomore Cohort using the weighted sample.

At your school, to what extent are the following true?

1. I have had disciplinary problems during the past year.
2. I don't feel safe at this school.
3. Students don't attend school.
4. Students talk back to teachers.
5. Students don't obey instructions.
6. Students fight with each other.
7. Students attack teachers.

Student responses to these seven questions were aggregated to the school level; for example, if 60 percent of students answered yes to question 3 at a specific school, then the school was coded as 60 percent. This means, in effect, that all students at this school are assigned this value. The value of the variable was coded high for a youth subcultural response. Thus, student disobedience is scored high. For each respondent, the values on each of the seven items were combined to form a single adolescent subculture variable ranging from 24 to 98 percent.

Finally, the variable was collapsed into three categories of youth culture, as shown in Table 7.2. This table displays the relationship between school-level variable and individual-level variables; that is, one variable characterizes an organization while the others characterize individuals.

We can observe in Table 7.2 that the existence of a strong youth culture in a school is related to the amount of homework, the amount of television, and, not surprisingly, to both sophomore and senior test scores. Students in schools that are characterized by a high adolescent subculture do less homework, watch more television, and score lower on cognitive tests than their counterparts attending schools with a less intense youth culture. Of course, these are only bivariate relationships and they might diminish if appropriate controls for home background or school type (public or private) were included. In fact, the adolescent subculture is most widespread in public schools. Of eighty-four Catholic schools in the sample, there were none in the high-youth-culture category and only one in the medium category. Of course, this may be the result of a high degree of selectivity in Catholic high schools as well as a higher degree of authority to enforce a school policy emphasizing discipline and control (see Coleman and Hoffer, 1987).

During the 1960s and 1970s, numerous researchers generated considerable support for Coleman's findings about the negative academic effects of the adolescent subculture. McDill and Rigsby (1973), for instance, compared the effects of various aspects of an adolescent value climate on student achievement relative to other characteristics, including home socioeconomic background, individual scholastic ability, individual values, and school-level socioeconomic context. (This study is reviewed and depicted as Figure 4.4 in Chapter 4.) McDill and Rigsby found a clear relationship between the adolescent value climate and math achievement, even after the other variables had been controlled simultaneously. Moreover, these researchers found that the adolescent climate was the only school-level variable accounting for some variation in achievement. Individual ability explained the greatest amount of achievement variation, followed by home socioeconomic status and personal values, and then by the adolescent subculture. The work of McDill and his associates was extended and further supported by the studies of Brookover and his colleagues (1979, 1982); Campbell and Alexander (1965); Kandel and Lesser (1969); Cusik (1973, 1983); Larkin (1979); Willis (1977), Clasen and Brown (1986); and Goodlad (1984). The conclusion is inescapable and McDill et al. stated it succinctly in 1967 (p. 199): "In those schools where academic competition,

intellectualism and subject matter competence are emphasized and rewarded by faculty and student bodies, individual students tend to conform to the scholastic norms of the majority and achieve at a higher level."

More recently, Goodlad (1984: 75) concludes that "junior and senior high school youth are excessively preoccupied with physical appearance, popularity in the peer group, and games and athletics." He notes that there is nothing new in these findings except perhaps "the apparent intensity of these nonacademic interests." Goodlad wonders "why we have taken so little practical account of them in school." He also declares that a "potential for explosion exists . . . in the present disjuncture between elements of the youth culture on the one hand and the orientation of teachers and conduct of school on the other" (p. 76).

Goodlad (1984) makes the point that the influence of peer groups upon individuals is growing as the influence of the family decreases. In our society, large increases in employed mothers and fathers, coupled with increases in divorce and single-parent households, creates a family ill-equipped to supplement the work of the school. The contemporary family has also seen its former influence upon children shift to the peer group. In a study of the daily lives of children, Boocock (1976) found that children spend most of their time outside schools with friends or alone, working or watching television, or "fooling around." Powell and Powell (1983) fear that the adolescent subculture is increasingly what school is all about, implying that schools might cease to exist if adolescent values and goals were somehow constrained. Such conclusions broadly resonate with Coleman's (1961: 51) warning that coeducation "may be inimical to *both* academic achievement *and* social adjustment."

❖ OPPOSITIONAL CULTURE AND RESISTANCE THEORY

Youth cultures are clearly more prevalent in inner-city public schools that are attended mostly by disadvantaged and high-risk students. Black and Hispanic youth in particular are subject to the most intense forms of antiacademic culture. In predominantly black and Hispanic schools across the country, students who aspire to succeed academically are harassed by their peers, and they come to experience the "fear of acting white" (Ogbu, 1986). The manifestation of violence and victimization depicted in Figure 7.2 is attenuated by nearly 50 percent in private schools (Nolin et al., 1995).

Sometime during the late 1970s and early 1980s, the adolescent subculture concept was expanded to include the concept of an "oppositional culture." It was first identified by Ogbu (1978), who distinguished between voluntary and involuntary immigrant minorities. Voluntary minorities were those groups who migrated to a country of their own free will whereas involuntary minorities were groups that had been enslaved (African Americans) or conquered (Native Americans). This view had actually been identified earlier by Judith Kramer in her classical sociological study, *The American Minority Community* (1970; see discussion in Chapter 3 of this book). The distinction is important for Ogbu in that he argues that voluntary minorities compare themselves to relatives in their homelands, and more often than not, this means that their life conditions including

educational and occupational opportunities are much improved. Involuntary minorities, on the other hand, lacking an identifiable foreign reference group, compare their life chances to that of the dominant group. For fairly obvious reasons, according to Ogbu this leads to resentment, anger, and detachment. In their study of nine high schools in two states, Steinberg, Brown, and Dornbusch (1996) confirmed Ogbu's thesis; black students were negatively influenced by their peers even in the face of positive parenting.

Black children learn from their parents at an early age (mostly by observation rather than parental advice) that their educational and occupational opportunities are limited by their race. Consequently, they come to resist and resent school and develop an oppositional attitude toward school that manifests itself as detachment and resentment and apathy. A key point of opposition theory is that black students who otherwise might strive to succeed in school are discouraged and dissuaded from doing so by their peers acting out of the norms associated with oppositional culture (Fordham and Ogbu, 1986). Ogbu argues that blacks are not socialized to succeed in an educational system dominated by whites, but rather are socialized to accept their oppressed and ascribed lower-status position, though not without the dignity of creating their own identity and culture. Fordham and Ogbu (1986: 177) concluded that black students discourage their peers, perhaps unconsciously, from emulating white people in academic striving, that is, "acting white." Oppositional culture theory is also known as cultural difference theory (see Chapter 3).

The "acting white" hypothesis suggests that if African American students were as motivated as whites, the achievement gap would narrow. This is exactly what the adolescent subculture theory implies except it generalizes beyond the black-white comparison. Of course, the basis of oppositional culture is quite different from that implied by the adolescent subculture. It is quite important, however, to note that oppositional theory was quickly generalized to social class by other theorists and researchers. Drawing upon social reproduction theory, Willis (1977) and Giroux (1981) argue that social class, more so than race, limits the opportunity for educational and occupational mobility of low-SES students and generates the oppositional or resistance culture among these students. Willis (1977), for example, found this to be true among working-class students (the "lads" as he called them) in England. This has also been shown to be the case in other ethnographic studies in the United States (MacLeod, 1995; Devine, 1996). In *The Declining Significance of Race*, Wilson (1978) affirms that in modern society social class is a more important factor in accounting for inequalities than race (see also, Wilson 1987). Thus, oppositional theory applies to both class and race.

Although oppositional theory is widely accepted and highly compelling, it does appear to require some fine tuning as empirical quantitative studies have failed to account for its presence or its usefulness in explaining why either blacks or low-SES whites do so poorly in school. Ethnographic studies have never failed to observe this in and out of school and one would have to be blind to not observe it in any inner-city school among both blacks and whites and others. Key to this, however, is that ethnographers and casual observers carefully choose what Devine (1996) calls lower-tiered

schools. Acknowledging that there is no precise definition of lower tiered, he points out that every community is well acquainted with these schools characterized by high rates of violence, absenteeism, lowest test scores, lowest SES context, metal detectors, highest dropout rates, and simply those schools that are referred to as the worst in the city (Devine, 1996). It is no surprise that if you visit one of these schools you will discover the oppositional culture.

Several problems therefore arise in attempting to conduct quantitative large-scale research on this construct. One problem is that oppositional culture turns into its more benign form of an adolescent culture as one moves beyond these lower-tiered schools. Second, one has to be careful in operationalizing oppositional theory. Blacks and lower-class whites do value education. They understand that it is the way to occupational success but at the same time perceive that the deck is stacked against them on the educational playing field. If you ask them if they value education, they will probably answer "Yes" and the data supports this over at least three decades (Gordan, 1972; Ainsworth-Darnell and Downey, 1998). The research challenge is to detect the existence of an oppositional culture that should manifest itself by students acknowledging the desire to be good students but being unable to pursue this value because of the pressure of the oppositional culture.

Several studies have attempted to measure various components of Ogbu's thesis using large-scale survey data from the National Educational Longitudinal Study (NELS) and the National Assessment of Educational Progress (NAEP). These studies (Ainsworth-Darnell and Downey, 1998; Cook and Ludwig, 1998) found that black students did not perceive that they would have fewer educational and occupational opportunities than whites. In fact, they reported that blacks appear to hold more proschool attitudes than whites. They did find, however, that blacks were perceived by teachers as putting forth less effort and that they were more disruptive than whites and Asian Americans. And by virtue of the self-reports of black students, they were more likely than whites and Asian Americans to get into trouble in school, and they did less homework. But on a whole set of proschool attitude measures, blacks did score higher than whites. These researchers also found that academically successful blacks reported that they were at least as popular as whites (that is, they were not put down for "acting white"). Finally, Ainsworth-Darnell and Downey (1998) found that the racial gap in school grades could not be explained by any or all of the resistance variables. Cook and Ludwig (1998) conducted essentially the same analysis with the same data set and found the same results.

These findings have generated considerable discussion in the sociology of education and educational policy communities. Ainsworth-Darnell and Downey (1998: 547) noted that the inconsistent results may be due to the fact that oppositional theory might only apply to the most severely apathetic and discouraged students: dropouts. Using the NELS data, they actually examined those students who had dropped out between the 8th and 10th grades and indeed found that African American dropouts reveal patterns of behavior and attitudes "much like the ones that Ogbu describes—frustrated with their occupational chances, pessimistic about their futures, and resistant to school goals." They downplayed the

importance of these findings, arguing that the oppositional theory should apply to the full range of African American students. This appears to be a mistaken appraisal. Ogbu's theory was developed and based on an all-black, inner-city, lower-tiered school, and the ethnographies have also been conducted in these types of schools. There is little basis for generalizing this theory, as it might apply to both blacks and low-SES white students, beyond these lower-tiered schools. Like so many findings in the sociology of education, this appears to be a specification effect; oppositional culture is a problem for low-SES youth (both whites and nonwhites) in lower-tiered schools and one of the causes of lower academic achievement (see Farkas, Lleras, and Maczuga, 2002: 150).

Another criticism regarding the null findings of Ainsworth-Darnell and Downey (1998) and Cook and Ludwig (1998) is that the choice of dependent variable was incorrect. Farkas, Lleras, and Maczuga (2002) argue convincingly that self-reported popularity among successful black students is not the appropriate variable to examine. Rather, oppositional theory rests on the notion that successful low-SES or black students will be pressured by their peers and hence, the correct dependent variable should be the frequency of hostile attacks by peers. To test this hypothesis, Farkas and colleagues employed the following variable from the 1998 NAEP data: My friends make fun of people who try to do well in school (strongly agree; agree; disagree; strongly disagree). Note that this question combines "being made fun of" with "trying to do well in school" that is at the center of the oppositional culture theory. Note also that Farkas et al. employed 4th grade data from NAEP (avoiding the 8th and 10th grade data) arguing (p. 150) that "fourth graders are more likely to answer without concern for impression management or for issues of adolescent identity than tenth graders" used by previous researchers. Farkas, Lleras, and Maczuga (2002: 150–151) found that, net of other variables employed as controls:

> Males experience significantly more peer opposition to school effort than do females. Blacks and Hispanics experience significantly more peer opposition than do whites . . . Students in Title I schools . . . are significantly more likely to have peers that discourage academic effort . . . The same is true among children who are eligible for the National Student Lunch Program.

Thus, Farkas et al. provide substantial support for an oppositional culture theory that can be applied to blacks and Hispanics, to males, and to low-SES students and low-SES schools.

In a reply, Downey and Ainsworth-Darnell (2002) argue that Farkas et al. did not employ the 8th and 10th grade NAEP data. They analyzed these two higher grade levels and found null results for the theory, but in fairness, Farkas et al. (2002: 153) had already noted that they never expected to find effects among students in these higher grades because "academically oriented adolescents . . . employ a variety of strategies to reduce the psychological pressure they are under [including] denying that a problem exists."

Downey and Ainsworth-Darnell (2002) also extended the research of Farkas et al. by demonstrating that the oppositional culture (using the variable, My friends make fun of people who try to do well in school) actually "explains" 11 to 15 percent of the black-white gap in test scores. They argue that this a small amount, but this is not convincing given the fact that there are many other vari-

ables that also explain this gap (see Chapter 2). In any event, the matter is not open and shut, although the Farkas et al. study does take us a long way toward confirmation.

Why is oppositional theory so important? There are two possible implications of oppositional theory assuming that it is true (even for only a certain subgroup of low-SES blacks and whites). One implication is that these groups are inherently responsible for their poor school performance. To succeed in school and beyond, members of the oppositional culture will need to alter their value system and their behavior to coincide with the value system of the schools and the rest of society. This is an extension of the notion that blacks and low-SES families are dysfunctional and that the solution is a middle-class life style (D'Souza, 1995). Recall that this was discussed in Chapter 4 under the culture of poverty or "deficit" theory.

Most social scientists have reservations about this line of thinking (Ainsworth-Darnell and Downey, 1998; Hallinan, 2001; Steele, 1990), claiming that it leaves out the fundamental sociological notion that location in society strongly influences one's value system and capacity to act. The alternative theory, far most receptive to the sociologist, is locating the problem in the social and economic material conditions that produce attitudes and behaviors that are either pro- or antischool. Thus, the sociology of education would direct attention to the stratification system of America that locates most blacks and low-SES students in crime-infested neighborhoods, badly funded schools, with underqualified teachers, or in a dysfunctional and fractured family structure. But even if the cause lies in the social context, intervention will involve cultural and individual modification to bring about greater congruence between youth and school cultures. Thus, the stakes are high in terms of remediation, but first it is necessary to confirm the theory.

❖ STUDENT ENGAGEMENT WITH SCHOOL AND ACADEMIC ACHIEVEMENT

In the 1990s, the terms student engagement or disengagement with school emerged as a synonym for the adolescent and oppositional subculture orientations that had been identified earlier by Coleman, Goodlad, Ogbu and others. It became increasingly clear that engagement or disengagement in the classroom was strongly related to student achievement and social development (Elmore et al., 1990; Newmann, 1992; Finn, 1993). Steinberg et al. (1996), much like Coleman, defined the real problems of school reform as lying *Beyond the Classroom*, by which he meant that student alienation and disengagement from schooling made efforts at school reform fruitless. Unlike earlier research that mostly described the adolescent subculture, the new research addressed two questions: (1) What factors influenced engagement? and (2) What was the effect of engagement on achievement relative to other home background and school factors?

Two major reform models have been employed to raise achievement in schools by directly combating the ill effects of youth cultures. These models are improving the academic environment or culture of the school and providing positive social support from parents, teachers, peers, and community members. The first model has come to be identified as academic press or academic climate, which we discussed in Chapter 4 (see McDill and Rigsby as depicted in Figure 4.4). It emphasizes the *academic* organization and culture of the school as defined by students, teachers, and administrators. The second model centers on the relationships that exist between students, parents, teachers, and the community. It emphasizes the *social* organization of the school.

Academic Press: This theory emerged at least as early as 1970 in the work of McDill and Rigsby (1973), who sought to explain the effects of the SES context of the school by identifying specific structural and cultural attributes of schools which provided an intellectual climate for promoting learning. Academic press, of course, also dates back to the late 1950s and the response of the scientific and educational community to the advances made by Russia in space exploration, and even earlier. Researchers and practitioners in this tradition argue that effective schools are those that emphasize high teacher expectations, high academic standards, clear achievement goals, quality instruction, an effective curriculum, more homework, and more time on instruction. Both the effective schools movement and the Catholic-public school studies discussed in Chapter 4 belong in this tradition. But, at the present time, it is clearly based largely on the issue of standards-based reform, including the professionalization of teachers, teacher expectations, and accountability (Darling-Hammond, 1997; Lee and Smith, 1999). It is hard to imagine any theory opposed to increasing academic press, and yet, concerns have been raised that increasing academic press and higher standards may increase school dropouts and student alienation, and reverberate back into negative youth cultures (McDill, Natriello, and Pallas, 1986).

Social Support for Learning: Several reform initiatives and theories fall under this rubric, but all have the common theme of providing more effective and positive connections between students and the broader community (parents, teachers, peers). School reform advocates have collectively agreed on the importance of the "personalization of learning and instruction" and the "creating of small communities of learning" as imperative for improving schools (Sizer, 1984, 1992; National Association of Secondary School Principals, 1996; Carnegie Council on Adolescent Development, 1989). Coleman's concept of social capital is pivotal to the social support theories. This notion (fully described in Chapter 3) argues that positive social relationships (supports) between children and parents, children and their friends, parents and other parents, parents and teachers, and teachers and students are the foundation for building functional communities which have been shown to increase students' achievement and development (Coleman and Hoffer, 1987; Bryk, Lee, and Holland, 1993). During the 1990s, this led to "an ethic of caring" theory of schooling (Noddings, 1988). And, many researchers have broadened the theory so that communal social organization is contrasted with bureaucratic, impersonal, and inefficient social organization (Bryk and Driscoll, 1988b; Lee and Smith, 1995).

In broadening the scope of social support theory, however, complications do arise since the theory can be conceived of at either the macro or the micro levels or both. Some researchers have obtained measures from teachers and/or students and aggregated them to the school level to create a school community variable. Defined at this level, the concept typically means that there are a set of shared values and shared activities that

are held by most participants internally but influence students' achievement externally by operating at the school level. This version of the concept is derived from Durkheim (1951) who argued that norms or normlessness in the larger society directed the behavior of individuals. Normlessness also operates at the individual (micro) level, however, when individuals perceive that the society (community, organization) does not allow them personally to achieve the generally agreed upon goals (Merton, 1957). This can occur for individuals who are excluded from the means to attain goals because of a lack of resources as is the case with economically disadvantaged students, or because of youth culture values that reject the academic values of the school. Generally, the research has been supportive of both the micro and the macro concepts of social support (Bryk and Driscoll, 1988b; Bryk, Lee, and Holland, 1993; Battistich et al., 1995).

Several studies have compared academic press with social support theories. Shouse (1996) found that academic press was a stronger predictor of student achievement than communal organization (the macro concept), but like so many studies that we have reviewed, he found that the effect of academic press was greater in low-SES schools. Moreover, he found that the influence of academic press in low-SES schools was greatest where the school did have a strong communal organization. Phillips (1997) critiqued many of the above studies for confounding the measurement of social support by allowing academic indicators to be included in the social support index, and vice versa.

Lee and Smith (1999) conducted a study in the Chicago public schools among 6th and 8th grade students to test the influence of the social support (at the micro level) and academic press theories, and in particular to test the extent to which social support effects are conditioned by the academic press of the schools. The dependent variables were mathematics and reading scores from the Iowa Test of Basic Skills in 1997. The major independent variables were social support for learning and academic press. The social support for learning was a composite measure from student responses regarding the amount of support they received from teachers, parents, peers, and the community. For example, the questions on the peer section asked students the degree to which their classmates "treat each other with respect,

work together to solve problems, help each other learn, don't care about each other (reversed), often disrupt classes (reversed), make fun of other students who do well in the class (reversed)." Social support for learning was a factor-weighted sum of the four social support scales. The academic press variable was a composite of a set of questions asked of both students and teachers. For example, there were four teacher questions asking teachers the degree to which their school "set high standards for schools performance." Students were asked about the extent to which their English and math teacher would "praise their efforts when they work hard." Figure 7.4 displays the results of their multilevel analysis for

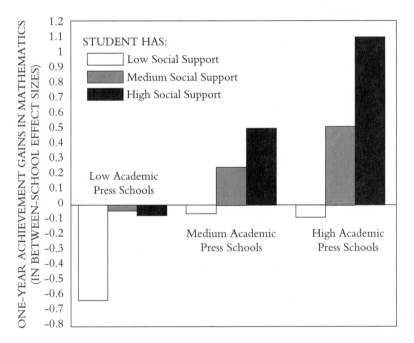

FIGURE 7.4 **Achievement Gains in Mathematics for Students with Varying Levels of Social Support in Schools with Different Levels of Academic Press**

Source: Valerie E. Lee and Julia B. Smith, 1999. "Social Support and Achievement for Young Adolescents in Chicago: The Role of School Academic Press." *American Educational Research Journal 36:* 933. Reprinted with permission.

mathematics (the results for reading are essentially the same).

In contrast to Phillips (1997), Lee and Smith (1999) found that both social support and academic press had moderate effects on student achievement in mathematics and reading.[2] Academic press conditions the influence of social support at the micro level. Students with medium to high levels of social support learn quite a bit so long as they are in schools with a medium to high academic press. In schools with a low academic press, however, even high levels of social support are insufficient to produce positive one-year gains. The authors (1999: 935) conclude that "a focus on the average relationship between social support and learning in schools may be misleading and a focus on only improving social support may be misguided." They also point out that raising standards (increasing academic press) will leave some students behind (as critics have argued) unless efforts are made to provide social support. As Figure 7.4 shows, Lee and Smith (1999: 936) conclude:

> Our results indicate rather clearly that when students are both supported and pressed, learning results. When either of these elements is lacking in children's learning environment, they learn less. When both are lacking, our findings suggest that children actually lose ground academically.

In more recent research, Marks (2000) also found evidence that social support

and academic press increased students' engagement with school. Furthermore, these restructuring practices reduced the effects of social background characteristics such as race and SES.

❖ EGALITARIANISM AND ADOLESCENCE

During the past century, our society has successfully moved toward universal, egalitarian schooling. In some respects, this achievement has exacerbated the problems associated with the adolescent subculture.

> At the turn of the century, [public schools] shared with private schools in the education of a small, elite student population preparing, for the most part, for higher education. Today, it educates an extraordinarily diverse student body from families varying widely in their expectations for education. Many of the boys and girls graduating from elementary schools and moving up into junior and senior high schools are not clients in any sense of the word. They go to school until the age of 16 or more because society requires it—and, of course, their friends are there. (Goodlad, 1984: 9)

In America, public schools are comprehensive, relatively nonselective, relatively egalitarian, and highly inclusive institutions. They accept the gifted and the disabled, the affluent and the poor, those who are motivated and those who are simply required to attend school. A great political achievement of this country is that there is virtually equal educational opportunity in terms of access to elementary and secondary schools. Accordingly, efforts at educational reform require utmost

---

[2] Lee and Smith actually confirm Phillips's results in that they were unable to show an effect of the social support index when they aggregated it to the school level, which is how Phillips conducted her analysis.

protection of the progress our society has made toward becoming more just.

Nonetheless, our commitment to equality and universality constrain the public schools to housing an increasingly powerful adolescent subculture. "Student inclusiveness is the reality most high schools must cope with: the students are *different* and they are *there*. At the level of institutional policy, schools accommodate to this situation by providing something for everyone" (Powell et al., 1985: 2). The result, according to these authors, is "the shopping mall high school," an educational institution characterized by *accommodation and mediocrity*.

Of course, private schools have been able to avoid this conflict of equality and quality. Generally, they have had the luxury of student selection, allowing them not only students of higher ability and higher socioeconomic status but also a less volatile adolescent subculture. In contrast, public schools must persist along the path of equality and universality; they must discover a way to either harness or diffuse the effects of the adolescent subculture. The challenge, therefore, is to create an *academic subculture* sufficiently powerful to counteract the adolescent and oppositional subcultures, yet politically sensitive enough to allay the fears of those groups whose relatively equal educational opportunities have been hard-won and recent. Weis (1985: 217–219) comes to this conclusion:

> Many of the recent reports on "Excellence in Education" tend to assume that student cultures can be manipulated easily. The production of "excellence," for example, has been linked in the various reports to a longer school day, pay increases for teachers, more rigorous teacher training, a "core" curriculum, less federal and/or state control,

increased attention to traditional academic subjects, and increased attention to science and technology. The attempt is to alter certain school-related factors, with the assumption that altering such factors will produce higher achievement scores among students. . . . Although the reports differ in some profound ways, they all assume student cultures can be *made* to change. This assumption—that student outcomes are a simple function of certain within-school factors and can be altered if only these factors are manipulated—is incorrect. Student outcomes are tied rather directly to the cultures students themselves produce within the institutions in which they reside. . . . Student cultures play a key mediating role in the production of student outcomes, and such cultures are not a simple response to practices either within or outside the schools. Student cultures are, rather, semi-autonomous and, as such, cannot be controlled easily or directly. None of the proposals for reform address these issues.

It is of course assumed that schools will not give in to youth cultures. In fact, as Waller (1932) long ago correctly observed, the problem is the conflict that results between "the spontaneous life of children" (p. 195) and "the established social order in the school" (p. 196). The culture of the school is more than academic. It is extremely authoritarian and students are powerless in the formal environment. The appropriate characteristics for successfully negotiating the role of student are passivity, compliance, patience, silence, receptivity, docility, and respect. In contrast, the role of teacher is characterized by power and authority, control, activity, and self-agency (see Boocock, 1980; Jackson, 1968).

Within the formal system, authority and control favor the teacher (Waller,

1932). For this reason, the conflict operates at the informal level. Research shows that students accept their docile role at the formal level only (and here it is not without public display). At the informal level, students employ all of the various ways in which social control can be sabotaged (Berger, 1963), including all of the trivial things that can go wrong with a pencil to much more serious and, often deadly, manifestations of fighting or simply refusing to cooperate (see Jackson, 1968; Csikszentmihalyi, Larson, and Prescott, 1977; Bayh, 1975; Holt, 1964, 1967; National Center for Education Statistics, 1992; National School Boards Association, 1993; Devine 1996). In all of this, however, the critical question is to what extent youth cultures and peer groups obstruct the learning and developmental process.

Peer groups may form and act in several different ways: (1) in the school, and beyond the school, as *youth cultures* described above; (2) in the classroom and outside of school entirely as *friendship choices;* and (3) in *extracurricular activities*. Unlike the study of differences between schools and homes (as discussed in Chapters 3–6), the effect of differences between peers is more difficult to assess. As we have seen above, it is entirely possible to measure the intensity of an adolescent subculture in the school and to then compare this variable with other school and home differences on student outcomes. With regard to the other two ways (friendships and *extracurricular* activities) in which peers may influence outcomes, however, it is more difficult to determine the quantitative or qualitative effect. The main obstacle lies in measuring the degree of involvement in *extracurricular* activities or the degree of involvement with friends.

Moreover, it is important to note that friendship patterns and *extracurricular* involvement may influence outcomes over and beyond the adolescent subculture and various home and school effects. For example, a low-SES student may attend a predominantly low-SES school with a very strong youth culture and very weak within school characteristics (low teacher quality and limited resources). This student may befriend a set of medium-SES peers who together form a small clique and safe academic haven in an otherwise ineffective school environment. This is surely not an uncommon example. The same is true for *extracurricular* activities where a single involvement such as athletics or orchestra may provide an alternative and more effective educational environment.

❖ FRIENDSHIP CHOICES

Several early studies examined the influence of friendship choices on achievement relative to other factors. Campbell and Alexander (1965) studied 1,400 male seniors in some thirty high schools to test a model claiming that the influence of school SES (that is, the structural quality of a school) was mediated largely through friendship choices. Specifically, their hypothesis was that the cultural norms of the school, as established by the adolescent subculture and the school curriculum and the extracurriculum, and polished by the SES context of the school, influenced academic outcomes through the intervening variable of friendships. In simple terms, students hang out with other students who share their interests, aspirations, and values, and it is the direct influence of the beliefs of friends (not the structure of the

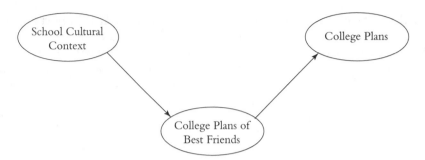

FIGURE 7.5   **Model of Friendship Influence on College Plans**

school) that determines academic out-comes. Figure 7.5 displays the resulting empirical model obtained by Campbell and Alexander. The culture of the school strongly influences the college plans of friends, which in turn influence the col-lege plans of each student. Note that there is no direct path between the school culture and college plans.

These results have been replicated in a number of large-scale studies (Alexander and McDill, 1976; Alexander, Cook, and McDill, 1978). For example, Alexander et al. (1978) found that peer educational expectations (along with parental expec-tations) mediated virtually all of the influ-ence of the socioeconomic background of students on track placement in high school (see Figure 6.3 and the related dis-cussion in Chapter 6). Said simply, a stu-dent's social class strongly affects the atti-tudes and values of his or her peers, and peers in turn strongly influence most ed-ucational outcomes (track placement, grades, test scores, educational plans, and educational attainment). Some peo-ple have identified this process as the "Wisconsin Model" of status attainment (Haller and Portes, 1973; Sewell et al., 1969, 1970). It is important to note, how-ever, that some researchers have not found support for this model (Wilson and

Portes, 1975) while others (Kerckhoff, 1976) have emphasized the importance of both structural as well as socialization factors in status attainment (see the dis-cussion in Chapter 6).

The significance of direct contact with peers was reviewed in Chapter 4, es-pecially the study by McPartland, which revealed that the only positive effects of a desegregated school for black children came when these students were actually in the same classes as white students (see Figure 4.5 and the related discussion). This powerful effect of peers also has im-plications for tracking. Critics of tracking argue that the influence of peer contact in college preparatory classes provides unfair advantages to students in nonaca-demic tracks that go beyond the actual differences in content (see Vanfossen, Jones, and Spade, 1987).

❖ EXTRACURRICULAR ACTIVITIES

To no small degree, the expansion of the extracurriculum at all levels of schooling is a direct response on the part of the school to the rise of the adolescent sub-culture. Extracurricular activities provide an acceptable institutionalized channel for the energies and nonacademic interests of the youth culture. Some critics argue that the extracurriculum has become the focus of schooling altogether (Goodlad, 1984; Powell et al., 1985).

It has been found that participation in extracurricular activities carries important benefits for students in terms of personal and social development, cognitive and affective outcomes, educational attainment, and adult attitudes and behavior (Holland and Andre, 1987; Otto, 1982; Braddock, 1981; Sweet, 1986; Broh, 2002). Participation in extracurricular activities has been linked to higher self-esteem, better grades, higher educational aspirations, improved race relations, lower delinquency rates, feelings of control over one's life, and greater interest in school (Otto, 1976a; Otto, 1976b; Spady, 1970; Camp, 1990; Biernat and Klesse, 1989; Holland and Andre, 1987; Eckert, 1989; Snyder and Spreitzer, 1992; Kinney, 1993; Broh, 2002).

In terms of the longevity of the effects and the potency of implications, Otto (1982) states that the research concerning *later* outcomes is even more conclusive than immediate effects. "The extent to which an adolescent participated in high school extracurricular activities positively affects a variety of later life outcomes beyond educational, occupational, and income achievements at age thirty-two." (p. 223). Participation in extracurricular activities was the strongest predictor of young adult social participation in community, religious, educational, political, and other realms (Lindsay, 1984). Otto (1982) also confirmed that high school activity participation has the strongest relationship to positive adult outcomes than any other factor in his analysis. In fact, Otto claims that this participation is a stronger predictor of

later adult outcomes than *immediate* outcomes for the adolescent.

The Office of Educational Research and Improvement (Sweet, 1986) concluded from research on a national high school sample that a positive relationship existed between participation in extracurricular activities and grade point average (GPA). A similar relationship was observed by McNamara et al. (1985). It appears that higher GPAs are comprehensively associated with higher levels of participation. Various types of student involvement—in the school, church, and community—were found to be related to more positive academic outcomes (Cheong, Toney, and Stinner, 1986). Thus, the value of extracurricular activities has been well documented.

Holland and Andre (1987) note that although correlations exist for each of the above relationships, some studies reporting these findings did not adequately control for preexisting background and initial differences between participants and nonparticipants. Given that participants and nonparticipants self-select themselves in or out of extracurricular activities, this may be an important qualification and an important question to address.

This problem is shown in Table 7.3, where the relationships between participation in extracurricular activities and grade point average and socioeconomic status are shown. (Only a portion of the large list of activities included in the original survey is shown in the table.) Sweet (1986) found that students with high levels of extracurricular participation have higher grades than do nonparticipating students. Likewise, the students who have high levels of participation are also high in socioeconomic status. This presents the classic case of selection bias and the potential spuriousness of the

TABLE 7.3

PERCENTAGES OF 1982 HIGH SCHOOL SENIORS PARTICIPATING IN EXTRACURRICULAR ACTIVITIES BY GRADE POINT AVERAGE AND SOCIOECONOMIC STATUS

Activity	Socioeconomic Status		GPA		
	Highest Quartile	Lowest Quartile	2.00 or Less	2.51– 3.00	3.50– 4.00
Any activity	85	75	68	81	96
Varsity athletics	44	29	30	35	42
Cheerleaders, pep clubs, majorettes	14	12	9	13	21
Debate or drama	19	9	9	13	19
Band or orchestra	16	10	9	14	23
Chorus or dance	22	18	18	19	24
Hobby clubs	21	18	21	20	16
Honorary clubs	25	9	3	7	75
Newspaper, magazine, or yearbook	25	15	9	20	33
Subject-matter clubs	22	20	16	18	37
Student council, government, political clubs	23	12	8	16	31
Vocational education clubs	14	39	23	24	20

Source: Adapted from D. A. Sweet, "Extracurricular Activity Participants Outperform Other Students," *OERI Bulletin* (September 1986).

relationship between participation and grades. Moreover, it is difficult to determine the direction of influence—does high participation lead to high grades, or do high grades lead to higher levels of participation?

Quiroz, Gonzales, and Frank (1996) have demonstrated that the problem is actually more complicated than originally thought. In their ethnographic study of high school students, they show that "participation in the extra curriculum is more than self-selection of individual students into a voluntary structure" (p. 1). What really happens is that the

extracurriculum is organized in a way that limits participation among some students and encourages participation among others. Performance "thresholds" (required GPA, attendance, tryouts, and so on) are formally employed by the school as a filter. In addition, teachers, counselors, and peers recruit students into extracurricular activities on a differential basis. Likewise, access to information regarding the opportunities available in the activities is differentially communicated according to social class and school track. "The consequence of these formal and informal processes is that a relatively small segment of the student high school population becomes *hypernetworked*, receiving the greatest numbers of opportunities to participate" (p. 1).

♦ CONTROLLED EFFECTS OF PARTICIPATION

Some research using causal model techniques has established that extracurricular participation does have causal effects on educational outcomes, independent of socioeconomic background and initial academic ability (Hanks and Eckland, 1976; Otto, 1975, 1976a, 1976b; Otto and Alwin, 1977; Braddock, 1981; Broh, 2002). For example, in a long-term study using the National Longitudinal Survey (NLS) of the high school class of 1972, Braddock (1981) found that for both black and white males, participating in high school athletics was positively related to academic self-esteem, educational plans, and educational attainment (after controlling for socioeconomic background and cognitive ability). Using the same data set, Hanks (1979) found these effects were much smaller for females.

In a recent study using the High School and Beyond data and controlling for background variables, McNeal (1995: 62) showed that extracurricular participation in athletics "significantly reduces a student's likelihood of dropping out, whereas participation in the academic and vocational clubs has no effect." Although lower-class students are less likely to participate in extracurricular activities (Sweet, 1986), the relationship between participation and positive outcomes is strongest among males from low-SES families (Spady, 1970; Snyder, 1969). Thus, there may be some important interaction effects of extracurricular activities. Broh (2002) shows that the effects of extracurricular participation vary accord-

ing to the type of extracurricular program (see also Hanson and Kraus, 1998). Using data from the National Educational Longitudinal Study (NELS), Broh (2002: 69) demonstrates that "participation in some activities improves achievement, while participation in others diminishes achievement." Specifically, Broh discovered that participation in interscholastic activities and music groups (controlling for a large set of background characteristics) are the only activities that consistently increase student grades and test scores. Student council participation increased grades but not test scores. But participation in intramural sports and vocational clubs consistently led to lower grades and test scores. All the other various forms of extracurricular participation had null effects. Moreover, Broh (2002: 69) was able to demonstrate that "interscholastic sports promote students' development [locus of control] and social ties among student, parents and schools [social capital], and these benefits explain the positive effects of participation on achievement."

Participation rates have consistently been found to be higher in smaller schools (Schoggen and Schoggen, 1988; Barker and Gump, 1964; Grabe, 1981; Lindsay, 1982). This has led numerous researchers to conclude that small schools provide a more favorable environment for personal and academic development. Of course, the value of small schools has been identified for reasons that transcend extracurricular activities (Goodlad, 1984; Fowler, 1992; Lee, 2000).

♦ EXTENT OF PARTICIPATION

Most previous studies have focused on participation in a single extracurricular activity, most notably, varsity athletics. The total number of activities in which students are involved has received much less attention. Since many students are involved in two or more activities, this should be a potent variable. In a study using the NELS data, Riordan (1997) found that 46 percent of eighth grade students were involved in two or more activities, 27 percent were involved in three or more activities. Remarkably, a full 16 percent were involved in four or more activities.

Studies exploring the extent of participation have found that the degree of involvement is positively correlated with academic and developmental outcomes (Feltz and Weiss, 1984; Spady, 1970; Otto, 1975, 1976b; Otto and Alwin, 1977; Burbach, 1972; Marsh, 1992). For example, Burbach found that personal feelings of powerlessness decreased as the number of extracurricular activities that students participated in increased. Feltz and Weiss (1984) demonstrated that the ACT scores of females increased in a linear fashion with greater levels of participation. Based upon a series of studies with young males, Otto (1976a: 222) came to this conclusion:

> [T]he extent of participation has a salutary effect on achievements, but also that extent of participation is the only variable in a rather complex set that had a consistent positive effect on all three socioeconomic achievements: education, occupation, and income.

Thus, previous research suggests the existence of a linear positive relationship between participation and academic and developmental outcomes.

Yet, we might question how excessive involvement affects the relationship. Specifically, we might hypothesize that the relationship is actually curvilinear—that is, that participation is positively related to these outcomes but only up to a certain extent of involvement, at which point the relationship reverses itself and becomes negative. Although this hypothesis has not been thoroughly tested, several critics have argued that time spent on extracurricular activities decreases a student's chances for doing well academically (Camp, 1990; Jeffreys, 1987).

Riordan (1997) tested this curvilinear hypothesis using the NELS data and separate scores for participation and leadership. The participation index represented the total number of activities that each student participated in among a set of sixteen total activities and a score could range from 0 to 16. This index was limited to only school-based activities that were academic in nature, and it eliminated varsity and intramural sports and cheerleading, religious organizations, and vocational clubs.

The analyses revealed that participation in extracurricular activities was positively related to variables such as test scores, amount of homework, self-esteem, and locus of control. This was only true, however, for participation values up to five. Values for extracurricular participation beyond this point produced a negative relationship. Thus, the relationship may be nonlinear. This result is neither puzzling nor surprising, suggesting that too much involvement is likely to result in less homework, less cognitive achievement, and less personal success.

❖ PEER SEXUAL HARASSMENT

Thus far, we have noted that peer influence may take shape in several positive—or negative—forms. Strong adolescent subcultures will negatively affect all students in terms of academic outcomes. Associations with academically minded peers will produce positive academic outcomes, and vice versa. Participation in extracurricular activities is related to positive educational outcomes for some students, at least up to a point, at which overinvolvement may create adverse academic and developmental results.

One area of great concern that creates only negative results is sexual harassment by peers. A 1993 national survey of 1,632 randomly selected public school students in grades eight through eleven found that sexual harassment in school is *epidemic*. The American Association of University Women (AAUW, 1993) commissioned Louis Harris and Associates to conduct this survey. They found that both boys and girls were victims of sexual harassment by peers, but that the

effects were more severe for girls. In addition, they learned that peer harassment is four times more common than sexual harassment of students by an adult. The study reported a large number of negative and significant educational, emotional, and behavioral results that accrue from sexual harassment including loss in self-esteem, fear of attending school, avoidance of certain classes or places in the school, lower grades, self-doubts, and difficulties in studying.

Sexual harassment begins as soon as school begins and peaks during the seventh grade. Figure 7.6 shows that from the sixth through ninth grade, 11 to 17 percent of girls reported being sexually

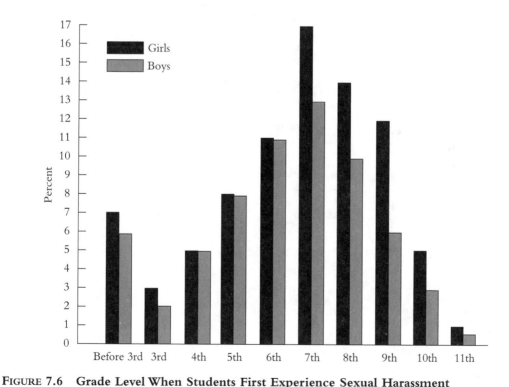

FIGURE 7.6   **Grade Level When Students First Experience Sexual Harassment**

Note: Based on the 81 percent of students who report some experience of sexual harassment in school.

Source: American Association of University Women, *Hostile Hallways* (Commissioned and Researched by Louis Harris and Associates, 1993), 8. Reprinted with permission.

harassed. The figures are only slightly lower for boys. What is the nature of the harassment? Figure 7.7 shows the variety of the student reports regarding specific types of sexual harassment across all grades. Where is peer sexual harassment occurring? The researchers found that 65 percent of the harassment occurred in the hall, 50 percent in the classroom, 43 percent outside the school but on

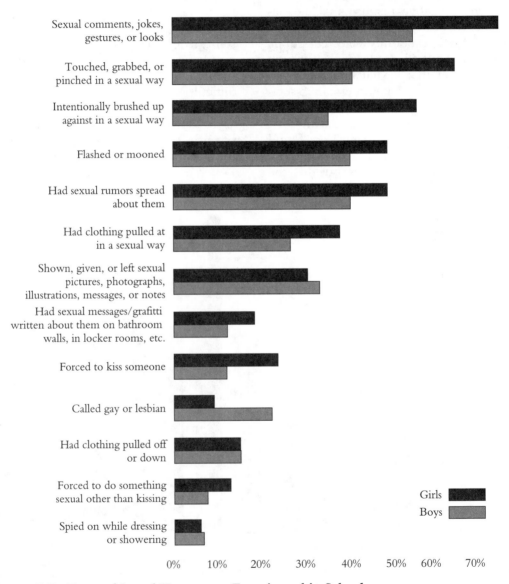

FIGURE 7.7 **Types of Sexual Harassment Experienced in School**

Source: American Association of University Women, *Hostile Hallways* (Commissioned and Researched by Louis Harris and Associates, 1993), 9. Reprinted with permission.

school grounds, 34 percent in the cafeteria, 26 percent on school transportation to and from school, 24 percent on field trips, 23 percent in the parking lot; smaller percents were reported in the locker room, on public transportation, and in the rest room. Note that many of these occurrences (but not all) are in formal school locations, presumably under the control of teachers.

An interesting finding of the study is that 66 percent of all boys and 52 percent of all girls admit that they have sexually harassed some other student. This finding is not surprising since four out of every five students said that they were sexually harassed at some point during their school career. In fact, "of the 59 percent of students who say that they have sexually harassed someone else in the school setting, 94 percent claim that they themselves have been harassed" (AAUW, 1993: 12). And when asked why they engage in sexual harassment, the vast majority of students say that "my friends encouraged me or pushed me into doing it" or "it's just part of school life" (AAUW: 11). Thus, sexual harassment is essentially a feature of the adolescent subculture.

In 2001, the AAUW (2001) asked Harris and Associates to replicate the 1993 study reviewed above. The results were essentially unchanged. In 2001, boys are slightly more likely to report that they had been sexually harassed, but they are still less likely than girls to have this experience. There has been a small decline in the percentage of students who indicate that they themselves have sexually harassed someone else (59 percent down to 54 percent). The only major change from 1993 to 2001 is that students reported that schools are much more likely now to have policies in place

and more information available on sexual harassment. But the unchanged reality is that large numbers of students in schools (especially girls) are subject to sexual harassment across all levels of school.

Shakeshaft et al. (1995) confirm that peer sexual harassment has become a central part of the adolescent subculture. As many as nine million students a year may be sexually harassed by their peers in school (Shakeshaft, Cohen, and Greenberg, 1996). Moreover, they note that very little is known regarding how this actually occurs. In an intense set of interviews and observations of 1,000 students in eight schools, Shakeshaft et al. (1995) report that the sexual harassment is indeed pervasive for most middle school and high school students. The harassment is primarily verbal and students feel powerless to control it. The researchers demonstrate how a seemingly harmless male-female encounter in front of student lockers can involve perverted and hostile forms of verbal harassment. They note that teachers were often observed to overhear such behavior and ignore it.

Those students most susceptible to peer sexual harassment were girls who were considered unattractive or physically mature and boys who did not fit the stereotypical male mold. Shakeshaft et al. (1995: 15) note that the harassment of boys often takes the form of homophobic insult:

> Boys are called fag, queer, pussy, old lady, sissy, or any name that links them to a female or feminine behavior. Fear of being labeled a homosexual is much more common than fear of actually being a homosexual. Boys don't want others to believe they are homosexual and work hard to make sure their behaviors fit the male norm.

Boys will often confront girls directly making sexual demands or innuendos. According to their interviews, Shakeshaft et al. (1995: 14) provide several examples of this process:

> To me they say "you are stacked!" It's annoying but at least they're not saying anything bad to me like being called Titty Fuck Queen.... They (boys) tell you to suck their body parts and stuff all the time.... In English class, right in front of the teacher, Joey will say, "I think I'm getting hard."

This reprehensible and pervasive interaction is undoubtedly central to today's version of the adolescent subculture. An interesting question to pursue at this point is whether peer sexual harassment is entirely a product of youth subculture or whether possibly it is supported by the formal institutions of the school.

❖ THE REPRODUCTION OF GENDER ROLES IN EXTRACURRICULAR ACTIVITIES

Throughout the book, we have devoted considerable attention to the role that schools may play in the social reproduction of social class. We have observed that the research is somewhat mixed— some studies show that the structure of schooling serves to maintain and extend social class differences, while others demonstrate that in the absence of schools, social class differences would increase dramatically. The research on tracking usually confirms the former contention, and the summer learning studies lend support to the latter argument. Interestingly, little attention has been given to the ways in which schools may reproduce gender differences in values and attainment. Instead, the focus of much research has been upon inequalities in school resources (AAUW, 1992; Lockheed and Klein, 1985).

Some studies have examined gender socialization as it occurs in the formal aspects of schooling—for example, gender stereotypes in textbooks (Saario, Jacklin, and Tittle, 1973) and in curriculum allocation (Gaskell, 1985). As we have noted above, however, recently there has been increasing interest in the extracurricular and other informal activities of the school. Several studies have determined that girls develop social and nurturing behaviors and boys develop competitive and achievement-oriented skills (Best, 1983; Borman and Frankel, 1984). Other studies have found that boys begin to manifest disdain for girls and that they come to occupy larger territories (Best, 1983; Thorne, 1986). Yet, the issue of the cultural reproduction of gender remains unresolved.

To fill this void, Eder and Parker (1987) conducted an extensive ethnographic study of this issue. They studied both formal and informal school activities that occurred during lunch and after school among middle school students. Their main aim was to discover the extent to which socialization toward traditional gender roles occurred during these informal and extracurricular times in school. "In general, traditional gender roles in our society emphasize the importance of occupational achievement and competition for males and attractiveness and interpersonal skills for females" (p. 202). And traditionally, males have learned these roles through athletic events while cheerleading has been the most prestigious activity for females. Has this changed as a result of Title IX and to what degree does it exist as early as middle school?

Indeed, Eder and Parker found that athletics was the most valued extracurricular activity for boys and that cheerleading was most valued for girls among these middle school students (see also Adler, Kless, and Adler, 1992; for similar findings among high school students, see Coleman, 1961; Kessler et al., 1985). These activities expose males and females to a very different set of values. For boys, the values of achievement, competition, aggressiveness, and toughness are essential. These characteristics are basic to the male adolescent subculture. For girls, the values of smiling, an attractive appearance, and a bubbly personality are emphasized. Thus, these values become essential to the female adolescent subculture (Eder and Parker, 1987). In a more recent study, Eder, Evans, and Parker (1995) demonstrate how this gendering process occurs daily in acts of gossip, teasing, and sexual harassment.

Most importantly, however, Eder and Parker conclude that "schools continue to play an important role in reproducing gender differences." (p. 211). Unlike other aspects of peer youth culture, which are clearly separate from the formal school curricula, this study demonstrates that the extracurricular activities of a school are readily incorporated into the informal peer culture. Eder and Parker suggest several reasons for this: (1) formal academic schooling is relatively nonparticipatory, whereas extracurricular activities provide high levels of student interaction; (2) extracurricular activities offer more opportunities for male-female interaction than is the case with academic work; and (3) extracurricular activities provide more visibility, and hence have greater impact on role modeling.

❖ SUMMARY

Unlike all of the previous chapters in this book, the conclusions that can be drawn here are relatively straightforward. Differences exist between peers both between and within schools, and these differences influence academic, attitudinal, behavioral, and developmental outcomes. All schools are subject to the negative effects of youth subcultures that emphasize and manifest antiacademic values, traditional gender roles, and sexual harassment. School reform would do well to concentrate on this variable alone rather than some of the more complicated factors such as per pupil expenditure and other between school differences that we have discussed earlier. Beyond the probative influence of the norms of the youth culture in schools, peer differences also exist in friendships and involvement in extracurricular activities. Here the research is both pro and con. Associations with friends who are academically oriented are obviously a positive influence, but the reverse is just as true for those students whose friends are part of the oppositional subculture. Likewise, participation in extracurricular activities has been shown to be positively related to a variety of academic and developmental outcomes. Yet, overinvolvement may cause negative results, and some extracurricular activities actually have negative effects on grades and test scores. Moreover, extracurricular activities usually reinforce traditional gender roles and are inequitable. Peer sexual harassment is quite pervasive both in and out of school and

contributes to the strength of adolescent and oppositional subcultures. It requires a zero tolerance control on the part of parents, teachers, and school administrators.

❖ KEY CONCEPTS

adolescent youth subcultures
perceived and preferred goal emphasis
   in schools for parents, teachers,
   and students
student victimization
oppositional culture
resistance theory
engagement and disengagement
academic press reforms
social support reforms
friendship choices as a mediating
   variable

the "Wisconsin model" of status
   attainment
the effects of extracurricular activities
selection bias in extracurricular activities
hypernetworked students
the extent of participation in extracurricular activities
types of extracurricular activities that
   influence achievement
peer sexual harassment
the reproduction of gender roles

❖ KEY STUDIES

Goodland (1984)
Coleman (1961)
Nolin et al. (1995)
Ogbu (1987)
Fordham and Ogbu (1986)
Ainsworth-Darnel and Downey
   (1998, 2002)
Farkas, Lleras, and Maczuga (2002)

Phillips (1997)
Lee and Smith (1999)
Campbell and Alexander (1965)
Sweet (1986)
Otto (1976, 1982)
Quiroz et al. (1996)
Broh (2002)
Eder and Parker (1987, 1995)

❖ REVIEW QUESTIONS

1. Contrast and compare the ideas of those who view youth cultures as functional or dysfunctional.

2. Drawing upon Figure 7.1, show how it appears that (1) students and teachers hold conflicting ideas about the goals of school, and (2) how it appears that teachers accommodate

the goals of school to the preferences of students. What are the implications of this analysis?

3. Drawing upon Coleman, describe how most students would best like to be remembered. How does this compare with the one best thing that students like about school (Goodlad)?

4. Describe Coleman's findings regarding the way in which youth cultures may condition the relationship of IQ and grades. What are the implications for the functional theory of stratification?

5. Describe the elements of "oppositional theory" and the empirical support that has been found for the theory.

6. Describe the results of the Lee and Smith (1999) study on social support and academic press.

7. Identify and describe the dilemma posed by youth cultures in a school context emphasizing egalitarianism.

8. Show a model and describe the way in which peer friendships mediate the cultural norms of the school.

9. Summarize how the problem of selection bias and hypernetworking may confound the study of extracurricular activities and their influence on school outcomes.

10. Summarize what is known regarding the effects of participation in extracurricular activities.

11. Discuss the nature of the relationship between the extent of participation and leadership in extracurricular activities and academic-developmental outcomes.

12. Describe the extent of sexual harassment in school. Provide specific information with particular attention to gender and grade-level differences and the type of harassment.

13. What do we mean by the reproduction of gender roles? To what degree does this form of social reproduction exist in the schools?

Chapter 8

MAXIMIZING ACHIEVEMENT AND EQUALITY

The broad goal in this chapter will be to generalize the specific results from previous chapters into a single coherent picture. Throughout this book, we have examined the conditions leading to greater academic achievement and greater equality in our schools. Chapter 2 presented a basic model (see Figure 2.2), and now I wish to reexamine that model in view of what we have learned in Chapters 3 through 7. It may be useful at this point to summarize some crucial relationships.

We have discovered that policies *within* schools have the greatest influence on achievement, especially policies regarding discipline, tracking, or ability grouping. Although the association between tracking and achievement is very high, it is likely that the overall achievement of all students within highly tracked schools may be lower than the average achievement of students in untracked schools (see Figure 8.2, p. 255). This paradox is central to the dual outcomes of achievement and equality and should not go unnoticed.

Bearing this in mind, note immediately that within school policies may have small but significant effects on increasing student equality if conditions such as untracking or cooperative learning are in place. Although there is no meta-analysis available, I estimate that the results of within school effects on equality are substantially less than the within school effects on achievement and only occur under the type of conditions noted above. I refer to tracking and cooperative learning only as examples. There are clearly other types of structures and processes that may be even more effective in producing more equal outcomes (see Lee and Smith, 1994 and Figure 8.1).

All of the factors that we have identified as home background—including the status characteristics of SES and race, along with family structure and functioning variables—have strong influences on both achievement and (in)equality. Specifically, positive valences (high SES, white, and so on) on these variables are related to positive increases in student achievement. Of course, the fact that SES influences achievement means that SES influences equality indirectly as a result of achievement differences. Equality of educational opportunity between groups (such as blacks and whites or high- and low-SES students) decreases to the extent that social background and home variables influence achievement.

In any event, home background factors and within school policies are the major determinants of educational outcomes. These are the forces that matter most regarding who succeeds or fails in school, and beyond school. Home background influences the type of school that a student attends (high-SES students attend suburban or private schools), and the type of school influences the within school policies (restructured schools track less), and the type of school and school policies affect the intensity of youth cultures in the school (for example, private schools and suburban schools have low levels of an oppositional subculture).

Throughout the book, we have seen that the differences between school types (Catholic versus public, for example) are significant only for students who are historically or traditionally or economically disadvantaged. For white middle-class students, the choice between one school and another school will have only minimal effects. This important specification effect of school type on achievement applies across a wide range of differences between schools (school size, class size, school resources, summer learning, the effect of academic press, the effects of oppositional culture, and reform curricula such as Success For All). Within school policies, however, do affect both key outcomes as we have already noted. Likewise, the adolescent subculture has negative effects on both achievement and equality. Youth cultures lower achievement for most students both in and out of school, and youth cultures decrease equality, especially as they operate to exacerbate and sharpen traditional gender differences.

❖ THE INFLUENCE OF SCHOOL RESTRUCTURING ON ACHIEVEMENT AND EQUALITY

In the debate over school reform, considerable time and effort are given to the effects of differences between schools on equality and achievement. This takes the form of both research and policy, and it involves such matters as school choice, private and public schooling, vouchers, desegregated schools, effective schools, magnet schools, and charter schools. Clearly, school reform and social reform should focus on within school policies, especially the way that classes are organized and the extent to which youth cultures are allowed to influence school outcomes. Moreover, this attention to within school policies should include an examination of those policies that decrease the influence of home background on achievement.

A study addressing many of these issues was conducted by Valerie Lee and Julia Smith (1994). They used the NELS data to examine the influence of restructuring practices within schools on both achievement and equality. Using data supplied by the school principal, they identified a list of thirty school policies that could be labeled as being traditional, moderate, or radical restructured reforms.[1] These practices, along with Lee and Smith's grouping of them, are shown in Figure 8.1. Traditional structures, such as having a PTA or parent-teacher conferences each semester, were practiced by the majority of schools in the sample. The radical restructuring practices, such as cooperative learning and mixed-ability classes in math and science, were in place only in a minority (9 to 30 percent)

[1] Lee and Smith drew upon two basic sources to group these practices: a set of criteria for restructuring developed by the Center on Organization and Restructuring of Schools at the University of Wisconsin, Madison, as well as the work of Bryk and Driscoll (1988a), which contrasted traditional bureaucratic schools with communally organized schools. For a more extensive and enhanced analysis, see Valerie E. Lee with Julia B. Smith (2001).

Structural Practice	Probability of Practice
Traditional Practices	
Departmentalization with chairs	.85
Common classes for same curricular track	.76
Staff development focusing on adolescents	.66
PTA or PTO	.64
Parent-teacher conferences each semester	.64
Focus on critical thinking in curriculum	.64
Common classes for different curricular tracks	.62
Increased graduation requirements	.62
Recognition program for good teaching	.56
Parents sent information on how to help kids study	.56
Moderate Practices	
Parent workshops on adolescent problems	.46
Student satisfaction with courses important	.42
Strong emphasis on parental involvement	.38
Strong emphasis on increasing academic requirements	.35
Student evaluation of course content important	.35
Outstanding teachers are recognized	.34
Emphasis on staff stability	.34
Emphasis on staff development activities	.32
Restructuring Practices	
Students keep same homeroom throughout HS	.30
Emphasis on staff solving school problems	.29
Parents volunteer in the school	.28
Interdisciplinary teaching teams	.24
Independent study, English/social studies	.23
Mixed-ability classes in math/science	.21
Cooperative learning focus	.21
Student evaluation of teachers important	.20
Independent study in math/science	.18
School-within-a-school	.15
Teacher teams have common planning time	.11
Flexible time for classes	.09

FIGURE 8.1 **Frequency of Structural Practices in the 820 Secondary Schools Studied, Classified as Traditional, Moderate, and Restructuring**

Note: Each figure in the "probability" column represents the likelihood that an average high school engages in each practice.

Source: Valerie E. Lee and Julia B. Smith, *High School Restructuring and Student Achievement* (Madison, WI: Center on Organization and Restructuring of Schools, 1994). Reprinted with permission.

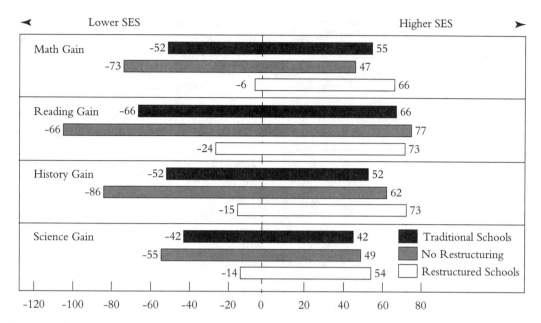

FIGURE 8.2   Percentage Gain in Achievement for Students of Different Social Class within Schools with Different Types of Practices

Source: Valerie E. Lee and Julia B. Smith, *High School Restructuring and Student Achievement* (Madison, WI: Center on Organization and Restructuring of Schools, 1994). Reprinted with permission.

of the schools. The question that the researchers asked was: What effect, if any, do restructured within school practices have on achievement and equality? Lee and Smith hypothesized that student achievement would be higher in the restructured schools *and* that the restructured schools would be more equitable than either the traditional or the moderate reform schools.

In their analysis of outcomes, Lee and Smith defined "restructured" schools as any school in the sample that had in place at least three of the twelve "restructuring practices" shown in Figure 8.1. Forty-six percent of the schools fell into this category. Twelve percent of the schools actually indicated that none of the thirty practices were in place. The remainder (42 percent) indicated that they had at least tried one of the practices labeled as traditional or moderate. The outcome measures were test scores in mathematics, reading, history, and science for the eighth and tenth grades. A measure of student engagement was also used but is excluded here. (The findings were consistent with those for achievement.) Figure 8.2 presents the results of the analysis.

Test score gain results are shown separately for each of the four cognitive tests and for high- and low-SES students. *The baseline in Figure 8.2 is the zero point that represents the average gain on each test by middle-SES students in the traditionally restructured schools.* Each bar shows the difference in gain from the eighth to the tenth grade for students of low SES (to the left) and high SES (to the right). For example, for mathematics in traditionally structured schools, high-SES students obtained gain scores that were 55 percent higher than the middle-SES students; low-SES students achieved gains that were 52 percent lower than the middle-SES students. By contrast, for mathematics in radically restructured schools, high-SES students obtained gain scores that were 66 percent higher than the baseline middle-SES students; low-SES students achieved gains that were 6 percent lower than the baseline middle-SES students. Although there is a great deal of complex information conveyed in Figure 8.2, several important patterns stand out.

First, the gains made by high-SES students reflect a very familiar pattern, regardless of the level of restructuring in the school. It is clear that the gains made by such students in restructured schools are no less than those made by similar students in the other schools. Thus, high-SES students are *not* affected negatively by within school restructuring. If anything, restructuring may actually increase achievement for the high-SES students. Most remarkable, however, is the fact that the gap between the high- and low-SES students was smaller in the schools with three or more radical restructuring practices. In fact, low-SES students in the restructured schools perform at levels very close to medium-SES students in the traditional schools. Thus, Lee and Smith demonstrate that it is possible to obtain both greater achievement and greater equality under certain within school conditions.[2] Notably, Lee and Smith also report that smaller schools in

their analysis demonstrated greater and more equitable test score gains than larger schools.

The alert reader will question whether these results are between rather than within school effects. After all, Lee and Smith have grouped a set of schools into three types—restructured, traditional, and no restructuring at all—which are reflected in Figure 8.2. In actuality, Lee and Smith conducted an analysis that allows for an assessment of both between and within school effects. This mode of analysis is called hierarchical linear modeling and is reviewed in Chapter 5. Fully two-thirds of the variance attributed to the structure of the schools lies within rather than between the schools.

As we have noted previously, certain schools or school systems (with certain within school policies) do bring about both higher levels of achievement and greater equality. Catholic schools do this relative to public schools in the United States (see Chapters 1 and 4) and Japanese schools do this relative to American schools (see Chapters 1 and 6). You will recall that in these studies, the influence of home background characteristics of students was somehow reduced considerably. Here, however, we see that under certain conditions, equality and achievement can be cultivated in both public and private schools. However, one of the problems with these previous studies (on Catholic schools and Japanese schools) as well as with the Lee and Smith study above is that insufficient knowledge has been obtained as to which

---

[2] Surprisingly, the researchers do report that restructured schools practicing *more than three* of the restructured policies in Figure 8.1 obtained a less equitable distribution of test

scores and an overall lower gain score. The implications of this are not discussed by Lee and Smith, but might possibly be due to a lack of structure from too much change at once.

of the within school policies is most responsible for the results.[3]

Lee, Smith, and Croninger (1995) have extended the above study. First, they report that the eighth to tenth grade findings endure from the tenth to the twelfth grade. The schools with the radical forms of restructuring in place are more effective: "Their students learn more, and learning is distributed more equitably" (p. 27). More importantly, however, Lee, Smith, and Croninger demonstrate quite convincingly that the results are due to five basic ideas of restructured schools: (1) small school size, (2) active learning, (3) heterogeneous grouping, (4) constructivist teaching, and (5) a strong academic ethos.[4] These findings replicate the results obtained by Bryk, Lee, and Holland (1993) in their study of why and how Catholic schools are able to produce greater achievement and greater equality than public schools.

Looking again at Figure 8.1, it might appear at first glance that the restructuring practices have little in common. In fact, these practices are closely associated with what has been identified as "communally organized" schools as opposed to traditional bureaucratic and hierarchically organized schools (Bryk

---

[3] The exception to this statement is the recent work of Bryk, Lee, and Holland (1993), which actually provides considerable conceptual material for the Lee and Smith research.

[4] The importance of heterogeneous grouping is not elaborated in the Lee, Smith, and Croninger (1995) paper, but is acknowledged elsewhere as part of the larger study (see Lee and Smith, 1993, 2001). Note carefully that a strong academic ethos is one of the driving forces behind these positive results and this implies that the negative effects of youth and oppositional subcultures have been overcome.

and Driscoll, 1988; Bryk, Lee, and Holland, 1993). Bureaucratic schools are characterized by large size, formalized rules and procedures, top-down decision making, and tracking. Among other things, bureaucratic schools are impersonal and alienating. By contrast, communal schools are smaller, more personal, more team oriented, and typically less tracked. In a comment on the Lee and Smith study, McLaughlin (1994) noted that the radical restructuring practices used in that research, although seeming to have little in common, all contributed to the same end: "a personalized school setting where teachers are able to know students as learners and as people" (p. 9).

❖ ONE SIZE MAY NOT FIT EVERYONE

A central problem with school reform and restructuring is that there is a strong tendency to overgeneralize the scope of the reform strategy. The restructuring practices identified in the Lee and Smith (1994) study cited above seem almost beyond criticism. And the results are very persuasive. But, we need to ask if these types of reform strategies will consistently produce equality and achievement across all types of schools. In fact, Mussoline and Shouse (2001) did ask this question and tested it using the same NELS data as Lee and Smith (1994).

Mussoline and Shouse (2001: 45) began with the fact that "several studies have suggested that low-SES urban schools attain greater effectiveness and higher achievement through the use of more traditional types of organizational and curricular arrangement, practices and understanding." For example, Hallinger and Murphy (1986) found that effective leadership in low-SES schools was more authoritative and traditional compared to effective leadership in high-SES schools that appeared to be more communal and collegial. Mussoline and Shouse reasoned that the context of low-SES schools was quite different from the context of high-SES schools and this context was badly matched to restructuring practices that were dependent on school context that was supportive. Specifically, they argued (2001: 48) that "the problem is essentially related to the deficits in human and social resources with which low-SES schools must often contend, as well as to the high complexity associated with many restructuring practices." In high-SES schools:

> Students' broader knowledge base increases the likelihood that some types of restructured practices will be effective (such as those that emphasize constructivist or student-centered learning and the acquisition of higher-order knowledge). Second, the availability of denser, more academically oriented social support structures in advantaged communities helps reinforce and facilitate schools' academic goals. In other words, a "safety net" is available to students in advantaged schools that reduces the potential risk of flawed, poorly executed, or highly complex instructional practices. In addition to lacking these social resources disadvantaged schools suffer from a dearth of certain kinds of human resources (such as high-quality teaching staffs and low rates of turnover and absenteeism among teachers) that are crucial to the successful implementation of many of the complex technical reforms often recommended by the advocates of restructuring.

Hence, Mussoline and Shouse hypothesized that disadvantaged schools may reduce the risk by focusing on incremental reform that would include improving their traditional teacher practices rather than introducing radical reforms. Given these assumptions, the researchers expected to find negative consequences for low-SES schools that attempted to implement more elaborate radical reform along the lines of Lee and Smith (1994) above.

To test their hypothesis, they examined data from the NELS survey, limiting their analysis to public schools and employing the tenth grade data for their analysis. They employed the multilevel modeling technique to determine the effect of school-level variables on achievement while controlling for a full array of individual-level variables. The key school-level variables were school average SES and whether the school was restructured or not (using the exact same measures as Lee and Smith above, namely, restructured schools were those using at least 3 of the 12 restructuring practices shown in Figure 8.1). They also broke the schools down into those that were very low SES, low SES, medium SES, and high SES.

The analysis supported the researchers' hypothesis. In public schools (Lee and Smith used both public and private schools) the influence of restructuring practices is not consistent across different SES contextual categories. In low-SES schools, and especially in very low SES schools, restructuring effects are significantly negative. On average, students achieve less in schools that serve mainly disadvantaged students, controlling for a set of individual variables such as SES and race, and other school-level variables such as academic press and the degree of shared community in the schools. The implication is that these students would be better served with an alternative form of reform, perhaps an improved set of traditional teacher practices combined with greater efforts at controlling the energies of the "oppositional culture."

This seems reasonable in light of the arguments made by Mussoline and Shouse concerning the lack of resources in these schools along with additional problems of an "oppositional culture" in low-SES schools, as discussed in the previous chapter. Mussoline and Shouse do not suggest that restructuring be withheld or discouraged in middle- or high-SES schools, and in fact, their analysis shows that the results are positive (though not significantly so) for these schools. Their point, well made, is that there are multiple avenues to greater school effectiveness, and they cite Cuban (1998), who noted that school "goodness" can be found in both traditional and progressive settings.

❖ THE INFLUENCE OF SCHOOL CHOICE ON ACHIEVEMENT AND EQUALITY

The debate over various forms of "school choice" policies is positioned front and center in educational reform. In contrast to the notion of restructuring, which focuses more upon individual schools rather than the entire system, choice is based upon the idea that there are fundamental things that are wrong with the entire public school system, beginning with the fact that allocation to a school is based upon residence. Although school choice plans can take a multitude of shapes, they all are alike in allowing parents to choose a school for their children from among all public and often private schools in a particular region (in some

cases, the region can be as large as the state of Minnesota). In this discussion, we use Chubb and Moe's (1990) market-oriented choice proposal, which is a broader concept than some policy options that use only vouchers.

At the present time, one-half million children attend public charter schools in the United States, and this amounts to less than one percent of the fall 2000 enrollment of all public and private school students (Hoff, 2001). Another 100,000 students are participating in some form of a voucher program. School choice has grown much more rapidly in other countries such as the Netherlands, Australia, Belgium, Spain, France, and the United Kingdom. In the Netherlands, for example, 76.3 percent of Dutch students attend a private school that receives public money, and this is true for the other countries but to a lesser degree (OECD, 2001). This has occurred largely because the political system in these countries agreed to offer tuition reimbursement to religious schools that follow a national curriculum and administer national tests. This is a model that is unlikely to move at the same pace in the United States for two reasons: (1) the constitutional separation of church and state, and (2) the country's resistance to a national curriculum.

Charter schools are generally confined to the public sector. That is, a charter school is provided an amount of money on a per pupil basis that is approximately equal to what it would have cost a city or a district to educate the student in a regular public school. In this case, the only issue is whether a student should have a choice or not. A more controversial form of school choice is a voucher program. In a voucher system, a student is given an amount of money (usually much less than the actual cost of a regular public school) to attend any school, either public or private. In theory, voucher funds would come from the public sector, but in practice, money for most ongoing voucher programs comes from private foundations who have grown impatient with progress in the public sector. This form of school choice complicates the issue in several ways. First, students who are provided with vouchers are more likely to attend religious (mostly Catholic) schools rather that independent private schools because the voucher will pay most if not all of the tuition. This raises the specter of whether government-financed education can be used at religious schools. Does this violate the First Amendment to the Constitution that prohibits the government from establishing (supporting) a religion? Currently, schools in Cleveland, Milwaukee, and in the states of Florida, Vermont, and Maine operate some form of a voucher system (Walsh, 2001). The matter of the constitutionality of voucher programs is currently being considered by the Supreme Court (for a good discussion of the legal and educational issues, see Viteritti, 1998).

◆ **PROPONENTS**

School choice plans focus on the way that schools are governed. According to Chubb (1994), a market-oriented choice policy operates as follows:

> The government makes a commitment to educating all children. Second, the government needs to have high standards for schools. Third, the government feeds responsibilities for actually delivering instructional services to others—to private schools, to groups of teachers, to groups of parents, to independent school operators. Parents are then not assigned to schools, but are free to choose among alternative providers of public education. A market then

comes into place in which innovation is encouraged, in which poor performers are weeded out through the choice process, in which efficiency is encouraged. And finally, the government takes responsibility for monitoring and regulating the process to see to it that the market operates properly.

School choice is premised on several assumptions: (1) some schools are better than other schools; (2) given a choice, parents will choose to send their children to the best school; (3) parents are knowledgeable about the quality of schooling; (4) the opportunities to choose a school will be equitably available to all parents; (5) all schools will strive to become better in order to be able to attract students; and (6) schools that do not improve according to the market will go out of business for lack of students. In effect, the concept of parental choice moves schooling into the capitalistic marketplace. Good schools will be innovatively created in order to attract students; bad schools will go out of business or be constrained to improve.

There is much debate about choice, but there are very few refined empirical answers at this point. We will examine several of the best studies below. Of course, the difficulty with this type of macroscopic proposal calling for a revolutionary transformation of schooling is that it is difficult to study. Let's try to project some results, however, in terms of achievement and equality.

Assuming that all segments of the population have equal access to the choice-making process, it seems reasonable to expect the following results:

1. A system of choice that is fair, equitable, and just will replace the current school choice system of buying a home to buy a school. That is, the idea of choosing a school is not new—what is new is that low-income families who do not have a choice under the present system would have an equal choice alongside their affluent counterparts. In theory, a parental choice plan would replace an existing Nozickian educational policy with one that is more in keeping with the philosophy of Rawls (recall Chapter 1).

2. It seems reasonably clear that the result of choice will be a set of prize-winning schools and students at one end and a group of "loser" schools and students at the bottom. Possibly, the overall achievement will be greater because of the students at the top schools and also because the bottom schools will attempt to get better in order to survive.

3. The existing achievement gap between the classes and the races should be reduced. Since the schools will be driven by the competition of a market economy, a widening of the spread of achievement scores should be expected. This inequality, however, in theory would be based upon merit and achievement rather than upon the invidious status characteristics of socioeconomic status or race. We also know that the effects of a "good" school are greater for disadvantaged students than for middle-class students; hence, minorities and low-income students should actually realize greater gains from a policy of choice than middle-class white students, which means that the inequality gap will be closed.

◆ OPPONENTS

What do the critics say? It is difficult to envision that low-SES and minority parents will indeed have equal access to the choice-making process. In fact, as I have intimated above, if equal access were

virtually guaranteed, the idea of choice would be at least minimally compelling. Once the process of social reproduction enters this picture however, we can probably assume that this will be politically unacceptable to the American white middle class, who will ultimately either oppose choice plans or will want at a minimum to have first choice.

Choice plans require extreme forms of selectivity. Chubb and Moe (1990: 221–222) have identified the factors needed in order for choice to work:

> Schools must be able to define their own missions and build their own programs in their own ways, and they cannot do this if their student population is thrust on them by outsiders. They must be free to admit as many or as few students as they want, based on whatever criteria they think relevant—intelligence, motivation, behavior, special needs—and they must be free to exercise their own, informal judgements about individual applicants.

Although Chubb and Moe clearly note that the above marching orders would be subject only to nondiscrimination requirements, the quote is boldly exclusive in every other regard. The negative implications for equality are ominous. School choice might increase the sorting and selecting of students by race and socioeconomic status, and thereby increase inequality and the potential for social conflict.

Astin (1992) has argued that schools are incapable of functioning in a market economy. Typically, successful organizations grow larger in order to accommodate the market and to increase profits. Schools obviously are non-profit organizations and are actually disinterested in growing larger. In lieu of growing larger, successful schools become more selective. Moreover, "since the size of successful schools in the educational marketplace does not usually increase, the least successful schools seldom go out of business: Students have to attend school *somewhere*" (Astin, 1992: 256). Astin argues that we can estimate the likely effects of parental choice programs by looking at American higher education. Higher education has been a choice system from the outset, and it is extremely stratified and elitist. This is true for public as well as private institutions.

Yet another problem with choice proposals is how the schools would function in a market economy, especially with regard to advertising (Astin, 1992). Several sticky issues will quickly arise: Will the costs of advertising for students inevitably lead to greater costs for schooling? Who will pay for this? How will the quality of information about schools that is conveyed in an advertising message be monitored for integrity?

Proposals for greater parental choice in the schooling of their children have a lot of political appeal. How can you argue for less freedom of choice? Who would possibly wish schools to be less accountable for their work? And doesn't choice seem to provide answers to these questions? But the issue will in fact require a close order examination to determine whether it will increase equality and achievement. In any event, the debate over school choice will continue on for the next decade and it is likely that some programs of choice will be implemented in most of the United States during this time. Assuming this is so, evaluation of these programs is essential. In theory, choice plans seem to offer the promise of greater equality; in practice, however, they might magnify the existing stratification system.

◆ SOME EMPIRICAL RESULTS

The results of voucher or charter programs are not limited to achievement outcomes for those students attending charter schools or participating in a voucher program. Both proponents and critics are interested also in the achievement results for those students who do not choose to apply for either of these types of programs. Proponents argue that the regular schools will be forced to improve while the critics see a problem as the best students exit the regular schools. Two studies below address this issue. Another important outcome is parent satisfaction with charter and voucher schooling and here the results are consistent. Parents desire more charters and vouchers, and those parents who have children participating in either a charter school or a voucher program are more satisfied with their schooling than comparable parents whose children attend the regular public schools (Gill et al., 2001; Peterson, 1999).

Two recent reports commissioned by the U.S. Department of Education conclude that charter schools are expanding, performing well, and most importantly, they are spurring regular public schools within the same district to improve through competition. In one study of forty-nine school sites in five states, the researchers report that they found the regular schools to have become more "consumer-service oriented" as a result of losing money from their budgets because of transfers into charter schools. The regular schools had added extra programs and services and were more responsive to parents and the community (Sack, 2001). As of 2000, the Education Department estimates that there are 2,100 charter schools in 36 states.

Arum (1996) found similar results by examining the influence of the size of the private school sector in a state on student outcomes in public schools. Theoretically, he hypothesized that competition from private schools would affect the organizational structure of public schools which in turn would influence student outcomes in public schools. By comparing the percentage of private to public schools in each state (range for private schools was 3 to 19 percent in 1980) along with student/teacher ratios (elements of organization) to student test scores outcomes, Arum was able to demonstrate that public school student/ teacher ratios responded to increases and decreases in the percentage of private schools in a state.

Employing the HSB survey and using 12th grade student outcomes in conjunction with aggregated state-level data, Arum (1996: 40, 42) concluded:

> [A]s school choice advocates argue—the presence of increased choices in the school marketplace has a beneficial influence on student performance in the public schools. Students learn more in public schools that face competition from the private sector. . . . Overall, results indicate that public school students have greater gains on test scores in states with a large competing private sector, and this result is largely explained by the increased resources available to public schools facing greater competition from the private sector.

Arum cautions that competitive forces do not change the behavior of public schools, but rather they appear to improve the schools by way of increased funding to decrease the student/teacher ratios. This is not exactly what choice proponents envision. The distinction is

that the public school improvement came from increased resources rather than adopting one or more of the characteristics of the private school model such as a communal environment or greater academic press (as discussed in Chapter 7) or one of the innovative restructuring elements. But choice advocates are not locked into a single vision of how competition might lead to positive results in the public sector. In this case, the public schools are constrained to implement one of the proven school reforms (class size) as a result of an increased private sector presence. When the private sector presence is small, there is little or no pressure to reduce the student/teacher ratio.

Empirical studies of student outcomes are more plentiful and more refined in voucher programs rather than for charter schools (for a complete discussion of the issues, see Peterson, 1999; Gill et al., 2001). In both cases, there are serious methodological challenges. As we have noted often in the book, the main problem is "section bias" and here it is especially perplexing. As in studies of public and private schools, students and parents who choose voucher programs or charter schools are likely to differ in systematic ways from students who remain in regular public schools. For this reason, observed differences in outcomes might result from preexisting differences. Of course, efforts are made to statistically control for observable background characteristics.

Fortunately, especially in the case of voucher programs, it is possible to employ a research design of random assignment that reduces the problem of selection bias. In large citywide voucher programs, of which there are at least seven, selection into the voucher program is determined by random lottery. Thus, the achievement outcomes of those students who win the lottery can be compared to those students who applied to but were not selected for the program (and who then must go on to regular schools without the voucher). To a large degree, we can assume that these two groups were equivalent at the outset. Also, because these are citywide programs, there are adequate numbers of students for each group, unlike charter schools where the numbers are often limited. For this reason, I confine the discussion to studies of voucher programs.

Four studies, in particular, are viewed as having the most carefully designed research plans (Gill et al., 2001). These studies were conducted on private citywide voucher programs in New York, New York, Dayton, Ohio, Charlotte, North Carolina, and Washington, District of Columbia. To be eligible for a voucher scholarship, students in each city were required to be entering grades one to five, attend a public school at the time of application, live within the city limits, and come from families with incomes sufficiently low as to qualify for a free school lunch.[5] As of 2000, these programs had been operational ranging from one to three years (Howell et al., 2000). The size of the voucher in each city ranged between $1,200 to $2,200 and could be applied toward tuition at any private school in the city.

The findings from these four voucher programs are remarkably consistent as well as perplexing. For African American students, the achievement gains in the voucher programs were significantly greater than for their counterparts in the regular public schools and were of modest size, ranging from 4 to 9 national percentile points in gains over two years. For all other racial/ethnic groups, the results are null (Gill et al., 2001). Latinos in New York and whites in Dayton did not score higher than their public school peers in the regular public schools. The perplexing part is that the other racial/ethnic groups were as disadvantaged as the African American students.

In summary, the results of these four evaluations show promising results for low-income African American students, but no benefit (and no harm) to other low-income Latino and white students. These programs will continue to be followed over the next several years and perhaps some answers will emerge as to why the positive effects are limited to African American students.

❖ SCHOOL CHOICE, SCHOOL EFFECTS, AND SCHOOL SELECTIVITY

The selectivity controversy surrounding the Catholic-public school debate, as well as the voucher and charter school debate, has been treated largely as a problem of evaluating self-selection bias in the composition of school populations. Two objections are raised: first, by researchers claiming that all existing individual attributes and endowments must be

---

[5] In reality, the yield from this selection process is not as simple as it may seem. The evaluations are complicated by noncompliance and attrition. Specifically, in each city only some students agreed to take up the voucher (takers) while others declined (decliners). And the takers and decliners differed along a variety of lines including SES, despite the benchmark of having to qualify for a free lunch. But, in fact, the research controlled for these relative differences statistically.

equated in order to separate the effects of different types of schools from the effects of individuals who choose to attend them; and second, by some policy types who claim that school choice is a narrow path that will be open only to a few students and all the rest will be left behind. Both of these concerns, though not without some basis, only address part of the problem.

The fact is that schools of choice are more effective in every way because they do select students who desire exactly what the school offers or supplies. Schools might offer greater safety, better teachers, unique programs, better facilities, or more opportunities for athletic development, or they might be closer to home, or further away from a neighborhood that is detrimental to academic success. The point is that schools are selective in terms of what they supply to students. According to Dreeben (2000: 126) attention to self-selection bias:

> [I]gnores selectivity from the supply side as a component of internal school structure and operation, while fastening on the demand (household choice) side of enrollment. . . . Making these values known [as in the publication of the school mission and philosophy] is part of the student selection process, of establishing self-definitions, or of establishing charters, . . . a practice also familiar to private or magnet, or vocational schools. . . . If schools claim to be academic and possess certain social and spiritual qualities, students and their parents interested in this kind of schooling . . . irrespective of background, will be more likely to seek admission than those looking for something different. From the pool of admission seekers, schools select students they believe will prosper under their academic regimen and form of social life. Selection occurs on both the supply and the demand sides.

This implies that school choice issues must attend to the manner in which schools choose students along with attention to the process by which students choose schools.

Thus, the proacademic choice that is made by parents and students is the key explanatory variable as to why schools of choice are more effective. This choice sets into motion a set of relationships among teachers, parents, and students that emphasize academics and deemphasizes youth culture values. This choice is all about the rejection of antiacademic values, which predominate our culture and our schools. Moreover, this rejection comes from the bottom up rather than the top down.

This proacademic environment is a function of the choice-making process that is made by students who attend charter schools or participate in voucher programs. In this regard, it is entirely different from a set of structures or programs that are put into place by educators. In "choice" schools, the academic environment is normative in a true sociological sense. It is a set of rules established by the subjective reality (definitions) of participants that takes on an objective reality as a set of social structural norms (Berger and Luckman, 1967). This idea is similar to that proposed by Bryk, Lee, and Holland (1993) of a "voluntary community" for public school policy which would resemble Catholic schools in every respect except for religion. Moreover, these academic definitions of school contradict the nonacademic definitions that students will otherwise bring to school and which come to constitute a youth culture. In effect, choice schools mitigate the single largest obstacle, which stands in the way of effective and equitable schooling, and they do this by using a fundamental sociological principle of how real social structures are created. Structures that are imposed and that contradict deeply cherished beliefs (regardless of how wrongheaded and problematic they may be) will be rejected out of hand by any group with substantial power in numbers such as students in schools.

The challenge of effective and equitable schooling in the next century is to overcome the resistance and the recalcitrance of youth cultures in and out of the school (Goodlad, 1984; Steinberg et al., 1996). This is not a new problem and undoubtedly predates the modern school, but the intensity and the complexity of the problem is new and it is the most important obstacle in the schools today. It is not just about youthful anti-intellectualism; it is not just about antisocial behavior; it is not just about athletics and rock concerts; it is not just about sexual harassment; it is not just about the contentiousness that comes from increased diversity in the schools; it is about all these things and more.

❖ ACCOUNTABILITY IN EDUCATION

The idea of holding a school accountable for student outcomes goes to the heart of why we study differences between schools. Hoffer (2000) describes the history, scope and, growth of accountability. He shows how with accountability we come full circle to the input-output production models that have been addressed throughout this book. Hoffer notes (2000: 530) that "the school is understood to transform inputs of various sorts into outputs through certain productive processes." Hoffer is well aware of the controversies over the black box of the educational processes, but he remarks that in practice these distinctions between educational processes (still troubling to researchers in the sociology of education) and outcomes are often blurred by those charged with conducting accountability in the schools. Students bear the main burden of formal outcomes assessment, which is then used as the indicator of system, school, and teacher effectiveness.

Accountability has always existed as an informal system whereby performances of teachers and the outcomes of students have been examined. Only over the past two decades has the system grown to a formal and quantitative stage. According to Hoffer (2000: 530):

> Accountability systems are intended to work as quality control mechanisms. In the current U.S. policy context, they can be viewed as an alternative to the kinds of market controls that an expanded system of school choice might provide (Ladd, 1996). The accountability system sends codified signals (e.g., test scores and drop-out rates) about school effectiveness to education administrators and to external constituencies. A school choice system, in contrast, sends signals of client satisfaction in the form of enrollment decisions. Market systems may lead to signaling structures similar to those used in accountability systems, but this is not necessarily the case.

There are clearly problems of identifying the value-added component that is made by schools in accounting for student learning. This, of course, is fraught with all of the difficulties and many more than are usually confronted by education researchers who have available better data (longitudinal) than school officials.

Assessment tools often lack adequate and valid information about the characteristics of schools or families that are available in many of the studies reviewed in this book. We have noted the difficulties of identifying "school effects" as separate from home effects and peer effects. Moreover, most assessments use a cross-sectional rather than a longitudinal design to measure outcomes. Ultimately, accountability must control for the problems associated with selection bias as discussed throughout this book; if one looks only at the final results at a given grade level on a cross-sectional survey, there is the real possibility that schools which may have done an effective and commendable job with low-performing students may be judged as substandard, whereas schools that have done very little with initially high-performing students may look spuriously like exemplary schools (see Meyer, 1996). And, as noted above, most local and statewide assessments do not include measures of the educational process such as opportunity-to-learn variables. Recent proposals for accountability have advocated a focus on these educational process variables, not only as intervening variables, but also as outcomes in themselves (Hoffer, 2000; Smith, Scoll, and Link, 1996).

A pivotal question in an accountability system is, Who is held accountable by whom and with what practical consequences? In the United States, formal standards vary from state to state and often from district to district. In contrast to many other industrialized nations, the United States does not have national standards in any area of the elementary or secondary school curriculum (Bishop, 1996). Generally, principals of schools are held accountable for average outcomes at their school, and increasingly incentives are being offered to principals for positive outcomes. Teachers are not held responsi-

ble for outcomes at the classroom level (at this time) and incentives are generally not available to teachers. "At all level of education, performance standards are most rigorously and systematically defined for students" (Hoffer, 2000: 532). That is, students are held accountable by the state (or district) with principals being the agents for the state. The consequences of attaining or failing to attain standards set by the state vary for both students and principals, but increasingly we are moving to a point where the assessment has become a "high stakes process." For students, failure to reach the standard means not graduating from high school, and for the principal it means looking for a new job. Teachers also are increasingly being held accountable in two ways: (1) through requirements in some states to pass a knowledge-based test, and (2) by the availability of data on the progress of students in their class (as opposed to schoolwide averages).

Hoffer provides a set of answers to the question of what accounts for the growth in formal accountability systems over the past decades. Again, informal accountability has always been part of educational systems, but formal accountability is a new phenomenon. According to Hoffer, drawing upon Callahan (1962) and Porter (1995), there are six main explanations for the rapid growth of accountability in education:

1. Support for education has passed into the realm of formal taxation mechanisms at the local, state, and national levels, and this has greatly expanded the constituencies of schools beyond the immediate sphere of the families served by the schools. In this process, education competes with other uses of tax dollars among the general public;

2. The expansion of higher education in the second half of the twentieth century increased the need for standardized information and credentials of students as seen in the SAT or ACT scores that are used extensively in college and graduate school admissions;

3. The Nation at Risk report (1983) and the expansion of NAEP to the state level, coupled with international comparisons of American schools in the mass media has led to a perceived crisis in schooling;

4. The growth of regional and national job markets has generated a need for more efficient and accurate exchange of information among employers about prospective employees;

5. Increasingly, families want to have more accurate information about the quality of schools that they are considering as communities of residence;

6. Computer and information processing has made it possible to compile, analyze, and distribute the information more quickly.

There is a clear distinction between the ongoing activities of educational research in the sociology of education and the educational policy and practice of conducting accountability with the goal of determining which school works best. Sociologists of education know that the difference between schools in accounting for variation of student learning is not large, and yet an entire industry of formal educational accountability moves forward under the assumption that school (not families, not peer groups) is responsible for student outcomes.

As this book goes to press, President Bush has just signed a massive education bill (ESEA, 2002), which greatly increases the role of the federal government in education with mandatory testing in all states from grades three to eight; greater accountability, especially toward providing both greater achievement and equality in the schools; more choice for parents; and increased teacher quality (see Schemo, 2001; Robelen, 2001, 2002; Bumiller, 2002). States and districts must ensure that students score at state-defined proficiency levels with a particular focus on racial, gender, and socioeconomic subgroups, and on those schools which make the least and most improvement on a year-to-year basis. One of the earmark features of the bill is the establishment of a twelve-year time period for significantly closing the gap in student achievement between racial and social class groups. Schools that persistently fail to make improvement will be subject to sanctions, and ultimately if no improvement occurs within five years, a school will be remanded over to the state for reconstitution. In addition, children in failing schools will be eligible for transfer to more successful public schools (that is, they will be provided a choice). The bill signals an expanded role of the federal government in public school education. Many of the budget requests accompanying the bill call for increased federal spending on charter schools, choice demonstration schools, and Title I grants to local agencies to turn around low-performing schools, improve teacher quality, and ensure that "no child is left behind."

◆ Sociological Studies of Accountability

Having noted above the difficulties of assessment using statewide testing, what do we know about the effects of reform and accountability and standards using research by sociologists of education? Muller and Schiller (2000) take up this question using data from NELS along with another data set from the National Longitudinal Study of Schools (NLSS). They begin by noting that accountability initiatives are the most recent in a long line of efforts by the federal and state governments to provide equality of opportunity as defined in this book (that is, reducing the gap between subgroups and raising achievement for all). Their study examined how state variations in testing policies (an essential component of accountability) influence educational outcomes for students.

They employ a unique application of the multilevel models that we have discussed previously to study the effect of variation in state-level policies (level 2) on student outcomes (level 1). Specifically, they addressed two questions: (1) What effect did testing policies have on the relationship of SES to outcomes? and (2) What effect did testing policies have on the average achievement of two educational outcomes? The decentralized nature of the American educational system means that there is great variation in the use of testing, especially with regard to the incentives. In some states, students are held responsible and cannot be promoted or graduate unless a standard is met; in other states, schools are held responsible and receive rewards or sanctions if the standard is not met. And the states vary in the extent of testing.

Muller and Schiller employed the NELS data to measure student outcomes along with both SES and teacher expectations as independent variables together with a set of background control variables. The outcomes were high school graduation and the number of advanced course work in mathematics (number of Carnegie credits). They chose these two outcomes because (1) they represent the low and high levels of the performance spectrum, and (2) they are more directly associated with the accountability issue. Muller and Schiller used three variables from the National Longitudinal Study of Schools (NLSS) to obtain indicators of state testing policies. This survey was conducted in the 1990s (independent of NELS) and asked questions of the Department of Education (DOE) in each state including the extensiveness of testing (grade levels and content areas), consequences for students (mandatory policies/guidelines/no guidelines), and consequences for schools (financial incentives; official recognition and sanctions, including loss of accreditation; and loss of control to higher educational authority).

Generally, Muller and Schiller discovered that more accountability measures (rather than less) had moderately favorable effects on students, especially academically vulnerable students. But the results are complex. To illustrate part of the results, they predict the results for a hypothetical "vulnerable" student under varying levels of state accountability testing policies. They defined such a student (2000: 208) "as one who came from a poor family (one standard deviation below the mean in SES), was enrolled in remedial mathematics class in the 8th grade, and was considered a risk of dropping out by his or her 10th grade teacher." This is a typically real student since all three of these strikes against the student are highly correlated between socioeconomic status, course enrollments, and teacher's expectations. Figure 8.3 shows the predicted results for this student on the two outcomes variables and different testing policies.

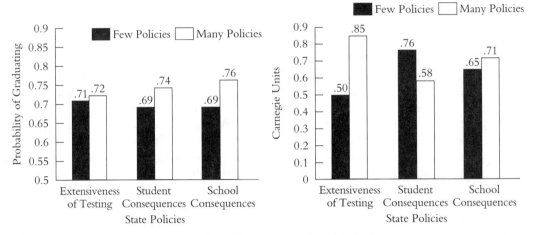

FIGURE 8.3   **The Predicted Outcomes of Accountability Practices with Consequences for Schools or Students for a Hypothetical Vulnerable Student**

Source: Chandra Muller and Kathryn S. Schiller, 2000. "Leveling the Playing Field? Students' Educational Attainment and States' Performance Testing." *Sociology of Education 73:* 209. Reprinted with permission.

Note first that in five of the six comparisons, the hypothetically disadvantaged student fares better (in terms of achievement) in a state with many testing policies as opposed to a state with few policies. Note also that in four of these five positive comparisons the magnitude of the difference is substantial. We would expect that the effect of these policies would be more consistent with regard to high school graduation since that is a main objective of the policies. We would not expect the vulnerable student to take many advanced courses and yet, as Figure 8.3 shows, there is an increase in the number of advanced courses taken by such a student in states with more testing and more policies with consequences for the school.

In addition to the results portrayed in Figure 8.3 showing the effects of state testing policies on average mean outcomes under the conditions described (a vulnerable student), the researchers also

examined the extent to which these state testing policies influence the issue of equality. To do this, they examined the way in which testing policy altered the effect of SES at the individual level on the two educational outcomes. Here is where the results become a bit more complicated.

They found that testing policies with consequences for schools actually increased the influence of SES (implying that it increased inequality among the students from different social classes). This finding is consistent with those who argue that disadvantaged students may be harmed (marginalized) by increased testing and accountability by being placed in lower-tracked classes so that they can meet minimal standards for the school (Muller, Katz, and Dance, 1999), or that they may be overchallenged academically and drop out (McDill, Nattriello, and Pallas, 1986). These two possibilities would be within schools processes. It is also possible that there is greater stratification between schools. Muller and Schiller state (2000: 210) "it could be an indicator of a more serious funneling of resources away from schools that serve poor communities, possibly to schools that serve populations that are more likely to perform well on state examinations."

By contrast, policies with consequences for students decreased the influence of SES, thereby increasing equality in the educational attainment of all students. This finding, however, held only for the likelihood of graduating, not for the Carnegie units. That is, the results also show that testing policies having consequences for students (rather than for schools) do work to increase equality among students by reducing the influence of home socioeconomic status of students on achievement. These results are in line with those who advocate increasing standards and establishing accountability systems based on student performance (Coleman, 1997; Porter, 1995). Theoretically, student accountability will require schools to help students at all levels to improve their academic performance.

A more recent study supports the Muller and Schiller research. Carnoy and Loeb (2003) computed an accountability measure that combined consequences for both schools and students and rated all 50 states on their strength of accountability. The study found that student test scores in mathematics improved more during the late 1990s when tougher accountability programs were in place than in states with weaker accountability systems. Moreover, there was no evidence that students were more likely to dropout or repeat grades in the states with the more demanding conse-

quences for both students and schools. A study demonstrating less promising results was reported by Amrein and Berliner (2002).

❖ SCHOOLS AS ENDS RATHER THAN MEANS

Three decades ago, Christopher Jencks and his colleagues (1972) exhaustively reanalyzed the original Coleman Report along with several other large-scale data sets to reassess the influence of family and schools on student outcomes. This book, *Inequality*, reported nothing different than what has been reviewed here, except that it did examine in depth the effects of schools on adult achievement in terms of occupation status and income. In the end, they concluded (1972: 255) that children are more influenced by what happens at home and on the streets than what happens in school; reformers have little control over what actually happens in the classroom and out of the classroom on a minute-by-minute basis; and "even when a school exerts an unusual influence on children, the resulting changes are not likely to persist into adulthood. It takes a huge change in elementary school test scores, for example, to alter adult income by a significant amount."

These results, again the same results we have found, suggested to Jencks and his colleagues that we should modify the way we think about schools. Specifically, we should abandon the "factory" model, which was then and has remained until now, the backbone of research, practice, and policy on schools. Schools are viewed as factories that take human raw material in the form of children and produce a product in the form of a more valuable material, that is, an employable adult. But our research from Coleman to the summer learning studies of Entwisle and Alexander leads us inescapably to the conclusion that the outcomes of schooling depend mostly on the characteristics of students at the very outset of and throughout their educational careers. "Everything else—the school budget, its policies, the characteristics of the teachers is either secondary or irrelevant." (Jencks et al., 1972: 256).

They ended their book with a somber and radical idea; namely that we should think about schools as ends in themselves rather than as means to some other end and that we should begin by describing and analyzing and practicing in schools by using a model that is more like families than like factories. Currently, policy makers, teachers, administrators, researchers, and parents are attempting to make schools more effective through practice, experimentation, and research in terms of achievement and equality. But, they fail to recall how onerous schools are for those who must attend them. Many schools are dull, depressing, and dangerous places. Schools have maintained a prisonlike atmosphere that has not changed much in 100 years in terms of formal organization and control of behavior.

This leads to the view that as many students as possible should be able to attend the school that they prefer and that they like. After all, some schools are exciting, much less dangerous, happy, and fun places to spend the day. Since students spend one-fifth of their lives in schools, we should spend at least one-fifth of our thinking on how to make all schools more pleasant places to be. This implies, as I have suggested in the above section on selection, that students should

be able to choose which school they wish to attend, at least within their district if not beyond. Choices would be made for varying reasons, most of which would be academic of course, but some parents and students would choose for other reasons as well. This would not mean that schools would become nonacademic in their orientation, but that each might be different. Once again, some children would choose to attend a school in their own neighborhood, but others would choose a school in another community, perhaps to escape a depressing neighborhood.

❖ ORGANIZATIONAL STRUCTURES AND SCHOOL REFORM STRATEGIES

What accounts for the apparent inability of the schools to move forward, to change, to reform, to resolve these conflicts that constrain and strain effectiveness? In education, the history of reform is mostly a set of commission reports gathering dust. In fact, with few exceptions (Common School, Progressive Education, Comprehensive High School), virtually every change in education can be traced to governmental intervention in the form of laws or subsidies or to parental and student revolt. And virtually every change (small or large) has been reversed eventually—that is, small schools → large schools → small schools; common curriculum → tracking → untracking.

Part of the problem, I believe, lies in a failure to recognize and account for the fundamental and unique conflict of goals identified in Chapters 1 and 7. Unlike the professions of law and medicine where clients and professionals share the same goals, professional educators and their clients are at odds with one another. Moreover, organizational change or reform requires an accurate conception of the organization. Yet the school as reformers often conceive it no longer corresponds to the school as it now exists (and perhaps it never did).

In the face of the recurrent failures of reform, scholars share a growing sense that the problems of education extend beyond the schools. Over the past decade, an array of social conditions circumscribing the schools and acting as obstacles to school improvement have been identified. Taken together, Goodlad (1984) and Coleman (1987) pinpoint the following conditions:

1. a growing number of employed parents;

2. a growing number of single-parent families;

3. a growing number of families broken by divorce;

4. a growing number of households without children;

5. decreases in the number of adults populating family units—that is, a sharp decline of the extended family;

6. decreases in church attendance and membership;

7. decreases in the solidarity of communities or neighborhoods;

8. fewer coalitions of legislators, parents, school board members, school administrators, teachers, business leaders, and others;

9. increasing segmentation in the educational profession;

10. increasing diversity of students in the schools;

11. increasing role and impact of television.

These social transformations, however accountable they may be for impeding school reform, cannot account for the failure of schools to clearly define their organizational structure and processes.

In *A Place Called School*, Goodlad (1984: 247) makes the point "that the didactics of the classroom can be—and indeed are—very much the same from school to school and yet often are presented within a context of considerable school-to-school difference in the eyes of principals, teachers, students, and parents." Goodlad (1984: 246) demonstrates that schools are really very much alike, especially with regard to those things commonly regarded as unique to schooling—namely, "the mechanics of teaching, the kinds of activities in which students are engaged in classrooms, the modes of learning encouraged, instructional materials, tests and quizzes, grouping practices, and classroom management."

Thus, those aspects of schooling that most distinguish it from other institutions *do not* differ significantly from school to school. Rather, it is those characteristics of schooling that are shared by other types of organizations and institutions (such as business, industry, government, the military, and so on) that *do* often differ from one school to another. And, Goodlad notes, these latter school characteristics (such as school size, sex ratio, the school's orientation to academic concerns, the informal adolescent norms, the relationship between teachers and principal) are less likely to be experienced by visitors and observers (that is, researchers). Understandably then, the real structural differences that do exist between schools have often been overlooked.

If some schools are more effective than others and if schools do not differ significantly in their curricula and instructional practices, then the differential outcomes must derive from structural differences that schools share with all organizations and institutions. Over the years, these structural differences in schools have been either undetected or disregarded. Instead, reforms have been directed more often at those matters where effective and noneffective schools do not differ, such as basic modes of instruction, the nature of classroom activities, and the mechanics of teaching. Sedlack et al. (1986) apparently agree with this appraisal of the situation:

> Not one of these [reform] proposals, however, takes into account the most fundamental variables in the educational process: the nature of the relationship between educators and their students and the extent to which students are actively engaged in the learning process. (p. ix)

❖ CREATING AN ACADEMIC SUBCULTURE

Historically, the central problem of school reform is the conflict that exists between the goals of teachers and students—a conflict between the life of the mind and that of the body, a life of reading, thinking, and intellectual sharing versus a life of playing sports, dancing, or just plain hanging out. I avoid presenting the student's interests as primarily sexual because I doubt the predominance of sexual motives. The adolescent value system is complex, genuine, healthy, physical, valuable, and suffused with practical rationality. In and of itself, it is functional and productive for adolescents in their overall sociohistorical situation. It is, however, dysfunctional with respect to the

cognitive academic development of adolescents and the academic goals of the school. This value conflict is at the heart of the crisis of schooling. Any successful strategy for reforming schools must discover acceptable ways to deactivate or reduce the energy of the adolescent value system or at least rechannel that energy into scholastic endeavors. Of course, the oppositional subculture extends the intensity of this conflict, bringing about the problems of animosity, detachment, violence, resistance, and deliberate sabotage of school activities.

One strategy for doing this, according to Goodlad (1984), is to reduce the size of our schools (not class size). His study of thirty-eight schools showed that the most effective schools were relatively small. He notes that other studies support this conclusion across a variety of academic outcome areas. "It appears to be more difficult in small schools for the more extreme peer group values to take hold" (p. 370). This idea is a relatively inexpensive school reform.

Goodlad (1984) proposes another strategy: that students begin school at age four and graduate from high school at age sixteen. This recommendation would help to reduce the conflict between educational and adolescent values, since that conflict begins around age twelve and reaches a peak between fifteen and eighteen. The idea would entail no additional costs. In fact, it would assist parents economically by saving the costs of day care for four-year-olds.

Coleman's (1961) solution was to channel the energies and values of youth toward the idea of academic competition. He found that academics, unlike sports, were an unrewarded activity and hence, they were pursued passively and reluctantly. He recommended offering more realistic rewards and prizes for academic achievement both within and between schools. With considerable foresight, he seems to have anticipated the "choice" movement whereby parents and students would be allowed to choose which school to attend rather than being assigned one. If appropriate rewards were tied to academic success, the best students would be attracted to this type of activity. And if a particular school or set of schools were to consistently outperform the other schools, more of the better students would be attracted to the schools where the academic subculture had become dominant. Unfortunately, this idea entails the possibility of creating a school system with an increasing degree of inequality.

Another approach is to separate potentially troublesome students from other students in the schools. Although this practice may seem undemocratic or inegalitarian, Hamilton (1986) notes that it is actually one of four important characteristics of successful dropout-prevention programs. Hamilton states that John Rawls's (1971) *Theory of Justice* helps to clarify a policy of separatism. Considering how inequalities might be justified in a democratic society, Rawls proposed that they could only be considered "just" if the inequality benefited those at the lowest level. Historically, this argument has proven ineffective as an educational policy. Ability grouping, for example, is now generally viewed as being more costly to those in the lowest groups in terms of both achievement and self-image (see Rosenbaum, 1980; Oakes, 1985; Lucas, 1999). In the case of potential dropouts, however, Hamilton (1986) believes that differential treatment can sometimes be justified providing that the "probable consequences of assignment to the lowest group [is] favorable and

acceptable to those students and their parents" (p. 158).

In their study of public and private schools, Coleman, Hoffer, and Kilgore (1982) report that Catholic schools provide a more effective learning environment and better academic outcomes than public schools. They concluded that "the constraints imposed on schools in the public sector seem to impair their functioning as educational institutions, without providing the more egalitarian outcomes that are among the goals of public schooling" (p. 185). And they strongly imply that the effectiveness of Catholic schools is due in large part to school policy, value consensus, and the authority of the school to impose a greater degree of order and discipline. The implication is that school officials can cultivate an academic subculture if they are free from certain external constraints and are able to draw upon a supportive parental community (see also, Bryk, Lee, and Holland, 1993).

In any event, the challenge is to create an academic subculture sufficiently powerful to counteract the persistent negative influence of the adolescent subculture. There is perhaps no single best way to accomplish this. Yet, we cannot go too far wrong by instituting the factors that have come to constitute an effective school, as discussed in Chapters 4 through 7.

❖ WHAT SHOULD INTERESTED PARTIES DO?

Despite the limitations in the scope of this book, we have covered a great deal of ground pertaining to how people concerned with the welfare of children in school might act. It is important to attempt to provide direction to these parties based upon the sociological research and theory that we have reviewed. In doing so, we skate on thin ice, for others might interpret the same data differently. Bearing this in mind, I will try to avoid those recommendations that are likely to be controversial, and I will focus on those resting on fairly solid ground.

◆ WHAT SHOULD PARENTS DO?

1. Regardless of their family situation or work situation, parents should recognize that parental presence and involvement with their children is crucial and provides children with whatever cultural, human, and social capital they have to give. Parents should spend the maximum time and effort they can on caregiving.

2. Parents should understand that differences between types of schools are much less important than differences within schools. Therefore, they should ensure that their child is appropriately (and fairly) placed in classes and groups (tracks) within the school. (If the existing system seems unjust, parents should work to untrack the school.)

3. Parents should learn to identify the negative effects of youth subcultures on the academic development of their child and to control, at least to some degree, the involvement of their child in certain peer groups. Children and young adults need peer groups to grow, but they do not need associations characterized by violence, sexual or racial harassment, and other forms of antisocial acts.

◆ WHAT SHOULD TEACHERS DO?

Teachers should come to fully embrace their critical role. The summer learning studies demonstrate clearly that teachers must be doing most things right since it is only when children are not in school that both achievement and equality decreases. This must be true despite the conflicting evidence regarding the extent to which teacher credentials and training are related to student outcomes. Teaching does make a difference because students, especially traditionally disadvantaged students, do learn when they are in school. Moreover, it appears that professional educators do teach in such a way as to minimize the inequalities that students bring with them to school. Yes, it is true that some students learn more than others, but this may be due to factors beyond the control of teachers— that is, the organization of schools and the structure and functioning of families.

Bear in mind that the elements really making a big difference in educational outcomes lie *between homes* and *within schools*. *Between school* differences are important, in the same way that any small but significant difference is important. A good teacher and/or a good classroom make a bigger difference. The same is true regarding the home. On the other hand, someday you may be in a position whereby you can influence the availability of a "good" school in your community, or you may need to advise a student who is either deficient in parental resources or disadvantaged by race, sex, or social class regarding a school choice. All other things being equal, a student is better off in a "good" school, even if the differences between a good school and a bad school are small. Keep in mind also that the difference between a good school and a bad school always has a greater impact for disadvantaged or deficient students.

◆ WHAT SHOULD SCHOOL PRINCIPALS AND OTHER ADMINISTRATORS DO?

1. Principals must learn to recognize the real cultural norms existing in their schools, especially those that are created and driven by adolescent and oppositional subcultures. Principals must harness the energies of the youth subcultures and direct them into the productive academic goals of the school. At a minimum, principals must institutionalize an academic ethos that recognizes both quality and equality. Barth (2002) argues that principals must be culture builders and that this is their most difficult and most important job. According to Barth (2002: 8), "culture building requires the will to transform the elements of school culture into forces that support rather than subvert the school's purposes."

2. Principals must clearly understand their own roles. Forming the most important group among school administrators, they are responsible for the way that the schools are organized. As school site managers, they increasingly have the authority to change the mode of school organization. Of course, they also have the authority to simply follow the rules of the school that have been established over the years. Unfortunately, many schools today are still governed by bureaucratic ethos and procedures, and rule following has evolved as the norm of school management. Some principals by contrast, may choose innovative school management, a course that requires leadership combined with courage, professionalism, and vision. Bureaucracy undermines such professionalism, and it drives out parents and alienates both teachers and students.

3. Positioned above school principals are superintendents, and between these two extremes are school boards and countless administrative personnel. All of the recommendations that apply to principals apply equally to these other administrators as well.

❖ CLOSING THOUGHTS

We need to pay more attention to the conception of the sociology of education held by John Meyer (1986), who points out that educational theory is *not* coterminous with theory in the sociology of education. Modern educational theory is rationalistic and rests upon modern social science, especially with regard to how to bring about greater equality and progress in society. Meyer presents this contrast:

> The main lines of thought in the sociology of education, rather, rise as sociological *commentary* on the institutionalized science of education. They parallel the system at every point, asking the sociological questions and expressing the sociological skepticism about it. Is the system really equal and meritocratic? . . . Does the rationalized system really work, or is it swamped by a variety of social forces? . . . Modern education . . . is designed . . . to create an equal citizenry and to legitimate any inequality on meritocratic grounds. The sociological critics raise the hypothesis that it does not do so, and that the old or new inequalities of estate and class and ethnicity and gender still live behind the educational legitimating mask. Access is, they suggest, based on status as much as merit. (pp. 343–344.)

We need to reapply *The Sociological Imagination* (Mills, 1959) and we need to demand more replicable research. No other discipline or profession (an exception perhaps being social work) creates and implements large-scale policy with so little replicable research and empirical support.

School reform is all about structural change, and the burden of this critical work falls collectively on the shoulders of principals, teachers, parents, policy makers, and researchers. Some of the changes might be relatively minor, such as establishing a recognition program for good teaching or a parental workshop to address youth problems. Other changes might be of enormous magnitude with probative consequences, such as increasing parental involvement in the school or in the home, or initiating and supporting an untracked school, or other forms of radical restructuring. School administrators *are* in positions to either conduct "business as usual" or to implement programs of structural and organizational change. The first route involves relatively safe work—discover the old rules and administer them firmly and gracefully. The second requires the kind of sociological knowledge that this book is about, but it also requires courage and vision.

❖ KEY CONCEPTS

restructuring
school choice
vouchers
charter schools
assessment

accountability
voluntary communities
proacademic choices
schools as ends rather than means
academic subcultures

❖ KEY STUDIES

Lee and Smith (1994)
Mussoline and Shouse (2001)
Arum (1996)

Hoffer (2002)
Muller and Schiller (2000)
Gill et al. (2001)

❖ REVIEW QUESTIONS

1. Describe the study on "restructuring" by Lee and Smith (1994).

2. Describe the study by Mussoline and Shouse (2001) and the manner in which it is related to the Lee and Smith (1994) research.

3. Drawing upon Hoffer (2000), explain how the rapid expansion of accountability has come about.

4. Summarize the results of the research by Muller and Schiller (2000). What are the implications for statewide assessments?

5. Describe the issues pro and con regarding school choice.

6. Discuss the notion of treating schools as ends rather than as means.

REFERENCES

Abington School District v. Schempp. 1963. 374 U.S. 203.

Adler, Patricia A., Steven J. Kless, and Peter Adler. 1992. "Socialization to Gender Roles: Popularity Among Elementary School Boys and Girls." *Sociology of Education* 65: 169–187.

Ainsworth-Darnell, James W., and Douglas B. Downey. 1998. "Assessing the Oppositional Culture Explanation for Racial/Ethnic Differences in School Performance." *American Sociological Review* 63: 536–553.

Alexander, Karl L. 2001. "The Clouded Crystal Ball: Trends in Educational Stratification." *Sociology of Education* Extra Issue: 169–177.

Alexander, Karl L., and Martha A. Cook. 1982. "Curricula and Coursework: A Surprise Ending to a Familiar Story." *American Sociological Review* 47: 626–640.

Alexander, Karl L., Martha Cook, and Edward L. McDill. 1978. "Curriculum Tracking and Educational Stratification: Some Further Evidence." *American Sociological Review* 43: 47–66.

Alexander, Karl L., and Bruce K. Eckland. 1974. "Sex Differences in the Educational Attainment Process." *American Sociological Review* 39: 668–682.

Alexander, Karl L., and Bruce K. Eckland. 1975. "Contextual Effects in the High School Attainment Process." *American Sociological Review* 40: 402–416.

Alexander, Karl L., and Doris R. Entwisle. 1995. "Schools and Children at Risk." In *Family-School Links: How do They Affect Educational Outcomes?* eds. Allan Booth and Judith Dunn. Hillsdale, NJ: Lawrence Erlbaum.

Alexander, Karl L., Doris R. Entwisle, and Susan L. Dauber. 1994. *On the Success of Failure: A Reassessment of the Effects of Retention in the Primary Grades.* New York: Cambridge University Press.

Alexander, Karl L., Doris R. Entwisle, and Linda S. Olson. 2001. "Schools, Achievement, and Inequality: A Seasonal Perspective." *Educational Evaluation and Policy Analysis* 23: 171–191.

Alexander, Karl L., Scott Holupa, and Aaron M. Pallas. 1987. "Social Background and Academic Determinants of Two-Year Versus Four-Year College Attendance: Evidence from Two Cohorts a Decade Apart." *American Journal of Education* 95: 56–80.

Alexander, Karl L., and Edward L. McDill. 1976. "Selection and Allocation Within Schools: Some Causes and Consequences of Curriculum Placement." *American Sociological Review* 41: 963–980.

Alexander, Karl L., Gary Natriello, and Aaron M. Pallas. 1985. "For Whom the Bell Tolls: The Impact of Dropping Out on Cognitive Performance." *American Sociological Review* 50: 409–420.

Alexander, Karl L., and Aaron M. Pallas. 1985. "School Sector and Academic Performance: When Is a Little a Little?" *Sociology of Education* 58: 115–128.

Alexander, Karl L., Cornelius Riordan, James Fennessey, and Aaron M. Pallas. 1982. "Social Background, Academic Resources, and College Graduation: Recent Evidence from the National Longitudinal Survey." *American Journal of Education* 90: 315–333.

American Association of University Women (AAUW). 1992. *How Schools Shortchange Girls*. Commissioned and researched by Susan Bailey, Wellesley College Center for Research on Women, Wellesley, MA.

American Association of University Women (AAUW). 1993. *Hostile Hallways: The AAUW Survey on Sexual Harassment in America's School*. Commissioned and researched by Louis Harris and Associates.

American Association of University Women (AAUW). 2001. *Hostile Hallways: Bullying, Teasing, and Sexual Harassment in School*. Commissioned and researched by Harris Interactive.

American Federation of Teachers. 1995. *What Secondary Students are Required to Know: Gateway Exam Taken by Average-Achieving Students in France, Germany, and Scotland*. Washington: American Federation of Teachers.

Amrein, Audrey L., and David C. Berliner. 2003. "High-Stakes Testing, Uncertainty, and Student Learning." *Education Policy Analysis Archives* 10 (18).

Apple, Michael W., and Lois Weis. 1986. "Seeing Education Relationally: The Stratification of Culture and People in the Sociology of School Knowledge." *Journal of Education* 168: 7–34.

Archer, Jeff. 2002a. "Focusing in on Teachers." *Education Week* 29 April 3: 36–39.

Archer, Jeff. 2002b. "Group Cites Needy but High-Performing Schools." *Education Week* 21 January 9: 3.

Armor, David. 1995. *Forced Justice: School desegregation and the Law*. New York: Oxford University Press.

Arum, Richard. 1996. "Do Private Schools Force Public Schools to Compete?" *American Sociological Review* 61: 29–46.

Ascik, Thomas R. 1984. "An Investigation of School Desegregation and Its Effect on Black Student Achievement." *American Education* 20: 15–19.

Astin, Alexander W. 1992. "Educational 'Choice': Its Appeal May Be Illusory." *Sociology of Education* 65: 255–259.

Astone, Nan Marie, and Sara S. McLanahan. 1991. "Family Structure, Parental Practices and High School Completion." *American Sociological Review* 56: 309–320.

Atkinson, Rick. 1990. "Kansas City's High Stakes Education Games: Enterprising Magnet Plan Seeks to Lure White, Suburban Students." *Washington Post*, May 13: A1, A16.

Austin, Gilbert R., and Herbert Garber, eds. 1985. *Research on Exemplary Schools*. Orlando, FL: Academic Press.

Baker, David P. 1993. "Compared to Japan, the U.S. Is a Low Achiever . . . Really." *Educational Researcher* 22 (April): 18–20.

Baker, David. P., Catherine Riegle-Crumb, Alexander W. Wiseman, Gerald K. LeTendre, and Francisco O. Ramirez. 2001. "Shifting Gender Effects: Opportunity Structures, Mass Education, and Cross National Achievement in Mathematics." Paper under review.

Baker, David P., and Cornelius Riordan. 1998. "The 'Eliting' of the Common American Catholic School and the National Educational Crisis." *Phi Delta Kappan* 80 September: 16–23.

Baker, David P., and David L. Stevenson. 1986. "Mothers' Strategies for Children's School Achievement: Managing the Transition to High School." *Sociology of Education* 59: 156–166.

Baker, Keith. 1991. "Yes, Throw Money at Schools." *Phi Delta Kappan* 72: 628–631.

Ballantine, Jeanne H. 1993. *The Sociology of Education: A Systematic Analysis*. 2d ed. Englewood Cliffs, NJ: Prentice Hall.

Baratz, Stephen S., and Joan C. Baratz. 1970. "Early Childhood Intervention: The Social Science Basis of Institutional Racism." *Harvard Educational Review* 40: 29–50.

Barbanel, Josh. 1992. "District in Amagansett Illustrates Anomalies of School Financing." *New York Times*, February 12: A23.

Barker, R. G., and P. V. Gump. 1964. *Big School, Small School: High School Size and Student Behavior*. Stanford, CA: Stanford University Press.

Barr, Rebecca, and Robert Dreeban. 1983. *How Schools Work*. Chicago: University of Chicago Press.

Barth, Roland S. 2002. "The Culture Builder" *Educational Leadership* 59: 6–11.

Bates, Percy. 1990. "Desegregation: Can We Get There From Here?" *Phi Delta Kappan* 72 (September): 8–17.

Battistich, V., D. Solomon, D. I. Kim, M. Watson, and E. Schaps. 1995. "Schools as Communities: Poverty Levels of Student Populations, and Students' Attitudes, Motives, and Performance." *American Educational Research Journal* 32: 627–658.

Battle. James. 1981. "Enhancing Self-Esteem: A New Challenge to Teachers." *Academic Therapy* 1: 541–550.

Bayh, Birch. 1975. *Our Nation's Schools—A Report Card: "A" in School Violence and Vandalism.* Washington: Government Printing Office.

Beck, Joan. 1990. "The Needs of Bright Children." *Providence Journal-Bulletin,* June 5: A-15.

Becker, Gary S. 1964. *Human Capital.* Chicago: University of Chicago Press.

Becker, Henry Jay, and Joyce L. Epstein. 1982. "Parent Involvement: A Survey of Teacher Practices." *Elementary School Journal* 83: 85–102.

Bell, Derrick A., Jr. 1980. *Race, Racism and American Law.* 2d ed. Boston: Little, Brown.

Bell, Derrick. 1983. "Learning From Our Losses: Is School Desegregation Still Feasible in the 1980s." *Phi Delta Kappan* 65 (April): 572–575.

Bennett, David. 1992. "Private Management for Public Schools: The Students Benefit." *Providence Journal-Bulletin,* June 16: A-13.

Benovaot, A., Y. Cha, D. Kamens, J. Mayer, and S. Wong. 1991. "Knowledge For the Masses: World Models and National Curricula, 1920–1986." *American Sociological Review* 56: 85–100.

Berger, Joseph. 1991. "New York Panel Backs School for Minority Men." *New York Times,* January 10: A1, B7.

Berger, Joseph, Thomas L. Connor, and M. Hamit Fisek. 1974. *Expectation States Theory: A Theoretical Research Program.* Cambridge, MA: Winthrop.

Berger, Joseph, and Morris Zelditch, Jr., eds. 1985. *Status, Rewards, and Influence.* San Francisco: Jossey-Bass.

Berger, Peter L. 1963. *Invitation to Sociology.* Garden City, NY: Doubleday.

Berger, Peter L., and Brigitte Berger. 1978. *Sociology: A Biographical Approach,* 2d ed. New York: Basic Books, see especially ch. 9.

Berger, Peter L., and Thomas Luckman. 1967. *The Social Construction of Reality.* Garden City, NJ: Doubleday-Anchor.

Bernstein, Basil. 1975. *Class, Codes and Control. Vol. 3.* London: Routledge and Kegan Paul.

Bernstein, Basil. 1996. *Pedagogy, Symbolic Control and Identity: Theory, Research, Critique.* London: Taylor and Francis.

Best, Raphaela. 1983. *We All Have Scars: What Boys and Girls Learn in Elementary Schools.* Bloomington: Indiana University Press.

Bidwell, Charles E., and Noah E. Friedkin. 1989. "The Sociology of Education." In *Handbook of Sociology,* ed. Neil J. Smelser, 449–471. Beverly Hills, CA: Sage Publications.

Bidwell, Charles E., and John D. Kasarda. 1980. "Conceptualizing and Measuring the Effects of School and Schooling." *American Journal of Education* 88: 401–430.

Biernat, N., and E. Klesse. 1989. *The Third Curriculum: Student Activities.* Reston, VA: National Association of Secondary School Principals.

Bilcer, Diane K. 1997. User's Manual, Version 1, Improving Chicago's Schools: The Teachers Turn, 1997; The Students Speak. 1997. Chicago, IL: Consortium of Chicago School Research, University of Chicago.

Billet, Roy O. 1932. *The Administration and Supervision of Homogeneous Grouping.* Columbus: Ohio State University Press.

Bills, David B. 1983. "Social Reproduction and the Bowles-Gintis Thesis of a Correspondence Between School and Work Settings." In *Research in Sociology of Education and Socialization,* Vol. 4, ed. Alan C. Kerckhoff, 185–210.

Bishop, John, H. 1996. "Signaling, Incentives, and School Organization in France, the Netherlands, Britain, and the United States." In *Improving America's Schools: The Role of Incentives,* eds. Eric A. Hanushek and Dale W. Jorgenson, 111–145. Washington, DC: National Academy Press.

Blake, Judith. 1985. "Number of Siblings and Educational Mobility." *American Sociological Review* 50: 84–94.

Blau, Peter M., and Richard A. Shoenherr. 1971. *The Structure of Organizations.* New York: Basic Books.

Boe, E., S. Bobbitt, L. Cook, G. Barkanic, and G. Maislin. 1998. *Teacher Turnover in Eight*

REFERENCES

Cognate Areas: National Trends and Predictors. Philadelphia, PA: Center for Research and Evaluation in Social Policy.

Bogenschneider, Karen, and Laurence Steinberg. 1994. "Maternal Employment and Adolescents' Academic Achievement: A Developmental Analysis." *Sociology of Education* 67: 60–77.

Boocock, Sarane S. 1976. *Students, Schools, and Educational Policy: A Sociological View*. Cambridge, MA: Aspen Institute for Humanistic Studies.

Boocock, Sarane S. 1980. *Sociology of Education: An Introduction*, 2d ed. Boston: Houghton Mifflin.

Borman, Kathryn M., and Judith Frankel. 1984. "Gender Inequality in Childhood Social Life and Adult Work Life." In *Women in the Workplace: Effects on Families*, ed. Sarah Gideonse, 55–83. Norwood, NJ: Ablex.

Bourdieu, Pierre. 1977. "Cultural Reproduction and Social Reproduction." In *Power and Ideology in Education*, eds. Jerome Karabel and A. H. Halsey, 481–511. New York: Oxford University Press.

Bourdieu, Pierre. 1987. "The Forms of Cultural Capital." In *Handbook of Theory and Research for the Sociology of Education*, ed. John G. Richardson, 241–258. Westport, CN: Greenwood Press.

Bowles, Samuel, and Herbert Gintis. 1976. *Schooling in Capitalist America*. New York: Basic Books.

Bowles, Samuel, and Herbert Gintis. 2002. Schooling in Capitalist America Revisited. *Sociology of Education* 75: 1–18.

Braddock, Jomills Henry. 1979. "Academics and Athletics in American High Schools: Some Further Considerations of the Adolescent Subculture Hypothesis." Center for Social Organization of the School, Report 275.

Braddock, Jomills H. 1981. "Race, Athletics, and Educational Attainment: Dispelling the Myths." *Youth and Society* 12: 335–350.

Braddock, Jomills H., Robert Crain, and James McPartland. 1984. "A Long Term View of School Desegregation." *Phi Delta Kappan* 66: 259–264.

Braddock, Jomills H., and James McPartland. 1988. "The Social and Academic Consequences of School Desegregation." *Equity and Choice* February: 50–73.

Bradley, Karen. 2000. "The Incorporation of Women into Higher Education: Paradoxical Outcomes." *Sociology of Education* 73: 1–18.

Broh, Beckett A. 2002. "Linking Extracurricular Programming to Academic Achievement: Who Benefits and Why? *Sociology of Education* 75: 69–91.

Bronfenbrenner, Urie. 1970. *Two Worlds of Childhood*. New York: The Free Press.

Bronfenbrenner, Urie. 1986. "Alienation and the Four Worlds of Childhood." *Phi Delta Kappan* 68: 431–436.

Brookins, Craig C., and Kofi Lomotey. 1989. "Independent Black Institutions: A Cultural Perspective." In *Visible Now: Blacks in Private Schools*, eds. Diana Slaughter and Deborah Johnson, 163–183. Westport, CN: Greenwood Press.

Brookover, Wilber, et al. 1979. *School Social Systems and Academic Achievement: Schools Can Make a Difference*. New York: Praeger.

Brookover, Wilber, et al. 1982. *Creating Effective Schools*. Holmes Beach, FL: Learning Publications.

Brooks-Gunn, Jeanne, Greg J. Duncan, Pamela Kato Klebanov, and Naomi Sealand. 1993. "Do Neighborhoods Influence Child and Adolescent Development?" *American Journal of Sociology* 99: 353–395.

Brown, Byron W., and Daniel H. Saks. 1975. "The Production and Distribution of Cognitive Skills Within Schools." *Journal of Political Economy* 83: 571–593.

Brown v. Board of Education. 1954. 347 U.S. 484.

Bryk, Anthony S., and Mary E. Driscoll. 1988a. *The High School as Community: Contextual Influences, and Consequences for Students and Teachers*. Madison, WI: National Center on Effective Schools.

Bryk, Anthony S., and Mary E. Driscoll. 1988b. *The School as Community: Theoretical Foundations, Contextual Influences, and Consequences for Students and Teachers*. Chicago: University of Chicago, Benton Center for Curriculum and Instruction.

Bryk, Anthony S., Valerie E. Lee, and Peter B. Holland. 1993. *Catholic Schools and the Common Good*. Cambridge: Harvard University Press.

Bryk, Anthony S., and Stephen W. Raudenbush. 1992. *Hierarchical Linear Models*. Newbury Park, CA: Sage Publications.

Bumiller, Elisabeth. 2002. "Focusing on the Home Front, Bush signs Education Bill." *New York Times,* January 9: A16.

Bumpass, Larry, L. 1984. "Children and Marital Disruption." *Demography* 21: 71–82.

Burbach, H. J. 1972. "An Empirical of Powerlessness Among High School Students." *High School Journal* 55: 343–354.

Burstein, Leigh. 1980. "The Analysis of Multi-Level Data in Educational Research and Evaluation." *Review of Research in Education* 8: 158–233.

Buzacott, J. A. 1982. *Scale in Production Systems.* New York: Pergamon.

Callahan, R. 1962. *Education and the Cult of Efficiency.* Chicago: University of Chicago Press.

Camp, W. 1990. "Participation in Student Activities and Achievement." *Journal of Educational Research* 83: 272–278.

Campbell, Donald T., and Julian C. Stanley. 1966. *Experimental and Quasi-Experimental Designs for Research.* Chicago: Rand McNally.

Campbell, Ernest Q., and C. Norman Alexander. 1965. "Structural Effects and Interpersonal Relations." *American Journal of Sociology* 71: 284–289.

Campbell, Jay R., Catherine M. Hombo, and John Mazzeo. 2000. *Trends in Academic Progress: Three Decades of Student Performance.* Washington: U.S. Department of Education, Office of Educational Research and Improvement, NCES 2000-469.

Carbonaro, William J. 1999. "Opening the Debate on Closure and Schooling Outcomes." *American Sociological Review* 64: 682–686.

Carnegie Council on Adolescent Development. 1989. *Turning Points: Preparing American Youth for the 21st Century.* New York: Carnegie Corporation of New York.

Carnoy, Martin. 1974. *Education as Cultural Imperialism.* New York: McKay.

Carnoy, Martin, and Henry Levin. 1976. *The Limits of Educational Reform.* New York: Longman.

Carnoy, Martin, and Susanna Loeb. 2003. "Does External Accountability Affect Student Outcomes? A Cross-State Analysis." *Educational Evaluation and Policy Analysis* 25 (forthcoming).

Celis, William III. 1990. "Oregon Considers Tax Credits to Aid Private Schooling." *New York Times,* August 22: A1, B6.

Celis, William III. 1992a. "A Texas-Size Battle to Teach Rich and Poor Alike." *New York Times,* February 12: A23.

Celis, William III. 1992b. "An Effort to Improve Schools: Pupils to Be Assigned on the Basis of Income." *New York Times,* January 23: A13.

Chall, Jeanne S., and Catherine E. Snow. 1988. "School Influences on the Reading Development of Low-Income Children." *Harvard Education Letter* 4: 1–4.

Cheong, Keywon, M. B. Toney, and W. F. Stinner. 1986. "School Performance of Migrant and Native Youth in Nonmetropolitan Areas of Utah." Paper presented at the annual meeting of the Rural Sociological Society.

Cherlin, Andrew J., ed. 1988. *The Changing American Family and Public Policy.* Washington: Urban Institute Press.

Cherlin, Andrew J., ed. 1992. *Marriage, Divorce, Remarriage.* Rev. ed. Cambridge: Harvard University Press.

Choy, Susan P., and Sharon A. Bobbit. 1993. *America's Teachers: Profile of a Profession.* Washington: Department of Education, Government Printing Office.

Chubb, John E. 1994. "It is Good Public Policy for Pre-collegiate Public and Private Education to be Supported by Indirect Subsidies such as Voucher Systems." A debate with Robert Chase, presented at the annual meeting of the American Educational Research Association.

Chubb, John E., and Terry M. Moe. 1990. *Politics, Markets, and America's Schools.* Washington: Brookings Institution Press.

Cicourel, Aaron V., and John I. Kituse. 1963. *The Educational Decision-Makers.* New York: Bobb-Merrill.

Civil Rights Act. 1964. Section 402.

Clark, Burton R. 1960. "The Cooling Out Function in Higher Education." *American Journal of Sociology* 65: 569–576.

Clark, Burton R., and Martin Trow. 1966. "The Organizational Context." In *College Peer Groups: Problems and Prospects for Research,* eds. Theodore M. Newcomb and Everett K. Wilson. Chicago: Aldine.

Clark, Reginald M. 1983. *Family Life and School Achievement.* Chicago: University of Chicago Press.

Clasen, D. R., and B. B. Brown. 1986. "The Relationship Between Adolescent Peer Groups and School Performance." Paper presented at the annual meeting of the American Educational Research Association.

Clotfelter, Charles T. 2001. "Are Whites Still Fleeing? Racial Patterns and Enrollment Shifts in Urban Public Schools." *Journal of Policy Analysis and Management* 20: 199–221.

Cogan, Leland S., William H. Schmidt, and David E. Wiley. 2001. "Who Takes What Math and in Which Track? Using TIMMS to Characterize U.S. Students' Eighth-Grade Mathematics Learning Opportunities." *Educational Evaluation and Policy Analysis* 23: 323–341.

Cohen, Elizabeth G. 1984. "Talking and Working Together: Status, Interaction, and Learning." In *The Social Context of Instruction: Group Organization and Group Processes*, eds. P. Peterson, L. C. Wilkinson, and M. Hallinan, 171–187. New York: Academic Press.

Cohen, Elizabeth G. 1994. *Designing Groupwork: Strategies for the Heterogeneous Classroom*, 2d ed. New York: Teachers College Press.

Cohen, Elizabeth G. 2000. "Equitable Classrooms in a Changing Society." In *Handbook of the Sociology of Education*, ed. Maureen T. Hallinan. New York: Kluwer Academic/Plenum Publishers.

Cohen, Elizabeth G., Terrence E. Deal, John W. Meyer, and W. Richard Scott. 1979. "Technology and Teaming in the Elementary School." *Sociology of Education* 52: 20–33.

Cohen, Elizabeth G., and Rachel A. Lotan. 1995. "Producing Equal-Status Interaction in the Heterogeneous Classroom." *American Educational Research Journal* 32: 99–120.

Cohen, Elizabeth G., and Rachel A. Lotan. 1997. *Working for Equity in Heterogeneous Classrooms*. New York: Teachers College Press.

Cohen, Elizabeth G., and Susan S. Roper. 1972. "Modification of Interracial Interaction Disability: An Application of Status Characteristic Theory." *American Sociological Review* 37: 648–655.

Cohen, Jacob. 1988. *Statistical Power Analysis for the Behavioral Sciences* (2E). Hillsdale, NJ: Lawrence Earlbaum Associates.

Cohen, Jere. 1983. "Peer Influence on College Aspirations with Initial Aspirations Controlled." *American Sociological Review* 48: 728–734.

Coley, Richard J. 2001. *Differences in the Gender Gap: Comparisons Across Racial/Ethnic Groups in Education and Work*. Princeton, NJ: Educational Testing Service.

Coleman, James S. 1961. *The Adolescent Society*. New York: The Free Press.

Coleman, James S. 1965. *Adolescents and the Schools*. New York: Basic Books.

Coleman, James S. 1966. "Equal Schools or Equal Students." *The Public Interest* 4: 70–75.

Coleman, James S. 1967. "Toward Open Schools." *The Public Interest* 9: 20–27.

Coleman, James S. 1968. "The Concept of Equality of Educational Opportunity." *Harvard Educational Review* 38: 17–22.

Coleman, James S. 1976. "Rawls, Nozick, and Educational Equality." *The Public Interest* 43: 121–128.

Coleman, James S. 1987. "Families and Schools." *Educational Researcher* 16 (September-August): 32–38.

Coleman, James S. 1988a. "Equality and Excellence in Education." In *Surveying Social Life*, ed. Hubert J. O'Gorman, 376–392. Middletown, CT: Wesleyan University Press.

Coleman, James S. 1988b. "Social Capital and the Creation of Human Capital." *American Journal of Sociology* 94 (Supplement): S95–S120.

Coleman, James S. 1990a. *Equality and Achievement in Education*. Boulder, CO: Westview Press.

Coleman, James, S. 1990b. *Foundations of Social Theory*. Cambridge, MA: Belnap Press of Harvard University Press.

Coleman, James S. 1991. *Parental Involvement in Education*. Department of Education, Policy Perspectives Series. Washington: Government Printing Office.

Coleman, James S. 1997. "Output-Driven Schools: Principles of Design." In James S. Coleman, Barbara Schneider, Stephan Plank, Katherine S. Schiller, Roger Shouse, and H. Wang. eds., Redesigning American Education. Boulder, CO: Westview Press.

Coleman, James S., Ernest Q. Campbell, Carol J. Hobson, James McPartland, Alexander M. Mood, Frederick D. Weinfeld, and Robert L. York. 1966. *Equality of Educational Opportunity*. Washington: Government Printing Office.

Coleman, James S., and Thomas Hoffer. 1987. *Public and Private High Schools*. New York: Basic Books.

Coleman, James S., Thomas Hoffer, and Sally Kilgore. 1982. *High School Achievement*. New York: Basic Books.

Coleman, James S., S. Kelly, and J. Moore. 1975. *Trends in School Segregation, 1968–1973*. Washington, DC: The Urban Institute.

Coleman, Sandy. 2002. "Foreign Study: Filipino Teachers Find Boston Classrooms Trying." *Boston Globe,* March 20: B1, B3.

Comber, L. C., and John P. Keeves. 1973. *Science Education in Nineteen Countries*. Stockholm: Almquist and Wiksell.

Comer, James P. 1988. "School-Parent Relationships that Work." *Harvard Education Letter* 4: 4–6.

Conant, James B. 1967. *The Comprehensive High School*. New York: McGraw-Hill.

Cook, Phillip J., and Jens Ludwig. 1998. "The Burden of 'Acting White': Do Black Americans Disparage Academic Achievement?" in *The Black–White Test Score Gap*, eds. Christopher Jencks and Meredith Phillips. Washington: Brookings Institution Press.

Cook, Thomas, et al. 1975. *Sesame Street Revisited*. New York: Russell Sage Foundation.

Cookson, Peter W. Jr., and Caroline Hodges Persell. 1985. *Preparing for Power: America's Elite Boarding Schools*. New York: Basic Books.

Cooper, H., B. Nye, K. Charlton, J. Lindsay, and S. Greathouse. 1996. "The Effects of Summer Vacation on Achievement Test Scores: A Narrative and Meta-Analytic Review." *Review of Educational Research* 66: 227–268.

Cooper, Harris M. and D. Y. Tom. 1984. Teacher Expectation Research: A Review with Implications for Classroom Instruction." *Elementary School Journal* 85: 77–89.

Corrigan, Thomas. 1994. Personal communication, June 9.

Coser, Lewis A. 1975. "Presidential Address: Two Methods in Search of Substance." *American Sociological Review* 40: 691–700.

Covello, Leonard. 1967. *The Social Background of the Italo-American School Child*. Leiden, Netherlands: E. J. Brill.

Crain, Robert L., and Rita. E. Mahard. 1983. "The Effects of Research Methodology on Desegregation Achievement Studies." *American Journal of Sociology* 88: 839–854.

Cremin, Lawrence. 1988. *American Education: The Metropolitan Experience 1876–1980*. New York: Harper and Row.

Csikszentmihalyi, Mihaly, Reed Larson, and Suzanne Prescott. 1977. "The Ecology of Adolescent Activity and Experience." *Journal of Youth and Adolescence* 6: 281–294.

Cuban, Larry. 1998. "A Tale of Two Schools." Education Week January 28: 48.

Cuban, Larry, and David Tyack. 1992. "Mismatch: Historical Perspectives on Schools and Students Who Don't Fit Them." In *Accelerated Schools* (ed.) Henry Levin.

Cubberly, Ellwood P. 1919. *Public Education in the United States*. Boston: Houghton Mifflin.

Cusik, Philip. 1973. *Inside High School: The Student's World*. New York: Holt, Rinehart, and Winston.

Cusik, Philip. 1983. *The Egalitarian Ideal and the American High School*. New York: Longman.

Dahl, Rene F. 1997. "Organizational Factors and the Continuation of a Complex Instructional Technology." In *Working for Equity in Heterogeneous Classrooms: Sociological Theory in Practice*, eds. E. G. Cohen and R. A. Lotan, 486–516. New York: Teacher College Press.

Darling-Hammond, Linda. 1984. *Beyond the Commission Reports: The Coming Crisis in Teaching*. Santa Monica, CA: Rand Corporation.

Darling-Hammond, Linda. 1997. *The Right to Learn: A Blueprint for Creating Schools that Work*. San Francisco, Jossey-Bass.

Darling-Hammond, Linda. 2001. *The Research and Rhetoric on Teacher Certification: A Response to "Teacher Certification Reconsidered."* New York: National Commission on Teaching & America's Future.

Darling-Hammond, Linda, Arthur E. Wise, and Stephen P. Klein. 1995. *A License to Teach*. Boulder, CO: Westview Press.

Davis, Julius A., and George Temp. 1971. "Is the SAT Biased Against Black Students?" *College Board Review* 81: 4–9.

Dawis, Rene V., and Yong H. Sung. 1984. "The Relationship Between Participation in School Activities to Abilities and Interest in a High School Student Sample." *Journal of Vocational Behavior* 24: 159–168.

Devine, John. 1996. *Maximum Security: The Culture of Violence in Inner-City Schools*. Chicago: University of Chicago Press.

Dillon, S., and J. Berger, 1995. "New Schools Seeking Small Miracles." *New York Times,* May 22: A1, B11.

DiMaggio, Paul. 1982. "Cultural Capital and School Success: The Impact of Status Culture Participation on the Grades of U.S. High School Students." *American Sociological Review* 47: 189–201.

Dinnerstein, Leonard. 1982. "Education and the Advancement of American Jews." In *American Education and the European Immigrant: 1840–1940*, ed. Bernard J. Weiss, 44–60. Urbana: University of Illinois Press.

Dougherty, Kevin. 1987. "The Effects of Community Colleges: Aid or Hindrance to Socioeconomic Attainment?" *Sociology of Education* 60: 86–103.

Dougherty, Kevin J., and Floyd M. Hammack. 1990. *Education and Society*. New York: Harcourt, Brace, Jovanovich.

Downey, Douglas B., and James W. Ainsworth-Darnell. 2002. "The Search for Oppositional Culture Among Black Adolescents." *American Sociological Review* 67: 156–164.

Doyle, W. 1992. "Curriculum and Pedagogy" In *Handbook of Research on Curriculum*, ed. P. W. Jackson, 486–516. New York: Macmillan.

Dreeben, Robert. 1968. *On What is Learned in School Today*. Reading, MA: Addison-Wesley.

Dreeben, Robert. 2000. "Structural Effects in Education: A History of an Idea." In *Handbook of the Sociology of Education*, ed. Maureen T. Hallinan. New York: Kluwer Academic/Plenum Publishers.

Dreeben, Robert, and Rebecca Barr. 1988. "Classroom Composition and the Design of Instruction." *Sociology of Education* 61: 129–142.

D'Souza, Dinesh. 1995. *The End of Racism*. New York: The Free Press.

Duncan, Beverly, and Otis Dudley Duncan. 1968. "Minorities and the Process of Stratification." *American Sociological Review* 33: 356–364.

Duncan, Greg J. 1994. "Families and Neighbors as Sources of Disadvantage in the Schooling Decisions of White and Black Adolescents." *American Journal of Education* 103: 20–53.

Durkheim, Emile. 1951. *Suicide*. Glencoe, IL, The Free Press.

Eckert, Penelope. 1989. *Jocks and Burn-outs: Social Categories and Identity in the High School*. New York: Teachers College Press.

Eder, Donna. 1981. "Ability Grouping as a Self-fulfilling Prophecy: A Micro-Analysis of Teacher-Student Interaction." *Sociology of Education* 54: 151–162.

Eder, Donna, Catherine Colleen Evans, and Steven Parker. 1995. *School Talk: Gender and Adolescent Culture*. New Brunswick, NJ: Rutgers University Press.

Eder, Donna, and Steven Parker. 1987. "The Cultural Production and Reproduction of Gender: The Effect of Extracurricular Activities on Peer Group Culture." *Sociology of Education* 60: 200–213.

Edmonds, Ralph. 1979. "Effective Schools for the Urban Poor." *Educational Leadership* 37: 5–24.

Educational Amendments. 1972. Section 901. Laws of the 92nd U.S. Congress, Second Session.

Education Week. 2003. *Quality Counts, 2003*. January 9: 106–181.

Eisenstadt, Samuel N. 1956. *From Generation to Generation*. New York: The Free Press.

Ekstrom, Ruth B. 1959. *Experimental Studies of Homogeneous Grouping*. Princeton, NJ: Educational Testing Service.

Elmore, Richard F., 1990. "Choice as an Instrument of Public Policy." In *Choice and Control in American Education*, eds. William H. Clune and John F. Witte. New York: Falmer.

Elmore, Richard F., and Associates. 1990. *Restructuring Schools: The Next Generation of Educational Reform*. San Francisco: Jossey-Bass.

Engle v. Vitale. 1962. 370 U.S. 421.

Entwisle, Doris R., and Karl L. Alexander. 1992. "Summer Setback: Race, Poverty, School Composition, and Mathematics Achievement in the First Two Years of School." *American Sociological Review* 57: 72–84.

Entwisle, Doris R., and Karl L. Alexander. 1994. "Winter Setback: The Racial Composition of Schools and Learning to Read." *American Sociological Review* 59: 446–460.

Entwisle, Doris R., and Karl L. Alexander. 1995. "A Parent's Economic Shadow: Family Structure Versus Family Resources as Influences on Early School Achievement." *Journal of Marriage and the Family* 57: 399–409.

Entwisle, Doris R., Karl Alexander, Aaron M. Pallas, and Doris Cadigan. 1988. "A Social Psychological Model of the Schooling Process Over First Grade." *Social Psychology Quarterly* 51: 173–189.

Entwisle, Doris R., and Leslie A. Hayduk. 1982. *Early Schooling*. Baltimore: Johns Hopkins University Press.

Epstein, Joyce L. 1987. "Parent Involvement: What Research Says to Administrators." *Education and Urban Society* 19: 277–294.

Epstein, Joyce L. 1996. "Effects on Student Achievement of Teachers' Practices of Parent Involvement." In *Literacy Through Family, Community, and School Interaction*, ed. Steven Silvern. Greenwich, CT: JAI Press.

Epstein, Joyce L., and Mavis G. Sanders. 2000. "Connecting Home, School, and Community." In *Handbook of the Sociology of Education*, ed. Maureen T. Hallinan. New York: Kluwer Academic/Plenum Publishers.

Erickson, Frederick. 1975. "Gatekeeping and the Melting Pot: Interaction in Counseling Encounters." *Harvard Educational Review* 45: 44–70.

ESEA (2002). "No Child Left Behind Act of 2001." Reauthorization of the Elementary and Secondary Education Act of 1965, signed into law January 2002. Washington, DC.

Esposito, Dominick. 1973. "Homogeneous and Heterogeneous Ability Grouping: Principal Finding and Implications for Evaluating and Designing More Effective Educational Environments." *Review of Educational Research* 43: 163–179.

Eve, Raymond A. 1975. "Adolescent Culture: Convenient Myth or Reality? A Comparison of Students and Their Teachers." *Sociology of Education* 48: 152–167.

Farkas, George, and Kurt Beron. 2001. "Family Linguistic Culture and Social Reproduction: Verbal Skill from Parent to Child in the Preschool and School Years." Paper presented at the annual meeting of the Population Association of America, Washington, DC.

Farkas, George, Robert Grobe, Daniel Sheehan, and Y. Shuan. 1990. "Cultural Resources and School Success: Gender, Ethnicity, and Poverty Groups Within an Urban School District." *American Sociological Review* 55: 127–142.

Farkas, George, Cristy Lleras, and Steve Maczuga. 2002. "Does Oppositional Culture Exist in Minority and Poverty Peer Groups?" *American Sociological Review* 67: 148–155.

Feltz, D. L., and M. R. Weiss. 1984. "The Impact of Girls' Interscholastic Sports Participation on Academic Orientation." *Review Quarterly for Exercise and Sport* 55: 332–339.

Fennessey, James, Karl L. Alexander, Cornelius Riordan, and Laura Hersh Salganik. 1981. "Tracking and Frustration Reconsidered: Appearance and Reality." *Sociology of Education* 54: 302–309.

Ferguson, Ronald F. 1991. "Paying for Public Education: New Evidence on How and Why Money Matters." *Harvard Journal of Legislation* 28: 465–498.

Ferguson, Ronald F. 1998. "Can Schools Narrow the Black-White Test Score Gap." In *The Black-White Test Score Gap*, eds. Christopher Jencks and Meredith Phillips. Washington, DC: Brooking Institution Press.

Findley, Warren G., and Miriam M. Bryan. 1971. *Ability Grouping: 1970 Status, Impact, and Alternatives*. Athens, GA: Center for Educational Improvements, University of Georgia.

Fine, Michelle, ed. 1994. *Chartering Urban School Reform: Reflections on Public High Schools in the Midst of Change*. New York: Teachers College Press.

Finley, Merilee K. 1984. "Teachers and Tracking in a Comprehensive High School." *Sociology of Education* 57: 233–243.

Finn, Jeremy D. 1993. *School Engagement and Students at Risk*. Washington: National Center for Education Statistics.

Finn, Jeremy D., and Charles M. Achilles. 1990. "Answers and Questions About Class Size: A Statewide Experiment." *American Educational Research Journal* 27: 557–577.

Firestone, William, and S. Rosenblum. 1988. Building Commitment in Urban Schools. *Educational Evaluation and Policy Analysis* 10: 285–300.

Firestone, William A., and Robert E. Herriot, 1982. "Prescriptions for Effective Elementary School Don't Fit Secondary Schools." *Educational Leadership* 40: 51–53.

Firestone, William A., and Bruce L. Wilson. 1985 "Using Bureaucratic and Cultural Linkages to Improve Instruction: The Principal's Contribution." *Educational Administration Quarterly* 21: 7–30.

Fischer, Claude S., Michael Hout, Marvin Sanchez Jankowski, Samual R. Lucas, Ann Swindler, and Kim Voss, 1996. *Inequality by Design: Cracking the Bell Curve Myth*. Princeton, NJ: Princeton University Press.

Flanders, Ned A. 1970. *Analyzing Teaching Behavior*. Reading, MA: Addison-Wesley.

Fleming, Jacqueline. 1984. *Blacks in College: A Comparative Study of Student Success in Black and White Institutions*. San Francisco: Jossey-Bass.

Foley, Michael, and Bob Edward. 1999. "Is It Time to Divest in Social Capital?" *Journal of Public Policy* 19: 141–173.

Fordham, Signithia, and John U. Ogbu. 1986. "Black Students' School Success: Coping with the 'Burden' of 'Acting White.'" *The Urban Review* 18: 176–206.

Fowler, William J., Jr. 1991. "School Size, Characteristics, and Outcomes." *Educational Evaluation and Policy Analysis* 13: 189–202.

Fowler, William J., Jr. 1992. "What Do We Know About School Size: What Should We Know? Paper presented at the annual meeting of the American Educational Research Association.

Fowler, William J., Jr., and Herbert J. Walberg. 1991. "School Size, Characteristics, and Outcomes." *Educational Evaluation and Policy Analysis* 13: 189–202.

Fraser, Steven, ed. 1995. *The Bell Curve Wars: Race, Intelligence, and the Future of America*. New York: Basic Books.

Friedenberg, Edgar. 1959. *The Vanishing Adolescent*. Boston: Beacon Press.

Friedenberg, Edgar. 1963. *Coming of Age in America*. New York: Random House.

Friedman, Stephen J. 2000. "How Much of a Problem? A Reply to Ingersoll's The Problem of Underqualified Teachers in American Secondary Schools." *Educational Researcher*, 29, #5 (June–July): 18–20.

Fuller, Bruce. 1986. "Defining School Quality." In *The Contributions of the Social Sciences to Educational Policy and Practice: 1965–1985*, eds. Jane Hannaway and Marlaine E. Lockheed, 33–70. Berkeley, CA: McCutchen.

Fuller, Bruce. 1987. "What School Factors Raise Achievement in the Third World?" *Review of Educational Research* 57: 255–292.

Fuller, Bruce, and Prema Clarke. 1994. "Raising School Effects While Ignoring Culture? Local Conditions and the Influence of Classroom Tools, Rules, and Pedagogy." *Review of Educational Research* 64: 119–157.

Fuller, Bruce, Richard Elmore, and Gary Orfield, eds. 1995. *School Choice: The Cultural Logic of Families, the Political Rationality of Institutions*. New York: Teachers College Press.

Fuller, Bruce, and Stephen P. Heyneman. 1989. "Third World School Quality: Current Collapse, Future Potential." *Educational Researcher* 18 (March): 12–19.

Furstenberg, Frank F., Jr., and Gretchan A. Condran. 1988. "Family Change and Adolescent Well-Being: A Reexamination of U.S. Trends" In *The Changing American Family and Public Policy*, ed. Andrew J. Cherlin, 117–155. Washington: Urban Institute Press.

Gaines, Donna. 1991. *Teenage Wasteland: Suburbia's Dead End Kids*. New York: Pantheon.

Gamoran, Adam. 1984. "Teaching, Grouping, and Learning: A Study of the Consequences of Educational Stratification." Ph.D. dissertation, Department of Sociology, University of Chicago.

Gamoran, Adam. 1986. "Instructional and Institutional Effects of Ability Grouping." *Sociology of Education* 59: 185–198.

Gamoran, Adam. 1987a. "Organization, Instruction, and the Effects of Ability Grouping: Comment on Slavin's 'Best-Evidence Synthesis.'" *Review of Educational Research* 57: 341–345.

Gamoran, Adam. 1987b. "The Stratification of High School Learning Opportunities." *Sociology of Education* 60: 135–155.

Gamoran, Adam. 1992. "The Variable Effects of High School Tracking." *American Sociological Review* 57: 812–828.

Gamoran, Adam. 1995. "Effects of Schooling on Children and Families." In *Family-School Links: How do They Affect Educational Outcomes*, eds. Allan Booth and Judith Dunn. Hillsdale, NJ: Lawrence Erlbaum.

Gamoran, Adam, and Mark Berends. 1987. "The Effects of Stratification in Secondary Schools: Synthesis of Survey and Ethnographic Research." *Review of Educational Research* 57: 415–435.

Gamoran, Adam, and Robert Dreeban, 1986. "Coupling and Control in Restructured Schools." *Administrative Science Quarterly* 31: 612–632.

Gamoran, Adam, and Robert D. Mare. 1989. "Secondary School Tracking and Educational Inequality: Compensation, Reinforcement, or Neutrality." *American Journal of Sociology* 94: 1146–1183.

Gamoran, Adam, Martin Nystrand, Mark Berends, and Paul C. Lepore. 1995. "An Organizational Analysis of the Effects of Ability Grouping." *American Educational Research Association* 32: 687–715.

Gamoran, Adam, Walter G. Secada, and Cora B. Marrett. 2000. "The Organizational Context of Teaching and Learning." In *Handbook of Sociology of Education*, ed. Maureen T. Hallinan. Kluwer Academic/Plenum Publishers.

Garber, Michael P. 1994. "The Michigan Compromise." *Education Week* 13 (May 11): 35, 44.

Gardner, John. 1961. *Excellence: Can We Be Equal and Excellent Too?* New York: Harper.

Gaskell, Jane. 1985. "Course Enrollment in the High School: The Perspective of Working Class Females." *Sociology of Education* 54: 48–57.

Geertz, Clifford. 1973. *The Interpretation of Cultures*. New York: Basic Books.

Gewertz, Catherine. 2002. "Qualifications of Teachers Falling Short." *Education Week* 21: 1, 18.

Gill, Brian P., P. Michael Timpane, Karen E. Ross, and Dominic J. Brewer. 2001. *Rhetoric Versus Reality: What We Know and What We Need to Know About Vouchers and Charter Schools*. Santa Monica, CA: RAND Distribution Services (MR-1118-EDU).

Giroux, Henry A. 1981. *Ideology, Culture, and the Process of Schooling*. London: Falmer Press.

Glass, Gene V. 2002. "Teacher Characteristics." In *School Reform Proposals: The Research Evidence*, ed. Alex Molnar. Tempe, AZ: Educational Policy Studies Laboratory, EPSL-0201-EPRU.

Glass, Gene V., and Mary Lee Smith. 1978. *Meta-analysis of Research on the Relationship of Class Size and Achievement*. San Francisco: Far West Laboratory of Educational Research and Development.

Glass, Gene V., and Mary Lee Smith. 1979. "Meta-analysis of Research on Class Size and Achievement." *Educational Evaluation and Policy Analysis* 1: 2–16.

Glastris, Paul, and Thomas Toch. 1989. "The Uncertain Benefits of School Choice." *U.S. News and World Report*, November 6: 79–82.

Goffman, Erving. 1959. *The Presentation of Self in Everyday Life*. Garden City, NY: Doubleday.

Goldhaber, Dan D., and Dominic J. Brewer. 2000. "Does Teacher Certification Matter: High School Teacher Certification Status and Student Achievement." *Educational Evaluation and Policy Analysis* 22: 129–145.

Gonzales, D. 1995. "A Bridge from Hope to Social Action." *New York Times,* May 23: A1, A14.

Gooding, Richard Z., and John A. Wagner. 1985. "A Meta-Analytic Review of the Relationships Between Size and Performance." *Administrative Science Quarterly* 30: 462–481.

Goodlad, John. 1984. *A Place Called School*. New York: McGraw Hill.

Goodman, Paul. 1962. *Growing Up Absurd*. New York: Random House.

Gordan, Chad. 1972. *Looking Ahead: Self-Conceptions, Race, and Family as Determinants of Adolescent Orientation to Achievement*. Washington: American Sociological Association.

Grabe, M. 1981. "School Size and the Importance of School Activities." *Adolescence* 61: 21–31.

Grannis, Joseph. 1975. "Beyond Labels: The Significance of Social Class and Ethnicity for Education." *Equal Opportunity Review* (July): 1–5.

Greeley, Andrew M. 1976. *Ethnicity, Denunciation and Inequality*. Beverly Hills: Sage.

Green, P. (1993). *High School Seniors Look to the Future, 1972 and 1992*. 1993. Washington, DC: U.S. Department of Education, Office of Educational Research and Improvement, NCES 93-473.

Green, P., J. Bernard, L. Dugoni, S. J. Ingels, and P. Quinn. 1995. *Trends Among High School Seniors, 1972–1992*. Washington, DC: U.S. Department of Education, Office of Educational Research and Improvement, NCES 95-380.

Greenberg, Paul. 1990. "Education Marches On, as it Eliminates Tracking." *Providence Journal-Bulletin,* April 23: A-9.

Greenwald, Rob, Larry V. Hedges, and Richard D. Laine. 1996. "The Effect of School Resources on Student Achievement." *Review of Educational Research* 66: 361–396.

Greer, Colin. 1972. *The Great School Legend*. New York: Basic Books.

Grissmer, D., and Kirby, S. 1997. "Teacher Turnover and Teacher Quality." Teachers College Record, 99: 45–56.

Grissmer, David W., Sheila Nataraj Kirby, Mark Berends, and Stephanie Williamson. 1994. *Student Achievement and the Changing American Family*. Santa Monica, CA: Rand Corporation.

Guthrie, James. W. 1979. "Organizational Scale and School Success." *Educational Evaluation and Policy Analysis* 1: 17–27.

Haertel, Edward J., Thomas James, and Henry M. Levin. 1987. *Comparing Public and Private Schools Volume 2*. New York: The Falmer Press.

Hafner, Anne, Steven Ingels, Barbara Schneider, and David Stevenson. 1990. *A Profile of the American Eighth Grader: NELS 88 Student Descriptive Summary*. U.S. Department of Education (OERI). Washington: Government Printing Office.

Haggstrom, G. W., L. Darling-Hammond, and D. Grissmer. 1988. *Assessing Teacher Supply and Demand*. Santa Monica, CA: Rand Corporation.

Hall, Richard, H. 1972. *Organizational Structure and Process*. Englewood Cliffs, NJ: Prentice-Hall, 1972.

Haller, Archibald O., and Alejandro Portes. 1973. "Status Attainment Process." *Sociology of Education* 46: 51–91.

Haller, E. J., D. H. Monk, A. Spotted Bear, J. Griffith, and P. Moss. 1990. "School Size and Program Comprehensiveness: Evidence from High School and Beyond." *Educational Evaluation and Policy Analysis* 12: 109–120.

Hallinan, Maureen T. 1989. "Sociology and Education: The State of the Art." In *Schools and Society*, 2d ed., ed. Jeanne H. Ballantine, 21–36. Mountain View, CA: Mayfield.

Hallinan, Maureen T. 1992. "The Organization of Students for Instruction in the Middle School." *Sociology of Education* 65: 114–127.

Hallinan, Maureen T. 1994. "Tracking: From Theory to Practice." *Sociology of Education* 67: 79–84, 89–91.

Hallinan, Maureen T. 1996. "Track Mobility in Secondary School." *Social Forces* 74: 999–1018.

Hallinan, Maureen T. 2000. "On the Linkages Between Sociology of Race and Ethnicity and Sociology of Education." In *Handbook of Sociology of Education*, ed. Maureen T. Hallinan. Kluwer Academic/Plenum Publishers.

Hallinan, Maureen T. 2001. "Sociological Perspectives on Black-White Inequalities in American Schooling." *Sociology of Education* Extra Issue: 50–70.

Hallinan, Maureen T., and Warren N. Kubitschek. 1999. "Conceptualizing and Measuring School Social Networks." *American Sociological Review* 64: 687–693.

Hallinger, Philip, and Joseph F. Murphy. 1986. "The Social Context of Effective Schools." *American Journal of Education* 94: 329–345.

Hamilton, Stephen F. 1986. "Raising Standards and Reducing Dropout Rates." In *School Dropouts: Patterns and Policies*, ed. Gary Natriello, 148–167. New York: Teachers College Press.

Haney, Walter. 1980. "Units and Levels of Analysis in Large Scale Evaluation." *New Directions for Methodology of Social and Behavioral Sciences* 6: 1–15.

Hanks, M. 1979. "Race, Sexual Status, and Athletics in the Process of Educational Achievement." *Social Science Quarterly* 60: 482–496.

Hanks, M. P., and Bruce K. Eckland. 1976. "Athletics and Social Participation in the Educational Attainment Process." *Sociology of Education* 49: 271–294.

Hanson, Sandra L., and Rebecca S. Kraus. 1998. "Women, Sports, and Science: Do Female Athletes Have an Advantage?" *Sociology of Education* 71: 93–110.

Hanushek, Eric A. 1989. "The Impact of Differential Expenditures on School Performance." *Educational Researcher* 18: 44–51.

Hanushek, Eric A. 1994. "Money Might Matter Somewhere: A Response to Hedges, Laine, and Greenwald." *Educational Researcher* 23: 5–8.

Hanushek, Eric A., John F. Kain, and Steven G. Rivkin. 2001. "Why Public Schools Lose Teachers." National Bureau of Economic Research. Cambridge, MA: Working Paper Number w8599.

Harvard Education Letter. 1985. 1 (February): 1–3.

Harvard Educational Review. 1968. "Equal Educational Opportunity." 38: 3–160.

Harvard Educational Review. 1969. "Science, Heritability, and IQ." Reprint Series, no. 4.

Harvard Educational Review. 1981. 51, no. 4.

Hauser, Robert M. 1971. *Socioeconomic Background and Educational Performance*. Washington: American Sociological Association, Rose Monograph Series.

Hauser, Robert M. 1974. "Contextual Analysis Revisited." *Sociological Methods and Research* 2: 365–375.

Hauser, Robert M., William H. Sewell, and Duane F. Alwin. 1976. "High School Effects on Achievement." In *Schooling and Achievement in American Society,* eds. William H. Sewell, Robert M. Hauser, and David L. Featherman, 309–341. New York: Academic Press.

Havighurst, Robert J. 1965. "Who Are the Socially Disadvantaged?" *Journal of Negro Education* 40: 210–217.

Hayes, Donald P., and Judith Grether. 1969. "The School Year and Vacations: When Do Students Learn?" Paper presented at the annual meeting of the Eastern Sociological Association, New York.

Heath, Shirley Brice. 1983. *Ways with Words: Language, Life, and Work in Communities and Classrooms.* Cambridge: Cambridge University Press.

Heath, Shirley Brice, and Milbrey Wallin McLaughlin. 1987. "A Child Resource Policy: Moving Beyond Dependence on School and Family." *Phi Delta Kappan* 68: 576–680.

Heath, Shirley Brice, and Milbrey Wallin McLaughlin. 1991. "Community Organizations as Family." *Phi Delta Kappan* 73: 623–627.

Hedges, Larry V., Richard D. Laine, and Rob Greenwald. 1994. "Does Money Matter?: A Meta-Analysis of Studies of the Effects of Differential School Inputs on Student Outcomes." *Educational Researcher* 23: 5–14.

Hedges, Larry V., and Amy Nowell. 1999. "Changes in the Black-White Gap in Achievement Test Scores." *Sociology of Education* 72: 111–135.

Hedges, Larry V., and Amy Nowell. 1995. "Sex Differences in Mental Test Scores: Variability, and Numbers of High Scoring Individuals." *Science* 269 (July 7): 41–45.

Hedges, Larry V., and Ingram Olkin. 1980. "Vote Counting Methods in Research Synthesis." *Psychological Bulletin* 88: 359–369.

Henig, Jeffrey R. 1994. *Rethinking School Choice: Limits of the Market Metaphor.* Princeton: Princeton University Press.

Henry, Jules. 1963. *Culture Against Man.* New York: Random House.

Herrnstein, Richard J., and Charles Murray. 1994. *The Bell Curve: Intelligence and Class Structure in American Life.* New York: The Free Press.

Hewitt, John P. 1998. The Myth of Self-Esteem. New York: St. Martin's Press.

Heyneman, Stephen P., and William A. Loxley. 1983. "The Effect of Primary School Quality on Academic Achievement in Twenty-Nine High and Low Income Countries." *American Journal of Sociology* 88: 1162–1194.

Heyns, Barbara. 1974. "Social Selection and Stratification Within Schools." *American Journal of Sociology* 79: 89–102.

Heyns, Barbara. 1978. *Summer Learning and the Effects of Schooling.* New York: Academic Press.

Heyns, Barbara. 1982. "The Influence of Parents' Work on Children's School Achievement." In *Families That Work: Children in a Changing World,* eds. S. B. Kamerman and C. D. Hayes. Washington: National Academy Press.

Heyns, Barbara. 1986. "Educational Effects: Issues in Conceptualization and Measurement." In *Handbook of Theory and Research for the Sociology of Education.* ed. John G. Richardson, 305–340. Westport, CN: Greenwood Press.

Heyns, Barbara, and Sophia Catsambis. 1986. "Mother's Employment and Children's Achievement: A Critique." *Sociology of Education* 59: 140–151.

Hiebert, Elfrieda H. 1987. "The Context of Instruction and Student Learning: An Examination of Slavin's Assumptions." *Review of Educational Research* 57: 337–340.

Hirschman, Charles, and Luis M. Falcon. 1985. "The Educational Attainment of Religio-Ethnic Groups in the United States." In *Research in Sociology of Education and Socialization,* Vol. 5, ed. Alan C. Kerckhoff, 83–120.

Hobson v. Hansen. 1967. 269 F. Supp. 401, DC Cir.

Hoff, David J. 2001. "School Choice Programs Growing More Rapidly Outside the U.S." *Education Week,* June 20: 5.

Hoffer, Thomas B. 2000. "Accountability in Education." In *Handbook of the Sociology of Education,* ed. Maureen T. Hallinan. New York: Kluwer/Academic Publishers.

Hoffer, Thomas B. 2000. "Catholic School Attendance and Student Achievement: A Review and Extension of Research." In

Catholic Schools at the Crossroads, eds. James Youniss and John J. Convey. New York: Teachers College Press.

Hoffer, Thomas B., Andrew A. Greeley, and James S. Coleman. 1985. "Achievement Growth in Public and Catholic Schools." *Sociology of Education* 58: 74–97.

Hoffer, Thomas B., Andrew A. Greeley, and James S. Coleman. 1987. "Catholic High School Effects on Achievement Growth." In *Comparing Public and Private Schools, vol. 2: School Achievement*, eds. Edwards H. Haertel, Thomas James, and Henry M. Levin. New York: The Falmer Press.

Hoffman, Lois H. 1980. "The Effects of Maternal Employment on the Academic Attitudes and Performance of School-Age Children." *School Psychology Review* 9: 319–335.

Holland, Alyce, and Thomas Andre. 1987. "Participation in Extracurricular Activities in Secondary School: What is Known, What Needs to be Known." *Review of Educational Research* 57: 437–466.

Holland, Spencer. 1991. "For Minority Males Only." *Daily News*, February 3: 31.

Hollingshead, August B. 1949. *Elmtown's Youth*. New York: Wiley.

Holt, John. 1964. *How Children Fail*. New York: Delta.

Holt, John. 1967. *How Children Learn*. New York: Pitman.

Howell, William G., Patrick J. Wolf, Paul E. Peterson, and David E. Campbell. 2000. "Test Score Effects of School Vouchers in Dayton, Ohio, New York City, and Washington, DC: Evidence from Randomized Trials." Paper presented at the annual meeting of the American Political Science Association. Washington, DC. Also available at http://data.fas.harvard.edu/pepg.

Hoxby, Caroline M. 2000. "The Effects of Class Size on Student Achievement: New Evidence from Population Variation." *The Quarterly Journal of Economics* 116: 1239–1285.

Hurn, Christopher J. 1993. *The Limits and Possibilities of Schooling*, 3d ed. Boston: Allyn and Bacon.

Ingersoll, Richard, M. 1999. "The Problem of Underqualified Teachers in American Secondary Schools." *Educational Researcher*, 28, #2 (March): 26–37.

Ingersoll, Richard M. 2001a. "Rejoinder: Misunderstanding the Problem of Out-of-Field Teaching." *Educational Researcher*, 30, #1 (January–February): 21–22.

Ingersoll, Richard, M. 2001b. "Teacher Turnover and Teacher Shortages: An Organizational Analysis." *American Educational Research Journal*, 37: 499–534.

Ingersoll, Richard, M. 2002. "Out-of-Field Teaching, Educational Inequality, and the Organization of Schools: An Exploratory Analysis." Center for the Study of Teaching and Policy. University of Washington, Document R-02-1, http://www.ctpweb.org

International Association for the Evaluation of Educational Achievement. 1988. *Science Achievement in Seventeen Countries: A Preliminary Report*. New York: Pergamon Press.

Jackson, Philip W. 1968. *Life in Classrooms*. New York: Holt, Rinehart and Winston.

Jacobson, Linda. 2001. "Sizing Up Small Classes." *Education Week*, February 28: 26–28.

Jacoby, Russell, and Naomi Clauberman, eds. 1994. *The Bell Curve Debate: History, Documents, Opinions*. New York: Times Books.

Jaynes, Gerald David and Robin M. Williams, Jr. 1989. *A Common Destiny: Blacks and American Society*. Washington: National Academic Press.

Jeffreys, Bradford J. 1987. "Variables Associated With Co-curricular Participation in Vocational Student Organizations." Ph.D. dissertation, Virginia Polytechnic Institute and State University.

Jencks, Christopher. 1985. "How Much Do High School Students Learn?" *Sociology of Education* 58: 128–135.

Jencks, Christopher, and Marsha Brown. 1975. "The Effects of High Schools on Their Students." *Harvard Educational Review* 45: 273–324.

Jencks, Christopher, and Susan Mayer. 1990. "The Social Consequences of Growing Up in a Poor Neighborhood." In *Inner-City Poverty in the United States*, eds. L. Lynn and M. McGeary. Washington: National Academy Press.

Jencks, Christopher, and Meredith Phillips eds. 1998. *The Black-White Test Score Gap*. Washington, DC: Brookings Institution Press.

Jencks, Christopher, Marshall Smith, Henry Acland, Mary Jo Bane, David Cohen, Herbert Gintis, Barbara Heyns, and Stephan Michaelson. 1972. *Inequality: A Reassessment of the Effect of Family and Schooling in America*. New York: Harper and Row.

Jensen, Arthur. 1969. "How Much Can We Boost I.Q. and Scholastic Achievement?" *Harvard Educational Review* 39: 1–123.

Kagan, Jerome S. 1969. "Inadequate Evidence and Illogical Conclusions." *Harvard Educational Review* 39: 126–129.

Kahl, Joseph A. 1953. "Educational and Occupational Aspirations of 'Common Man' Boys." *Harvard Educational Review* 23: 186–203.

Kahlenberg, Richard D. 2000. *All Together Now: Creating Middle Class Schools through Public School Choice*. Washington: Brooking Institution Press.

Kamin, Leon. 1974. *The Science of Politics and I.Q.* Potomac, MD: Erlbaum Associates.

Kandel, Denise B., and Gerald S. Lesser. 1969. "Parental and Peer Influences on Educational Plans of Adolescents." *American Sociological Review* 34: 212–223.

Karabel, Jerome, and A. H. Halsey. 1977. "Educational Research: A Review and an Interpretation." In *Power and Ideology in Education,* eds. Jerome Karabel and A. H. Halsey, 1–85. New York: Oxford University Press.

Kash, Marilynn M., and Gary D. Borich. 1982. "Teachers." In *Improving Educational Standards and Productivity,* ed. Herbert J. Walberg. Berkeley, CA: McCutchan.

Kelly, Dennis. 1991. "Separate Classes to Create Equality." *USA Today,* February 20: 8D.

Kerckhoff, Alan C. 1976. "The Status Attainment Process: Socialization or Allocation?" *Social Forces* 55: 368–381.

Kessler, S., D. Ashenden, R. Connell, and G. Dowsett. 1985. "Gender Relations in Secondary Schooling." *Sociology of Education* 58: 34–47.

Kessner, Thomas. 1977. *The Golden Door: Italian and Jewish Immigrant Mobility in New York City 1880–1915*. New York: Oxford University Press.

Kinney, David A. 1993. "From Nerds to Normals: The Recovery of Identity Among Adolescents from Middle School to High School." *Sociology of Education* 66: 21–40.

Kluger, Richard. 1976. *Simple Justice*. New York: Knopf.

Kohn, Alfie. 1998. "Only For My Kid." *Phi Delta Kappan* 79 April: 569–577.

Kohn, Melvin L. 1977. *Class and Conformity: A Study of Values,* 2d ed. Chicago: University of Chicago Press.

Kopka, T. L. C., and R. A. Korb. 1996. *Women: Education and Outcomes*. Washington, DC: U.S. Department of Education, National Center for Education Statistics.

Kozol, Jonathan. 1991. *Savage Inequalities*. New York: Crown.

Kramer, Judith. 1970. *The American Minority Community*. New York: Crowell.

Kulik, Chen-Lin C., and James A. Kulik. 1982. "Effects of Ability Grouping on Secondary School Students: A Meta-Analysis of Evaluation Findings." *American Educational Research Journal* 19: 415–428.

Ladd, H. F. 1996. *Holding Schools Accountable: Performance-Based Reform in Education*. Washington: Brookings Institution Press.

LaGumina, Salvatore. 1982. "American Education and the Italian Immigrant Response." In *American Education and the European Immigrant: 1840–1940,* ed. Bernard J. Weiss, 61–77. Urbana: University of Illinois Press.

Lareau, Annette. 1989. *Home Advantage: Social Class and Parental Intervention in Elementary Education*. New York: The Falmer Press.

Lareau, Annette. 1995. "Assessing Parent Involvement in Schooling: A Critical Analysis." In *Family-School Links: How do They Affect Educational Outcomes?* eds. Allan Booth and Judith Dunn. Hillsdale, NJ: Lawrence Erlbaum Associates.

Larkin, Ralph W. 1979. *Suburban Youth in Cultural Crisis*. New York: Oxford University Press.

Lee, Valerie E. 2000. "School Size and the Organization of Secondary Schools." In *Handbook of the Sociology of Education,* ed. Maureen T. Hallinan. New York: Kluwer/Plenum Publishers.

Lee, Valerie E., and Anthony S. Bryk. 1988. "Curriculum Tracking as Mediating the Social Distribution of High School Achievement." *Sociology of Education* 61: 78–94.

Lee, Valerie E., Anthony S. Bryk, and Julia B. Smith. 1993. "The Organization of Effective

High Schools." In *Review of Research in Education* 19: 171–267, ed. Linda Darling-Hammon. Washington: AERA.

Lee, Valerie E., and Robert G. Croninger. 1994. "The Relative Importance of Home and School to the Development of Literacy Skills for Middle-Grade Students." *American Journal of Education* 102: 286–329.

Lee, Valerie E., et al. 1991. "Family Structure and Its Effects on Behavioral and Emotional Problems in Young Adolescents." Paper read at the annual meeting of the Society for Research in Child Development.

Lee, Valerie E., and Susanna Loeb. 2000. "School Size in Chicago Elementary Schools: Effects on Teachers' Attitudes and Students' Achievement." *American Educational Research Journal* 37: 3–31.

Lee, Valerie E., and Julia B. Smith. 1993. "Effects of School Restructuring on the Achievement and Engagement of Middle-Grade Students." *Sociology of Education* 66: 164–187.

Lee, Valerie E., and Julia B. Smith. 1994. *High School Restructuring and Student Achievement*. Madison, WI: Center on Organization and Restructuring of Schools.

Lee, Valerie E., and Julia B. Smith. 1995. "Effects of School Restructuring and Size on Early Gains in Achievement and Engagement." *Sociology of Education* 68: 241–270.

Lee, Valerie E., and Julia B. Smith. 1997. "High School Size: Which Works Best, and for Whom?" *Educational Evaluation and Policy Analysis* 19: 205–227.

Lee, Valerie E., and Julia B. Smith. 1999. "Social Support and Achievement for Young Adolescents in Chicago: The Role of School Academic Press." *American Educational Research Journal* 36: 907–945.

Lee, Valerie E. with Julia B. Smith. 2001. *Restructuring High Schools for Equity and Excellence: What Works*. New York: Teachers College Press, Columbia University.

Lee, Valerie E., Julia B. Smith, and Robert G. Croninger. 1995. "Understanding High School Restructuring Effects on the Equitable Distribution of Learning Mathematics and Science." Paper read at the annual meeting of the American Sociological Association.

Lee v. Weisman. 1992. 112 Supreme Court 2469.

Lenski, Gerhard. 1989. *The Religious Factor: A Sociological Study of Religion's Impact on Politics, Economics, and Family Life*, rev. ed. Garden City, NY: Anchor.

Lewis, Oscar. 1966. "The Culture of Poverty." *Scientific American* 215: 19–25.

Lieberman, Ann. 1995. "Practices That Support Teacher Development: Transforming Conceptions of Professional Learning." *Phi Delta Kappan* (April): 591–596.

Lieberman, Ann, ed. 1992. *The Changing Context of Teaching: Ninety-First Yearbook of the National Society for the Study of Education* (Vol. 1). Chicago: University of Chicago Press.

Lieberson, Stanley. 1980. *A Piece of the Pie: Black and White Immigrants Since 1880*. Berkeley: University of California Press.

Lindsay, Paul. 1982. "The Effect of High School Size on Student Participation, Satisfaction, and Attendance." *Educational Evaluation and Policy Analysis* 4: 57–65.

Lindsay, Paul. 1984. "High School Size: Participation in Activities, and Young Adult Social Participation." *Educational Evaluation and Policy Analysis* 6: 73–84.

Linn, Robert L., George F. Madaus, and Joseph J. Pedulla. 1982. "Minimum Competency Testing: Cautions on the State of the Art." *American Journal of Education* 91: 1–35.

Lockheed, Marlaine E. 1985. "Sex and Social Influence: A Meta-Analysis Guided by Theory." In *Status, Rewards, and Influence*, eds. Joseph Berger and Morris Zelditch, Jr., 406–427. San Francisco: Jossey-Bass.

Lockheed, Marlaine E., and Susan S. Klein. 1985. "Sex Equity in Classroom Organization and Climate." In *Handbook for Achieving Sex Equity Through Education*, ed. Susan S. Klein, 189–217. Baltimore: Johns Hopkins University Press.

Louis, Karen Seashore, Helen M. Marks, and Sharon Kruse. 1996. "Teachers' Professional Community in Restructuring Schools." *American Educational Research Journal* 33: 757–798.

Lucas, Samuel R. 1999. *Tracking Inequality*. New York: Teachers College Press.

Lynd, Robert, and Helen Lynd. 1929. *Middletown: A Study in American Culture*. New York: Harcourt, Brace, and World.

MacLeod, Jay. *Ain't No Makin' It*. 1995. Boulder, CO: Westview Press.

Madaus, George F., Peter Airasian, and Thomas Kellaghan. 1980. *School Effectiveness: A Re-*

assessment of the Evidence. New York: Mc-Graw Hill.

Madaus, George F., Thomas Kellaghan, Ernest A. Rakow, and Denis J. King. 1979. "The Sensitivity of Measures of School Effectiveness." Harvard Educational Review 49: 207–230.

Manlove, Jennifer S., and David P. Baker. 1995. "Local Constraints on Opportunity to Learn Mathematics in High School." In Restructuring Schools: Promising Practices and Policy, ed. Maureen H. Hallinan, 133–153. New York: Plenum.

Marks, Helen M. 2000. "Student Engagement in Instructional Activity: Patterns in the Elementary, Middle, and High School Years." American Educational Research Journal 37: 153–184.

Marsh, Herbert W. 1992. "Extracurricular Activities: Beneficial Extension of the Traditional Curriculum or Subversion of Academic Goals?" Journal of Educational Psychology 84: 553–562.

Marsh, Herbert W. 1993. "Relations Between Global and Specific Domains of Self." Journal of Personality and Social Psychology 65: 975–992.

Martin, Jane Poland. 1992. The Schoolhome. Cambridge: Harvard University Press.

Martin, Jane Poland. 1995. "A Philosophy of Education for the Year 2000." Phi Delta Kappan (January): 355–359.

Massey, Douglas S., and Nancy A. Denton. 1993. American Apartheid: Segregation and the Making of the Underclass. Cambridge: Harvard University Press.

McCann, R. A., and S. Austin. 1988. "At-Risk Youth: Definitions, Dimensions, and Relationships." Paper presented at the annual meeting of the American Educational Research Association, New Orleans.

McDill, Edward L. et al. 1967. "Institutional Effects on the Academic Behavior of High School Students." Sociology of Education 40: 181–199.

McDill, Edward L., Gary Natriello, and Aaron Pallas. 1986. "A Population at Risk: Potential Consequences for Tougher School Standards for Student Dropouts." In School Dropouts: Patterns and Policies, ed. Gary Natriello, 106–147. New York: Teachers College Press.

McDill, Edward L., and Leo C. Rigsby. 1973. Structure and Process in Secondary Schools: The Academic Impact of Educational Climates. Baltimore: Johns Hopkins University Press.

McKnight, Curtis C., F. Joe Crosswhite, John A. Dossey, Edward Kifer, Jane O. Swafford, Kenneth J. Travers, and Thomas J. Cooney. 1987. The Underachieving Curriculum: Assessing U.S. School Mathematics From an International Perspective. Champaign, IL: Stipes.

McLanahan, Sara S., and Gary Sandefur. 1994. Growing Up with a Single Parent: What Hurts, What Helps? Cambridge: Harvard University Press.

McLaughlin, Milbrey W. 1994. "Somebody Knows My Name." Issues in Restructuring Schools. Center on Organization and Restructuring of Schools. Madison: University of Wisconsin, 9–11.

McLaughlin, Milbrey W., and Ida Oberman. 1966. Teacher Learning: New Policies, New Practices. New York: Teachers College Press.

McNamara, James F., P. A. Haensley, A. E. Lupkowski, and E. P. Edlind. 1985. "The Role of Extracurricular Activities in High School Education: A Chart Essay on Survey Findings." Paper presented at the annual meeting of the National Association for Gifted Children (ERIC document reproduction service #ED268712).

McNeal, Ralph B., Jr. 1995. "Extracurricular Activities and High School Dropouts." Sociology of Education 68: 62–81.

McPartland, James M. 1967. "The Relative Influence of School Desegregation and Classroom Desegregation on the Academic Achievement of Ninth Grade Negro Students." Baltimore: Johns Hopkins University, Center for the Social Organization of Schools.

McPartland, James M., and Edward L. McDill. 1982. "Control and Differentiation in the Structure of American Education." Sociology of Education 55: 77–88.

McV. Hunt, J. 1969. "Has Compensatory Education Failed? Has It Been Attempted?" Harvard Educational Review 39: 130–152.

McVicar, D. Morgan. 1993. "Superintendents Vow to Fight Sundlun Budget." The Providence Journal-Bulletin, March 11: A1, A11.

Mercer, J., P. Iadacola, and H. Moore. 1980. "Building Effective Multiethnic Schools:

Evolving Models and Paradigms." In *School Desegregation: Past, Present, and Future*, eds. W. G. Stephan and J. R. Feagin. New York: Plenum.

Mercy, James A., and Lala Carr Steelman. 1982. "Family Influence on the Intellectual Attainment of Children." *American Sociological Review* 47: 532–542.

Merton, Robert L. 1957. *Social Theory and Social Structure*. Glencoe, IL, The Free Press.

Metz, Mary H. 1978. *Classrooms and Corridors: The Crisis of Authority in Desegregated Secondary Schools*. Berkeley: University of California Press.

Metz, Mary H. 1989. "Real School: A Universal Drama Amid Disparate Experiences." *Politics of Education Association Yearbook: 1989*: 75–91.

Meyer, J., and Hannon, Michael. 1979. *National Development and the Work System*. Chicago: The University of Chicago Press.

Meyer, John W. 1977. "The Effects of Education as an Institution." *American Journal of Sociology* 93: 55–77.

Meyer, John W. 1986. "Types of Explanation in the Sociology of Education." In *Handbook of Theory and Research for the Sociology of Education*, ed. John G. Richardson, 341–359. New York: Greenwood.

Meyer, John W., and Brian Rowen. 1977. "Institutional Organizations Formal Structure as Myth and Ceremony." *American Journal of Sociology* 8: 340–363.

Meyer, R. H. 1996. "Value-Added Indicators of School Performance." In *Improving America's Schools: The Role of Incentives*, eds. E. A. Hanushek and D. W. Jorgenson. Washington: Brookings Institution Press.

Mickelson, Roselyn Arlin. 1990. "The Attitude-Achievement Paradox Among Black Adolescents." *Sociology of Education* 63: 44–61.

Mickelson, Roselyn Arlin. 2001. "Subverting Swann: First- and Second-Generation Segregation in the Charlotte-Mecklenburg Schools." *American Educational Research Journal* 38: 215–252.

Miech, Richard, Marylyn J. Essex, and H. Hill Goldsmith. 2001. "Socioeconomic Status and the Adjustment to School: The Role of Self-Regulation During Early Childhood." *Sociology of Education* 74: 102–120.

Miller, Lamar P., ed. 1986. *Brown Plus Thirty: Perspectives on Desegregation. Proceedings of a conference on the Thirtieth Anniversary of the 1954 Supreme Court Decision in Brown v. The Board of Education of Topeka, Kansas. New York, NY: September 11–14, 1984*. Published by New York University, Metropolitan Center for Educational Research, Development and Training. (See also, *Brown Plus Forty* by same publisher.)

Mills, C. Wright. 1959. *The Sociological Imagination*. New York: Oxford University Press.

Milne, Ann M., David E. Myers, Alvin S. Rosenthal, and Alan Ginsburg. 1986. "Single Parents, Working Mothers and the Educational Achievement of School Children." *Sociology of Education* 59: 125–139.

Mincer, Jacob. 1974. *Schooling, Experience, and Earnings*. New York: National Bureau of Economic Research.

Moles, Oliver C. 1990. "Disadvantaged Parents' Participation in their Children's Education." Paper presented at the annual meeting of the American Educational Research Association.

Monk, David H. 1987. "Secondary School Size and Curriculum Comprehensiveness." *Economics of Education* 6: 137–150.

Monk, David H. 1992. "Education Productivity Research: An Update and Assessment of Its Role in Education Finance Reform." *Education Evaluation and Policy Analysis* 14: 307–332.

Monk, David H. 1994. "Subject Area Preparation of Secondary Mathematics and Science Teachers and Student Achievement." *Economics of Education Review* 12: 125–142.

Morgan, D. L., and D. F. Alwin. 1980. "When Less is More: School Size and Social Participation." *Social Psychology Quarterly* 43: 241–252.

Morgan, Stephan L. 2001. "Counterfactuals, Causal Effects Heterogeneity, and the Catholic School Effect on Learning." *Sociology of Education* 74: 341–374.

Morgan, Stephan L., and Aage B. Sorenson. 1999. "Parental Networks, Social Closure, and Mathematics Learning: A Test of Coleman's Social Capital Explanation of School Effects." *American Sociological Review* 64: 661–681.

Mosteller, Frederick. 1995. "The Tennessee Study of Class Size in the Early School

Grades." *The Future of Children* 5 (Summer/Fall): 113–127. Los Altos, CA: The David and Lucille Packard Center for the Foundation of Children.

Mosteller, Frederick, Richard J. Light, and J. A., Sachs. 1996. "Sustained Inquiry in Education: Lessons Learned from Skill Grouping and Class Size." *Harvard Educational Review* 66: 797–842.

Mosteller, Frederick, and Daniel P. Moynihan, eds. 1972. *On Equality of Educational Opportunity*. New York: Random House.

Moynihan, Daniel P. et al. 1965. *The Negro Family: The Case for National Action*. Washington: Government Printing Office.

Muller, Chandra, and Kathryn S. Schiller. 2000. "Leveling the Playing Field? Students' Educational Attainment and States' Performance Testing." *Sociology of Education* 73: 196–218.

Muller, Chandra, Susan Roberta Katz, and L. Janelle Dance. 1999. "Investing in Teaching and Learning: Dynamics of the Teacher-Student relationship from Each Actor's Perspective." *Urban Education* 34: 292–337.

Murchan, Damian P., and Finbarr C. Sloane. 1994. "Conceptual and Statistical Problems in the Study of School and Classroom Effects: An Introduction to Multilevel Modeling Techniques." In *In Search of More Effective Mathematics Education*, eds. Ian Westbury, Corinna A. Ethington, Lauren A. Sosniak, and David P. Baker, 247–272. Norwood, NJ: Ablex.

Murnane, R. 1987. "Understanding Teacher Attrition." *Harvard Educational Review*, 57: 177–182.

Murrell, Peter, Jr. 1992. "Afrocentric Immersion: Academic and Personal Developments of African American Males in Public Schools." In *Freedom's Plow: Teaching for a Multicultural Democracy*, eds. Theresa Perry and James Fraser. New York: Routledge.

Mussoline, Lawrence J., and Roger C. Shouse. 2001. "School Restructuring as a Policy Agenda: Why One Size May Not Fit All." *Sociology of Education* 74: 44–58.

National Association of Secondary School Principals (NASSP). 1996. *Breaking Ranks: Changing an American Institution*. Reston, VA: In partnership with the Carnegie Foundation for the Advancement of Teaching.

National Center for Education Statistics (NCES). 1992. *Digest of Education Statistics 1992*. Washington: Government Printing Office.

National Center for Education Statistics (NCES). 1995. *Use of School Choice*, prepared by Edith McCarthur et al. Washington: Department of Education, NCES 95-742R.

National Center for Education Statistics (NCES). 1999. *Highlights for TIMSS: Overview and Keys Finding Across Grade Levels*. Washington: NCES 1999-081R. See also, http://www.nces.ed.gov.timss.

National Center for Education Statistics (NCES). 2002. *Qualifications of the Public School Workforce: Prevalence of Out-Of-field Teaching 1987–88 to 1999–00*. Washington: U.S. Department of Education. See also, http://nces.ed.gov/pubs2002/2002603.pdf.

National Commission on Excellence in Education. 1983. *A Nation at Risk: The Imperative of Educational Reform*. Washington: Government Printing Office.

National Commission on Teaching and America's Future. 1997. *Doing What Matters Most: Investing in Quality Teaching*. New York: NCTAF.

National Education Association. 1986. Resolution adopted by the NEA Representation Assembly. Washington, DC.

National Education Association. 1987. *Status of the Public American School Teacher: 1985–86*. Washington: National Education Association.

National Institute of Education. 1984. *School Desegregation and Black Achievement*. Washington: Office of Education Policy and Organization.

National Organization for Women. 1991. *Public Education Programs for African-American Males: A Women's Educational Equity Policy Perspective*. New York: NOW Legal Defense and Education Fund.

National School Boards Association. 1993. *Violence in the Schools*. Alexandria, VA: National School Boards Association.

Natriello, Gary, Aaron Pallas, and Karl L. Alexander. 1989. "On the Right Track? Curriculum and Academic Achievement." *Sociology of Education* 62: 109–118.

Neisser, Ulric, Gwyneth Boodoo, Thomas J. Bouchard, Jr., A. Wade Boykin, Nathan

Brody, Stephan J. Ceci, Diane F. Halpern, John C. Loehlin, Robert Perloff, Robert J. Sternberg, and Susana Urbina. 1996. "Intelligence: Knowns and Unknowns." *American Psychologist* 51: 77–101.

Newmann, Fred M., ed. 1992. *Student Engagement and Achievement in American Secondary Schools*. New York: Teachers College Press.

Nisbet, Robert. 1975. *The Twilight of Authority*. New York: Oxford University Press.

Noddings, Nel. 1988. "An Ethic of Caring and Its Implication for Instructional Arrangements." *American Journal of Education* 96, 215–231.

Nolin, Mary Jo, Elizabeth Davies, Westat, Inc., Kathryn Chandler. 1995. *Student Victimization at School*. Washington: National Center for Education Statistics.

Nord, C. W., J. Lennon, B. Liu, and K. Chandler. 2000. *Home Literacy Activities and Signs of Children's Emerging Literacy, 1993 and 1999*. Washington: U.S. Department of Education, National Center for Education Statistics, Statistics in Brief (NCES 2000-26).

Nozick, Robert. 1974. *Anarchy, State, and Utopia*. New York: Basic Books.

Nye, Barbara A., J. Boyd-Zaharias, B. D. Fulton, et al. 1994. *The Lasting Benefits Study: Grade 7*. Nashville: Center for Research in Basic Skills, Tennessee State University.

Nye, Barbara, Larry V. Hedges, and Spyros Konstantopoulos. 2000. "The Effects of Small Classes on Academic Achievement: The Results of the Tennessee Class Size Experiment." *American Educational Research Journal* 37: 123–151.

Nye, Barbara, Larry V. Hedges, and Spyros Konstantopoulos. 2001. "The Long-Term Effects of Small Classes in Early Grades: Lasting Benefits in Mathematics Achievement at Grade 9." *The Journal of Experimental Education* 69: 245–257.

Oakes, Jeannie. 1985. *Keeping Track: How Schools Structure Inequality*. New Haven: Yale University Press.

Oakes, Jeannie. 1994. "More Than Misapplied Technology: A Normative and Political Response to Hallinan on Tracking." *Sociology of Education* 67: 84–89, 91.

Oakes, Jeannie, Adam Gamoran, and Reba N. Page. 1992. "Curriculum Differentiation: Opportunities, Outcomes, and Meanings." In *Handbook of Research on Curriculum*, ed. P. W. Jackson, 570–608. New York: Macmillan.

Oakes, Jeannie, and Martin Lipton. 1992. "Detracking Schools: Early Lessons From the Field." *Phi Delta Kappan* 73 (February): 448–454.

Ogbu, John U. 1978. *Minority Education and Caste*. New York: Academic Press.

Ogbu, John U. 1986. "The Consequences of the American Caste System" In *The School Achievement of Minority Children*, ed. Ulrich Neisser. Hillsdale, NJ: Lawrence Erlbaum.

O'Kelly, Charlotte, and Larry Carney. 1986. *Women and Men in Society*, 2d ed. Belmont, CA: Wadsworth Publishing.

Olneck, Michael R., and David B. Bills. 1980. "What Makes Sammy Run? An Empirical Assessment of the Bowles-Gintis Correspondence Principle." *American Journal of Education* 89: 27–61.

Orfield, Gary, and Franklin Monfort. 1992. *Status of School Desegregation: The Next Generation*. Arlington, VA: National School Boards Association.

Organization for Economic Cooperation and Development (OECD). 2001. *Education at a Glance*. Washington, DC. Also available at www.sourceoecd.org.

Otto, L. B. 1975. "Extracurricular Activities in the Educational Attainment Process." *Rural Sociology* 40: 162–176.

Otto, L. 1976a. "Extracurricular Activities and Aspirations in the Status Attainment Process." *Rural Sociology* 41: 216–233.

Otto, L. 1976b. "Social Integration and Status Attainment Process." *American Journal of Sociology* 81: 1360–1383.

Otto, L. B. 1982. "Extracurricular Activities." In *Improving Educational Standards and Productivity*, ed. Herbert J. Walberg. Berkeley, CA: McCutchan.

Otto, L. B., and D. F. Alwin. 1977. "Athletics, Aspirations, and Attainments." *Sociology of Education* 42: 102–113.

Owen, David. 1985. *None of the Above*. Boston: Houghton Mifflin.

Page, Ellis B., and Gary M. Grandon. 1979. "Family Configuration and Mental Ability: Two Theories Contrasted with U.S. Data." *American Educational Research Journal* 16: 257–272.

Pallas, Aaron M., Doris R. Entwisle, Karl L. Alexander, and M. Francis Stluka. 1994. "Ability Group Effects: Instructional, Social, or Institutional?" *Sociology of Education* 67: 27–46.

Parelius, Robert James, and Ann Parker Parelius. 1987. *The Sociology of Education*, 2d ed. Englewood Cliffs, NJ: Prentice-Hall.

Parsons, Talcott. 1959. "The School Class as a Social System." *Harvard Educational Review* 29: 297–318.

Parsons, Talcott. 1964. "Youth in the Context of American Society." In *Social Structure and Personality*. London: The Free Press of Glencoe.

Parsons, Talcott, and Edward Shils. 1951. *Toward a General Theory of Action*. New York: The Free Press.

Pedersen, Eigel, Therese A. Faucher, and William W. Eaton. 1978. "A New Perspective on the Effects of First Grade Teachers on Children's Subsequent Adult Status." *Harvard Educational Review* 48: 1–31.

Peng, Samuel S., and Ralph M. Lee. 1992. "Home Variables, Parent-Child Activities, and Academic Achievement: A Study of 1988 Eighth Graders." Paper presented at the annual meeting of the American Educational Research Association.

Persell, Caroline Hodges. 1977. *Education and Inequality: The Roots and Results of Stratification in America's Schools*. New York: The Free Press.

Peterson, Paul E. 1999. "Top Ten Questions Asked About School Choice." In *Brookings Papers on Educational Policy 1999*, ed. Diane Ravitch. Washington: Brookings Institution Press.

Peterson, Penelope L., Sarah J. McCarthy, and Richard F. Elmore. 1996. "Learning From School Restructuring." *American Educational Research Journal* 33: 119–153.

Phillips, Merideth. 1997. "What Makes Schools Effective? A Comparison of the Relationship of Communitarian Climate and Academic Climate to Mathematics Achievement and Attendance During Middle School." *American Educational Research Journal*, 34: 633–662.

Plank, Stephen B. 2000. *Finding One's Place*. New York: Teachers College Press.

Ponessa, Joan M. 1992. "Student Access to Extracurricular Activities." *Public Affairs Focus* 23: 1–11.

Pong, Suet-ling. 1998. "The School Compositional Effect of Single-Parenthood on 10th Grade Achievement." *Sociology of Education* 71: 24–43.

Pong, Suet-ling and Aaron Pallas. 2001. "Class Size and Eighth-Grade Math Achievement in the United States and Abroad." *Educational Evaluation and Policy Analysis* 23: 251–273.

Porter, Oscar F. 1990. *Undergraduate Completion and Persistence at Four-Year Colleges and Universities*. Washington: National Institute of Independent Colleges and Universities.

Porter, T. M. 1995. *Trust in Numbers: The Pursuit of Objectivity in Science and Public Life*. Princeton, NJ: Princeton University Press.

Portes, Alejandro. 1998. "Social Capital" Its Origins and Applications to Modern Sociology." *Annual Review of Sociology* 6: 65–78.

Powell, Arthur G., Eleanor Farrar, and David K. Cohen. 1985. *The Shopping Mall High School*. Boston: Houghton Mifflin.

Powell, Barbara S., and Arthur G. Powell. 1983. "For Girls, Schools of Their Own." *Independent School* 43: 55–58.

Providence Journal-Bulletin. 1994. "Michigan Will Pay for Schools with Sales and Cigarette Taxes." March 21: A5.

Public Agenda. 2001. *Teachers, Parents Find Smaller Schools Appealing, but See Other Education Reforms As More Pressing*. New York: www.publicagenda.org.

Purkey, Stewart C., and Marshall S. Smith. 1983. "Effective Schools: A Review." *The Elementary School Journal* 83: 427–452.

Putnam, Robert, D. 1995. "Tuning In, Tuning Out: The Strange Disappearance of Social Capital in America." Paper presented at the annual meeting of the American Political Science Association, Chicago.

Quiroz, Pamela Anne, Nilda Flores Gonzales, and Kenneth Frank. 1996. "Carving a Niche in the High School Social Structure: Formal and Informal Constraints on Participation in the Extra Curriculum." *Research in Sociology of Education and Socialization* 11.

Ramirez, F., and Rubinson, R. 1979. "Creating Members: The National Incorporation of Education." In *Nation Development and the World System*, eds. J. Meyer and M. Hannon. Chicago: University of Chicago.

Rasell, Edith, and Richard Rothstein, eds. 1993. *School Choice: Examining the Evidence*. Washington: Economic Policy Institute.

Ravitch, Diane. 1999. "Reading Wars." Paper presented at the John F. Kennedy School of Government, Harvard University, September 21.

Rawls, John. 1971. *A Theory of Justice*. Cambridge: Harvard University Press.

Rehberg, Richard A., and Evelyn R. Rosenthal. 1978. *Class and Merit in the American High School*. New York: Longman.

Remmers, Hermann H., and Don H. Radler. 1957. *The American Teenager*. Indianapolis: Bobbs-Merrill.

Renwick, W. 1985. "New Zealand: System of Education." In *International Encyclopedia of Education*, eds. T. Husen and T. Postlethwaite. Oxford: Pergamon Press.

Resnick, Daniel P., and Lawrence B. Resnick. 1985. "Standards, Curriculum and Performance: A Historical and Comparative Perspective." *Educational Researcher* 14 (April): 5–20.

Rich, Dorothy. 1987. *Schools and Families: Issues and Actions*. Washington: National Education Association Press.

Richard, Alan. 2002. "Cambridge Becomes Latest District to Integrate by Income." *Education Week* 21 January 9: 11.

Richardson, John G. 2000. "The Variable Construction of Educational Risk." In *Handbook of the Sociology of Education*, ed. Maureen T. Hallinan, New York: Kluwer Academic/ Plenum Publishers.

Riehl, Carolyn. 2001. "Bridges to the Future: The Contributions of Qualitative Research to the Sociology of Education." *Sociology of Education* Extra Issue: 115–134.

Riesman, David, with Nathan Glazer and Reuel Denney. 1951. *The Lonely Crowd*. New Haven: Yale University Press.

Riessman, Frank. 1962. *The Culturally Deprived Child*. New York: Harper and Row.

Riordan, Cornelius. 1985. "Public and Catholic Schooling: The Effects of Gender Context Policy." *American Journal of Education* 93: 518–540.

Riordan, Cornelius. 1990. *Girls and Boys in School: Separate or Together?* New York: Teachers College Press.

Riordan, Cornelius. 1994. "Single-Gender Schools: Outcomes for African and Hispanic Americans." In *Research in Sociology of Education and Socialization*, ed. Aaron M. Pallas, 10: 177–206.

Riordan, Cornelius. 2000. "Trends in Student Demography in Catholic Secondary Schools, 1972–1992." In *Catholic Schools at the Crossroads*, eds. James Youniss and John J. Convey. New York: Teachers College Press.

Riordan, Cornelius. 2002. "Gender Gaps Among First Time Kindergarten Children in the Public Schools: The Importance of Entry Age and Motor Skills." Paper presented at the annual meeting of the American Educational Research Association.

Riordan, Kate E. 1997. "Participation and Leadership Behavior in Extracurricular Activities and Academic and developmental Outcomes." State College, PA: Pennsylvania State University. M.A. Thesis.

Rist, Ray C. 1970. "Student Social Class and Teacher Expectations: The Self-Fulfilling Prophecy in Ghetto Education." *Harvard Educational Review* 40: 411–451.

Rist, Ray C. 1977. "On the Relations Among Educational Research Paradigms: From Disdain to Detentes." *Anthropology and Education Quarterly* 8: 42–49.

Rist, Ray C., and Ronald J. Anson, eds. 1977. *Education, Social Science and the Judicial Process*. New York: Teachers College Press.

Rivkin, Steven G. 1994. "Residential Segregation and School Segregation." *Sociology of Education* 67: 279–292.

Robelen, Erik, W. 2001. "Education Bill Ready to Face Final Hurdles." *Education Week*, 20 June 20: 1, 34–35.

Robelen, Erik, W. 2002. "ESEA to Boost Federal role in Education." *Education Week* 21 January 9: 1, 28, 29.

Robinson, V. 1985. *Making Do in the Classroom: A Report on the Misassignment of Teachers*. Washington: Council for Basic Education and the American Federation of Education Statistics.

Robinson, W. S. 1950. "Ecological Correlations and the Behavior of Individuals." *American Sociological Review* 15: 351–357.

Rogoff, Natalie. 1953. *Recent Trends in Occupational Mobility*. New York: The Free Press.

Roscigno, Vincent, and James Ainsworth-Darnell. 1999. "Race, Cultural Capital, and Educational Resources: Persistent Inequalities and Achievement Returns." *Sociology of Education* 72: 158–178.

Rosen, Bernard. 1959. "Race, Ethnicity and the Achievement Syndrome." *American Sociological Review* 24: 47–60.

Rosenbaum, James E. 1976. *Making Inequality*. New York: Wiley.

Rosenbaum, James E. 1980. "Track Misperceptions and Frustrated College Plans: An Analysis of the Effects of Tracks and Track Misperceptions in the National Longitudinal Survey." *Sociology of Education* 53: 74–88.

Rosenberg, Bella. 1993. "Opening Comments on Equity and Excellence." *Conference on Equity and Excellence in Education: The Policy Uses of Sociology,* jointly sponsored by the U.S. Department of Education and the Sociology of Education Section of the American Sociological Association.

Rosenberg, Morris. 1965. *Society and the Adolescent Self-Image*. Princeton: Princeton University Press.

Rosenberg, Morris, Carmi Schooler, Carrie Schoenbach, and Florence Rosenberg. 1995. "Global Self-Esteem and Specific Self-Esteem: Different Concepts, Different Outcomes." *American Sociological Review* 60: 141–156.

Rosenberg, Morris, and Roberta G. Simmons. 1972. *Black and White Self-Esteem: The Urban School Child*. Washington: American Sociological Association.

Rosenholz, Susan J. 1985. "Modifying Status Expectations in the Traditional Classroom." In *Status, Rewards, and Influence,* eds. Joseph Berger and Morris Zelditch, Jr., 445–470. San Francisco: Jossey-Bass.

Rosenshine, Barak V., and Norma Furst. 1971. "Research on Teacher Performance Criteria." In *Research on Teacher Education: A Symposium,* ed. B. Orthane Smith. Englewood Cliffs, NJ: Prentice Hall.

Rosenthal, R., and R. L. Rosnow. 1984. *Essentials of Behavioral Research: Methods and Data Analysis*. New York: McGraw-Hill.

Rosenthal, Robert, and Lenore Jacobson. 1968. *Pygmalion in the Classroom*. New York: Hold, Rinehart and Winston.

Ross, Catherine E., and Beckett A. Broh. 2000. "The Roles of Self-Esteem and the Sense of Personal Control in the Academic Achievement Process." *Sociology of Education* 73: 270–284.

Ross, Catherine E., and John Mirowsky. 1989. "Explaining the Social Patterns of Depression: Control and Problem-Solving—or Support and Talking?" *Journal of Health and Social Behavior* 30: 206–219.

Rossell. R. 1992. *The Carrot and the Stick*. Philadelphia: Temple University Press.

Rowen, Brian. 1990. "Commitment and Control: Alternative Strategies for the Organizational Design of High Schools." In C. B. Cazden, eds., *Review of Research in Education* 16 (353–389). Washington, DC: American Educational Research Association.

Rowen, Brian, and C. Miskel. 1999. "Institutional Theory and the Study of Educational Organizations." In *Handbook of Research in Educational Administration,* eds. J. Murphy and K. S. Louis. San Francisco, CA: Jossey-Bass.

Rutter, Michael, et al. 1979. *Fifteen Thousand Hours*. Cambridge: Harvard University Press.

Ryan, William. 1976. *Blaming The Victim,* rev. ed. New York: Vintage.

Saario, Terry N., Carol Nagy Jacklin, and Carol Kerr Tittle. 1973. "Sex Role Stereotyping in the Public Schools." *Harvard Educational Review* 43: 386–415.

Sack, Joetta L. 2001. "Ed. Department Finds Charter Schools Spur Existing Schools to Improve." *Education Week,* June 20: 32.

Sadker, Myra, and David Sadker. 1994. *Failing at Fairness: How America's Schools Cheat Girls*. New York: Scribner's Sons.

Sadker, Myra, David Sadker, and Susan Klein. 1991. "The Issue of Gender in Elementary and Secondary Education." *Review of Research in Education* 17: 269–334.

Sadovnik, Alan R., Peter W. Cookson, and Susan F. Semal. 1994. *Exploring Education*. Boston: Allyn and Bacon.

Salganik, Laura Hersh, and Nancy Karweit. 1982. "Voluntarism and Governance in Education." *Sociology of Education* 55: 152–161.

Scarr, Sandra, and Richard A. Weinberg. 1978. "The Influence of 'Family Background' on Intellectual Attainment." *American Sociological Review* 43: 674–692.

Schafer, Walter E., and Carol Olexa. 1971. *Tracking and Opportunity*. Scranton, PA: Chandler Press.

Schafer, Walter E., and Kenneth Polk. 1972. *Schools and Delinquency*. Englewood Cliffs, NJ: Prentice Hall.

Schaub, Maryellen, and David P. Baker. 1991. "Solving the Math Problem: Exploring Mathematics Achievement in Japanese and American Middle Schools." *American Journal of Education* 99: 623–642.

Schaub, Maryellen, and David P. Baker. 1994. "What Makes for Effective Mathematics Instruction? Japanese and American Classroom Compared." In *In Search of More Effective Mathematics Education*, eds. Ian Westbury, Corinna A. Ethington, Lauren A. Sosniak, and David P. Baker. Norwood, NJ: Ablex Publishing Corporation.

Schaub, Maryellen, and David P. Baker. 2002. "Is 'Social Capital' the 'Self-Esteem' of the 1990s? A Commentary" *Annual Review of Sociology of Education*, forthcoming.

Schemo, Diana Jean. 2001. "Senate Approves a Bill to Expand the Federal Roll in Public Education." *New York Times*, December 19: A27.

Schendel, Jack S. 1968. "The Psychological Characteristics of High School Athletes and Non-Participants in Athletics." In *Contemporary Psychology of Sport*, ed. G. S. Kenyon, 79–86. Chicago: Athletic Institute.

Schmidt, Peter. 1994. "Plan to Return Boston to Neighborhood Schools is Proposed." *Education Week* (June 15): 5.

Schmidt, Peter. 1995a. "Accord Set in Desegregation Case in Kansas City." *Education Week* (March 1): 1.

Schmidt, Peter. 1995b. "Urban Officials' Views on Desegregation Surveyed." *Education Week* (July 12): 7.

Schmidt, W. H., and C. C. McKnight. 1998. *Facing the Consequences: Using TIMMS for a Closer Look at U.S. Mathematics and Science Education*. Dordrecht, The Netherlands: Kluwer Academic Publishers.

Schmidt, William H., Curtis C. McKnight, Richard T. Houang, Hsingchi Wang, David E. Wiley, Leland S. Cogan, and Richard G. Wolfe. 2001. *Why Schools Matter: A Cross-National Comparison of Curriculum and Learning*. San Francisco, CA: Jossey-Bass.

Schofield, Janet. 1989. *Review of Research on School Desegregation's Impact on Elementary and Secondary School Students*. Commissioned by the State of Connecticut Department of Education. Eric Document, #ED3198825.

Schoggen, Phil, and Maxine Schoggen. 1988. "School Voluntary Participation and High School Size." *Journal of Educational Research* 81: 288–293.

Schultz, Theodore W. 1961. "Investment in Human Capital." *American Economic Review* 51 (March): 1–17.

Schwartz, Frances. 1981. "Supporting or Subverting Learning: Peer Grouped Patterns in Four Tracked Schools." *Anthropology and Education Quarterly* 12: 99–121.

Sedlack, Michael W., Christopher W. Wheeler, Diana C. Pullin, and Philip S. Cusick. 1986. *Selling Students Short: Classroom Bargains and Academic Reform in the American High School*. New York: Teachers College Press.

Selakovich, Daniel. 1984. *Schooling in America: Social Foundations of Education*. New York: Longman.

Sewell, William H., Archibald O. Haller, and George W. Ohlenhorf. 1970. "The Educational and Early Occupational Attainment Process: Replications and Revisions." *American Sociological Review* 35: 1014–1027.

Sewell, William H., Archibald O. Haller, and Alejandro Portes. 1969. "The Educational and Early Occupational Attainment Process." *American Sociological Review* 34: 82–92.

Sewell, William H., and Robert M. Hauser. 1976. "Causes and Consequences of Higher Education: Models of Status Attainment Processes." In *Schooling and Achievement in American Society*, eds. William H. Sewell, Robert M. Hauser, and David L. Featherman, 9–27. New York: Academic Press.

Shakeshaft, Charol, Ellen Barber, Mary Ann Hergenrother, Yolanda Johnson, Laurie Mandel, and Janice Sawyer. 1995. "Peer Harassment and the Culture of Caring in the Schools." Paper presented at the annual meeting of the American Educational Research Association.

Shakeshaft, Charol, Audrey Cohen, and Selma Greenberg. 1996. In *Loco Parentis: Sexual Abuse of Students in Schools*. New York: Routledge.

Shouse, Roger. 1996. "Academic Press and Sense of Community: Conflict and Congruence in American High Schools." In *Research in Sociology of Education and Socialization,* ed. A. M. Pallas. Greenwich, CT: JAI press, 173–202.

Shouse, Roger. 1999. "The Impact of Traditional and Reform-Style Practices on Student Mathematics Achievement: Evidence From the National Longitudinal Study." Paper presented at the John F. Kennedy School of Government, Harvard University, September 21.

Simon-McWilliams, Ethel, ed. 1989. *Resegregation of Public Schools: The Third Generation.* Portland, OR: Network of Regional Assistance Centers and Northwest Regional Educational Laboratory.

Sizer, Theodore R. 1964. *Secondary Schools at the Turn of the Century.* New Haven: Yale University Press.

Sizer, Theodore R. 1984. *Horace's Compromise: The Dilemma of the American High School.* Boston: Houghton Mifflin.

Sizer, Theodore R. 1992. *Horace's School: Redesigning the American High School.* Boston: Houghton Mifflin.

Slavin, Robert E. 1983. *Cooperative Learning.* New York: Longman.

Slavin, Robert E. 1987a. "Ability Grouping and Student Achievement in Elementary Schools: A Best Evidence Synthesis." *Review of Educational Research* 57: 293–336.

Slavin, Robert E. 1987b. "Ability Grouping in Elementary Schools: Do We Really Know Nothing Until We Know Everything?" *Review of Educational Research* 57: 347–350.

Slavin, Robert E. 1989. "Achievement Effects of Substantial Reductions in Class Size." In *School and Classroom Organization,* ed. Robert E. Slavin, 247–257. Hillsdale, NJ: Lawrence Erlbaum.

Slavin, Robert E. 2002a. "Evidence-Based Education Policies: Transforming Educational Practice and Research." Dewitt Wallace-Reader's Digest Distinguished Lecture, presented at the Annual Meeting of the American Educational Research Association, New Orleans, LA.

Slavin, Robert E. 2002b. "Randomized Evaluation of Success for All: Design Issues." Paper presented at the Annual Meeting of the American Educational Research Association, New Orleans, LA.

Smith, Marshall S. 1972. "Equality of Educational Opportunity: The Basic Findings Reconsidered." In *On Equality of Educational Opportunity,* eds. Frederick Mostellor and Daniel P. Moynihan, 234–342. New York: Random House.

Smith, M. S., B. W. Scoll, and J. Link. 1996. "Research-Based School Reform: The Clinton Administration Agenda." In *Improving American's Schools: The Role of Incentives,* eds. E. A. Hanushek and D. W. Jorgenson. Washington: National Center for Educational Statistics.

Snyder, Eldon E. 1969. "A Longitudinal Analysis of the Relationship Between High School Values, Social Participation, and Educational-Occupational Achievement." *Sociology of Education* 42: 261–270.

Snyder, Eldon E., and Elmer Spreitzer. 1992. "Social Psychological Concomitants of Adolescents' Role Identities as Scholars and Athletes: A Longitudinal Analysis." *Youth and Society* 23: 507–522.

Sociology of Education. 1982. 55, nos. 2/3.

Sociology of Education. 1983. 56, no. 4.

Sociology of Education. 1985. 58, no. 2.

Sorensen, Aage B. 1970. "Organizational Differentiation of Students and Educational Opportunity." *Sociology of Education* 43: 355–376.

Sowell, Thomas. 1977. "New Light on the Black I. Q. Controversy." *New York Times Magazine* (March 27): 56–63.

Sowell, Thomas. 1981. *Ethnic America: A History.* New York: Basic Books.

Spady, W. 1970. "Lament for the Letterman: Effects of Peer Status and Extracurricular Activities on Goals and Achievement." *American Journal of Sociology* 75: 680–702.

Spady, William G. 1974. "Mastery Learning: Its Sociological Implications." In *Schools, Society and Mastery Learning,* ed. J. H. Block, 91–116. New York: Holt.

Spring, Joel. 1955. "Education as a Form of Social Control." In *Roots of Crisis,* eds. Clarence Karier, Paul Violas, and Joel Spring. Chicago: Rand McNally.

State of California. 1986. A Bill to Establish California Commission to Promote Self-Esteem and Personal and Social Responsibility. Sacramento, CA: Assembly Bill Number 3659, Chapter 1065, September 23.

State of Rhode Island. 1994. "An Act Relating to Educational Reform: Guaranteed Student Entitlement." In General Assembly, 94-H9115, January.

Stedman, Lawrence C., and Marshall S. Smith. 1983. "Recent Reform Proposals for American Education." *Contemporary Education Review* 2: 85–104.

Steele, Claude M., and Joshua Aronson. 1998. "Stereotype Threat and Test Performance of Academically Successful African Americans." In *The Black-White Test Score Gap*, eds. Christopher Jencks and Meridith Phillips. Washington: Brooking Institution Press.

Steele, Shelby. 1990. *The Content of Our Character: A New Vision of Race in America*. New York: Harper Perennial.

Steelman, Lala Carr, and James A. Mercy. 1980. "Unconfounding the Confluence Model: A Test of Sibship Size and Birth Order Effects on Intelligence." *American Sociological Review* 45: 571–582.

Steelman, Lala Carr, Brian Powell, and Robert M. Carini. 2000. "Do Teacher Unions Hinder Educational Performance? Lessons Learned from State SAT and ACT Scores." *Harvard Educational Review* 70: 437–466.

Stein, Maurice R. 1960. *The Eclipse of Community*. New York: Harper and Row.

Steinberg, Laurence, B. Bradford Brown, and Sanford M. Dornbusch. 1996. *Beyond the Classroom: Why School Reform Has Failed and What Parents Need To Do About It*. New York: Simon & Schuster.

Steinberg, Stephen. 1981. *The Ethnic Myth: Race, Ethnicity and Class in America*. Boston: Beacon Press.

Stephan, Walter G. 1978. "School Desegregation: An Evaluation of Predictions Made in *Brown v. Board of Education*." *Psychological Bulletin* 85: 217–238.

Stevenson, David Lee, and David P. Baker. 1991 "State Control of the Curriculum and Classroom Instruction." *Sociology of Education* 64: 1–10.

Stevenson, David Lee, and David P. Baker. 1992. "Shadow Education and Allocation in Formal Schooling: Transition to Formal School-ing in Japan." *American Journal of Sociology* 97: 1639–1657.

Stevenson, David, Kathryn Schiller, and Barbara Schneider. 1994. "Sequences of Opportunities For Learning." *Sociology of Education* 67: 184–198.

Stiefel, Leanna, Robert Berne, Patrice Iatarola, and Norm Fruchter. 2000. "High School Size: Effects on Budget and Performance in New York City." *Educational Evaluation and Policy Analysis* 22: 27–39.

St. John, Nancy. 1975. *School Desegregation: Outcomes for Children*. New York: Wiley.

Sui-Chu, Esther How, and J. Douglas Willms. 1996. "Effects of Parental Involvement on Eighth Grade Achievement." *Sociology of Education:* 126–141.

Sweet, D. A. 1986. "Extracurricular Activity Participants Outperform Other Students." *OERI Bulletin* (September).

Taeuber, Karl. 1990. "Desegregation of Public School Districts: Persistence and Change." *Phi Delta Kappan* 72 (September): 18–24.

Tammivaara, Julie Stulac. 1982. "The Effects of Task Structure on Beliefs about Competence and Participation in Small Groups." *Sociology of Education* 55: 212–222.

Teachers College Record. 1995. "Forty Years After Brown" 96 (summer).

The Education Trust. 2002. *The Funding Gap*. Washington, DC. The Education Trust, Inc. http://www.edtrust.org/main/main/reports.asp

Thomas, Gail E., Karl L. Alexander, and Bruce K. Eckland. 1979. "Access to Higher Education: The Importance of Race, Sex, and Social Class." *School Review* 87: 133–156.

Thorne, Barrie. 1986. "Girls and Boys Together, But Mostly Apart: Gender Arrangement in Elementary Schools." In *Relationships and Development*, eds. William H. Hartup and Zick Rubin, 167–184. Hillsdale, NJ: Lawrence Erlbaum.

Thorne, Barrie. 1993. *Gender Play: Girls and Boys in School*. East Brunswick, NJ: Rutgers University Press.

Tidball, M. Elizabeth. 1989. "Women's Colleges: Exceptional Conditions, Not Exceptional Talent, Produce High Achievers." In *Educating The Majority*, eds. C. S. Pearson, D. L. Shavlik, and J. G. Touchton. New York: Collier Macmillan.

Tinto, Vincent. 1987. *Leaving College*. Chicago: University of Chicago Press.

Toch, T. 1996. "Why Teachers Don't Teach: How Teacher Unions are Wrecking Our Schools." *U.S. News and World Report*, February 26: 62–71.

Tomlinson, Tommy M. 1988. *Class Size and Public Policy: Politics and Panaceas*. Washington: Department of Education.

Trent, William T., Jomills Henry Braddock II, and Ronald D. Henderson. 1985. "Sociology of Education: A Focus on Education as an Institution." In *Review of Research in Education*, Vol. 12, ed. Edmund W. Gordon, 295–336. Washington: American Educational Research Association.

Trow, Martin. 1961. "The Second Transformation of American Secondary Education." *International Journal of Comparative Sociology* 2: 144–166.

Tryneski, J. 1997. *Requirements for Certification of Teachers, Counselors, Librarians, Administrators for Elementary and Secondary Schools*. Chicago: University of Chicago Press.

Twentieth Century Fund. 1983. *Making the Grade*. New York: The Twentieth Century Fund.

Twenty-First Century Education Commission. 1992. *Educating All Our Children*. Providence, RI: March.

Tyack, David. 1974. *The One Best System*. Cambridge: Harvard University Press.

Tyack, David, and Elizabeth Hansot. 1990. *Learning Together: A History of Coeducation in America*. New Haven: Yale University Press.

Uhlenberg, Peter, and David Eggebeen. 1986. "The Declining Well-Being of American Adolescents." *The Public Interest* 82: 25–38.

Uhlig, Mark A. 1987. "Learning Styles of Minorities to Be Studied." *New York Times*, November 21: 29.

United Nations Children's Fund (UNICEF). 1993. *The State of the World's Children, 1993*. New York: Oxford University Press.

Usdansky, Margaret L. 1996. "Single Motherhood: Stereotypes vs. Statistics." *New York Times*. February 11: E4.

Useem, Elizabeth L. 1992. "Middle Schools and Math Groups: Parents' Involvement in Children's Placement." *Sociology of Education* 65: 263–279.

U.S. Bureau of the Census. 1990. *Household and Family Characteristics*. Current Population Reports, Series P-20, No. 447. Washington: Government Printing Office.

U.S. Bureau of the Census. 1992a. *Marital Status and Living Arrangements*, CPR Population Characteristics, Series P-20, No. 468. Washington: U.S. Government Printing Office.

U.S. Bureau of the Census. 1992b. *Public Education Finances: 1989–90*. Washington: Government Printing Office.

U.S. Department of Education. 1992. *Digest of Education Statistics, 1992*. Washington: National Center for Education Statistics, Office of Educational Research and Improvement.

U.S. Department of Education. 2000. *Trends in Educational Equity of Girls and Women*. Written and researched by Yupin Bae, Susan Choy, Claire Geddes, Jennifer Sable, and Thomas Snyder. Washington: Office of Educational Research and Improvement, NCES 2000–03.

Valentine, Charles A. 1968. *Culture and Poverty*. Chicago: University of Chicago Press.

Valentine, Charles A. 1971. "Deficit, Difference, and Bicultural Models of Afro-American Behavior." *Harvard Educational Review* 42: 137–157.

Vaishnav, Anand. 2002. "Desegregation by Income Gets Wary Reception in North Carolina." *Boston Globe*, June 3: A1, A6.

Vanfossen, Beth E., James D. Jones, and Joan Z. Spade. 1987. "Curriculum Tracking and Status Maintenance." *Sociology of Education* 60: 104–122.

Velez, Willima. 1985. "Finishing College: The Effects of College Type." *Sociology of Education* 58: 191–200.

Viteritti, Joseph P. 1998. "School Choice and State Constitutional Law." In *Learning from School Choice*, eds. Paul E. Peterson and Bryan C. Hassel. Washington: Brookings Institution Press.

Waitrowski, Michael D., Stephen Hansell, Charles R. Massey, and David L. Wilson. 1982. "Curriculum Tracking and Delinquency." *American Sociological Review* 47: 151–160.

Walberg, Herbert J. 1985. "Educational Strategies That Work." *New Perspectives* (U.S. Commission on Civil Rights) 17 (winter): 23–26.

Walberg, Herbert J. 1986. "Synthesis of Research on Teaching." In *Handbook of Research on Teaching*, 3d ed., ed. Merlin C. Wittrock, 214–229. New York: MacMillan.

Walberg, Herbert J., and Kevin Marjoribanks. 1976. "Family Environment and Cognitive Development: Twelve Analytic Models." *Review of Educational Research* 46: 527–551.

Walberg, Herbert, J., Roseann Pascal, and Thomas Weinstein. 1986. "Effective Schools Use Homework Effectively." *Educational Leadership* 43 (May): 5–8.

Walberg, Herbert J., and Herbert J. Walberg III. 1994. "Losing Local Control." *Educational Researcher* 23 (June–July): 19–26.

Wallace, Walter. 1971. The Logic of Science in Sociology. Chicago: Aldine-Atherton.

Waller, Willard. 1932. *The Sociology of Teaching*. New York: Wiley.

Walsh, Mark. 1991. "Under Court Order, Girls Admitted to Schools for Black Boys in Detroit." *Education Week,* 11 (Sept. 4): 1, 24, 25.

Walsh, Mark. 2001. "Supreme Court to Hear Pivotal Voucher Case." *Education Week* 21 (Oct. 3): 1, 32, 33.

Walters, Pamela Barnhouse. 2001, "Educational Access and the State: Historical Continuities and Discontinuities in Racial Inequality in American Education." *Sociology of Education* Extra Issue: 35–49.

Wasserman, Miriam. 1970. *The School Fix: NYC, USA*. New York: Outerbridge and Dienstfrey.

Webb, Rodney B., and Robert R. Sherman. 1989. *Schooling and Society*, 2d ed. New York: MacMillan.

Webster, Murray, Jr., and James E. Driskell, Jr. 1983. "Beauty as Status." *American Journal of Sociology* 89: 140–165.

Wehlage, Gary, and Robert A. Rutter. 1987. "Dropping Out: How Much Do Schools Contribute to the Problem?" In *School Dropouts: Patterns and Policies*, ed. Gary Natriello, 70–88. New York: Teachers College Press.

Weick, Karl E. 1976. "Educational Organizations as Loosely Coupled Systems." *Administrative Science Quarterly* 21, 1–19.

Weick, Karl E. 1982. "Administering Education in Loosely Coupled Systems." *Phi Delta Kappan* 63, 673–675.

Weis, Lois. 1985. "Excellence and Student Class, Race, and Gender Cultures." In *Excellence in Education*, eds. Philip G. Altback, Gail P. Kelly, and Lois Weis, 217–232. Buffalo, NY: Prometheus Books.

Weiss, Heather. 1987. "Family Support and Education in Early Childhood Programs." In *Family Support Programs: The State of the Art*. eds. S. L. Kagan, D. Powell, B. Weissbourd, and E. Zigler. New Haven: Yale University Press.

Wells, Amy Stuart. 1990. "Experiment Pioneered the School Choice Concept." *New York Times,* August 22: B6.

Wells, Amy Stuart. 1995. "Reexamining Social Science Research on School Desegregation: Long Versus Short Term Effects." *Teachers College Record* 96: 691–706.

Wells, Amy Stuart, and Robert L. Crain. 1994. "Perpetuation Theory and the Long-Term Effects of School Desegregation." *Review of Educational Research* 64: 531–556.

Wenglinsky, Harold. 2000. *How Teaching Matters: Bringing the Classroom Back Into Discussions of Teacher Quality*. Princeton, NJ: Educational Testing Service, Policy Information Center. http://www.ets.org/research/pic/teamat.pdf

Westbury, Ian. 1989. "The Problems of Comparing Curriculums Across Educational Systems." In *International Comparisons and Educational Reform*, ed. Alan C. Purves, 17–34. Alexandria, VA: Association for Supervision and Curriculum.

Westbury, Ian. 1992. "Comparing American and Japanese Achievement: Is the United States Really a Low Achiever?" *Educational Researcher* 21 (June–July): 18–24.

Westbury, Ian, Corinna A. Ethington, Lauren A. Sosniak, and David P. Baker. 1994. In *Search of More Effective Mathematics Education*. Norwood, NJ: Ablex.

What Works, 2d ed. 1987. Washington: Department of Education.

Wheelock, Ann. 1992. *Crossing the Tracks: How "Untracking" Can Save America's Schools*. New York: New Press.

Will, George F. 1995. "Milwaukee Students are Captives to School Voucher Foes." *Boston Sunday Globe,* September 10: A-7.

Willie, Charles V. 1993. "Using Multiple Paradigms in the Development of Educational Policy." Paper presented at the Conference on Equity and Excellence in Education: The Policy Uses of Sociology, jointly sponsored by the U.S. Department of Education and the Sociology of Education Section of the American Sociological Association.

Willingham, W. W., and N. S. Cole. 1997. *Gender and Fair Assessment*. Mahwah, NJ: Lawrence Erlbaum Associates, Inc.

Willis, Paul. 1977. Learning to Labor: *How Working Class Kids Get Working Class Jobs*. New York: Columbia University Press.

Willms, J. Douglas. 1985. "Catholic-School Effects on Academic Achievement: New Evidence from the High School and Beyond Follow-Up Study." *Sociology of Education* 58: 98–114.

Wilson, Alan B. 1959. "Residential Segregation of Social Classes and Aspirations of High School Boys." *American Sociological Review* 24: 836–845.

Wilson, Bruce L., and Thomas B. Corcoran. 1988. *Successful Secondary Schools*. New York: The Falmer Press.

Wilson, Kenneth L., and Alejandro Portes. 1975. "The Educational Attainment Process: Results from a National Sample." *American Journal of Sociology* 81: 343–362.

Wilson, William J. 1978. *The Declining Significance of Race: Blacks and Changing American Institutions*. Chicago: University of Chicago Press.

Wilson, William J. 1987. *The Truly Disadvantaged: The Inner City, the Underclass and Public Policy*. Chicago: University of Chicago Press.

Wise, Arthur E., and Tamar Gendler. 1989. "Rich Schools, Poor Schools: The Persistence of Unequal Education." *The College Board Review* 151: 12–17, 36–37.

Witte, John F. 1992. "Public Subsidies for Private Schools: What We Know and How to Proceed." *Educational Policy* 6: 206–227.

Wolfle, Lee. 1985. "Postsecondary Educational Attainment Among Whites and Blacks." *American Educational Research Journal* 22: 501–525.

www.abell.org

www.census.gov/govs/school/00fullreport.pdf

www.nctaf.org

Zajonc, Robert B. 1976. "Family Configuration and Intelligence." *Science* 192: 227–236.

Zborowski, Mark, and Elizabeth Herzog. 1962. *Life is with People: The Culture of the Shtetl*. New York: Schocken.

Zill, Nicholas. 1988. "Behavior, Achievement, and Health Problems Among Children in Stepfamilies: Finding from a National Survey of Child Health." In *Impact of Divorce, Single Parenting, and Stepparenting on Children*, eds. E. Mavis Hetherington and Joseph D. Arasteh, 325–368. Hillsdale, NJ: Lawrence Erlaum.

Zill, Nicholas. 1996. "Family Change and Student Achievement: What We Have Learned, What It Means for Schools." In *Family-School Links: How Do They Affect Educational Outcomes?* eds. Allan Booth and Judith F., 139–174. Dunn. Hillsdale, NJ: Lawrence Erlbaum.

Zill, Nicholas, and Carolyn C. Rogers. 1988. "Recent Trends in the Well-Being of Children in the United States and Their Implications for Public Policy." In *The Changing American Family and Public Policy*, ed. Andrew J. Cherlin, 31–115. Washington: Urban Institute Press.

Zimiles, Herbert, and Valerie E. Lee. 1991. "Family Structure and Educational Progress." *Developmental Psychology* 27: 314–320.

CREDITS

I acknowledge here the following sources for granting permission to quote text excerpts that appear in the book:

Karl L. Alexander, Martha Cook, Edward L. McDill. 1978. "Curriculum Tracking and Educational Stratification: Some Further Evidence." *American Sociological Review* 43: pp. 64–65. Copyright 1978 by the American Sociological Association.

Richard Arum. 1996. "Do Private Schools Force Public Schools to Compete?" *American Sociological Review* 61: 29–46. Copyright 1996 by the American Sociological Association.

Elizabeth G. Cohen. 2000. "Equitable Classrooms in Changing Society." In Handbook of the Sociology of Education, ed. Maureen T. Hallinan. New York: Kluwer Academic/Plenum Publisher.

James S. Coleman. 1966. "Equal Schools or Equal Students." *The Public Interest* 4: 71.

James S. Coleman. 1967. "Toward Open Schools." *The Public Interest* 9: 22–23.

James S. Coleman. 1976. "Rawls, Nozick, and Educational Equality." *The Public Interest* 43: 121–122.

Rober Dreeban. 2000. "Structural Effects in Education: A History of an Idea." In the Handbook of the Sociology of Education, ed. Maureen T. Hallinan. New York: Kluwer Academic/Plenum Publishers.

George Farkas and Kurt Beron. 2001. "Family Linguistic Culture and Social Reproduction: Verbal Skill from Parent to Child in the Preschool and School Years." Paper presented at the annual meeting of the *Population Association of America*, Washington, DC.

Adam Gamoran, Walter G. Secada, and Cora B. Marrett. 2000. "The Organizational context of Teaching and Learning." In *Handbook of Sociology of Education*, ed. Maureen T. Hallinan. Kluwer Academic/Plenum Publishers.

Maureen T. Hallinan. 1989. "Sociology and Education: The State of the Art." In Jeanne H. Ballantine, ed., *Schools and Society*, 2nd ed. Mountain View, CA: Mayfield Publishing Company, p. 23.

Maureen T. Hallinan. 1994. "Tracking: From Theory to Practice." *Sociology of Education* 67: pp. 79, 84, 90. Copyright 1994 by the American Sociological Association.

Maureen T. Hallinan. 2000. "On the Linkages Between Sociology of Race and Ethnicity and Sociology of Education." In *Handbook of Sociology of Education*, ed. Maureen T. Hallinan. Kluwer Academic/Plenum Publishers.

Eric A. Hanushek. 1989. "The Impact of Differential expenditures on School Performance." *Educational Researcher* 18: 44–51.

Barbara Heyns. 1974. "Social Selection and Stratification Within Schools." *American Journal of Sociology* 79: pp. 1435, 1449. Copyright 1974 by the University of Chicago Press.

Thomas B. Hoffer. 2000. "Accountability in Education." In *Handbook of the Sociology of Education*, ed. Maureen T. Hallinan. New York: Kluwer/Academic Publishers.

Lawrence J Mussoline and Roger C. Shouse. 2001. "School Restructuring as a Policy Agenda: Why One Size May Not Fit All." *Sociology of Education* 74: 44–58.

Valerie E. Lee and Julie B. Smith. 1997. "High School Size: Which Works Best, and For Whom?" Educational Evaluation and Policy Analysis 19: 212.

Anne M. Milne, David E. Myers, Alvin S. Rosenthal, and Alan Ginsburg. 1986. "Single Parents, Working Mothers, and the Educational Achievement of School Children." *Sociology of Education* 59: pp. 131, 134. Copyright 1986 by the American Sociological Association.

Aaron M. Pallas, Doris R. Entwisle, Karl L. Alexander, and M. Francis Stluka. 1994. "Ability Group Effects: Instructional, Social, or Institutional?" *Sociology of Education* 67: p. 43. Copyright 1994 by the American Sociological Association.

Cornelius Riordan. 1990. *Girls and Boys in School: Together or Separate?* New York: Teachers College Press, pp. 135–146. Copyright 1990 by Teachers College, Columbia University. All rights reserved. Reprinted with permission.

Ray C. Rist. 1977. "On the Relations Among Educational Research Paradigms." *Anthropology and Education Quarterly* 8: pp. 42, 44. Reproduced by permission of the American Anthropological Association.

Charol Shakeshaft, Ellen Barber, Mary Ann Hergenrother, Yolanda Johnson, Laurie Mandel, and Janice Sawyer. 1995. "Peer Harassment and the Culture of Caring in Schools." Paper presented at the annual meeting of the American Educational Research Association.

Herbert J. Walberg and Herbert J. Walberg III. 1994. "Losing Local Control." *Educational Researcher* 23 (June–July): 19–26.

Ian Westbury. 1989. "The Problems of Comparing Curriculums Across Educational Systems." In *International Comparisons and Educational Reform*, ed. Alan C. Purves, 17–34. Alexandria, VA: Association for Supervision and Curriculum.

Lois Weis. 1985. "Excellence and Student Class, Race, and Gender Cultures." In Philip G. Altbach, Gail P. Kelly, and Lois Weis, eds. *Excellence in Education*. Buffalo, NY: Prometheus Books, pp. 217–218. Reprinted by permission of the publisher.

INDEX